PENGUIN BOOKS

THE WORLD OF THE GIFTED CHILD

Priscilla L. Vail lives and works in Bedford, New York, where she is a reading specialist at the Rippowam-Cisqua School. Her articles have appeared in *Instructor* magazine and *Independent School*. She has been a book reviewer for the *Journal of Learning Disabilities*, and her verse has appeared in *The New York Times*.

The World of the Gifted Child

Priscilla L. Vail

PENGUIN BOOKS

Penguin Books Ltd, Harmondsworth,
Middlesex, England
Penguin Books, 625 Madison Avenue,
New York, New York 10022, U.S.A.
Penguin Books Australia Ltd, Ringwood,
Victoria, Australia
Penguin Books Canada Limited, 2801 John Street,
Markham, Ontario, Canada L3R 1B4
Penguin Books (N.Z.) Ltd, 182–190 Wairau Road,
Auckland 10, New Zealand

First published in the United States of America by
the Walker Publishing Company, Inc., 1979
First published in Canada by
Beaverbooks, Limited, 1979
Published in Penguin Books 1980

LIBRARY OF CONGRESS CATALOGING IN PUBLICATION DATA
Vail, Priscilla L
The world of the gifted child.
Reprint of the 1979 ed. published by Walker, New York.
Includes index.
1. Gifted children—Education. I. Title.
[LC3993.V34 1980]   371.95   80-10255
ISBN 0 14 00.5546 0

Printed in the United States of America by
Offset Paperback Mfrs., Inc., Dallas, Pennsylvania
Set in Garamond

Excerpt from *Collected Poems 1913–1962* by E. E. Cummings reprinted by permission
of Harcourt Brace Jovanovich, Inc. Table of contents and excerpts from *Charlotte's
Web* by E. B. White reprinted by permission of Harper & Row, Publishers, Inc.;
copyright 1952 by E. B. White. Excerpt from *The Bad Island* by William Steig reprinted by permission of Windmill Books, Inc., Robert Kraus, Publisher; copyright
© William Steig, 1969. Excerpt from "First Lesson" (originally appeared in *The New
Yorker*) in *Times Three* by Phyllis McGinley reprinted by permission of Viking Penguin Inc.; copyright © Phyllis McGinley, 1959. Excerpt from *The Common Reader* by
Virginia Woolf reprinted by permission of Harcourt Brace Jovanovich, Inc.

To
　　　Donald
and our children
　　　Melissa, Polly, Lucia, and Angus

"I would rather learn from one bird how to sing
Than teach ten thousand stars how not to dance."

e.e. cummings

Acknowledgments

My thanks go to all the people who, individually and through their organizations, have helped me write this book. Sometimes gourmet cooks will pretend to give you their recipes while actually leaving out vital ingredients. Not so my friends who have generously shared their insights, practical knowledge, understanding, and time.

Margaret Mayo–Smith, Charlotte Goodhue, Anne and John Zinsser, and a legion of Lukes have given me courage, criticism, and copy.

Waldo Jones, head of our lower school, and Sam Parkman, our headmaster, are wise educators and treasured friends. I am grateful to them, my colleagues at Rippowam-Cisqua, and the children, all of whom have been my teachers.

The National Association of Independent Schools has always championed the cause of gifted children, explicitly and implicitly. Through their conferences, and their magazine *Independent School*, they reach a tremendous number of educators, and are always willing to take a strong philosophical stand. I am grateful to them for having been the first to publish the article that appears as the basis of Chapter One of this book and for exploring the question of language development in their publications and their meetings. Special recognition is due to Blair McElroy, an editor of superhuman ability and warmth, and Gordon Clem, quiet guardian of childhood.

The Orton Society sheds the light of understanding on the problems of language-disabled children. I have learned so much at Orton conferences and was proud to present some of the ideas in Chapter Eight at their World Conference on Dyslexia in Dallas, Texas, in November, 1977, under the title *Limerence; Language, Literature and Listening*. I give special thanks to Aylett R. Cox, a wise, humorous, and articulate teacher; Alice Ansara, an editor who gives her time and intellectual energy without reserve, and Katrina de Hirsch and Jeannette Jansky, who have built a beacon with their work.

I am grateful and proud that Henry Collis, director of the National Association for Gifted Children in London, was willing to vault the Atlantic Ocean and write the foreword for this book. Such a feat is no surprise considering his soaring mind, limitless agility, and his ties with Jane Burditt and Lucy Stanton, who, as Educator's Ally, Inc., in Bedford, New York, plan conferences, arrange meetings, and spread the word.

To Elizabeth Bauserman go my thanks for seemingly infinite amounts of patience and perfect typing.

A toast to two wizards of words: Edward Streeter, author, tease, and mentor, and my editor Richard Winslow at Walker, who, were he listed under W, might be described: wise, willing, wonderful —wry and rarely wrong.

Priscilla L. Vail
August, 1978

Foreword

In contrast to the tired and sometimes jealous jargon which hits the headlines in describing gifted children, this book is a balanced testament of sound common sense. The author is fortunate to have been able to write with one eye on the growing processes of her own gifted daughter, but this has not in any way narrowed her vision to the development of one child. The view is wide, the findings sound, and the observations meaningful. In short, we have here an amalgam of varied information as valuable to parents as to teachers and well worth reading by anybody interested in children.

It is good very early on to meet Lucia's sense of humor, for here is the saving grace of many a clever child. In a crisis the lighter touch can prove the finest aid to evasive action, as I found myself many times when I was a headmaster. If a child was brave and witty enough to try to lower the temperature by not being as serious as the situation seemed to demand, I invariably succumbed. It is not a question of being impertinent but can illustrate the insight given to socially gifted children to see through the adult glare and dig down into the friendliness which should always be on call.

This deep understanding of themselves and of what other people are really thinking is a characteristic which becomes very marked as gifted children tackle the dark ages of adolescence. Their problems can be deep seated and call for endless patience. How fully I agree with the author in the way she expresses this. And how wrong the world can be in its ready opinion of children in their formative years—the terror (not insolence) that can bring a laugh at the wrong moment, the eagerness to help a teacher that is a cry for companionship and not an attempt to curry favor, the brilliant child who is three or four years ahead intellectually but far behind emotionally. How easy for those who do not understand to regard the child as an uncomfortable freak whose lopsided development is beyond repair. As this book makes so very clear, gifted children are human beings and must be given every chance to grow up physically, emotionally, intellectually, and socially. Then they can lead balanced lives, at ease in the company of people with normal intelligence, yet finding scope in their work to reach a potential which can make a very powerful contribution.

At home, it is not an easy task to see the end product when facing sleepless nights, defiance in face of correction, and the aloofness of total withdrawal. But when reading this book, parents can take great comfort from what can emerge when parents are patient and tolerant, almost at times to the breaking point. The British National Association for Gifted Children has had unique opportunities since 1966 of glimpsing homes and their problems. Every week parents write and give accounts quite similar to those you will read about, only more of ours come from deprived families. Some of these parents view the prospect of having a brilliant child with apprehension and incredulity. This is taken straight from one letter I had: "We don't know if his development is in any way unusual, but by 2¼ his vocabulary was over 500 words and by 2½ over 900, at 3½ he used words like 'swivel, dissolve, muscle and shipshape.' So agile that the fence has been reinforced several times and the garden looks like a detention centre. So inquisitive that all drawers within reach have been tied up with string for two years. So determined that he regards any form of direct control as a challenge and then it is like coming up against a reinforced concrete wall. So observant that at 2½ he picked up half a biscuit and said 'that's a semi-circle' and then half a sandwich and said 'that's a triangle.' Can you help us decide whether this is a perfectly normal little boy?"

What is most important, and this is well brought out in Part II, "How They Live," is that gifted children must feel that they are wanted and that they are loved like their brother and sister. They are particularly in need of cuddling when small, of a great deal of talking to before they speak, and of being gently helped to develop as fast as nature makes easily possible. To force a child because a parent may be obsessed with an unfulfilled ambition of his own is just as bad as to hold a child back so as to make him conform. This latter trait must seem strange to Americans, but I do occasionally run across parents in poor areas who regard it as a stigma to have an intellectually gifted child. They fear there will be bullying at school and jeers from the neighbours. The easiest solution seems to be to try to make him appear less brainy and more average. My experience therefore bears out entirely the vulnerability of some parents which is implicit in this chapter.

Parents are often perplexed by the way their children become obsessed with some idea or some problem and will withdraw utterly into themselves and concentrate for hours on end. They are consumed with a burning interest which nothing should interrupt. However, at school a few hours later they may switch off entirely, like an electric light, because of lack of rapport with the teacher. Burning zeal has given way to restless frustration. How very right, then, Priscilla Vail is to give top priority to the need at school for a "goodness of fit" (in that telling phrase by Herbert Birch). If a gifted child feels at home in his classroom, relates well to his teacher, and is given demanding enough work he can be an inspiration to teach and an exciting challenge to his peers.

But there is only a hairline between high endeavor and depressing languor. On this point many useful individual case histories are quoted and much sound advice is given, but the overriding factor is that parents must be in harmony with the school. If they find this is impossible because their child is showing none of the zest they see at home, they must somehow be loyal to the school in front of the child or say nothing. In approaching the school they must remember they never see Johnnie when they are not there, and that children can behave very differently away from home. Before criticizing the teacher they must be frank with themselves and ask whether the root cause is in fact too much pressure at home or too much questioning on the school day and then putting too much credence in the stories they are told, perhaps touched up with lurid elaborations of any self-respecting imagination. Gifted children are intensely sensitive to prying and many collisions occur between parent and teacher because it is not accepted at home that, just as Father is not pestered with questions about the office, so should Junior not be bothered overmuch about how his day has gone at school.

Most teachers try to help each child according to his ability but gifted children whom they cannot motivate are a plain nuisance, especially if they are immature socially. Without the comparison of other children, parents may not realize and just clamor for acceleration. Occasionally a teacher driven to distraction bursts out with a condemnation of the work done as proof the child is *not* gifted. This can well be a false assumption because achievement and potential do not always go in double harness. Or teacher and parent may have overlooked that the child has a shortness of auditory attention which is leading to various problems. He cannot easily listen to what is said and will be worse off still if there is the background noise which is almost unavoidable in many school situations.

The problems that can be encountered at school and at home come out many times in this book, which also stresses the joy which the majority of gifted children can bring to those they meet. Their zest and sparkle can embellish their surroundings. They love life and life loves them. That is the happy message which predominates, but we must also take to heart the poignant passages, for these tell of gifted children in need. It is easy to forget in making generalizations that with every child, gifted or otherwise, the most telling factors in his life are the horizon and the climate which surround him when he is at his desk at school.

Whatever money is allocated from the Office of Education in Washington to meet the needs of gifted children, whatever enrichment programs are arranged locally, whatever well-intentioned teachers talk about at conferences, whatever far-reaching research is undertaken, nothing avails unless the child himself is able to thrive in his own personal school world. If there is fear or frustration, is the system at fault or could it be the failing of one teacher?

I have heard cynics say, "Why help gifted children? They have everything" or "Why not look after the slow learners and leave those lucky ones to teach themselves?" If all gifted children were mature, placid, evenly balanced intellectually, and socially adjusted, this could often happen to a reasonable degree, although few would reach their full potential. Unfortunately, some of these children are bewildered and have anything but a robust outlook. They are extremely sensitive and painfully allergic to sarcasm or feeling that they are in the way. Let an eleven-year-old boy whom I know well describe in his words what happened to him. He called his poem The Wall.

They laughed at me.
They laughed at me and called me names,
They wouldn't let me join their games.
I couldn't understand.
I spent most playtimes on my own,
Everywhere I was alone,
I couldn't understand.

Teachers told me I was rude,
Bumptious, over-bearing, shrewd,
Some of the things they said were crude.
I couldn't understand.
And so I built myself a wall.
Strong and solid, ten foot tall,
With bricks you couldn't see at all,
So *I* could understand.

And then came Sir,
A jovial, beaming, kindly man,
Saw through my wall and took my hand,
And the bricks came tumbling down,
For *he* could understand.

And now I laugh with them,
Not in any unkind way,
For they have yet to face their day
And the lessons I have learned.
For eagles soar above all birds,
And scavengers need to hunt in herds,
But the lion walks alone,
And now I understand.

We can understand too a great deal better when we have digested the recipes for success which Priscilla Vail so deftly sets out. Are there still teachers so out of touch with modern thinking that they are unsympathetic to children who are gifted? If they exist let other faculty members gently nudge *The World of the Gifted Child* their way with a muttered, "Well, there is a book which *you* won't read."

Who knows? It may quietly vanish from the faculty library and perhaps in a few weeks' time there are signs that the ranks of those like "Sir" in the poem are happily reinforced. One teacher has become much wiser. Gifted children need no longer dread his coming. There is now a goodness of fit.

Henry Collis
July, 1978

Contents

Prologue

This book is born of a combination of past experience, current concern, and hope for the future of gifted children.

As each child is a gift, so each child comes with distinguishing gifts. For some, the balance makes for a tranquil passage through life. For others, the balance produces frustrations, dreams, and energies which resemble the tides of the sea in their power and relentlessness.

Giftedness brings its own particular set of pleasures and perils. My husband and I have learned about some of them through our own family life. As a teacher and a parent I want to share what insights I have with others who are concerned with children: educators, parents, physicians, those who plan community projects, and enlightened caretakers who want to protect and support gifted children so they may grow into whole people.

Gifted children have intense emotional and social needs that are frequently sacrificed to intellectual or academic concerns, particularly when educators get into the act. Being a teacher myself, I feel a license to criticize my own profession which I might deny to an outsider.

PROLOGUE

My current worry is that as giftedness nudges other special educational needs aside in the popular and professional press, two things are happening. The first is a denigrating of the needs of gifted children. This springs from a philosophical discomfort with the idea of favoritism for an endowed elite. We prize equality so highly that superlative performance is often suspect. Paradoxically this coexists with ready applause for superheroes in sports, moneymaking and daredeviling. The idea of singling out one element of the population for special support is mistrusted unless the element is below the average. It is idealistically comfortable to help the underdog. Topdog is supposed to take care of himself.

The second cause for my concern is the limelight recently thrown on a group of children labeled "the gifted and talented." Suddenly these children are the focus of a great deal of governmental and professional attention. Their lives will be microscopically examined, they will be the objects of studies, and the recipients of hot, new, educational materials. This may be wonderful, or it may not. It all depends on whether the live child is found in the program or sacrificed to it.

In order to understand how we can best nurture gifted children, we first need to know who they are and how we can recognize them. Then we must see how they live, within their families, with their friends, and in their world, and what role school plays in their lives. We can then consider what additional nourishment they need. Finally, we can look at the lives of nine gifted people, five male and four female, who range in age from six to seventy-five, and listen to their words and wishes.

I intentionally blur the boundaries between genius, prodigy, gifted child, and bright kid because, even using the most sophisticated available diagnostic instrument, I'm not sure it is possible to make accurate distinctions, particularly when the children are young. Chapter Two will take up this question in greater detail. Although the philosophy and suggestions in this book were written primarily about gifted children, there is nothing here to harm a child who might be more accurately described as able or bright.

Each time my life has been touched by the people who appear on these pages I have received a gift.

PART I

Who They Are

Chapter 1

Lucia's Story

The first thing we have to remember about gifted children is that they are children. Like other children, they grow, lose their baby teeth, cry, laugh, and suffer the glories and pains of growing up. People are sometimes intimidated by their intelligence and think that just because they have giant vocabularies or understand quadratic equations they have the world by the tail. Not so.

Our gifted child introduced us to the wonders and problems of her life. As my husband and I—and her schools—tried to provide the best possible environment for her, we learned a lot about all gifted children. We learned from the good choices we made when we used our common sense; and more important, we learned from our mistakes. We learned why some current theories about educating the gifted don't have much to do with live children.

Lucia was the third of three daughters born to us at two-year intervals. She was an impatient baby, eager to be rid of the trappings of infancy. She hated being in a buggy or a basket. While her disposition improved when she could sit up and see more, she was

3

frustrated until she could walk. Then, she had both vistas and independence, and she began to laugh.

She played with all of the usual household toys, and her early talking didn't seem unusual, given the constant companionship of her very verbal older sisters. In spite of this facility, she kept many of her thoughts and accomplishments to herself in a kind of emotional and intellectual privacy. She was a passionate small person with what seemed like quirkily adult ways of seeing the world.

She did ordinary nursery school things in nursery school and appeared to be doing the same in kindergarten. No one knew she could read until one spring morning when she announced to the class at playground that everyone would be having cupcakes and chocolate milk the next day. Queried on her source of information, she was stopped short. Having blown her cover, she had to admit that she had read it on the teacher's desk.

After recess, the teacher sat down with her to give her some other things to read, ranging from first-grade books through *The Wizard of Oz*. She could read them all with ease and comprehension. No one had taught her. She said she just knew how, and indeed she did.

The school found this extraordinary. We tried to play it down because, although our fourth-grade daughter was whizzing along academically, our second-grade daughter was having a devilish time learning to read and spell.

Summer came, with its puppets, costumes, bathing suits, picnics, and library cards. Lucia enjoyed them all and made the September journey to the shoe store with enthusiasm and excitement about entering first grade.

No more than two weeks had gone by before the school called to schedule an appointment right away. They came right to the point. There was no way they could keep Lucia in the first grade.

She already knew all the work planned for the rest of the year, not only in reading, but in math and in general information and concepts. Her being so far ahead was demoralizing to the other children, and some parents had also complained. (In 1961, competition was rampant in rigorous schools. It involved class standing as well as marks, and it began as early as first grade.) Some parents argued that it wasn't fair for their children to have to compete with someone who already knew the material.

The teacher didn't feel she could keep Lucia. No, she wasn't making any trouble. She was cooperative and seemed glad to be there, but surely she would soon be bored, and discipline problems would follow.

We agreed that boredom is a threat to curiosity and that curiosity deserves protection. However, we wondered whether Lucia couldn't be given some projects to do while the group was working on skills she already had. We were told that this wasn't possible. It would be poor for classroom morale and discipline and would single her out and separate her from the group. (How strange this now sounds, given today's flexibility in many classrooms.)

What was to be done, then, with our cheery little misfit? The school suggested moving her forthwith into second grade. This raised many questions in our minds. Would she be accepted as a member of the class, joining them late, younger, and with some sort of favored status? Surely the kiss of death. Would second-grade work be right for her? She was already reading comfortably at third-grade level and above.

How much of a handicap would a full year's deficit be to Lucia in sports? Her athletic ability was only average for her own age, and sports are important for establishing a place in the group. What about always being a year younger than your classmates in terms of psychological development, activities, and boy-girl relationships?

We could see from our fifth grader that these concerns would be upon us in no time. The decision we made now would have to

5

carry us over more than just the next year. It would be foolish and harmful to sidestep a present problem if it meant putting up obstacles for the future.

The school acknowledged all these potential difficulties but recommended—insisted actually—that Lucia be moved on Monday. They felt they were dealing with an exceptional intellect that was in a period of vigorous growth. If they didn't stimulate her mind at such a moment, Lucia, with her passionate and purposeful nature, could be turned away from learning for life—something the school was unwilling to risk.

We were all thinking and trying hard up to this point. Then we all made a wrong assumption. "Because she is so smart," they said, "she will be able to figure out the social problems." We agreed.

Lucia went into second grade and, after some preliminary skirmishing, was fairly well accepted. Her classmates enjoyed her sense of humor and the stories and plays she made up. She was known in the group for being musical as well as smart. That seemed to take away some of the sting. She did well enough in sports, and the work was all right, even though it presented very little challenge. We didn't mind that because we were glad that she had enough physical and mental energy left at the end of the day for extracurricular and creative pursuits.

Lucia had smooth sailing through second, third, fourth and part of the fifth grade. Then the trouble began.

At first, it just seemed to be an energetic wave of showing off. Hoping it was a phase, we decided to ride it out. The school thought she had gotten too big for her britches and decided to crack down. Later, we and Lucia came to understand that all of a sudden, she saw her classmates moving away from her to some new level. She used her tried and true humor and song and dance routines to call them back to where she was. They, having reached a new level, saw her antics as a pain in the neck and drew even farther away. The problem got worse.

Sixth grade was really bad. Although she was doing excellent academic work, Lucia was friendless, rude, and seemingly uncaring. Moodiness, sarcasm, and antagonism were the order of the day. Her humorous tongue developed a deadly edge honed by practice. She was no joy to others and no joy to herself. Everyone was concerned.

That spring I went to hear the fifth and sixth graders sing. Music had remained a constant joy for Lucia. I looked at the sixth graders lined up on the stage—tall, faces growing in that bone-expanding way that heralds adolescence. Boys were getting thicker through the chest, and girls had bosoms. Then there was Lucia, flat of chest, delicate of face like—yes—like all the fifth graders.

I wondered whether she should be back with her contemporaries and shared my thoughts with the school. They said that, even though she was having a very bad time socially and emotionally, her academic work was excellent. The dangers of boredom were mentioned again, and I got the familiar, "A kid as smart as she is will figure all this social stuff out." We weren't convinced, and got their blessing to talk the idea over with Lucia.

We suggested a move, and her initial reaction (as it was to everything) was negative. We said that she might feel better being with people her own age, even though she was so good at her work. We told her honestly that the school was afraid she might get bored repeating a year, but that we didn't feel she was enjoying her work, or her life, very much. She didn't really seem to be getting much out of it except good marks.

Memorial Day weekend brought the imminence of final exams. Lucia's sisters did diligent things with Latin verbs and history dates. Lucia played with her hamster, stayed up late, and played the radio—loud. She failed four out of six exams and greeted the

7

news with a matter-of-fact, rather cheerful, "Well, I guess I'll have to stay back."

Her own age group accepted her more kindly than one might have expected. They all grew bosoms together. And, though she read the same stories and studied the same history as she had the year before, she brought such different perceptions to them that they seemed new.

New, also, was the experience of feeling a certain way about a character or event and finding that other people did, too. That had never happened to her in school before.

No matter how smart you are, you can't be twelve when you're eleven. You don't feel like a twelve-year-old when you're eleven. If you try, you're a fake twelve, and you miss being eleven. You have to go back later and pick up what you've missed, like a dropped stitch. The more rows you knit beyond the dropped stitch, the harder it is to weave it back up. That was Lucia's next task.

Lucia's high scores, high marks, and highest possible percentiles in standardized testing all gave the appearance of a brilliant child working at full capacity. Her great facility with words continued to help her learn quickly and easily from books.

Verbal expression—written, oral, and dramatic—was a happy outlet for her creative energies. It was tempting to encourage her to go on in these fields by fostering vertical growth in her strong area. But concentration on vertical growth is not what the gifted child needs.

Lucia graduated from elementary school at the end of ninth grade and went off for one year to an extremely demanding boarding school, which gave a surface appearance of individuality and creativity.

While showing us around, the headmaster said, "We have nothing here to force standardized behavior on our students—no uniforms, no one set of academic requirements. We have a community of individuals—all very different. Children this bright and this creative are free thinkers and enjoy being different from one another."

What he didn't say, and what we forgot, is that children of this age seek out kinds of conformity because they need the safety of a group code. It may appear in shared tastes for styles of dress, slang, or antagonisms, but it is part of every adolescent group.

When so much is shifting inside, the child needs visible, external confirmation that others are like him.[1] He already feels different and perhaps frighteningly alone. The world of adult support should provide ways for him to feel more connected, not more isolated.

When the adult world denies the existence and value of such conformity, it doesn't disappear. Instead, it goes underground, and the more subtle it is, the more rigid and binding its requirements, and thus the harder it is to discard or outgrow.

In Lucia's school, once again, adult expectations, based on assessment of intellectual capacity, worked to deny rather than enhance normal progression through developmental stages.

The head said, "Young people with this kind of intellect have different emotional needs from other young people. They are so quick to see, and to understand, that they are really much older than their chronological age. They don't need as much emotional support or time. They need more intellectual challenge."

Wrong. These children who are so quick to see patterns and grasp implications need even more chances to grow emotionally. Enhanced perception means enhanced perception of both pain and joy, not just joy, and of the discrepancy between how you see yourself and how the world sees you.

Bringing these two images into focus is one of the major tasks of growing up, as it is one of the manifestations of autonomy. Any time the trusted adult world reinforces the discrepancy in the two

---

[1] I use the masculine pronoun throughout the book because the constant use of "he or she" is cumbersome, and I wanted to settle on one. I flipped a coin.

WHO THEY ARE

images by ignoring or denying its existence, it makes pain for the child. Any time the trusted adult world can say, by implication or words, that "growing up is just as hard for you as it is for anyone else," it demonstrates acceptance and understanding from which the child can draw real support.

In this respect, dealing with the gifted is very like dealing with the learning-disabled. The learning-disabled child's bluffs and camouflages seem to say, "If they find out how bad I am at that, they won't like (or accept) me any more." The gifted child may be worrying, "If they find out that inside of me I'm not made of magic and excellence they won't like (or accept) me any more." The underlying question for both is, "If I'm not what they think I am, do I exist?"

One of the first tasks for a teacher who deals with a learning-disabled child is to acknowledge his disability while accepting him, simultaneously, as a person. We must treat our gifted students with the same understanding and acceptance.

Socially, the gifted child starts with an extra handicap. The world is apt to view success with a mistrust born of jealousy and to withhold encouragement and acceptance. Many people find it hard to be kind and natural with someone rich, famous, or smart. By withholding, or remaining somewhat aloof, they can say, "You're not any better than I am."

Intellectually, the gifted child should not march in lock step with everyone else. His mind must not be shackled. His curiosity must be protected and his growth encouraged. Some ways of doing this promote equilibrium; others do not. We should never diminish the child's gifted area in order to create a balance. Neither should we encourage growth in only one area, thereby creating a monolith.

Alexander Calder's graceful mobile makes an appropriate metaphor for a gifted child. The center of balance is the core of the child. The long wire or thread holding a large, heavy object can be seen as the child's astonishing facility in whatever form it may take—math, science, art, or language, to name a few. In a mobile, the long wire or thread is balanced by two shorter wires or threads holding smaller, lighter objects. It is to these that people working with the gifted must turn their attention.

The child instinctively turns to the primary weight. It is his nature, or his calling, and he must be precisely taught in whatever field this happens to be. Unaided, he may turn exclusively in this direction, preventing balance. How much better to encourage him to find and explore the areas that will provide the secondary counterweights, bringing synergy to this mobile.

Here, the adult, parent, friend, or teacher introduces the child to knowledge or ways of thinking that he might *not* find on his own. Do parents and teachers need specific training in this technique, or do they simply need to enlarge their point of view while holding fast to common sense?

As I mentioned earlier, some adults feel intimidated or defensive with very bright children. And parents of such children are sometimes afraid to involve themselves in the child's thinking and learning, partly out of awe, and partly for fear of damaging something rare. Intellectually, this is probably a needless concern, for a vigorous mind will respond to new exposures with new growth. More important, being treated with awe by one's parents is a burden few children can tolerate. A child feels safest when his parents are kindly but firmly in charge. Without this, the boundaries all children need to test and press against are missing. Of course the boundaries and limits must expand as the child develops, but they cannot expand if they haven't been set. Remember that children need to grow socially and emotionally as well as intellectually.

Since one mark of the gifted mind is its ability to see patterns and relationships that less nimble minds might miss, the job of helping the child find secondary counterweights is less difficult or frightening than it might seem initially. The child whose genius lies in music may find fascination in mathematics or molecular structure.

11

Rhythm in sports or design may provide complementary enjoyment. Perhaps literature, pantomime, or hieroglyphics would intrigue him as a different kind of symbolic representation.

The child with a gift for history might be fascinated by geology or astronomy as a way of comprehending the enormous. Perhaps painting and sculpture as a way of knowing about people, or electronics and communications as sources of information, would provide a complement.

The whole world can be a game of attribute blocks. The gifted mind makes a lifelong search for combinations, which are endless.

Something to do, as well as something to think about, should be on the smorgasbord, whether it be cooking, painting, carving, weaving, playing an instrument, athletics, or carpentry. Gifted children have an enormous faculty for taking in information. We have to remember to give them widely varied opportunities for giving it out, too. Later chapters deal with some specific suggestions.

Caretaking, also vital, can involve smaller children, other people, community projects, plants, or a pet. Responsibility, affection, and being needed as a giver of care and nurture contribute powerfully to a positive emotional base. Caretaking forges a bond between the child and the world which the gifted child needs badly.

Because his perceptions are keen, and because he sees that he is separate from other people in his area of specialty, he needs specific opportunities to join himself to his world. Isolation is frightening to any child, and a special peril for a gifted child.

We had seen these needs, appetites, and fears firsthand and were gradually learning to understand and anticipate them.

Lucia wanted to come home after her year in boarding school to finish her secondary education at the local high school. Her experience away had not been a happy one and yet she had fulfilled her academic obligations with distinction. We were perfectly willing to follow her wish, and we and her little brother were delighted at the prospect of having her at home. The high school was a new world to her, which she entered enthusiastically. However, by midwinter the school recommended that she graduate at the end of the year. Her daily work, college board scores, National Merit placement, and the course work she had already completed indicated she had outgrown what they could offer.

There we were again in a familiar situation, one which was both complimentary and discouraging. It seemed that schools were penalizing students for outstanding work. Fortunately, Lucia remembered the lessons she had learned and wisely decided not to go to college a year early. Instead, she graduated from high school and spent a year in New York where she studied music and got a part in an off-Broadway production of *Dracula*. Blood-sucking, Beethoven, and baby-sitting were the three major ingredients of a very happy postgraduate, precollege year. Possessed by theater fever, she was admitted to the drama school of an eastern university, where she planned total immersion in theater arts. But she had a jolt one day when someone mentioned the Renaissance. She realized she didn't know whether it was a person, a place, or a thing. She saw that her education was a patchwork because of her several shifts, and decided it was time to learn some of the knowledge shared by educated people. Once again she changed institutions, this time ending up in a rigorous liberal arts program in a highly demanding college. She has just graduated with honors and is setting forth to tackle the world.

We have generalized one cardinal rule and three pleas to other families from our experiences.

The rule: Hold fast to common sense.

Three pleas:

First, try to see the gifted child primarily as a developing child. His special learning pattern is an extra, not the main thing.

Second, provide extra opportunities for emotional growth.

13

With a strong inner base, the child will be able to use his extra-ordinary mind even more effectively. Without it, he is just a circus performer who does breathtaking stunts, but not a whole person.

And third, introduce the child to many different kinds of thinking and doing so that he can develop the counterweights to keep his mobile balanced.]

Chapter 2

Catching Quicksilver:
Can We Identify the
Gifted Child?

The first obstacle to identifying giftedness is a sense of embarrassment about it, both educationally and socially. The impact of such thinking on education has been either to deny that there is a group of children who are gifted, or to assume that because they are gifted they can be self-educators, use their time in school to help slower children, or do their learning outside of school where it won't have to embarrass anyone else. Apart from this philosophical problem, schools haven't wanted to single such children out because they didn't really have anything different to do with them once they had been identified.

John Silber, president of Boston University, said at the 1977 graduation exercises:

We are engaged in a headlong flight from the best.
Our flight from excellence is not a failure in our general ability to per-

form, nor is it the consequence of a general desire to accept the mediocre. It is something different and strange. It is profoundly philosophical: we have begun to reject the very notion of excellence as a social ideal. Out of a well-intentioned but inept concern with the equality of opportunity, we tend to reject anything if it exceeds the grasp of anyone.

Paradoxically, this rejection of excellence does not mean the end of competition. Adults and children alike still seek glory even though they may be content with laurels won from modest feats. But the wish for applause and recognition is different from the arduous pursuit of excellence. It is a mistaken assessment of quality to confuse the two, like thinking that zircons are diamonds. Denial of giftedness is a game of ostrich. Either one of these attitudes, alone, is a setback for the cause of gifted children. Together they create a gigantic obstacle.

Socially, there are equivalent problems. Some parents seek recognition vicariously through their children's achievements, and others who describe their own children as gifted are considered braggarts or liars. Competitive blood floods the cheeks of other parents required to listen to such hymning. The stage-mother, my-son-the-doctor stereotype, has fed humorists from Molière to Woody Allen.

Approaching the problem from the opposite point of view, a parent may be reluctant to have a child seem different from other children. The prodigy/freak association is automatic to some people. They may not want their child to have to take such a risk on the block, or in his sidewalk life. Henry Collis, director of the National Association for Gifted Children in London, says this reluctance is characteristic of many middle-class and lower-middle-class English families. They consider it somewhat shameful to have produced a gifted child, and often encourage the child to underachieve and conceal his ability in order to protect the family name. This is undoubtedly true, too, in some parts of the United States.

In addition to nationality, much depends on the age and cultural bias of the parents. One message of the sixties certainly was, "Away with tradition. Grow your hair. Don't dress like your parents. Be an individual. Be real." At the same time, a partner to that admonition was, "Dress just like your peers. Don't be special. Be real." Many people who grew up during those years are now of an age to be parents themselves. Some have changed their thinking, some have not.

But whatever best describes the social dilemma of the parents, woe be unto the child who proclaims himself gifted. Would even Lloyd's of London have a policy to insure his life on the playground?

A first step to improving our accuracy in identifying gifted children may be to rid ourselves of this sometimes hypocritical embarrassment and look without fear on "a society characterized by an aristocracy of achievement arising out of a democracy of opportunity."[1]

Perhaps the term *gifted* itself presents the problem. The Menuhin School in England is a school for musically gifted children, whose I.Q. scores, incidentally, range from 93 to 166. The school's admissions committee compares children to water, ice being at zero with the water getting progressively warmer. Most children might be described as poachers, or simmerers. Some might be considered boilers, but when water finally boils, part of it turns to steam. What the school unashamedly seeks are "steamers." We might all be better off if we borrowed their word since it doesn't imply its own opposite. Steamer versus nonsteamer is one thing. But gifted versus ungifted or nongifted makes an insulting distinction.

[1] George C. Robb, *Retrospects and Prospects* (London, 1975). This paper was presented at a conference held in London in 1975 and attended by delegates from fifty countries. The bibliography in the appendix includes the title of a volume of the papers presented there.

17

WHO THEY ARE

Whatever the reason for our embarrassment, we must overcome it and seek out reliable ways to identify the gifted children in our midst. Those who are trying to run identification programs in large school systems deserve our understanding and any help we can offer, for theirs is arduous and important work. The larger the scale, the more difficult the task, since accurate identification depends on understanding a human being, while operating a large program must depend on checklists, test scores, and figures. But complicated human beings seldom fit statistical formulae.

In a small school where teachers and students know one another well, meeting at meal time and on the playground as well as in class, the job is much easier. But the informality of a small setting does not guarantee accurate identification, and a responsible educator must be able to validate a subjective hunch. It is difficult to quantify something as mercurial as giftedness.

Let us look at some of the descriptions and criteria of giftedness, and current methods and instruments for pinpointing it, and consider their good and bad points. Then let us consider some characteristics common among people who have proven themselves gifted in hopes that this approach will help those concerned with identification to find ideas compatible with their needs.

In an effort to identify a future leadership pool and to encourage new programs, the United States Government has isolated and described the five following categories of giftedness:

1. *Intellectual*. This includes either academic achievement demonstrated by high performance or intellectual potential as indicated by an IQ score. While high intelligence surely goes hand in hand with giftedness, an IQ score can be obtained through many different kinds of instruments, some with a much greater reputation for accuracy than others. For instance, the validity of scores obtained through use of a group IQ test is poorly established, to say the least, as is the use of one final numerical score to describe an individual intellect. The reason for this is that a final number—

or full scale, to use professional terminology—is determined by combining subtotal scores from both verbal tests and performance tests. Each of these two numbers, in turn, is determined by combining the results of subtests in these two categories. The discrepancies or consistencies among these subtest scores are much more revealing than the final number, which may reflect dilution of a high score on one side by a low score on the other, or an even performance in all areas. But the final number gives no indication of its determiners. A brilliant engineer may have a very high score on the performance side and have a low verbal score. By averaging the two together it would be possible to arrive at a numerical indicator of average ability. In the same way, a well-organized and consistent student with good ability in a school setting might, through evenness of performance, score a higher number than the engineer, without any accompanying brilliance. A skillful interpreter can tell a great deal by looking at the subtest scores of a skillfully administered and scored test, but the test results are valid in direct ratio to the skill of, first, the test-giver, and then the interpreter. A well-administered test, knowledgeably interpreted, may indicate giftedness, but not certify it. I know of no test—and I doubt that there is one—that measures the strange combination, or balance, of drives and talents that produces not the numerical validation of giftedness, but rather that true miracle, a gifted person.

2. *Creative*. There are those who believe this can be measured by a standardized test. I am reluctant to join them.

3. *Leadership*. While a truly valuable gift, this, too, both transcends and escapes standardization, in my opinion. It also may be chrysalid or dormant at various times of personal development.

4. *Visual and Performing Arts*. At first glance this may seem easier to identify because there is an end product—the talents are easy to perceive and enjoy. But to distinguish between early developing of a minor talent and burgeoning genius seems a difficult distinction,

not predictable by timetable. A bud of something enormous does not always show as such. Similarly, a talent may grow to its ultimate capacity quickly and then stop, not heralding any further growth. The precocious child is not always gifted, nor is the gifted child always precocious.

5. *Psychomotor.* Athletes are a group that is permitted and even encouraged to excel in this country and culture. They are spotted early and given a great deal of encouragement. They are apt to have excellent coaching available either through school or municipal programs. Their teachers are quite familiar with their achievements and their parents can safely be publicly proud. Society accepts, supports, and encourages these children, and they may even get college scholarships on the basis of their muscles. Many fine athletes are also intelligent, but by no means are all good athletes intellectually inclined.

The government's method for identification leaves us with this syllogism. People who have shown themselves to be gifted are apt to have high IQs and certain character traits. Giftedness can come in the five areas listed. Therefore, anyone who is good in one of the five areas, whose IQ score falls in a given range, and who shares some of the specified character traits, is gifted.

There are two problems with using this syllogism for identifying gifted children. First, many people who have later proven to be gifted would not have been identified in school years and second, it includes too many people, exposing us to the "danger of lowering our standard of excellence through a confusion of criteria."[2]

Suppose we accept these criteria, which say that the athlete, the leader, the student, the achiever, the painter, and the musician are all gifted. Who's left?

Of course it is frequently easier to find flaws in an existing

[2]Ibid.

system than it is to design a new one. The government guidelines sprang from good intentions. They should not be rejected out of hand for their flaws any more than they should be accepted automatically because they have been published. The question we must continue to ask is whether these criteria work. Would they have identified many children we now know to be gifted?

I believe the child will keep his rightful place as the focus of our attention if we consider some traits gifted children frequently share, ways in which these traits may cluster together, and how the children use these traits in dealing with the world. I believe we will learn more by considering the effects of some of these traits, and watching *how* they are used, than we can by simply listing them in any kind of diagnostic checklist.

What follows does not pretend to be all-inclusive, but it will provide some descriptions. Those who work with gifted children (identified or not) may recognize some combinations and qualities. Some traits will seem positive, some negative. This is logical and honest because real people have both. In Chapter Four we will consider some of the delights and difficulties the gifted child faces in dealing with others in the world, but first, let's try to recognize a "steamer."

Some Traits of Gifted Minds

1. The first trait I associate with gifted minds is that *new material seems more recognized than learned*. It's as though the information, or concept, was already there and merely waiting to be quickened to life by being mentioned. This will probably be obvious in the early grades in school and may be embarrassing to the child. When algebraic equations are being explained for the first time to a class

21

of students who respond with head-scratching and knitted brows, yet one student nods with recognition and understanding, the others will surely notice. He may doodle or look out the window as camouflage.

The same kind of thing may happen to the verbally gifted child when something such as literary criticism is introduced as an art or a field of inquiry. The comment on one child's report card said, "Trying to interest Michael in sixth-grade literature is like trying to interest King Kong in a banana." It is hard for the child to handle the fact that he recognizes instantly while his peers are still struggling.

2. Another way in which a gifted mind reveals itself is in *noticing patterns:* intervals in music, shape and space in sculpture, ratio in numbers, attributes in fiction, repetitions in history. The ordinary mind can be trained to recognize these. The gifted mind does it practically automatically and delights in cross-referencing, associating the rhythm of a scherzo with the angles of a building, or the newly formed government with the shape of a constellation. Gifted children are frequently early readers, which is not surprising, since reading involves recognizing and taking meaning from patterns of visual configuration and linguistic construction.

Unconsciously and effortlessly, the gifted mind plays constantly with analogy. It is not much of a trick to solve the problem hot:cold::wet:——, but this is only the beginning. A look at the makeup of most advanced fields of inquiry shows that they require and rest on analogous thinking. This is as true of the sciences as it is of philosophy or history or art. And it certainly is true in mathematics, of which only a small part is memorization. Once the processes of computation are mastered, mathematics demands thinking, not rote memory. Intervals, comparisons, and processes come into play. Therein lies the joy and creativity. The same holds true for music (which is closely related to mathematics), architecture, literature, or science. This is why it is important to introduce

22

the child to areas other than the one of his primary interest, so he will be aware of many possible leap-froggings.

A later chapter explores ways of finding and playing with patterns to be found in children's literature. For reasons outlined there, I believe this can be immensely comforting and rewarding to the gifted child. Patterns are around us everywhere in things we hear, see, and feel, in ways we react, and in the ways our bodies work. They are inside of us and around us in all of our environment.

3. *Energy*—this is really hard to live with! I refer to physical energy and psychological energy. Each carries impact—each is finite. Gifted children frequently need less sleep than others. No one seems to know the reason for this, but it is a trait many gifted children share. When this is understood and well managed, it needn't ruin family life. A greater than usual supply of psychological energy is the mark of many gifted people, allowing them to move at a rate greater than normal, and furthermore to continue after others have stopped. It is unrealistic and unfair to expect everyone else to keep up. Chapter Six is devoted to activities the child can pursue on his own. If the rest of the family is zonked from the trip to the museum, they can guiltlessly take off their mental shoes and relax, while the energy-generator keeps going.

4. *Curiosity* is hard to live with, too. It goes hand in hand with energy. It requires protection because it is noble and important and yet it can be annoying to a weary parent. When it annoys, it arouses a negative response. This, of course, jeopardizes it, pulling the child in two directions—wanting to get along with his parent or parents, and exercising something that insists on living.

5. *Drive and concentration*. While these are not identical qualities or manifestations, they are companions, and so I couple them. For the person who can sustain concentration for a long time it is vital to have opportunities to do so. The realities of most school situa-

tions cannot provide this, because it would be unbearable torture and unreasonable expectation for everyone else. But since we recognize what a large percentage of time is nonschool time, it will be a great relief to the child capable of long concentration to be given such chances. To be denied them, or to have the family schedule restrict them, is like wakening the child who needs eight hours of sleep a night after only four, or asking Frank Lloyd Wright to limit himself to Lincoln logs. Nascent talents and abilities must be given room and opportunity to grow or else they rankle and disturb, making for restlessness or depression.

6. *Memory*. In working with disabled children who are having trouble with memory, teachers use multisensory activities, incorporating eyes, ears, and fingers simultaneously. In this way three avenues of experience are harnessed to one specific goal and the child has a triple shot at success. As teachers, we try to join an unfamiliar fact, or concept, to one already grasped. We link the new one to something already there. Similarly, in working with children who have sparse or damaged language, we emphasize pairing, finding as many ways as possible to connect the incoming unfamiliar with the known. We work with opposites, synonyms, categories, and so forth. We teach as many ways to pair as possible. It is as though we were laying single strips of Velcro, as many as would fit, and then presenting new things as the second Velcro strip. Looking at the ways in which the disabled must work to stock their memory stores may help us understand why the gifted child remembers so much. Earlier we talked about analogy, learning, and cross-referencing of patterns, at which the gifted child is so nimble. The child who starts with an ample number of learned or recognized concepts, and is agile at connections, is like a bundle of waiting Velcro. There are so many places for incoming information to stick that, of course, it sticks firmly, in turn creating more sticking places for the next information.

Memory and memorizing are often thought of together, and

this brings us to a seeming paradox. While the gifted child may remember many, many things, oddly enough, he may not be known for accuracy. Strict, rote, fact memory work may not be in harmony with the quicksilver way his mind works. Memorizing the multiplication tables may have little appeal for the child who is playing with algebra in his head. While creative thinking is a higher skill than computational accuracy, the gifted child needs both to use the full range of his ability.

7. *Empathy.* The genuinely sympathetic person seems to understand others intuitively. The dictionary defines intuition as "the direct perception of truths, facts, etc., independently of any reasoning process." This is related to the kind of recognition mentioned as the first trait, but when coupled with empathy it relates to the understanding of other people's feelings, and when coupled with concepts, it relates to the cognitive as opposed to the emotional realm. Look for the person gifted in empathy as a diagnostician, a teacher, a psychiatrist, an actor, the friend to whom you take your woes, the very best hostess—all those who know how to draw others out, and who know how to comfort and heal. Since this is not a skill one can measure with a formal test, thank God, it has no numerical equivalent. It does not show on an I.Q. score, and yet is unmistakable. One can study manuals on the interpretation of body English or practice sociological diagramming, and one may strive to become a more understanding person, but although genuine empathy, based on intuitive insights, can be exercised and refined, I do not believe it can be taught.

8. *Heightened perceptions.* For the possessor, this trait is distinctly a mixed blessing (as giftedness itself may be) in that it amplifies the painful as well as the joyful, discord as well as harmony.

Gifted children usually set extremely high standards for themselves, and their heightened perceptions can throw a painfully bright light on the discrepancy between what they would like to accomplish and what they as children can in fact accomplish. This can result in a fear of failure and because failure is so painful, they may seek safety in refusing to risk.

Heightened perceptions combined with the ability to see patterns allows the child to see, intellectually, many things with which he is not ready to cope emotionally. One example is an early awareness of the discrepancy between the wished-for and the actual. Annemarie Roeper, headmistress of the Roeper City and Country Schools for Gifted Children in Bloomfield Hills, Michigan, believes this may account for the fear of death these gifted children show. This fear comes earlier to them than to their peers and seems of a greater intensity. Acceptance of the inevitability of death is a difficult emotional task for all people, but in the case of the gifted child there is a greater than normal distance between his intellectual capacity to understand and his emotional ability to accept.

His heightened perceptions allow him no room to hide from the discrepancy between his own view of himself and the world's view of him. Fusing these two images is one of the tasks of growing up for all children, but the closer the two are, the easier the task, and the farther apart they are, the more difficult the task.

9. *Invulnerability.* Current literature would say that giftedness provides invulnerability to peer pressure. There are those who believe that because the gifted child differs intellectually from his peers he has a self-confidence that makes him impervious to the opinions of his peers, and immune to social pressure. Because he does not need to pursue popularity, the argument goes, he never need be a follower in order to be accepted. This is partly true.

The musical child who is composing in a new dimension will not be diverted from his explorations by the musical tastes of his contemporaries. However, in matters other than music, I believe he is just as vulnerable to peer pressure as anyone else, and perhaps more so, given his heightened perceptions and his emotional needs. Friendships are as important to the gifted child as they are to all children and friendship depends on acceptance.

10. *Divergent thinking*. As opposed to convergent thinking, this describes an enjoyment of open-ended, unanswerable questions, seeing the infinite as a treat, not a threat. While the divergent thinker is aware of what is there, he is also aware of what is missing. Think back to the example of looking at sculpture and seeing the space as well as the form or mass. In current literature on gifted children, divergent thinking is a term used as a synonym for creative thinking. It implies the power and freshness of originality.

It would be foolish to say, "Now we have a list of traits. People with these traits, or six out of the ten traits, or four out of the ten traits, are gifted and others are not." What we can say is that people who have been recognized as gifted have clusters of these traits. These work together in some mysterious alchemy to produce a gifted person. We may learn to recognize gifted children more easily than we have in the past if we think about clusters of these traits and consider the components of giftedness. We may look with more understanding eyes than before at the child who is a bother. Not all these traits are easy to live with, and the actions and thoughts they generate may rock the boat.

What group of people has been the most successful in recognizing giftedness?

Harold C. Lyon, director of education for the gifted and talented, U.S. Office of Education, reported to the World Conference on Gifted Children in London, 1975, that "We find that teachers miss 50 percent, particularly the creative youngsters, when you ask them to nominate the gifted and talented in the classrooms." Another paper presented at the same conference stated, "Parents correctly identified 76 percent of a group of Gifted Children while their teachers identified only 22 percent."

Simply the fact that these statistics, prepared by respected people and presented at a conference of leaders in the field, are so far apart illustrates the difficulty of the task. The job is complicated, as are the criteria and the children themselves.

We must not rely on the schools alone to identify gifted children, for reasons we will explore in Chapter Five. We mustn't depend on the government to do it because their categories are at once too rigid and too inclusive. They don't separate out that thin band of excellence which is found in every category from diamonds to cream, but take instead too large a number, particularly when athletes, leaders, and test-takers are all included. Orwellian perils abound. How dangerous to identify a group as the leadership elite when all late bloomers are eliminated. In order to function responsibly, we need to understand what a numerical score represents and we must be familiar with these categories, because they are part of our current language, but we must be aware of their dangers and limitations, while taking from them what is valid.

Parents and other children usually recognize something out of the ordinary. We must pay attention to what they say. As we read more, think more, observe more, we will continue to raise our own levels of awareness. As enlightened, concerned people (teachers, doctors, parents, and others), we can begin to trust our own ability to recognize giftedness when it crosses our path. We must use both objective measurements and subjective opinion. I do not believe that any single handy, reliable checklist or laboratory test is going to come along to do our recognizing for us. Human capacity is too complex for that, and for its complexity, variety, and surprises, particularly in giftedness, praise be!

Chapter 3

Hidden Talents: Disabled Gifted Children

Some gifted children come in disguise and are hard to recognize. There are those with learning disabilities, gifted children who are trapped in inhospitable socioeconomic conditions, and gifted minds imprisoned in bodies that do not serve them well.

Hidden in Learning Disabilities

Since schools put high value on verbal skills, a child who has trouble with reading, writing, or spoken expression may seem low in intelligence and therefore less valuable. And should he happen to do well in other conceptual fields such as engineering, science, or mathematics, he may be thought to be simply stubborn or lazy. "If only Charley would try as hard in English as he does in physics, he might get into a decent college."

History is filled with stories of those who did very poorly in school and subsequently made great contributions to knowledge and society. Winston Churchill, Thomas Edison, William James, Woodrow Wilson, Harvey Cushing, and Albert Einstein are some well-known examples. We can learn from their stories just which language skills were difficult for them, and how these difficulties surfaced, masking the giftedness which lay beneath.

The problems Edison, Wilson, Cushing, and James shared come under the umbrella of visual association or visual memory. Edison was tutored at home by his mother for several years before he was allowed to begin school, which was not until he was eight years old. In spite of early help, he had great trouble learning the letters of the alphabet, and reading and writing were always difficult for him. Correspondence written in his late teens betrays appalling weaknesses in writing and spelling, and, although the drawings in his scientific notebooks were complicated, he appears to have limited his written words to a small number with which he had learned to be comfortable.

Woodrow Wilson did not learn the letters of the alphabet until he was nine, and he was eleven years old before he learned to read. All the while his verbal output was large and of very high quality. Harvey Cushing was plagued by spelling disorders all his life which ceased to bother him once he was free of school and could go about his business of brain surgery. Throughout his life, letters and papers were typewritten for him, and the errors he made in handwritten correspondence only served to make him seem more lovable and human. William James, avid reader and prolific writer, wrote, "I am myself a very poor visualizer, and find that I can seldom call to mind even a single letter of the alphabet in purely retinal terms. I must trace the letter by running my mental eye over its contour in order that the image of it shall have any distinctness at all."

Churchill's reputation for eloquence is surely established. Look back then at his early performance in school and see his failing grades in English, his stuttering and, perhaps underlying his scholastic troubles, a difficulty in word-finding and word retrieval. The ability to deliver the needed word at the proper time is prerequisite to ease of expression. Some people are frequently plagued by a tip-of-the-tongue aphasic feeling which hinders not only their conversation but their written expression. A bright person with this type of difficulty may compensate by developing a huge store of synonyms and paired associations, so that when a needed word is elusive another related word will surface to take its place. Martha frequently has trouble finding a target word but, at six, she is already quick at association. When she needed her sock last week she called it a foot-mitten. A speaker or writer who depends on this strategy will float from lexicon to lexicon, producing originality of expression, freshness of imagery, and the surprise of poetry. Churchill may be one who transformed early aphasic problems into subsequent eloquence.

Einstein seems to have made his conceptual leaps directly, shortcutting the usual path of using words to formulate and refine thoughts. He was four before he spoke, did not read until he was nine, and his early school record was very poor. Later he said of himself, "The words of the language, as they are written or spoken, do not seem to play any role in my mechanism of thought. The psychical entities which seem to serve as elements in thought are certain signs and more or less clear images which can be voluntarily reproduced and combined. . . . "[1] Or as Georgia O'Keeffe said in a 1977 interview for The New York Times, "It's as if my mind created shapes I don't know about."

Do obstacles and achievements only exist in the past?

Sam is nine years old and lives in Santa Fe, New Mexico, with his mother, who is a silversmith. His father left the United States

[1]Lloyd J. Thompson, M.D., "Language Disabilities in Men of Eminence," The Bulletin of the Orton Society, XIX, 1969; and Richard L. Masland, M.D., "The Advantages of Being Dyslexic," The Bulletin of the Orton Society, XXVI, 1976.

during the Vietnam War when he was unable to reconcile his beliefs with government requirements for military service, and has not been a part of Sam's life since babyhood. Sam's mother chose the Southwest as an area with a moderate climate, affordable for a two-person family of very limited financial resources. She has a gentle disposition and highly developed aesthetic awareness. She graduated from college with high honors in the history of art and she has accumulated an excellent collection of books. But she saves her aesthetics and refinement for her studio and shop. Home is a pigpen.

Sam had an accident when he was six months old which severely impaired the sight in his right eye. He is physically clumsy and, since his mother is a preoccupied, very permissive parent, Sam is apt to be dirty and disheveled. He makes his own breakfast, and lunch when he thinks of it. Relics of his culinary adventures decorate his clothing. Often he smells bad. He is brilliant, stubborn, and severely disabled. Three subjective statements? Hardly.

Sam gets his current events from television and has learned a great deal about history from studying the pictures in his mother's art books. And his knowledge is not compartmentalized in discrete units; he makes connections. He will talk for hours about the similarities and differences between Egyptian and Roman military equipment. He will tell you more than you could possibly care to know about various ways cities managed sewage disposal and how Leonardo's inventions resemble some very complicated ancient Egyptian and modern American machinery. He delights in connections and analogies, and has made surprisingly few incorrect assumptions. Although he has learned so much from studying pictures, and he is a nine-year-old third grader, he is just beginning to learn to read.

Sam went to kindergarten at age five. Having spent most of his life alone, or with his mother, the sight of so many other children confused and exhausted him. He didn't fit in. He was clumsy, and therefore unwelcome in the block corner. The toy kitchen held little interest for him since he had the run of a real one at home. He was very poor at scissor and crayon work, disgusted with the fruits of his own efforts, and therefore reluctant to try again. He enjoyed music, but being clumsy, bumped into other people at rhythms and could not learn to skip. The one thing he loved was the hat collection. Each one was a passport to a world of make-believe where he would gladly spend the day. His teachers worried about this and tried to coax him back to the group. Sam wouldn't be coaxed.

He went on to first grade and great failure. He could not learn his letters. They changed shape before his very eyes and represented a trap—a distraction from knowledge, not a tool for its acquisition. When his teacher tried to work with him alone he would close his eyes, put his head down on the desk, or fall off the chair. The other children isolated him. He stayed in the back of the room, silent, different, and friendless. His teacher's notes for her final report read, "Sam can't seem to learn—in a world of his own—doesn't seek out other children—flakey mother—poor eyesight—needs glasses?—retarded?"

Sam went to second grade and Kim came into his life. She was a student teacher from the learning disabilities program in a nearby college. She was scheduled to work with some small groups and was also offered the challenge of working with Sam, alone, four days a week. Resourceful, idealistic, and stubborn, she tried phonics, she tried sight words, she tried tracing, she tried primers. Sam closed his eyes, pretended to sleep, and continued to fall off his chair. But one day he gave himself away while she was reading him a story. He pretended not to care but she knew he was listening. Then a strange thing happened. If this were a fairy tale, Sam would have smiled at Kim and changed overnight into a motivated, eager, affectionate student. Sam did just the opposite. When Kim came into the room he would bump into her. During their lesson time he would yawn right in her face, and since he was unwashed, with disheveled hair and unbrushed teeth, it was very unpleasant. He seemed to be making himself as difficult and unattractive as possible to see if she would keep on trying. He learned as little from her as he could—but just enough to keep her coming back and assure him a piece of a story. Kim was discouraged. Her supervisor told her to give up on Sam, his teachers didn't think he was worth her time, yet Kim had a hunch he was bright. She saw beyond his test score and surface appearances. Sam's camouflage was doomed.

Kim read to him while he pretended not to notice, guided his hand to make him trace his letters, painstakingly taught him to recognize letters, one by one. She withheld the day's story until he had given some correct responses. Given a correct response, she would read a small bit to him, require another response, and read again. Myths and legends were his passion, and *Norse Gods and Giants* came to be their daily textbook. Letter tracing, then a paragraph about Loki, phonics cards—"L—Loki—/L/" went their lessons, then a big piece of the story with time to look at the pictures and talk. More and more, almost against his will, Sam revealed to Kim the working of his mind, the clarity of his thinking, and the depth of his knowledge. Yet he continued to start each day's lesson with some such insulting challenges as falling off the chair, spilling Kim's purse accidentally-on-purpose, or yawning in her face.

Kim requested permission to work with him again in third grade. The year had not gone far before she realized Sam had backed her into a corner. He would break his pencil point by bearing down too hard, or he would erase and tear the paper. He would listen to the story, but when the time came for letter cards, Kim realized she was leaning forward; Sam was reclining. She was active; he was passive. Her own irritation and anger finally overrode the techniques she had learned in college. She exploded, "Sam, I've had it. You're a smart kid, and you're faking. Letters are hard for you, but you can do them if you stop copping out. I can't learn *for* you. No more help. No more stories till you shape up. I'm going to work with someone else." She picked up the book of myths and moved to the other side of the classroom. No response from Sam that day. No response all week. On Monday Kim and Sam pretended not to notice each other, but when she opened her purse at the end of the day she found this note:

"OK I wul red tumowor."

True to his word, Sam is struggling. He can decode three- and four-letter words now, he has memorized a hundred sight words, and can spell some of them. He and Kim are working their way through a tedious reading series for practice. Neither one pretends this is literature, but both agree it is necessary. They have an alliance against incapacity. Kim brought a high school physiology book to their lesson. She read the text, he studied the diagrams. After they had studied the chapter on preventive medicine he began to wash.

Sam loves science, biography, history, literature, and art and is discovering that he can gain access to them on his own. He is still disabled, and doubtless will always have to make a conscious effort to interpret the letters on a page, but some of his chains have been broken. His school acknowledges his intelligence. We cannot know the future, but Sam has a chance.

Hidden in Poverty

Families, schools, and community resources in economically depressed areas have special reasons for learning how poverty affects the nurture of a gifted child, how it creates distractions from recognizing giftedness, what can be done to raise levels of awareness, and what happens when unrecognized giftedness combines with lack of opportunity.

In many families where money is limited, children still receive intellectual and cultural nourishment, but the less affluent the parents, the harder it is for them to provide such costly things as tickets to plays and concerts, or music lessons. While free opportunities exist, it takes energy, time, and accurate reading to search them out, three commodities that may be scarce. Working parents may have little energy left at the end of the day for playing games, reading stories, or going on excursions.

Urban families generally live together in a small space where privacy and quiet are at a premium. There may be few opportunities for the gifted child to experiment, to be noticed, and to be recognized as gifted. When space is crowded and people are tired, families are apt to turn to television, the universal pacifier.

What about schools? Most economically depressed urban areas have old and overcrowded buildings that lack modern facilities and offer few, if any, enrichment extras. The dropout rate is high. Professional recruitment presents problems. Teachers must concentrate on discipline and physical safety before they can turn to teaching and learning. In such a climate the gifted child whose curiosity is still awake will find mischief, either in school or outside of it. The bored child with a nimble mind and restricted opportunity always finds trouble!

What about the community? Those who deal with children and social situations in economically depressed areas may not recognize giftedness because, having had little training in identifying a gifted child, they are not looking for one. Leaders of neighborhood organizations, social workers, clergy, parole officers, and guidance counselors, to name but a few, constantly deal with local problems of health, housing, crime, safety, drugs, and welfare. These usually require immediate attention. Time and energy are finite, and both have more demands on them than can be met.

Learning about gifted children may seem a low priority, or merely an academic exercise.

Yet if gifted children in these neighborhoods could be recognized and reached, they themselves could do much to help solve problems which their presence may aggravate. If their capacities for problem solving and their energies could be funneled to their own communities, the children's needs to be caretakers could be met and the problems they cause with their unchanneled restlessness would cease to exist. People concerned with social problems would find a new group of assistants replacing an old group of adversaries.

How might a community begin to raise the level of awareness of giftedness? Newspapers, radio, and television reach deeply into the neighborhoods they serve. If editorial staffs and program planners are themselves aware of giftedness and want their particular constituencies to share their awareness, it will happen. In the wake of such educational efforts, parents, community program planners, those in health, education, and welfare also become more aware. As the mesh of the sieve becomes finer, the chances of the gifted child slipping through unnoticed become fewer, and society stands to become richer.

In many ways the city and the country present different problems. But the gifted child in an economically distressed rural family may also remain unrecognized because, as is the case with his city counterpart, no one is looking for him.

Ben is one of three sons who lives with his family in a small town in the western part of New Jersey where people pride themselves on being hard-working and take satisfaction in the absence of "all them city things." The town library is in part of a house next to the post office. The school building is old, but well maintained. The town is run on a relatively small annual budget and no funds are available for educational experimentation. Most of the teachers have lived nearby all their lives, and few faculty members have had the money or inclination to continue their own studies after entering their profession.

Ben's parents own one car, which they share to get to work. His father is a maintenance man for a small manufacturing company and his mother is a hairdresser. Although there are two salaries, neither one is large; there is a mortgage to be paid on the house, and Ben's two remaining grandparents need financial assistance. On Saturdays Ben's mother takes the car to work. There is no public transportation, so Ben, his two brothers, and his father generally stay home and attend to chores around the place. On Saturday nights the family usually does the weekly marketing and then goes bowling or to a movie at the shopping mall twelve miles away, or else stays home and watches television. They get good reception on three channels and can usually see sports, situation comedies, and police shows. They cannot pick up any noncommercial educational channels. Two radio stations come in clearly. One gives continuous news, the other mingles local tidings with assorted music.

Ben's restlessness, energy, ideas, and questions are a constant irritation to his family. He is a leader in his class, but other boys' parents are beginning to mistrust him. They are afraid of what he'll think up next, and his pranks are taking an ominous turn as he grows physically stronger and his body is better able to keep up with his imagination. When he was fourteen he went on a shoplifting spree that lasted nearly all fall. He didn't need the things he took; it was the challenge of not getting caught that intrigued him. He moved from the mundane to the spectacular. He started pinching gum and Life Savers, and progressed to other things he and his friends could use such as transistor batteries and, of course, cigarette lighters. "I can get it for you wholesale," was the cry. His ultimate triumph came on a Saturday evening at the Caldor branch in the shopping mall. He swiped a pink, size 44, D cup bra. Just loitering at the ladies' underwear counter long enough to get it was a challenge. He had to keep a straight face and try not to be too noticeable—quite a trick for a gawky boy in a place where no gawky boy belonged. Once safely in the parking lot, he put it on and did bumps and grinds under the neon lights to the delight and applause of his friends. Then he threw the bra away and never stole another thing. It was too easy; the challenge was gone. He did, however, study the fine art of lockpicking. One night he walked the mile and a half to school, where he unlocked and opened every door, both inside and out—front door, science lab, record room, the principal's office, every door that had a lock. He left them all open wide, returned home, and went to sleep. The next day the school officials were horrified. Nothing had been stolen or vandalized, but they knew their safety was only thanks to the goodwill of the lockpicker. Now Ben's mind is occupied with CB radios, illegal fireworks, motorcycles, beer, and practical jokes. School bores him; team sports aren't nearly as interesting as the pranks he thinks up on his own. The dividing line between practical jokes and juvenile crime is not always clear and certainly not fair. It shifts from decade to decade, interpreter to interpreter, and social class to social class. Ben is bright and bored—a deadly combination.

A society guarantees problems for itself when it offers no appropriate channels for the energies of gifted children. As it is true in the physical sciences, it is true in human nature: energy is virtually impossible to extinguish. It can be harnessed, transformed, or stored, but not destroyed. Youthful energies—expression or suppression?

Hidden in Physical Disability

There are at least three ways in which a gifted mind can be imprisoned in a malfunctioning body. Physical immobility can stem from such neuromuscular diseases as cerebral palsy, and paralysis

39

or distortion can be the legacy of disease or injury. Sensory impairment such as blindness or deafness can reduce the sources from which the mind takes nourishment. Debilitating chronic illness can produce peaks and valleys of physical energy whose patterns are confusing to all.

Those who are denied physical mobility, but whose capacity for intake is undisturbed, have difficulty finding sufficient stimulation or social acceptance, and they long for the companionship of kindred spirits. This combination drove Jean, the young woman we will meet in Chapters Four and Nine, to ask Virginia Gildersleeve for admission to Barnard.

While Beethoven and Milton proved through music and literature that sensory impairment need not prevent aesthetic expression, these two examples are exceptional indeed. It is a step forward for our society that today there are facilities and programs for students with sensory impairment at most universities and many graduate schools. While such programs do not guarantee success, they do promise opportunity.

A child whose giftedness is likely to remain hidden is the one who suffers from a debilitating chronic illness. Unexplained fatigue may be interpreted as laziness or poor attitude. Surprising surges of energy at odd times lead teachers and parents to say, "She's just stubborn," or "She's just not motivated," or "She can do it when she wants to." Feeling this way, they are unsympathetic when the child can't or won't, and annoyed rather than delighted by energetic accomplishments which happen at unscheduled times.

Debby had a chronic low-grade urinary infection which remained undetected until she was seventeen. From age thirteen on she complained of fatigue and minor aches and pains that seemed to have no physical origin. She asked for frequent excuses from athletics saying she got the chills outside. When she could wangle an excuse from scheduled activities, or was allowed to stay home from school, she would draw. People who saw her work said, "She's just trying to get out of doing those other things so she can stay home and play with her pencil"; "A little exercise is what that girl needs to get the blood moving"; "No wonder she's pale and weak, sitting around like that all the time."

Her artistic talent was acknowledged but thought to be either seducing her away from "real life" or simply a cop-out. Her school grades were miserable. She didn't seem to bring energy, interest, or stamina to the academic fare and this made her teachers impatient and finally uninterested.

When Debby contributed ten drawings to a benefit being held for the nearby hospital, not only were they all sold, but the art critic for the newspaper praised her as an important new talent. "See what I mean," said her teacher. "When she *wants* to do something well, she can." Debby had neither the energy to meet such expectations nor the strength to fight back, so she withdrew, with the result that her drawing caused resentment rather than delight.

When she was about to enter her senior year of high school the doctor who had always given her her annual physical examination retired from practice. Debby went to a new doctor, who discovered that she had a low-grade infection. He considered Debby a legitimate patient, not a malingerer. He cured her illness and Debby bloomed. Her cheeks turned pink, her energy soared, her appetite was robust for the first time in years, and she had staying power. Her schoolwork improved dramatically without diluting her artistic output or development. People had come to assume that Debby would be wan and passive in her approach to life and had forgotten to look for the cause.

Similar stories can be told about children who suffer from such things as petit mal or chronic congestion of nose, ears, and sinuses. Of course, not all are gifted. Some are of average or below-average capacity. Not every naughty boy is gifted, nor is every child with language difficulty a Churchill or an Einstein, but it behooves us to remember Debby and Ben and Sam when we deal with children who displease and disappoint us.

Considering how many times we fail to recognize giftedness in children who are intact, it is no surprise that we frequently miss it in the disabled. We must raise our own levels of awareness and become better players in this game of hide and seek, ceasing to equate physical maneuverability and mental agility.

PART II

How They Live

Chapter 4

Give and Take

The gifted child has much to give his family, his friends, and his world. In return he needs their support and understanding. We must consider his relationships with each of these groups separately, in spite of occasional overlap, since they differ in intensity, duration, and frequency. We must also explore the special opportunities and special perils that attend each of the three; otherwise the opportunities may remain unrealized and the perils may catch the unwary by ambush.

The Gifted Child and His Family

WHAT HE CAN GIVE THEM

The gifted child will bring joy, energy, and originality to family life. These are his treasures, but they may be difficult gifts to accept or assimilate and are not guaranteed to promote domestic tranquility. When the mother of five-year-old Douglass describes

45

his early childhood, her voice blends exhaustion and awe. He was always active and seemed determined to conquer his world. His forays to the end of the crib or the far side of the wastebasket were marked by a determination Sir Edmund Hillary would have recognized instantly. In banging his mug on his highchair and pouring the milk from the mug to the floor, there was not only a delight in action and noise, but a determination to make the milk descend, and a thrill of mastery when it did. When he crept off on his first independent journey around the corner into the hall—and then urgently needed to return to his mother's side—the return trip had more a quality of reclaiming a territory than running for cover. As he investigated the new and returned to plant the flag on the previously explored, nothing was safe: cupboards, ashtrays, sisters' belongings, pocketbooks, and closets all yielded new and exciting treasures which he rearranged in novel combinations. Doesn't every woman rejoice at finding a fork in her purse? Although this child's delight in the world was contagious and, by his example, his family learned to see the novel in the familiar, it was hard to survive the combination of apartment living, ceaseless exploration, and Douglass's scant need for sleep. Infrequent short naps were all he required or would tolerate. The sharing of parental duties and allocating a generous amount of money for hiring baby-sitters saved the mother, father, and two sisters, not to mention Douglass. Now that he is five, his vigor and originality continue, but his concentration span is longer, his energies are more directed, and his scientific searches seem more like investigations than all-out invasions.

We must not confuse this child's activities, ceaseless and energetic though they were, with the restlessness of hyperactivity. His were attempts to bring the world under control, to understand it and master it. Hyperactivity is a distraction from mastery, not a step toward it.

The gifted child treats his family to a spectacle of accomplishments. These come physically as he moves out into his world using his body for exploration, intellectually as he sizes up opportunities and risks, and verbally as he learns to share his perceptions. One can say similar things about all babies. Families wait for such milestones and enjoy them with each child. But the family usually recognizes an extra dimension with the gifted child. He may walk early, as Douglass did, or, understanding the risks involved in taking off on two small feet, may wait a seemingly indecent length of time. But either his walking or his waiting will have an energetic rather than a passive quality. Words are tools of investigation and mastery, and the gifted child will probably use them at an early age, bringing delight and amusement to both speaker and listener.

The gifted child's supreme gift to his family is himself. He will share his energy and zest for exploration, and proudly parade his independence unless these have been pinched or malnourished by an unsympathetic environment. While this sounds fine on paper, it can be exhausting or maddening to live with. Lucia said, when nearly eight, "I know what I want for my birthday . . . a clothes allowance." "A clothes allowance? At your age? Whatever for?" "I don't like those boring things you make me wear. So I looked up in the Sears Roebuck catalogue and figured it out. If I just had a clothes allowance I could wear what I want." "Really? What would you buy?" The reply came solemnly, "A black dress with diamond buttons, red shoes, and a big umbrella. I could get it all for $44.37. I figured it out." Imagine the ensuing daily battle over Buster Brown oxfords with a young lady who had discovered slingbacks and rhinestones.

WHAT HIS FAMILY CAN GIVE HIM

The first thing the family of a gifted child must to do is acknowledge him as a person. This sounds obvious, but sadly, it's not automatic.

47

HOW THEY LIVE

Last spring in our school we had a call from a mother who was interested in the possibility of enrolling her child. She described him as an extraordinarily bright little boy and she wondered if we would be able to meet his academic needs. He had turned eight, was in the second grade, and she said he was bored in his present school. Admissions work is usually done in the spring, and there was nothing unusual about the call or the request. An appointment was scheduled.

It was an unusual and frightening session. The mother referred to the child variously as "my eight-year-old who does algebra in his head," "my son who is a math whiz," "my gifted child," and "the middle one who is gifted." She described his abilities, his achievements, and his test scores, but by the end of the conference, which lasted nearly an hour, she had never once used his name! We had to ask her what it was. And she clearly didn't understand the impact of our question, so totally had he become an anonymous achiever, or perhaps, her achievement.

Having acknowledged him as an individual, the gifted child's family can give him a strong connection with his world by relying on him to be a giver of care as well as a receiver. Family life provides countless opportunities for caretaking—of pets, plants, or other family members. Begun early, this tradition will be helpful throughout life. It needn't be outgrown and it needn't be shackled to the mundane. While an exotic teenage poet would probably have scant interest in taking care of a troop of Girl Scouts, she might be intrigued by the idea of growing specimen orchids or raising unusual fish. The responsibility for other living things is what forges the link.

The gifted child needs to share chores and duties as well as treats. (It goes without saying that this must be fair and not Cinderella-esque). He needs to participate in ordinary family activities as one member of the group. Joining in the telephone call to a distant grandmother, helping with the dishes, working with

48

everyone else on the Hallowe'en pumpkin, sharing the sadness that comes with loss and the anticipation of a longed-for event, talking *and listening* at the family dinner table are the kinds of group experiences the gifted child needs.

The gifted child's family can give him a reassuring acquaintance with limits and rules. This will help him structure and temper his world. Since his perceptions are acute, he sees how many things might go awry. The security of rules in his domestic life can help him tame fears of external or internal forces that might otherwise be overwhelming. Although he needs rules and requirements, he will, like all children, press at the limits, probably with extra momentum. This may intimidate individual family members, or sometimes the whole group, unless they are aware that such a possibility exists and resist the temptation to treat one child differently.

The gifted child may feel lonely because he is distinct among his contemporaries in his area of giftedness. He must not be made to feel secretive or embarrassed about his talent, and family life can provide an arena where he can display it unabashedly. This is true no matter whether the talent lies in performing, reasoning, creating, or understanding. A child loves to hear a parent say, "Will you help me? I need you." To honor a child's special quality, depend on it, don't simply praise it. Family life can give the child an opportunity to exercise it without embarrassment.

The gifted child's family must remember the depth and extent of his potential concentration and the extra power he brings to his pursuits. This combination needs scope, which his family can provide.

Sometimes the parents will need to help the child plan projects that match his level of ability and manual dexterity. This is not to say he should be held to a babyish level or have his plans thwarted. But the gifted child often has grandiose dreams; he may expect and demand perfect performance of himself and be frustrated and angry when he falls short. Cooperative planning can help a child avoid this disaster. The nine-year-old boy who envisioned himself the one Saturday creator of a television set agreed to make a radio first. He had a successful experience with the intracacies of electronic diagrams and music at the end of the day. Steered away from what would have been certain disaster, this child has legitimate confidence in his ability to try the next step.

There will also be fortunate times when the child can realistically create and attempt on his own. If he is not creating his own obstacles, he should be left alone to work out his plans and projects independently.

Stimulation is important, and the gifted mind will make imaginative use of variety. The arts, nature, history, athletics (which needn't be competitive) all can reinforce one another and expand the child's receptive and expressive limits.

As interest in gifted children grows on a national scale, it is growing locally too. Many communities have Saturday programs for gifted children which offer this kind of variety, and many welcome all members of a family. The appendix includes a list of organizations and publications related to gifted children in different areas of this country. A call to a nearby group should provide current information about opportunities in a specific community. The family of a gifted child who keeps in touch with current community activities and attitudes will be able to choose those that harmonize with the family's child-raising philosophy.

The family must evaluate whatever teaching the child receives in his area of primary interest, seeing that it is precise, of the highest available quality, and demands the child's best performance. Whether the field is gymnastics, music, science, or poetry, the child must learn obedience to the discipline of his field as well as delight in its company.

While gifted children can learn from explanations and teaching, they can also hypothesize independently, as Sam the dyslexic boy

50

in Chapter Three demonstrated. Then they need a way or place to test new hypotheses without ridicule. Such opportunities are just as important as an unending series of trips, and family life can provide them.

The child's need for privacy and enrichment are not contradictory. While he needs new experiences, new ideas, and new words as food for his intellect, he needs time, space, and privacy to play with them and internalize them. Providing the privacy in addition to the enrichment is a step some parents are embarrassed to take. Caught up in the tempo of lessons and trips, they think the child needs constant doses, and they feel guilty leaving him alone. The child's family must guarantee his privacy. He cannot do it for himself.

Living with a gifted child is not easy. It's like being invited to accompany an explorer. The reluctant or frightened parent will ignore the invitation. The cooperative parent will accept and pack for the trip. However, this is not a Sunday hike up a gentle hill. It is more like an attempt to scale the southwest face of Everest. It requires reservoirs of stamina, courage, and humor, which are the gifts the child needs to receive from his family.

SPECIAL PERILS, SPECIAL OPPORTUNITIES

It is difficult for the gifted child, his brothers and sisters, and his parents to meet their own various needs and still strike the balance most healthy families develop. For instance, it is natural for any child to try to have his own way and want to come first. The gifted child, with his extra impetus, may knock down those around him as he plays this classic game. If he always wins, he will be uneasy with himself, and the rest of the family will be resentful. A gifted child is encouraged to become a bully or a prima donna if his needs and accomplishments dominate family life. Harking back to an earlier image, three or five mobiles can swing in the same room with grace and fluidity. They may be big or small, multicolored or monochromatic, depicting sailboats, paper moons, birds, orbs, or anything. As long as they are all mobiles, it doesn't matter. Set a wind-up helicopter loose in the room, and it's a different story.

It is hard for brothers or sisters of a gifted child to feel that their talents are equally appreciated unless the parents take special care. Those whose qualities are unacknowledged will naturally resent those who are favored by recognition, and jealousy will destroy family happiness. Abigail was an outstanding mathematician who loved music, literature, and any challenge to her mind. She was intellectually aggressive, yet loving and gentle in her feelings about people. Even though she was admired for her achievements, throughout her childhood she was shy and lonely. She couldn't get a tennis ball over the net until she was fourteen and, while she longed for invitations, she was bashful about extending them. She won the highest academic awards her school could bestow, and she was a National Merit scholar. But her accomplishments seemed to isolate her from other people and she often wished they were less noticed. So did her young sister, Jenny.

Jenny could walk into a room full of people, know exactly what was going on and say something to each person which showed she understood his feelings. She could make anyone laugh, and put anyone at ease, young or old, boy or girl. She found rhythm in design and athletics. She could ski, swim, and play tennis, but academics were torture to her. Jenny was jealous of Abigail's scholastic success and Abigail was puzzled and annoyed by her little sister's social ease, athletic ability, and designer touch. Since these things came easily to Jenny, she thought they were fun but not valuable. She thought things had to be difficult in order to matter. Report cards came out six times every year between September and June, and each arrival demanded a juggling act on the part of the parents. Abigail's grades must be honored and praised. It would have been wrong to give them less attention than they deserved for they were the product of unusually fine work, and intellectual accomplishment was Abigail's way of extending her hand to the world. But to interpret Jenny's miserable grades as a similar reflection of the person inside would have been to label her worthless. The report cards had to be praised and underplayed simultaneously and without hypocrisy. The parents had to encourage Abigail to trust herself, to admire her sister's strengths and try not to feel threatened by someone two years her junior who still watched *The Flintstones*. They had to encourage Jenny to trust her own judgment and ability in spite of no formal confirmation of their worth from the academic world. These two sisters learned compassion for each other and because their parents genuinely valued each child's qualities, they, in turn, learned to be proud of each other's successes. When all members of a family honor different kinds of strengths, everyone is richer. Most parents do these things instinctively unless they are talked (or shamed) out of them by those who think gifted children should be treated differently from others.

A subtle peril threatens parents of gifted children, who risk a peculiar kind of loneliness and isolation in their child-raising. The whole world is sympathetic to the family of the child on the muscular dystrophy poster. Benefits for retarded children sell out weeks in advance. Emotionally disturbed or learning-disabled children and their families can find opportunities to share their experiences and join in programs. A sympathetic ear is usually available. But try this one. Call up a friend whose child is doing creditable, average work in school and say, "I'm so worried about Johnny. He's four years ahead of his age in math and I just don't know how to handle him." Or, "The school thinks Tom ought to go to college two years early. What do you think? What should I do?" It's a quick way to lose conversational companions. Discuss labor pains, communism, your neighbor's love affair, or the recent earthquake and all is well, but introduce the dilemma of raising a gifted child and you've cleared the room. Not only must you avoid discussing the attendant problems, but you'd better not be too specific about recent successes. The threat of loneliness is as real for the parents as it is for the child.

SPECIAL OPPORTUNITIES

The world needs people who are gifted in all three dimensions of human potential: the aesthetic, the ethical, and the rational/scientific. These labels, used by the English educator G. H. Parkyn in an address to the first World Conference on Gifted Children in London in 1975, are a memorable, simple description of a complicated balance. Since the happiness of the family group—perhaps even its survival—requires that the qualities of the gifted child be balanced with or against those of the other members, a unique opportunity exists here for the gifted child and his family. A group in which all three elements are represented has greater richness than one that cultivates only one or two. New ideas and thoughts can be considered in the special light that characterizes each. As the gifted child makes a particular contribution in the area which matches his talent, he covers that base, freeing the others in his family to expand in other directions. One person's talent or knowledge thus becomes not only something to be shared and admired, but also a force for new growth in other areas.

By providing opportunities for each family member to exercise all three facets of his own nature, each individual group member will have the same internal balance that is desirable for the group as a whole. The mobiles will swing without collision.

The Gifted Child and His Friends

It takes great restraint for adults not to interfere with children's choice of friends. However, except in cases of extreme unsuitability or danger, they must not usurp this privilege, although for reasons we will explore, some choices may seem puzzling.

WHAT HE CAN GIVE THEM

The gifted child brings himself, first, as the most important contribution. Since he is probably content in his own company, as most gifted children are, his offer of friendship is a step toward another person, not a flight from solitude. It is a valued gift rather than a defense against boredom.

As always, he brings energy and originality, which may not produce as many repercussions in friendship as they do in family life. Peers seem more willing to accept them, and if the going gets rough, it's possible to make new friends. Different interests may appear, new activities may have special appeal as the child grows, and the unwritten and strict code that dictates custom and costume may shift. The child is free to trade in his jeans, but not his genes.

If the gifted child seeks among his friends someone to share a particular interest, his contribution to the relationship will be depth of knowledge and the example of sustained enthusiasm. However, he may well prefer privacy in his special field, or only wish to share it with professionals.

WHAT FRIENDS CAN GIVE HIM

When adults are concerned that the gifted child's friends aren't up to his level, they must remember the frequent discrepancy between his level of intellectual functioning and his level of social maturity. A gifted child, trying so hard to measure up to his own standard of success, realistic or fantastic, can find supreme comfort in undemanding companionship. Trading baseball cards, forming clubs, sharing comic books (yes, gifted children like them, too), going to the movies, buying pizza, batting a ball, discussing disc jockeys, are all nonintellectual, normal pastimes, satisfying to a growing child. It is fun to hack around.

The gifted child needs surcease as well as stimulation. The electric, the quick, the advanced are a joy and a flint, but it is exhausting to be constantly stimulated, and nothing is sadder than the helpless creature whose gears are stuck in overdrive. Our child needs comfortable times that are not solitary. I believe this accounts for some of the puzzling alliances one sees from time to time.

Mike is a quiet boy whose electronic engineering will probably rescue the world from all its ills some day. He is in his mid-teens. When he gets home from school in the afternoon he likes to go to see Teddy, a ten-year-old neighbor. He tosses a ball with him, helps him build models, and sometimes they play with Teddy's massive collection of G. I. Joe paraphernalia which Mike passed down to him. Teddy throws himself into the make-believe and Mike finds refreshment in a bit of nostalgia. Needless to say, Teddy adores Mike, who teases him unmercifully, and both boys take nourishment from the friendship.

Susannah used to invite Maude Hart over every Saturday. Susannah's dynamism fairly rocked the planet. There was nothing she wouldn't try. Maude Hart (who was always called by both names) was a pudding of a child with tight braids, a plump face, and few ideas. Why then did Susannah beg for her week after week? Susannah was the youngest in her family. Everyone else was forceful, verbal, and independent. While she shared their talents, she stood no chance of persuading any of them to obey her. With her companion, she could call out, "Maude Hart, stand there," and Maude Hart would oblige while Susannah played out the game of the day around her, moving her from place to place as the occasion demanded, like a piece of scenery shrubbery. Maude Hart was delighted to stand in for a soldier or a lilac bush, and the two girls spent many days together—completely free from argument. Although her family would groan at the sight of Maude Hart, Susannah loved her and needed her.

A gifted child's friends may give him stimulation through a common interest. Children who share an interest, be it weather forecasting, fashion design, the Dallas Cowboys, or CB radio, contribute to one another's lives. The sharing is probably more important than the ball team chosen or the hobby itself, even though the interest may not match adult expectation.

Sometimes, of course, the interest or activity will offer rich, intellectual challenges. This is apt to be the case when a friendship jumps a generation. Warmth, leadership, knowledge, and encouragement to dare usually characterize such a relationship. Both life and literature provide examples of one older person who believes in a younger one, sharing insights and setting expectations.

A physician, renowned for his work in respiratory diseases, saw mostly adult patients in his New York City practice. Then a four-year-old boy needed his help on a regular basis for nearly two years. A tremendous bond sprang up between the two. The doctor, who was treated with awed respect by his patients and colleagues, would laugh with delight as the little boy would run past waiting room tables displaying *Forbes* and *Fortune* magazines, calling out, "Hi! I'm here. Look what I got." The child always brought his greatest treasure of the moment. The older man would examine it and then share some of his treasures in return. He gave the child a course in anatomy, showing him x-rays, explaining in detail what the pictures revealed, describing diseases and telling what kinds of medicines would help which ones. He taught the child to use a stethoscope, how to measure blood pressure, and to use long Latin names for many parts of the body. Although the little boy's illness led to some frightening episodes, and although the treatment involved both lengthy, tiring travel to the doctor's office and painful injections, the child looked forward to the visits and relished his special relationship with the older man, thinking of him first as a friend, and next as a doctor. He understood and remembered his anatomy lessons and delighted in using the complicated terms the doctor taught him. If this were the script of a thirty-minute television show, the boy would win a scholarship to Harvard Medical School and the proud aged doctor would give him his own black bag in a deathbed scene, passing the mantle of healing from one generation to another. But this is a true story. After the boy's treatment was completed, the family moved halfway across the country. The boy's health remains good, and, while the young and old friend have vivid memories of one another, their current relationship is limited to Christmas cards. However, the child will never forget that a learned older person, with rooms full of mysterious shiny equipment, shared his knowledge and his time, recognizing the child's level but never stepping down to it, and instead, explaining adult mysteries in adult language.

When Virginia Gildersleeve was dean of Barnard College she arranged college admission for a young woman in her late twenties who was badly crippled from poliomyelitis, surely one of the first informal experiments in continuing education. Dean Gildersleeve believed in the young woman's ability to complete a college education and to reach her goal of going on to medical school and becoming a practicing physician. What a welcome contrast this made to other reactions of incredulity, pessimism, or ridicule. Virginia Gildersleeve had had a particularly close relationship with her own father. He had had faith in his daughter's ability to do unusual and difficult things. He had shared his ideas and thoughts with his child in much the same way the elderly physician had explained anatomy to the little boy, and he encouraged her to express her thoughts in return. Having had her own mind and dreams thus dignified in her own youth, Dean Gildersleeve knew how to do the same for others. The faith she demonstrated not only contributed warmth to the friendship between the college

dean and her unusual student, but helped the young woman believe in herself at difficult times as she struggled to make her dream
come true. The rest of her story is told in Chapter Nine.

The biographies of distinguished people frequently pay grateful
attention to the role of an older, learned person whose friendship
reached across a chronological gap to touch a younger person's
mind and spirit. It may have been someone outside the family,
such as the doctor and college dean mentioned here; it may have
been a parent, as was the case with Virginia Gildersleeve; or it may
have been a grandparent, as was the case so beautifully described in
Blackberry Winter by Margaret Mead. Her grandmother's companionship, faith, and high expectations encouraged the young girl's
explorations. Such strong, intimate relationships between people
of different generations can set the direction of a whole life. In 1968
a White House task force was established for the express purpose
of interviewing a group of people whose lives were particularly
successful according to criteria of professional achievement and
community respect to see what elements might be common to
their various stories. "They all said that some individual had shed
his rank and status and built an intimate one-to-one human relationship encouraging them to take risks and try new things they
would not have tried without that kind of encouragement."[1]

We adults must not only notice the effect of such relationships
on the children of the past but must be aware of how we may fill
such spots for the children among us now.

SPECIAL PERILS, SPECIAL OPPORTUNITIES

Sadly, gifted children may suffer intense, unsatisfied longings
for friendship, since their awareness of the ways in which they are

[1]Harold C. J. Lyon, *Realizing Our Potential* (London, 1975). Paper presented at
World Conference on Gifted Children, London, 1975.

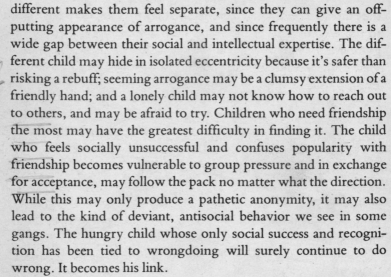

different makes them feel separate, since they can give an off-putting appearance of arrogance, and since frequently there is a wide gap between their social and intellectual expertise. The different child may hide in isolated eccentricity because it's safer than risking a rebuff; seeming arrogance may be a clumsy extension of a friendly hand; and a lonely child may not know how to reach out to others, and may be afraid to try. Children who need friendship the most may have the greatest difficulty in finding it. The child who feels socially unsuccessful and confuses popularity with friendship becomes vulnerable to group pressure and in exchange for acceptance, may follow the pack no matter what the direction. While this may only produce a pathetic anonymity, it may also lead to the kind of deviant, antisocial behavior we see in some gangs. The hungry child whose only social success and recognition has been tied to wrongdoing will surely continue to do wrong. It becomes his link.

The socially timid gifted child may try to conceal his special talent in an attempt to become or remain "one of the boys." Peter, the ballet dancer we will meet in Chapter Nine, tried this for a while. However, talents have a way of refusing to stay hidden. Popularity is an ephemeral prize at best, and meaningless if its price is the denial of gifts.

It is as difficult to predict the reasons for the miracle of a strong intimate friendship as it is to predict the reasons for giftedness itself, but it is wonderful to have one good friend. True friendship provides immunity from loneliness without sacrifice of self.

The Gifted Child and His World

WHAT HE CAN GIVE HIS WORLD

Once again, the gifted child offers vigorous originality. The novel ideas of gifted young thinkers may seem dangerous when they threaten traditional patterns and they may appear iconoclastic to those who cling to the status quo. Accordingly, their mental gymnastics will be accepted or rejected, depending on the point of view of the interpreter. On Charlotte's sixth-grade report card her English teacher called her original. Her sports teacher called her rebellious. Her mathematics teacher saw productive determination where her science teacher saw truculence. "Fresh" was used twice, once as a compliment and once as a reprimand. What one person called "energetic" another labeled "aggressive."

Until recently aggressiveness was suspect and unacceptable, particularly in girls. Now we seem to be growing more honest about its existence and its value. A gifted child's mental or physical explorations may seem personally aggressive when in fact they are thrustings into ideas, not thrustings against people.

Living in contemporary society is like sitting in the center of a giant corn-popper. The pot is bubbling on all sides, and things that previously looked like little brown objects with stable properties are exploding, changing shape and size, expanding and expanding. It is exciting, the results are beautiful and tasty, but the change is complete, and it is hard to say just where change will happen next. Each day seems to bring new discoveries about the human brain, past forms of life previously unknown, new theories on artificial creation of life, and all the empirical and philosophical controversy such topics generate. These few examples indicate some of the many directions thought and discovery could take.

The advent of space exploration, electronic discoveries, and technical sophistication have pushed us into a new era in which patterns of support and dependence have changed. For the first time ever tradition and culture give adults no experiential edge. Things are unfamiliar and unpredictable to all of us together. In their perception of patterns, the originality of the patterns they see, and their novel approach to traditional problems, gifted children developing into gifted adults may help us form the questions we need to ask about the future as we try to determine where our civilization should go next.

WHAT HIS WORLD CAN GIVE HIM

The most important thing the world can give to gifted children is a welcome and an acknowledgment of their human needs as well as of their intellectual capacities. Does this sound platitudinous? The acceptance that one group of sixth graders in a California school accorded a newcomer from New York proved to be a mirage. The group acknowledged his astonishing mathematical superiority, called attention to it, relied on it, and spoke of it proudly as a hallmark of their group. At the same time, they isolated him in this one area and turned him into their mascot. Since a mascot, by definition, is simply an object of affection, a toy or an amulet, this, of course, dehumanized him.

The child's world must acknowledge him as a human being, not as a notch in a belt or a feather in a hat. While this is a need all children share, the gifted child's own accomplishments, being outstanding, may work to his own detriment if they, alone, are the means by which his world recognizes him. If the world can accept the gifted child's extra dimension, he can accept it more easily himself. The combination of passion, energy, drive, and concentration, and his scant need for sleep are apt to exhaust most people in his world. Rather than creating delight, these traits are apt to irritate. "Why can't you————, just like everyone else?" The gifted child whose world has not accepted him is probably asking the same question of himself.

Additionally, a gifted child may be puzzled and feel faintly guilty about his extra endowment. It's the flip side of the "Why me?" we recognize in survivors and victims in other contexts. When one has less than others, "Why me?" is a natural question and is answered with sympathy by society. When one has more than others, "Why me?" is frequently answered with some version of "Why you indeed?" Scant comfort. In accepting the child, the world admits his qualities and removes his need to feel guilty, giving him license to use his energy for growth rather than for expiation or disguise.

The world can give the gifted child a mirror off which to bounce his various reflections so he may choose which ones are accurate and which ones are only temporarily satisfying dramatic exercises. As a little child, Claire was by turns the intrepid explorer, the detective, the monster, and, in later years, the egghead, the dilettante, and the embodiment of ennui. At seventeen she was in real danger because she had not held back one corner of her mind for realistic appraisal. She couldn't tell which pose was real and which a masquerade. The gifted child who finds welcome, acceptance, and reflection in the world around him will be able to resist the Circean call to eccentricity. While it may seem fun to play Greta Garbo or Oscar Wilde temporarily, it is frightening to be marooned in make-believe.

The gifted child's world can provide opportunity and exposure. This needn't mean extensive travel through the Himalayas; it can happen in neighborhoods, cities, villages, or country towns. It's a question of the point of view. If financial strictures preclude travel, libraries have books and records, children have feet and one another, and television broadcasts some excellent materials. Neighborhood excursions can yield a wealth of information and provoke profound questions. There is a sunset every day, but we frequently run out of time to notice it.

SPECIAL PERILS, SPECIAL OPPORTUNITIES

The gifted child is in danger of feeling like Superman, invulnerable and invincible. One four-year-old child, who frequently sees frontier where his family sees only peril, set off on an independent foray into the world, absorbed in his exploration, confident of his destination, and unperturbed at the prospect of a return trip. He lives close to a dangerously busy highway and to a swamp. When they realized he was missing, his family scoured the house and the neighborhood. He had been scolded severely several times in the recent past for running away, and they couldn't believe he had done it again. They were sure some dreadful trap had caught him. They finally found him several miles away, standing in a clump of trees. At first they were filled with joy at seeing him safe and alive and said, "We're so relieved to find you. What are you doing here?" He said, "I wanted to see the owl. I have one in my book." Indeed, his father remembered that six or eight months ago he had spotted an owl in this very tree and had shown it to the little boy. Relief turned to anger. "But you know you're not allowed to run away. We've told you and told you." "But I wasn't running *away*," protested the child, "I was coming to see the owl." He didn't understand their concern any more than they understood his insouciance.

An athletically gifted child may come to feel invincible. This feeling encourages prowess and prowess is nourishing. With it, a child sees himself not as a leaf carried on the stream, but rather as a determining oar in the water. All to the good. The danger here is that physical prowess is so often displayed in a competitive arena. The child becomes accustomed to a cycle of win-develop-compete-win and, being gifted, wins many times. Winning then becomes part of his identity, in his own mind, as well as in that of eager coach, proud parents, and admiring onlookers. Thus, when the inevitable moment comes to lose, it is as though a genuine part of his identity is lost. It is not an event; it is an amputation.

Intellectually, a subtle peril exists for the gifted child who is trying to explain new insights. Original ideas are difficult to express and even great thinkers may have trouble developing new symbols. Using old symbols in new ways is confusing to those of us who are trying to interpret by habit. We are used to certain symbols and patterns and don't stop to think about them every time we see or hear them. When the thinker or artist comes along who uses the familiar in unfamiliar ways, we are apt to react with suspicion or discomfort. e. e. cummings was initially considered crazy and dangerous, as were Stravinsky and Frank Lloyd Wright. Very few major contributors to science, philosophy, or the arts found acceptance early in their careers.

Finally, unless concerned adults are alert, gifted children are in danger of being exploited. They are being discovered as a new profitable commercial market and the "maximizers" and the "utilizers" smell gold.

For good or ill, we are a nation of bandwagoners with a cultural reflex demanding that once a condition is labeled, society must develop methods for either succumbing to it or curing it. From clean laundry to bad breath, we mobilize. Giftedness is no exception. Many of the materials being developed for gifted children to use at home, in school, or as independent projects are delightful and instructive. We and the children in our care should welcome them and learn how best to use them. But we also face an avalanche of "identificational instruments" and kits purportedly designed to foster creativity but which, in reality, are packaged and sold by humorless pedants.

In one three-week period my professional and personal mail included advertisements for over twenty-five items labeled specifically for gifted children. They ranged from materials for a set of classroom science experiments, which appeared to be of very high quality, to *Crossword Puzzles for Gifted Children, Grade 2*. The latter was actually a repackaging of a softcover book of the same crossword puzzles previously labeled for grade four. Another brochure assured me that if, as a teacher, I needed to spend funds allocated for materials for gifted children, or G/Ts as they were called, I could order the new lit kit containing condensed paperback versions of the classics complete with comprehension questions. They further assured me that "flowchart-wise," over 50 percent of their offerings were materials for G/Ts.

There is nothing intrinsically evil about giving fourth-grade crossword puzzles to a second grader, and abridged versions of complicated stories can be appropriate, but surely truth in labeling is as important here as it is in the supermarket. We should know what ingredients are in the nourishment we buy for children's minds as well as what goes into the food we buy for their bodies.

Will it be long before we have such terms as "Gift-Speak" to describe the utterances of gifted children, followed by "Insta-Gift-Speak," a kit to help a child be among the first to qualify for a new program? As British society was humorously divided into "U" and "non-U," will we be "G" and "non-G"?

Gifted children need protection from such exploitation. The power and freshness of their genuinely creative thinking must be protected, and their humor and creativity must be insulated from those materials that cap creativity while claiming to unlock it. They need people who insist on seeing them as real live people, not "ideational models" or percentages of populations.

Whether learning-disabled, retarded, handicapped, or gifted, it is inevitable that once a special category of student is identified, people have to be found to fit the description. School districts have money to be spent on their behalf, teachers have been specially trained and hired to cope with them, and educational materials have been developed and must be bought. With all this ready and waiting, each district needs to produce some such students in order to keep up with neighboring districts and keep the grant money flowing. Think what would happen to land values if the Elmwood District said, "We have only three gifted children this year. We don't need that program," while Oakwood was saying, "Gifted children make up 33 percent of our student body. We need more facilities." Families would surge to Oakwood, hoping there was some miraculous mineral in the drinking water.

It is heartening that gifted children and their needs are being given their rightful turn in the spotlight and that many adults are working wisely and enthusiastically on their behalf. But it would be destructively naive to assume altruism and quality in all the programs and materials which today claim to be for the gifted.

While it is not simple to live with a gifted child, humor and resilience can make the way easier for all concerned. Those who learn to understand and accept the drives these children have can share an adventure. To return to our earlier image of accompanying an explorer, new sights and experiences will be ours if we will go with him to a land we could not find on our own.

Chapter 5

A Goodness of Fit: The Gifted Child and School

Just as a choral director would be sure to hand a soprano score to a soprano, and an Olympic aspirant would only train with equipment appropriate to his physical size and level of skill, the gifted child will blossom best in a school which provides a "goodness of fit." This phrase, attributed to the late Herbert Birch, New York physician and professor, describes an ideal match of student need and academic offering. In stressing the harmony of the combination rather than the merit of a particular program or child, this concept underscores the flexibility and understanding gifted children require.

No single institution, family, or school can be expected to meet all of the needs of any child. The school certainly cannot do it alone. But the family, the school, and the student himself (in a manner appropriate to his age) can cooperate in meshing available opportunities and the student's academic, social, and emotional requirements to create a "goodness of fit." A brief review of recent

69

educational changes may help us understand what the school can and cannot promise the gifted child.

In times past, parents expected schools to concentrate on the child's intellectual training, but now schools are expected to provide for the whole child. More and more, parents depend on schools to function in loco parentis, taking responsibility for the child's social and athletic life as well as his intellectual and moral growth, psychological well-being, and his plans for the future. The guidance office is frequently busier than the library.

Changes have come in facilities as well as in functions, giving us many different kinds of schools. The rapid growth of the suburbs and the popularity of large families in the fifties and sixties spawned new schools in existing communities and new schools in new communities. At this moment in this nation we have public schools, parochial schools, and independent schools, all operating at elementary, junior high, and high school levels. They are urban, rural, well supported, well equipped, poorly supported, poorly equipped, with every variety of size, student body, and faculty. Some are close to colleges that offer teacher-training programs and hence have a steady flow of student teachers or apprentices. Some are well equipped with libraries, stages, music and art rooms, gymnasiums, darkrooms, and sometimes computers. Some schools are isolated, others are centrally located but lack facilities. Because of such great variety, and the variety of the children themselves, it would be foolish to try to devise an ideal curriculum for a gifted child here. But we can consider ways to tailor a goodness of fit between the gifted child and whatever school he may attend, whether the combination is ideal, workable, or miserable.

It is ideal when the school and the child are together by choice. A family may hope to choose a particular public school by buying or renting in one residential area. When this works out, all is well, but recent history shows that because of busing, or redistricting, or taxpayer revolts, there is no guarantee of permanence.

A Goodness of Fit

Some families prefer independent schools. Students come by choice and the school is free to accept or reject an applicant. Of course this does not guarantee perpetual peace but it makes a healthy beginning, and since there is mutual freedom to change, no one is in a trap. Each year the contract is renewed if both sides so wish.

In some instances there is no choice at all.

The wise family will try to work in harmony with whatever school the child attends. They will acknowledge what the school does well and voice their appreciation. Thoughtful educators will respond in kind. Once a cooperative climate has been established, school, family, and student can decide which areas of the child's life may need more attention or different levels of activity and parcel out the responsibility. The child himself should have an active stake in his own learning and not simply be the passive recipient of planning and attention.

Traditionally, the child's academic needs are met in school with the family lending support at home. Social needs are taken care of by both school and family. The responsibility for meeting emotional needs rests primarily with the family, whose efforts are supported by teachers in the school. In spite of good intentions on all sides, however, the boundaries sometimes shift. The following stories of five children show different ways this can happen.

Michael was in the sixth grade in an independent boys' school in the Midwest. It was strong in traditional academics, and offered an outstanding athletic program. Discipline was firm, studies were carefully sequenced, and grades were given and posted regularly. Michael was an able student and an excellent athlete. The school met his needs well in these two areas, but Michael was also a gifted pianist, and had a gentle, loving side to his nature. After much deliberation, the school agreed to allow Michael to substitute piano (lessons and practice) for one of the regularly scheduled daily study halls. In addition, his family enrolled Michael in a

71

Saturday program at their community nature center where he not only learned about animals and plants but shared in their maintenance and care. All the children in the program were given opportunities to take both plants and animals home during the week, loving them and tending them, to be sure, but also keeping scientific records. No grandparent has ever been prouder of offspring than Michael was of the hamsters born at his house. The mother hamster's chart was a careful record of gestation period, diet, onset and length of labor, time of delivery, and observations of the general health of mother and babies. Cooperative planning by Michael's teachers and family created a goodness of fit between the child and his education. He loved his school day, particularly after piano instruction became a part of it, and both his affective needs and his needs for independent study were satisfied by the nature center program.

Martha was in the fourth grade in an open classroom, public elementary school in the outskirts of a northeastern city. The atmosphere was permissive and the arts were heavily emphasized. The curriculum was individualized and students seemed to use the discovery method for everything from the principles of gravity to the multiplication tables. Martha was high-strung, artistic, and independent, and happy in a school that catered individually to her rapid pace and creative spurts. However, the school and her family wisely decided that Martha needed some firm, recognizable structure, too. So she joined a children's choir, which provided a very disciplined artistic group activity, and she began what is now a valuable coin collection. She loved the beauty of some of the coins and also learned to appreciate their history, how they were made, and their relative value. She created highly appealing methods of display and thoroughly enjoyed acquiring large amounts of precise information.

Jeffrey's school urged him to join a Saturday club for gifted children on a university campus two hours away from his home. Fascinated by computers, he had learned all that the teachers in his own school could teach him. He was capable of astounding feats and needed the kind of advanced facilities available only at the university. It seemed a miracle that an appropriate program existed. Jeffrey's parents were unsophisticated and afraid to be different. They were frightened by the school's suggestion, interpreting it as a version of expulsion. They were afraid of the people Jeffrey might meet, and what their neighbors would say. They wondered how to explain that Jeffrey wouldn't be around for local Saturday events such as bowling and Little League. They wondered if people would think they were trying to show off. They worried about the expense. But they agreed to give it a try. The experiment was a total success! Jeffrey continued to enjoy his classmates, got in an appropriate number of disciplinary scrapes for playing rowdy games of floor hockey in the corridor, and received his greatest intellectual nourishment away from school with other people who understood his thoughts.

The foregoing are all happy stories. Unfortunately, conflict and antagonism sometimes prevent cooperation.

When the choice does not exist, a family may try to change the character of a school. Such efforts seldom help the child since educators rarely welcome parental interference with curriculum.

Where controversy seems imminent, the child's best interests are served by a thoughtful family who is more interested in the child's well-being than in having the last word. Realistically, the family is the child's primary resource, and it is easier for a family to modify its schedule or change the activities it emphasizes than it is for a school to do so.

In situations where a goodness of fit is difficult or impossible to arrange, it may help the family to remember that although school is a legal requirement, and therefore an inescapable reality for the child and his family, and although it absorbs the central block of the child's time on Mondays through Fridays, it doesn't take it all.

There are the years before school, and the hours and days when school is not in session. For example, in New York State, schools are required to be in session 181 days, six hours per day. That leaves eighteen other hours in every day and even adolescents seldom sleep more than ten of those. There are 184 days, virtually half the calendar year, when there is no school at all.

This realization made life bearable for Eric, who hates school. He is in seventh grade in public school in a medium-sized town in Mississippi. His mother is an operating room nurse at the local hospital. His father has a debilitating heart condition and cannot work. Eric is a mathematician and a contemplator, small for his age, and not particularly athletic. He would be very comfortable with college mathematics, but those in charge of his school program rigidly insist on his taking the same math courses as his classmates, and no others. They say it is good for him to be treated the same as everybody else. They point out that he is not particularly well liked by the other students and does not do well in athletics. "He'd better learn to make a place for himself, just like everybody else. No special favors." They feel that the example of an inactive father has encouraged the boy to be different—"too much thinking—an oddball." They resent his mother's efforts to change his curriculum and mistrust her for the clarity of her thinking, her knowledge, and the ease with which she expresses herself. She is a threat and they are jealously guarding their prerogatives. Eric is trapped. He is required by law to attend this school. He cannot physically leave it. He needs to remember that he has time before and after school to do as he wishes; to think, explore, experiment, and read. He continues to play games of strategy with his father and they have joined a club to play chess by mail. He got a dog for his birthday. During school hours, Eric has to insure his intellectual privacy by handing in his assignments promptly and by being unobtrusive. His junior high school sentence has nearly been served.

Paul's school was also reluctant to promote his intellectual growth but for different reasons. His parents wanted to enroll him in first grade in a nearby independent school. He was nearly five, could read well, and had good number concepts. However, since the head of the lower school felt he was chronologically young and socially extremely immature, she offered him a place in kindergarten instead. For the first three months of school, Paul was a bystander. After Thanksgiving he began to try to join in activities in the block corner and made small experiments with messy paint and conversation. By February he had a friend. Unsatisfied, his family wanted him to have more workbooks. Both his teacher and the head of the lower school gave examples of how Paul was growing as a person but the family did not share their enthusiasm or understand their priorities. Without telling them, Paul's parents hired a private tutor to work with him every afternoon in reading and arithmetic. Paul began to suck his thumb in school, and went back to the sidelines. The school voiced concern over his regression, but the parents remained silent about the afternoon lessons. In May Paul's mother called to say he would not be returning the following year. They had found a school willing to put him in the third grade. It seems unlikely that Paul will be given the chances for emotional and social growth he needs so badly and to which he was beginning to respond.

Identification of Gifted Children in School

Schools that offer special programs for gifted children generally rely on two measures for identification: marks and money.

High academic achievement is the most commonly used yardstick even though it alone does not certify giftedness.

When good marks are the result of a fine mind growing in an academically challenging situation, hymns of thanksgiving should fill the air, and student and school should be left in peace. But if the school lacks academic rigor, the same grades don't mean the same thing. Furthermore, it is always vital to consider how much of the student's personal energy is directed to report card success. If high grades are one of several elements in a child's life, they indicate balance. If high grades are the major goal of the child's life, they indicate distortion. The Grind is both caricature and cliché. A student who is socially timid may find schoolwork a safe and polite way of hiding from people. In such a case, he invites impoverishment rather than enrichment from his academic labors.

As good marks do not always indicate giftedness, so mediocre or low grades do not always indicate dullness. If the work is too easy, or requires conformity instead of thought, the gifted child may be bored and may not score well. If he is interested in the social doings of his classmates and is not being intellectually stimulated, his energies will flow in social directions. If he is at odds with his teacher, he may be unwilling to apply himself. If he is afraid of not satisfying his own expectations, he may refuse to try as a way of avoiding failure. Each of those attitudes will result in poor grades which are not caused by poor intellectual endowment. We considered the disabled gifted child in Chapter Three, but it is important to mention again that schools value verbal skills. A child with modest verbal skills may be highly gifted in other areas that are not reflected in marks. Unless we understand the reasons behind high or low academic performance we cannot interpret the goodness of fit between the child's ability and his report card.

All too often, when a school system decides to offer a special program for gifted children, the number of available dollars determines the makeup of the group. A school with a generous allocation of funds will probably identify many. A school with limited funds may not dare to identify more than a few. This is not necessarily an accurate way to select or reject a child as gifted. In one

Westchester County town gifted children were an unknown until $2,500 became available for an elementary level program. Then followed a well-publicized school board dispute. One faction spoke against the entire program because they did not feel the preparation was sufficiently detailed. The winning faction felt that since the money was available, there was no risk in going ahead. Students for that program were to be selected on the basis of IQ scores obtained from a group administered test and standardized test scores. Finally, "the program itself shall determine the number of pupils selected for inclusion." What effect will this have on the children? Are those chosen by this method in fact the gifted children in the school? Will they cease to be gifted next year if the cash flow dries up and become de-gifted or dys-gifted? Budgets are a reality of life, and doubtless the planners of this program are well-intentioned, but the episode illustrates one reason why schools are not always accurate in identifying their gifted students and why we must not rely solely on them to make such decisions.

What is likely to be the impact on the rest of the school when one group is identified as gifted? Usually there is a different reaction in each group within the school: faculty and administration, other students, and parents.

The size of the budget will influence or determine the reaction of faculty and administration. If the budget is ample and facilities and extra personnel are available, the faculty may well react with joy and pride. Intellectual vigor is contagious and a teacher who is part of an academically outstanding institution can enjoy the stimulation. However, if a group of special children is identified and there is inadequate funding, the teachers and administrators may be far from jubilant. Resistance will generate such comments as "Mainstreaming is the ideal," "This is supposed to be a democracy, isn't it?" "The bright ones can do it on their own." The addition of one more special program or individualized curriculum may seem overwhelming if present class size and demands on time have already led to faculty fatigue.

Other students will probably accept the identification of a special group more easily than either teachers or parents. Children know when another child has an extra dimension, and are usually forthright about acknowledging it. If children are assured that their own contributions are valuable, they will not resent others being singled out for something different. If artistic talent, athletic ability, academic achievement, and citizenship are all recognized, each student can feel enriched, not diminished, by another's special gifts.

Parents react vigorously when a school labels one group of students as gifted. Those whose children are chosen show their pride according to their personalities; they may preen, boast, glow quietly, or be embarrassed. Parents whose children are not chosen usually react as people do when they are excluded, again depending on their personalities. They may object to the concept of identification, to the instruments used, to the children chosen, or to the teachers who were responsible for the selection. But whatever they specifically object to, or whatever form the objection takes, the chances are that they will be hurt or angry. The danger is that they may take out their disappointment on their own child or children, pressuring them to try harder to get on the list. Adult reactions of jealousy, resentment, or denial will spill over onto the children and bring about a childhood mirroring of adult negatives.

Ideally, a parent-education program precedes a program of identification. When schools make the effort to help interested parents understand the problems as well as the blessings of giftedness, much potential jealousy will disappear. When parents understand why a program is necessary for gifted children they are likely to respect it, support it, and may even volunteer to serve in it. Teachers are a necessary part of such a parent-education program, and as they share their professional knowledge with nonprofessional parents they too will raise their own levels of understanding of giftedness, and recognize what the school can and cannot give each gifted child.

The Teacher

The success of the program depends on the teacher.

This cannot be said too often or too loudly. The teacher's personal style and point of view are more important than the number of courses taken or certificates received. In addition to being knowledgeable about subject matter, the teacher must enjoy meeting special needs, admire independent thinking, and welcome challenge.

Most teachers have homerooms or teach special disciplines such as mathematics, history, a foreign language, science, or English. They must juggle the needs of regular students and those of children with special requirements. Oddly, the presence of gifted children in regular classes will arouse the same set of responses as the presence of disabled children. Both represent special needs. Some teachers will be exhilarated, and their creativity will be stimulated. Others will try hard and their success will be in direct ratio to their flexibility and imagination. Others who feel threatened by giftedness will resent the child.

We know that the divergent thinking described in Chapter Two is a common trait of gifted minds. The student whose responses to straightforward questions spring from divergent thoughts is a delight to the teacher who admires independence but is an unwelcome challenge to a teacher who likes to dispense knowledge and hear it parroted. Oblique answers and unusual ideas are threatening to a teacher whose goal is to control. There will probably be no goodness of fit between such a teacher and a gifted child.

Power and excitement will characterize the relationship between a gifted child and a supportive teacher. Encouragement can lead a child to love a subject he might never have thought appealing. This can happen in the classroom or outside of it. Adult willingness to share an enthusiasm is contagious. If enthusiasm is coupled with both knowledge and experience, the child can learn from the adult. If the adult has enthusiasm, and incomplete knowledge, the older and the younger can explore together. No adult is ever made smaller in a child's eyes by saying, "I don't know." The child is honored when the adult says, "I don't know, let's try to find out together."

Three Approaches

There are three philosophical approaches to the education of gifted children: acceleration, segregation, and enrichment.

ACCELERATION

This was a frequent choice in the past. It seemed easy and convenient since it was available and didn't require extra money. But as more people understand the social and emotional perils involved, the disadvantages are being recognized.

It is very difficult for a child to be separated from his chronological peers, even though his intellectual capacity in certain fields may extend well beyond their grasp. We know that children pass through certain developmental stages on their way to autonomy. Children in an accelerated program who try to skip over some of these stages miss the accompanying activities. Lucia leapfrogged over the era of the secret club, missing the fun of the membership list, election of officers, selection of the password, location of meetings, and then the agony of trying to think up a suitable secret. There is a year in school when such clubs flourish. Children who are one year older have outgrown them, and children one year younger don't know how to put them together. How sad it was for her to be too young to be included when it was de rigueur, and alone in needing it when others had outgrown it! In rushing to close a permanent chronological gap, the child who tags after others' pleasures misses his own.

An intellectually gifted sixth-grade reader still needs to read sixth-grade stories with other sixth-graders to share a common emotional reaction. His reading needn't be restricted to this, but must include it.

The child who is conceptually brilliant in mathematics or science needs to be with his age group at least part of the time for this reason. Unless the child is included in classroom explanations, he may accumulate his mechanical skills in a haphazard way. Since he appears to know so much at an advanced level, people may incorrectly assume that he has understood each earlier level. Brilliant minds need accuracy and discipline. The ability to see new patterns or to extend an idea beyond the reach of ordinary minds is dazzling, and anyone with the smallest element of P. T. Barnum in him is surely going to be tempted to pyrotechnics. Without precision and an understanding of hierarchical process the child's performance can be impressive, but superficial cleverness may keep him from profound understanding. Real skill depends on discipline.

From the opposite point of view, technical accuracy without brilliance produces the reliable but not the profound. The gifted child needs the accurate mechanical skills of his field as well as the original thoughts in order to develop his talent to its utmost capacity. Using both meanings of the word prevent (impede and precede) we can say that facileness prevents profundity.

The social and emotional drawbacks to acceleration outweigh the advantages of arriving at the end of formal schooling one or two years ahead of schedule.

81

HOW THEY LIVE

Segregation means separate programs. We should consider examples of those that physically remove students from their regular school, those that exist within the regular school, those devoted to one particular academic discipline, and finally, those that exist because of the special nature of the school itself.

One public school program in a northeastern city provides that students in the district who qualify as gifted shall attend their regular school three days a week and be transported to a special center two days a week. There they work on projects deemed to be stimulating. Those in charge of the program assume that because the children are clever they will catch up on Monday with whatever happened in their absence on Thursday and Friday. This program is only two years old and may ultimately prove successful. However, so far it has aroused tremendous uneasiness and resentment in the community. Parents are competing ferociously to have their children included. Local psychometricians can scarcely keep up with the demand for testing. Monday through Wednesday teachers are resentful. "I'm good enough to teach him and watch over him in the beginning of the week but I don't qualify on Thursday and Friday." "What am I supposed to do?" "He'll get all that extra stuff over there in that special place, I don't need to do anything different for him." Teachers who are trying to organize a dramatic program or build a varsity team find half their people missing, and the students, both the selected and the leftovers, are thoroughly confused.

Some segregation programs take place within the regular framework. Schools, either public or independent, which group students by ability automatically offer this in their honors sections or tracks, whichever term they choose to use. In secondary school this works well. Students remain with their contemporaries, and can still eat lunch or play basketball with friends who may not be

82

A Goodness of Fit

in their calculus class. Teachers enjoy teaching advanced sections. There is seldom a discipline problem, and the students are usually receptive and quick to understand. However, for elementary school years, this kind of segregation is usually not appropriate.

Some segregation programs exist for a special purpose, such as the SMPY (Study of Mathematically Precocious Youth) at Johns Hopkins University in Baltimore. This program attempts to identify seventh-grade children with extraordinary mathematical abilities and then to act as a catalyst. Although some direct teaching is involved, the main goal is to spot these children and help them accelerate their studies. Frequently a child is encouraged to go straight to college, without reference to his chronological age. A recent example is Eric Jablow, who joined the study at age eleven and now, a college graduate at fifteen, has entered Princeton where he hopes to earn a doctorate in mathematics. Although SMPY is philosophically comfortable with the kind of acceleration which isolates a child from others of his chronological age and which fosters growth in only one area, they also promote some extracurricular after-school, weekend, and summer programs.

Finally there are segregation programs that are defined by the very nature of the schools.

Hunter College Campus Schools in New York City is an example. Founded roughly one hundred years ago, and operating under the aegis of the New York City Board of Higher Education, this school has 1200 high school students whose IQs, as measured by the Stanford-Binet, are frequently 155 or 160. Students in this school are with their chronological and intellectual peers every day. This is an exciting and rare opportunity. However, according to Dr. Bernard Miller, director of the school, there are not nearly enough openings to satisfy the number of applicants. "It's a wonderful school but it's practically impossible to go here."

Since independent schools are free to choose their student body and curriculum without state control, they can tailor programs to

83

specific groups or needs, depending on student body, faculty, and community expectation, and can readjust to achieve goodness of fit.

Roeper City and Country School is a coeducational school for gifted and talented students in Bloomfield Hills, Michigan, with an enrollment of 500 students, 307 in the elementary division and 193 in grades seven through twelve. By nature and title this school exists for a distinct population. It goes without saying that their academic standards are high, and it is interesting to note that in their admissions policy and their curriculum they do not look for a single score or a single focus, but stress instead combinations of talents, observation and manipulation of patterns, and the development of the child as a human being.

Independent day schools can offer segregation to gifted children, as Roeper does, if that is what the community requests and is willing to support. Or they can represent an alternative to public education which, by philosophy and teaching methods, can accommodate gifted students and other students too.

Marcus was miserable in his local public school near Philadelphia. As early as second grade his giftedness in mathematics was unmistakable. When he reached third grade his school was either unable or unwilling to offer him the kind of teaching he needed. He grew frustrated and bored. His family had always believed in public education and felt that independent schools were somehow un-American. However, their child's unhappiness forced them to investigate some of the nearby alternatives. Feeling traitorous to their own ideals, they switched him in midyear to a country day school. He joined a class of eighteen children, one of whom had severe learning disabilities, three of whom needed extensive remedial reading, and the rest of whom were solid or outstanding scholars. Following the lead of a strong teacher, the children enjoyed one another, and while recognizing their various differences, neither mocked those in difficulty nor salaamed the very able. They willingly made room for Marcus in the group. A special mathematics curriculum was designed for him, and he did his other work with the rest of his class. His family was thrilled with the democratic spirit reflected in the balance and activities of the whole class, and overcame their initial feeling that independent education was equivalent to social snobbery.

Many nationally known secondary schools offer segregation of the gifted by the very nature of their student body. A child must be very able in order to be admitted to such schools as Exeter, Andover, and those special purpose public high schools that still exist. Many incoming students each year will have scored in the ninety-ninth percentile in the Secondary School Aptitude Tests (SSAT). Segregation is doubled in a boarding school which requires living twenty-four hours a day with intellectual and chronological peers. Here lies the value of the school's freedom to select its student body. A wise school will orchestrate a good balance of rational/scientific, aesthetic, and ethical/moral strengths in the student body as well as the faculty. The gifted boy or girl who goes to such a school should find a combination of intellectual challenge and opportunities for healthy social and emotional development.

Enrichment

Enrichment can be provided in three ways. Independent projects can be available during school hours as part of a child's curriculum. Wise planners realize that enrichment doesn't mean more math dittos, but fewer, once the child has demonstrated understanding of a concept. Extracurricular activities can also be a regularly scheduled part of the academic day and there can be after-school, Saturday, or weekend projects. These three approaches are not mutually exclusive, they do not conflict with one another or with the regular curriculum, and they need not be expensive.

In elementary school, where children work in a self-contained classroom, an imaginative teacher can provide enrichment as a part of the curriculum. Something such as a special project on dinosaurs could be available to those whose work is completed, or perhaps a unit on Morse and semaphore code could replace some regular assignments. There is no limit to suitable ideas. (Some of the suggestions in Chapter Seven on group activities may be helpful.) It is as easy to supply enrichment in a traditionally arranged elementary classroom as it is in an open classroom. The teacher's priorities are more important determiners than the arrangements of the tables and chairs.

Enrichment can still be part of the regular school day in middle grades when children generally have a homeroom and go out to different rooms and teachers for separate subjects. The homeroom teacher can provide brain-teasers for children to work on alone, in pairs or in small groups. Some of these can doubtless be incorporated into particular subject matter. A teacher can stock some of the excellent commercially developed games of logic, vocabulary, or pattern, and a creative teacher will develop many original ones. Middle school teachers who do not have homeroom groups can do the same thing. This is not to suggest that a Scrabble game in every bookcase will take care of the gifted children from September through June. Of course more is needed. But it is important to remember that enrichment can take place in many hours of school and home life. It needn't be limited to a special period of the day. Children's lives needn't resemble television programming with special slots for housewife time, the children's hour, and family viewing. The whole day can be prime time.

When they reach high school, students have more freedom to choose their courses. Independent study projects can be arranged more easily than in earlier years. Since students are more likely to carry out such projects successfully, administrators are more likely to endorse them. In addition, honors sections are frequently available and no stigma is attached to membership. The student whose enthusiasm for school has been sustained by enrichment in elementary years will enjoy the flexibility and additional course offerings in grades nine through twelve.

It is wonderful when a teacher or tutor can work on a regular basis with a group of children who share a common interest. If the school's point of view permits, such opportunities can be arranged. Meetings might be scheduled in study hall periods or replace other preordained events. A group of four or five mathematically gifted students, poets, artists, or scientists can accomplish a great deal while having a splendid time. Publishing a school newspaper proved to be just such an opportunity for one multi-aged group of students and a very gifted teacher. He challenged them to produce one whole issue using nothing but advertising, propaganda, and opinion. The students were intrigued by the idea, adored playing with the appropriate language, and were delighted with their end product. (Needless to say, they are all astute propaganda spotters now.)

Extracurricular activities such as art, shop, music, or drama provide an excellent opportunity for the gifted child to develop some of the counterweights mentioned earlier. The child's view of the world becomes larger and he increases the number of expressive capabilities at his command. All children need this enrichment, but for the reasons discussed earlier, the gifted child's needs are particularly intense. Ideally, this should be part of the regularly scheduled academic day or week and available to all ages.

Brentwood College of Education in Brentwood, England, was host to an experimental program run by Sidney Bridges and described in *The Gifted Child and the Brentwood Experiment*.[1] Gifted children who attend their regular schools during the week would come to the college on Friday afternoons for special activities. The

[1]S. Bridges, *The Gifted Child and the Brentwood Experiment* (London: Pitman's Educational, 1975).

purpose of the project was to provide companionship and intellectual nourishment without interrupting the children's regular lives. The first report of the project states:

It is to this work that we owe the first unequivocal statement by gifted children that while they loved being with their intellectual peers for part of their week, they would not wish to separate from their own class full-time.[2]

After-school or weekend groups can offer companionship, challenge, variety, and big blocks of time. Participants can work on drama, chess, electronics, art, music—there is no limit to interesting subject matter. A recent brochure describing an independently sponsored Saturday program for gifted children in Westchester County, New York, listed astronomy and celestial navigation, pot gardening, mathematical puzzles, maintenance and repair of common household appliances, magic, and madrigal singing.

The National Association for Gifted Children in London has a successful program of Saturday Clubs. In their words, a Saturday Club is a gathering of children, on a regular basis, most of whom are gifted in one way or another. These groups were started for children needing greater opportunity for self-fulfillment than is normally experienced in their everyday lives. Here is how the current brochure describes their scope and curriculum:

SCOPE OF THE CLUB

This is undoubtedly a real, if indirect, value of the club in the sense that it offers some parents new insights into their own children's needs and into hitherto unrealised ways of meeting them.

It is worth noting, too, that outside professional observation of this experiment during the first year gave rise to encouraging and supportive recommendations for future developments, underlining and strengthening the initial success.

[2]George C. Robb, *Retrospect and Prospect: A British View.* Paper given at World Conference on Gifted Children (London, 1975).

The Saturday Club is primarily for gifted children needing greater opportunity for self-fulfilment than is normally experienced in their everyday lives. An essential value of this process must lie within activity in the company of their peers. This simple definition, however, poses a dilemma. Should the gifted be separated from their natural associates (siblings at the least) for the occasion of their visit to the Saturday Club? *Can* they be so separated? By what standards or testing procedures are they to be so selected!

The association does not recognise any valid specific test for defining 'giftedness'. Nor is it thought desirable to separate siblings during periods of intense and, hopefully, satisfying self-fulfilment such as is afforded by the Saturday Club.

The membership of the club is therefore open to children generally realised to be in need of 'stretching' to a higher level than normally available to them, *and* their brothers and sisters if accompanying them.

There is currently no test in use, yet experience has shown that between parents' awareness, obvious manifestations of ability, and the naturally selective process of personal interest the resulting balance is about right. Siblings of lower ability do not appear to be any problem in managing the club and are welcomed. So far, without testing or other formality the club has maintained an ability intake higher than average. The age range is from 5 years without an upper limit. In practice this has settled itself at about 14. Children from all types of schools attend the Saturday Club, with those from the maintained sector (state schools) greatly in the majority.

CURRICULUM

The range of subjects offered by the club must necessarily vary from time to time with the facilities and staff available, as well as with experience. Nevertheless, the following activities are usually offered:

    Art, Crafts, Woodworking, Pottery,
    Trampoline, Net & ball games,
    Board games, Photography, Drama, Music,
    Creative writing, Academic subjects

There are no formal work programmes culminating in examinations, nor are particular examinations elsewhere recognised as targets. The activities of the club are largely socially cohesive and aimed at self-fulfilment and interest rather than specific attainment.

Who should lead enrichment groups? The qualifications are the same as they are for teachers—knowledge, curiosity, and openness are of greater value than paper certificates. Teachers may wish to work with advanced students in their particular subjects. Parents, community members, or industries may enjoy serving as mentors and are an extremely valuable resource, heretofore insufficiently tapped. Business organizations and professional people sometimes offer apprenticeships. Interested students with adequate background can apply. In addition, industries, professional people, and citizens with a field of expertise are often willing to teach and supervise specific projects. Individual mentors may want to demonstrate their professional knowledge or they may prefer to share an avocation. The cost of a mentor's services ranges from high pay, with the cost of the sessions being shared by the participants, to modest or token payment, to volunteer participation. Chapter Seven gives more detailed information.

Summary

Families whose children are required to attend one specific school should systematically figure out what the school does well, which of the child's needs are being met within the school, and which require more attention. Life is easier when the desired balance is born of cooperation between faculty and school.

Families with the luxury of choice may decide whether acceleration, segregation, or enrichment seems most likely to suit a particular child, recognizing that each institution offers its own adaptation and each child will bring to it unique skills and needs.

A GOODNESS OF FIT

As soon as the rigid concept of the one perfect program, the one perfect school, or the one perfect gifted child is abandoned, the way is clear for flexible teachers and families to create a goodness of fit between the child and his education.

PART III

What Else They Need

For balanced growth the gifted child needs things to do alone, things to do as a member of a group, and wide exposure to stories and language.

The following suggestions are intended to provide supplementary, not primary, fare. It is important to include the old favorites along with the new ideas because omitting them might seem to denigrate their importance. Also, a familiar idea in an unexpected context can often be the catalyst for an original thought.

Do not treat these next three chapters as a Cordon Bleu recipe in which every ingredient must be used. Rather, use them as you would a menu in a Chinese restaurant, choosing appetizing offerings from categories A, B, and C. Here is a browsing ground for those who plan for gifted children: teachers, parents, community leaders—and the children themselves.

Chapter 6

Solo Activities

Why are they necessary and why is it difficult to provide them?

The gifted child's extra energy needs outlets, opportunities, and channels. When people around him are tired out, he needs things he can do on his own so others can rest without feeling guilty.

Creativity and fine soup have much in common. Really good soup is made up of a principal ingredient, a blend of seasonings to enhance the flavors, and liquid to put the various flavors in touch with one another. Here is how the best cook I know makes her famous turkey soup. She starts with the Thanksgiving carcass, which goes into a heavy pot with water, carrots, celery, onion, thyme, salt, and pepper. Once it has come to a boil and been skimmed, she lets it simmer overnight. By morning the taste and bouquet have been doubled, as the volume has been reduced by half. A long simmer in a securely lidded container produces better soup than a vigorous, short boil with lots of opening and looking. As warmth, privacy, and time are preconditions for soup, so they are, too, for creativity.

WHAT ELSE THEY NEED

At the World Conference on Gifted Children in London in 1975, A. H. Passow, Columbia University professor of education, explored four recognizable phases of creativity. While it may seem inappropriate to chart something as mysterious as creativity, these four steps are well worth considering.

1). preparation
2). incubation
3). illumination
4). verification

The first and the last depend on the outside world. The third comes unbidden and cannot be scheduled or prearranged. Incubation requires soup-pot privacy.

Why is it hard for gifted children to find privacy? Physical limitations of time and space are factors, and also an insidious adult weakness. Many adults are not comfortable in their own company. They fear solitude and fill their time with activities that guarantee companionship. Most little children, and particularly gifted children, do not start out with this fear. They know how to have a wonderful time by themselves. But the adult who hates solitude himself feels guilty watching a child play alone, and intrudes on his privacy with suggestions, conversations, and interruptions. Thus, adult inadequacy robs the child of the chance to enjoy a natural gift.

Here are some activities a child can pursue on his own, with indications of what I would consider appropriate ages where necessary. They will be divided into three categories in an attempt to avoid the pitfall of the endless list.

I. incorporative
II. associative
III. generative

SOLO ACTIVITIES

I. Incorporative Activities

Incorporative is a word with several meanings. The *American College Dictionary* gives three: to suck up or drink in, to engross wholly, and to take in without echo or recoil. Here are five incorporative activities.

1. *Reading* is the obvious first. A reader can acquire factual information independently, find out how to do almost anything, and have unlimited aesthetic nourishment. Most gifted children like to read, are willing to try different kinds of stories, and move easily from fiction to fact. Since Chapter Eight is devoted to literature and the gifted child, this space will focus on more factual reading.

All children like having their own magazine subscription. Here are some which gifted children, among others, enjoy. Young children roughly from the ages of four to ten enjoy *Highlights for Children*, 2300 W. Fifth Ave., P. O. Box 269, Columbus, Ohio 43216. Each issue contains things to do as well as stories and features and the magazine received a Certificate of Merit from The National Association for Gifted Children. The child who has outgrown *Highlights* will be ready for *World*, published by the National Geographic (National Geographic World, Dept. 00278, 17th and M Sts. N.W., Washington, D.C. 20036). This is beautifully laid out, with a balance of text, photography, trompe l'oeil, suggested activities, and a regular feature titled "Kids Did It." It is published monthly and a year's subscription costs $5.85. Children from roughly eight to adult enjoy it. For children from roughly ten and up there is a magazine called *Games*, which features puzzles, games, contests, self-tests, and brainteasers. A year's subscription costs $5.97 and the address is P. O. Box 10147, Des Moines, Iowa 50349. For the older child, or the sophisticated mathematician, *Scientific American*, P. O. Box 5919, New York, N.Y. 10001, will provide information, challenge, and delight. If the gifted child in your care has a particular interest—astronomy, computers, motorcycles, or basketweaving—browse through a magazine store or the nearest public library. There are periodicals for nearly every subject. Not only are the articles informative, but nearly all special interest magazines have classified sections announcing both products and upcoming events.

Gifted children need frequent reassurance that they are like other human beings and that we all share common physiology and surroundings. They, like other children, like to understand their bodies. For this I recommend the *Brown Paper School Books*, published by Little, Brown for elementary school children. Here are their eight current titles:

1. *Blood and Guts*
2. *I Am Not a Short Adult*
3. *Everybody's a Winner*
4. *My Backyard History Book*
5. *The I Hate Mathematics Book*
6. *The Book of Think*
7. *The Reason for Seasons*
8. *The Night Sky Book*

Little, Brown also publishes *The Great Perpetual Learning Machine*, a book that overflows and defies categories. It is a collection of thoughts, projects, and puzzles for children alone or in groups.

The teenage gifted child who wants to expand a special mechanical or mathematical interest through independent study should investigate International Correspondence Schools, Scranton, Pa. 18515. They will send a catalogue on request which lists such selections as electrical engineering, electronics, drafting, chemical engineering, surveying and mapping, and house planning and design.

The local librarian is a valuable friend for the gifted child. He or she can show the child how to find materials in a special field of interest, and explain the mysteries of card catalogues and stacks.

The child should also be shown how to keep his own card catalogue. The gifted child, in all likelihood, will read widely, and, delighting as he does in associations and patterns, will cross reference in an unusual way. A card file can help him retrieve information quickly and accurately. Children from roughly the age of eight learn to do this with precision and pleasure. They enjoy the mechanical skills of alphabetizing, using bibliographical form, and categorizing.

It is important to remember that not all independent reading must be of high intellectual caliber. The gifted child needs surcease, occasional nostalgia, and current jokes. He may need to relax with his reading in the same way some of the children in Chapter Four needed to relax with their friends. *Mad* magazine may sometimes be more appropriate than masterworks.

Reading, valuable as it is, is not the only path to knowledge, however.

2. *Television,* our cultural whipping boy, offers some exciting material. Many presentations are appropriate for gifted children. The trick lies in choosing what to watch. Here is a system which works well and requires decision making, evaluation, and thinking, things that television theoretically deadens. When the weekly paper or monthly guide arrives, ask the child to sit down and read it, or read it with him if he is too young to do it alone. Then ask him to circle in red Magic Marker whatever shows he thinks would be good and would fit the family time allowance for television. Go over the choices with him, encouraging him to explain his reasons, discuss the differences between various programs offered simultaneously, and see the patterns and balance of what he has chosen for a week. Invite his predictions of what the various shows will be like, and be sure to listen to his opinions afterwards if you do not, or cannot, watch the program with him. As an example, here is what one nimble-witted ten-year-old boy chose for a week in July—a season when the offered fare is thought to be so thin.

WHAT ELSE THEY NEED

Sunday: 7:00 P.M. *The Hardy Boys and Nancy Drew.*

Before and after comments: "I like mysteries." "I always know they'll get out OK, but I still always get scared in the middle. It's like not being sure even though you really know."

8:00 P.M. *Evening at Pops,* Arthur Fiedler and the Boston Pops with Henry Mancini.

Before and after comments: "I like the way they play. They put surprises in—like the way they play the Rudolph the Red-Nosed Reindeer part in that Christmas record." "Hey—he's the Pink Panther guy!"

Monday: 7:00 P.M. *The Brady Bunch.*

Before and after comments: "Can Sam come over and watch it with me?" "It wasn't bad."

7:30 P.M. *The Muppets.*

Before and after comments: "I love that show." "I love that show."

Tuesday: 8:00 P.M. *West Side Story.*

Before and after comments: "It's hard to choose. There's a National Geographic show, and they're usually good, and there's baseball. I'll choose this because I have the record." "It was good. I love that 'Hey Officer Krupke' song. I wonder who won the ballgame."

Wednesday: 6:30 P.M. *I Love Lucy.*

Before and after comments: "Sometimes I just like to watch something dumb." "It was funny—dumb, but funny."

8:00 P.M. *Nova.*

Before and after comments: "They have good stuff." "Do you think that's true, about people affecting plants? I never thought about that before. In a way it's creepy. I think I'll try."

100

Thursday: 7:30 P.M. *In Search of Hypnosis.*

Before and after comments: "Maybe I can learn how to hypnotize *you*." "I'm glad you can't be hypnotized if you don't want to be."

8:00 P.M. *World: Three Days in Szczecin.*

Before and after comments: "Is Poland a free country?" "What happens to people in our country who go on strike?"

Friday: 6:00 P.M. *Zoom.*

Before and after comments: "I like seeing other kids on TV." "I liked it. You know what was funny—the younger kids were better than the older kids. They never looked embarrassed."

8:00 P.M. *Baseball.*

Before and after comments. "Tonight's going to be a good night." "I know what went wrong. They shouldn't have changed pitchers when they did."

Saturday: 7:30 P.M. *The Price is Right.*

Before and after comments: "I like to know how much things cost." "How old do you have to be to get on that show?"

8:00 P.M. *Great Performances,* The Berlin Philharmonic.

Before and after comments: "I love that music." "I don't watch the screen much. I mostly just listen."

Television can be used as an awakener instead of an anaesthetic, as this ten-year-old child clearly demonstrated. Others in his family use it in much the same way. His mother frequently watches *Sunrise Semester,* college courses taught by the faculty of New York University, and his older brother and father, excellent tennis players themselves, like to watch televised tennis matches. Although it is intellectually fashionable to scorn television, it is snobbery to assume that high availability automatically indicates low quality. Rejecting the offerings of a whole medium because some of the selections are poor is throwing out the baby with the bathwater.

3. *Radio.* The same comments and system apply to radio. For the gifted child who is a music lover, classical or contemporary, a good radio is an invaluable companion. Consult your local newspaper for program selections and look ahead to see what's coming. For lovers of classical music, *Musica,* Box 1266, Edison, N.J., lists a thousand AM and FM stations in the United States alphabetically according to state and city, and gives the days and hours of concerts. It costs $3.95 plus 75 cents postage.

Children who enjoy mystery stories should try *Radio Mystery Theater.* Time and station vary regionally.

As with television, shopping through the schedule, choosing, contrasting, and evaluating add an extra dimension to listening which the gifted child welcomes. And, as noted with respect to friends, activities, and reading, sometimes the gifted child needs blandness and surcease.

4. *Puzzles* come in many forms. Gifted children who enjoy visual puzzles will spend happy hours working to assemble jigsaw or three-dimensional-object puzzles or using elastic bands and a geoboard to duplicate complicated printed patterns. This is both a visual and a mathematical puzzle, one of the many possibilities for those who enjoy playing mathematical games and meeting mathematical challenges. Bookstores carry those that are currently popular and generally available. In addition, there is an excellent selection in a catalogue published by Creative Publications, 3977 East Bayshore Rd., P.O. Box 10328, Palo Alto, California 94303. The catalogue itself is a thing of beauty. The books of mathematical puzzles and games of strategy, probability, and pattern are appropriate for groups as well as individuals; detailed descriptions of several are found in Chapter Seven.

The electronic age and miniaturization have given us a host of quiet individual games to be played with calculators, computers, and on television screens. The Creative Publications catalogue offers games for children from grades four and up to play with pocket calculators. The computer games of *Chess Challenger, Checker Challenger,* and *Gammonmaster* Backgammon can be tested and purchased at good-sized camera stores. If $300 is within the family budget of a gifted child who enjoys chess, *Boris,* the portable chess computer, is available. Hand-eye coordination games of television screen handball, tennis, and hockey can be bought at television stores, or at much lower cost at a toy store, under the name Telstar.

Children who enjoy paper and pencil puzzles will enjoy and learn from paperback puzzle books in four series published by Lee Publications, 815–25 E. Market St., Louisville, Ky. 40232: *Yes and Know, Game Books, Guess and Show,* and *Cross and Know.* The answers are printed in invisible ink, which appears when the *Yes and Know* pen (included) is used.

Dover Publications has an excellent book of *Storybook Mazes* which offer a maze accompaniment to each of the fairy tales in the collection. Bookstores generally carry a large selection of books of mazes. *Altair Design* books provide opportunity for original design.

Older gifted children may happily tackle double crostics or crossword puzzles such as those found in the *New York Times.* In fact, one student at an independent school in New York City developed such skill that he taught a course in crossword puzzles at the New School for Social Research in New York.

5. *Collections.* The gifted child, delighting as he does in patterns, cross references, and combinations, may become intrigued by collecting. Here is unlimited opportunity for investigating, searching, categorizing, trading, and displaying. Although the term *collector's item* calls to mind black tie affairs, glass cases, limousines, and Limoges, it needn't be limited to that. Collections can contain things that nature provides free to the finder, things

that must be bought, things that are of current popular interest, or things that are alive. Here are some specifics.

Rocks or leaves make interesting collections and are available for the picking. The country child need only step outside his door. The city child can either go to the country on a day excursion, or simply go to the park. The child who is interested in rocks will find *Rocks and Minerals,* a Golden Press Nature Guide, $1.95, a good book to begin with. The child who wants to collect leaves will find *Trees,* in the same series, helpful. A leaf collection requires the further step of pressing and drying, a learning process in itself. For the child who has access to the seashore, a shell collection is a natural. Two splendid books for identifying shells and marine life are *Seashells of the World,* in the Golden Press Nature Guide Series, and *The Sea Beach at Ebb Tide* by Augusta F. Arnold, published by Dover Publications.

Once the category has been chosen and the collection begun, the young collector must decide how to display it, how to label the various components, and how far to expand it. Box lids can be divided into compartments with cardboard strips and Scotch tape. They can be lined with adhesive-backed paper, in any pattern from marble to gingham, to make effective display cases and can be covered with a layer of plastic wrap to protect the contents.

The Styrofoam packing boxes used for such things as jelly jars are already compartmentalized and can usually be obtained without cost by asking for them at a specialty food shop or supermarket with a gourmet section. If a modest financial outlay is appropriate, go to the hardware store and buy one of the small metal chests of compartmentalized drawers used to keep screws, nails, nuts, washers, and bolts. They make ideal holders for small items and each species can have its own spot and its own label.

If the child is in a position to spend money for collecting, he might enjoy stamps or coins. Each of these has an enthusiastic cadre; there are bulletins, clubs, magazines, and meetings devoted to the subject. For specific local information, check the Yellow Pages of the telephone book under the headings coins, stamps, and hobbies. It is easy to start one of these collections with a modest outlay; it is expensive to expand it as far as the imagination of the gifted child would like to take it.

Two gifted children I know like to collect things of current popular interest. Franklin, who is ten years old, has an enormous collection of baseball cards which he keeps in four shoeboxes and one plastic album the size of a looseleaf notebook. Each album page has twelve see-through pockets per side, designed specifically for baseball cards. He loves to change it around, sometimes arranging his album pages by teams, sometimes by positions and men who play them, or sometimes by the size and weight of the players. He is constantly sorting, shifting, and recategorizing. Today's front page pitcher may find himself in a shoebox tomorrow. Franklin spends contented hours with his collection learning facts, playing with combinations, and according to his taste of the moment, bestowing honor or exile.

Another child, who is also ten, collects commercials and advertising slogans. She has a huge bulletin board on which she tacks those that catch her eye. She has a good ear for music and mimicry and has tape recorded a thirty-minute original medley of commercials beginning with "I Love New York" and ending, "Pop-pop, fizz-fizz, oh what a relief it is—this tape is over." She used considerable skill putting them together and the result sounds almost like a Gilbert and Sullivan patter song.

The gifted child who lacks an opportunity for caretaking may find satisfaction as well as interest in a collection of such live things as tropical fish or plants. His need to be a giver of nurture as well as a receiver of care is powerful and he can take emotional nourishment from such an experience.

Here is a way to begin which works well. Find a good-sized pet shop and go there with the child, a notebook, and a pencil. Look at all the possibilities, write down the necessary equipment, cost, and space required for each, and go home. Away from the seductive appeal of a glistening tank, bubbling water, and darting fish, or the wistful look in the homeless hamster's eye, the child will find it easier to evaluate the alternatives and make his decision. He may decide he'd rather grow varying species of herbs and violets than clean out a cage every day. Then set aside whatever physical space will be required, arrange the financing, whether through loan or piggy bank, and finally, having done the planning, return to the store to make the purchase.

Whatever the category, a collection can provide hours of solitary enjoyment, intellectual nourishment, and sometimes even a dignified new word; there is weight in ichthyologist, numismatist, and philatelist.

II. Associative Activities

Associative activities encourage the child's natural proclivity for playing with analogy. His whole world teases him with its attributes, as he finds ways to combine the new with the already familiar or to put familiar things together in novel partnerships. Here are four such activities.

The first is a book for the child to write about himself. As a teacher, I have used this with reading-disabled children who had never before found anything very interesting in the printed word. I have also used it with extremely able, imaginative children who wanted to soar.

In writing this book, the child forges a three-link chain connecting the written word, the world around him, and himself. It offers infinite opportunities for original thinking and, once begun, will be read and reread, for children, like adults, enjoy reading about themselves. Here is how to set up ten pages.

Page 1 is about the child's birthday. At the top write the old rhyme.

> Monday's child is fair of face.
> Tuesday's child is full of grace.
> Wednesday's child is full of woe.
> Thursday's child has far to go.
> Friday's child is loving and giving.
> Saturday's child must work for a living.
> The child born on the Sabbath Day
>   Is blithe and bonny, merry and gay.

At the bottom write a line that says, "I am a _____ child." In case the poor child is a Wednesday, Thursday, or Saturday child, conclude with a line that says, "I do/do not believe this old poem."

Page 2 shows the child how to find his place in the Chinese calendar. It says, "The Chinese calendar names years for animals. The calendar is on a 12-year cycle. Here are some recent years. Now you can figure out your own year: 1977, Dragon; 1976, Rabbit; 1975, Tiger; 1974, Ox; 1973, Rat; 1972, Pig; 1971, Dog; 1970, Rooster; 1969, Monkey; 1968, Sheep; 1967, Horse; 1966, Snake." End with a line that says, "I was born in the year of the _____." Add as much interpretation of these animals' characteristics as the child enjoys.

Page 3 does the same thing with zodiac information. A current horoscope column from your local newspaper adds zest.

Page 4 is about the child's name and says, "This is my name in code." There are spaces for him to write his name in Morse Code, semaphore or nautical flag code, a code substituting numbers for letters, and finally, a space for him to write in code a word he likes to use in describing himself. Morse Code and semaphore can be found in an encyclopedia and the substitution code can be an original invention.

Page 5 says, "When I go out to buy clothes, I like to _____, but

WHAT ELSE THEY NEED

I hate to _____," and "When I get up on Saturday morning, I like to put on _____ and this is how I look [illustration]."

Page 6 provides an opportunity to put dislikes and unpleasant things on paper. Many children are surprised that this is permissible. For them, this page opens up a whole new world. For others, it is just plain fun. It says:

I do not like to eat _____.
I do not like to wear _____.
I do not like to go to _____.
I do not like to listen to _____.
I do not like to see _____.
I do not like the feeling of _____.
I hope I never have to _____ again.

Be sure to make the blank spaces big enough to accommodate lots of ideas.

Page 7 is called "Bon Appetit." It says: "My favorite breakfast is _____; my favorite lunch is _____; my favorite snack is _____. My mother says _____ is bellywash, but I love it."

Page 8 is titled "Initial Reactions," and says, "Write your initials in the space below. Now choose descriptive words that start with these initials, and you will have a new name."

Page 9 is called "Here I Go." It says, "Write Yes or No: I slither ____, I crawl ____, I tiptoe ____," and so forth. Other verbs I have used are march, dance, wobble, gyrate, cavort, wiggle, vacillate, twist, and perambulate.

Page 10 uses the same yes or no format and is called "I Do, I Do." It says: "I lacerate, recount, verbalize, embellish, blush, respirate, imagine, create, tease, exacerbate, exaggerate. I bring joy!"

Should you want samples and suggestions for other pages, you will find them in *Supplement to a Teacher's Notebook: Alternatives for Children with Learning Problems* by Migdail and Vail, published by the National Association of Independent Schools, 4 Liberty

Square, Boston, Mass. 02109, $2.00. It includes a section on storywriting which the gifted have used in particularly imaginative ways. Most children are usually eager to think up ideas for many new pages on their own.

The second suggestion is *Treasure Hunt,* an open-ended, non-competitive game which provides hours of enjoyment. It can be played by a group or by one child alone. Choose any one of the thousands of shapes and patterns that surround us. Circles and symmetry are two examples. Listing them by word, or simple drawing, the child discovers where and how frequently the chosen pattern can be found. His whole world is the hunting ground. For example, consider how many circles a careful observer could find in the kitchen, or how much symmetry is in human bodies, plants, flowers, shells, architecture, and design, from the chassis of an automobile to the grapefruit display at the supermarket. Keeping track is entertaining and finding shapes or patterns in unexpected places provides a thrill of surprise. The Creative Publications catalogue mentioned earlier uses *Math in Nature* as its design theme. The results are surprising and lovely.

The third suggestion is drawing while listening to music, which can produce surprising results. Sometimes it is more fun to draw to many different pieces and kinds of music. Another kind of fun lies in hearing the same piece five or six times and drawing something different from each hearing. Contrasting the results with one another is an intriguing way to interpret mood and association. Most children are not reluctant to draw unless their natural willingness has been extinguished by a rigid art program in school, or by adult mockery.

The fourth is category albums, or collages. They are entertaining to make and can be unusual and eye-catching. The child needs paper, scissors, paste, and a stack of old magazines and catalogues. A category can be suggested in advance and adhered to, or an older child may delight in keeping the category secret, making the collage or album, and challenging others to find the common denominator.

The fifth suggestion is tricks. Chapter Seven has specific suggestions about magic, which the gifted child can learn and practice alone or in a group. Here is another suggestion particularly appropriate to the child who is alone at bedtime or in the evening, *Hand Shadows to Be Thrown Upon the Wall: A Series of Novel and Amusing Figures Formed by the Hand* by Henry Bursill, Dover Publications.

Dover Publications has a comprehensive group of books which teach tricks. They are inexpensive and the directions are clear.

III. Generative Activities

Generative activities are those that result in a specific product. Why are they important? Think in the imagery of pipes and water tanks. The gifted child has huge equipment for taking in. It is as though his pipes are many and of a very wide diameter. He needs many pipes leading out, and a generous supply of faucets, to prevent a flood or an explosion. Generative activities turn on the faucets.

There is another value which must not be overlooked. They give the child an additional way to meet a world not always friendly to him. Jealousy and fear often generate resentment of a gifted child. The brilliant mathematician or the satiric poet may frighten many people. But his home-baked brownies, a lovely piece of needlework, or a musical rendition doesn't. And a slight detectable flaw (a good possibility in cooking, sewing, or instrument playing) makes the creator seem more human rather than less, a welcome shift for the gifted child.

Nine specific generative activities follow.

SOLO ACTIVITIES

1. *Playing a musical instrument.* The joy and nourishment of music has been described through the ages. If a gifted child is musically inclined, have plenty of time for him to play and practice. If he is interested but doesn't know how to play, try to provide an introductory series of lessons. While he is still experimenting, rent his instrument instead of buying it. That will give him more leeway and allow him to try several, if need be, before deciding on one. If he already knows how to play, and enjoys ensembles, explore the series of records titled *Music Minus One*, published and packaged by Music Minus One, 43 West 61 St., New York, N.Y. 10023. These are available for almost every instrument, and go from beginning to advanced levels.

2. *Drawing, painting, or sculpting.* As with music, if the child is already skillful, give him time and privacy. If he is interested but hasn't yet chosen a medium, go with him to an art store, and let him browse through their introductory level materials. Here are some typical offerings.

For the child who would like to try sculpture, Caran d'Ache has a set of ten blocks of perpetually soft colored clay for $10.80. *Paris Craft,* an instant papier mâché, is available for $4.00.

For the very young painter, there is an excellent item by Talens called Poster Blocks. These are large blocks of tempera paints which come in a set of six for $8.95. Since the blocks are big, the children can use big brushes, which are better suited to little hands than the tiny brushes usually found in watercolor sets. Acrylic paints can be used on anything, paper, cardboard, glass, or even stones. A modular set can be bought for $8.00.

The child who would like to draw but doesn't know quite how to start should look at the Grumbacher series in which my favorite is *The Art of Drawing Animals.* (This series can be found in any art store or hobby shop.) For $5.00 the child gets a book, paper, four pencils, a sharpener, an eraser, and two smudgers. A child who wants less instruction might buy a beginner's drawing set. A typical one contains five pencils differing in hue and hardness, erasers, and smudgers and costs $7.25.

3. *Athletics*—practicing and polishing an athletic skill: skating, gymnastics, dance, shooting baskets, or whatever the child particularly likes. Since so much depends on whether the child lives in the city or the country, what facilities are close enough for him to reach on his own, and what his personal inclinations are, I will simply mention the category and not try to be specific.

4. *Writing*. The gifted child needs many opportunities to express himself. Writing is an ideal one. It can take the form of original poetry, stories, plays, or a journal. Or he may enjoy copying some favorite selections and illustrating them or illuminating the first letter of each line. An ideal vessel is the blank books now available at stationery stores or counters for roughly $4.00. They come with attractive covers, they look like real books, but the pages are blank.

5. *Building:* models, dioramas, electronic wonders, collages. The purpose can be aesthetic delight, historical accuracy, precision, scientific knowledge, experimentation, or any combination of the above.

Take the child who is interested in building models to a hobby shop rather than to the plastic model department of a discount store for this reason. It is very hard to assess the level of manual dexterity required simply by looking at the picture on a box. Discouragement and frustration result when a goodness of fit is lacking between the child's skill and the agility required. A good hobby shop will give reliable recommendations. Logix-kosmos has a science experiment set called *Electronics* in which the child first builds a console, and then through building increasingly complicated circuits learns how to make such things as a lie detector, automatic light switch, and two-transistor radio. This is available at toy stores. If a doll house has greater appeal than a police siren, try *All About Doll Houses*, published by Bobbs-Merrill.

Don't forget Lego, which, although initially expensive, is beautifully made, lasts forever, has intriguing components, and can be
used to make almost anything. A gifted child can spend hours
imagining and creating.

6. *Cooking*. Whether the palate inclines to vegetarian fare,
soups, crepes, Chinese, Mexican, German, French, or down-
home food, there is a cookbook. A word of caution: many cookbooks written for children have bland or sugary foods with such
whimsical labels as Red Riding Hood's Applesauce or Seven
Dwarf Cookies. The gifted child is usually well able to enjoy and
prepare more sophisticated and nutritious offerings. Bypass the
junior cookbooks and go instead to such specialties as quiches or
Chinese cooking. With a little help and experience, the gifted child
will find his favorite toy—patterns—and understand why certain
ingredients are necessary and how they work together. He will
understand intellectually as well as enjoy gastronomically.

7. *Gardening*. Since so much depends on where the gifted child
lives, this is hard to describe in detail. However, there are two
cardinal rules: keep it small, and insure success. The country child
who is given a six-by-six-foot plot of earth and six packages of
seed from the hardware store has more than a beginner can manage and will be turned away for life. Little children like to garden
in little pots. Hanging shelves for window gardening are inexpensive, available at garden supply shops, and keep the project
in one location. One such garden, planned and tended by a nine-
year-old girl, had a top shelf with four different kinds of ivy, another with two varieties each of begonia and African violets, and a
bottom shelf of herbs which were a mainstay of the family salad
bowl. Sprout gardening is quick, tidy, and tasty. Equipment is
inexpensive and available in hardware stores, health food stores,
and some garden shops. Terrariums give room for a huge variety
of species in a small space and they accept but do not require constant attention.

WHAT ELSE THEY NEED

8. *Photography*. Because this is expensive and requires a dark-room, a great deal of equipment, and initial supervision, I simply mention it. The visually acute gifted child whose family has plenty of space and money may find it an ideal occupation and one that will bless them in return with beautiful results.

9. *Handcrafts*. These include sewing, weaving, ceramics, leatherwork, carving, macramé, to name but a few. Mercifully, sex-related cultural taboos are losing their power. Both boys and girls can enjoy all the above. There are five publishers whose handcraft and how-to books are favorites of mine because their directions are clear, their offerings are varied, they are inexpensive, and they encourage the reader to try something that might initially seem difficult. Doubtless there are other fine publications unknown to me which do the same things, but here are my personal preferences.

1. Sunset Hobby and Craft Books
   Lane Publishing Co.
   Menlo Park, California 94025
      sample crafts: Bonsai, leather, macramé, sewing

2. McCall's
      sample title: *Golden Do-It Book*. This offers a wide variety of short, accomplishable projects. Their needlecraft suggestions are particularly well done.

3. Time-Life Encyclopedias.
      sample title: *Gardening Under Lights*

4. Drake Home Craftsman's Books
      sample titles: *Making Toys in Wood, A Woodcarver's Primer, Understanding High Fidelity*

5. Dover Publications
      sample titles: *Fruit and Vegetable, Iron-On Transfer Patterns*, Dover Coloring Books: *Seashore Life, Garden Flowers*, and

so forth. These make excellent embroidery outlines and are a blessing to the craftsperson who delights in using unusual combinations of color, stitchery, or collage, but does not draw well.

Two books that are not part of any series are *The Ashley Book of Knots*, published by Doubleday, and *Sculptured Needlepoint Stitchery* by Ella Projansky (Scribner's). Knots have historical uses, and are practical as well as decorative. Gifted boys and girls enjoy learning their history and associations as well as learning how to make them and for what use each is appropriate. Mrs. Projansky is an accomplished needlewoman who, like a gifted child, delights in novel combinations and unusual patterns. She brings a freewheeling spirit to the geometric grid of canvas. Her book not only shows how to make various stitches but through the examples she gives she teases the reader's imagination and encourages originality.

Once again—a craft does not belong to one sex or the other. Joy in creating something new is for both boys and girls.

If the ideas in this chapter carry out the purpose for which they are listed, they will not be the end of a search, but the beginning of new plans.

Chapter 7

Group Activities

Belonging is a need and right of every gifted child. In early years group activities offer companionship and a place to develop social skills. In adolescence the common bond of group membership provides attachment to the world and feelings of similarity and safety. When a young person's feelings are turbulent and he finds himself changing, sometimes against his own will, he is apt to feel bizarre and unlike anyone else. Already feeling different because he is gifted, he may be unable to bear additional loneliness. Group activities use a natural resource we have on hand: one another. They needn't be expensive or solemn; they should provide enjoyment and tease the imagination.

The gifted child (particularly if he is an only child) needs to know how to belong to a group and not just how to be the leader. Martin is a brilliant man who is now in his late forties. An accomplished student all the way through school, he delighted in scientific knowledge and precision. Although he was ambitious, he was also kind. He enjoyed being a leader and his classmates fell into the habit of electing him class president. In his senior year he was president of the student body. Having the habit of leadership, he spoke with authority and walked with assurance. When he went to college, his classmates again chose him as a leader. After graduation he went steadily to the top in his business life, once again a leader. Yet our compassion should go out to him. He is a man who knows how to lead and control, but not how to partici-pate. He and his wife are master and servant, not partners. His children were obedient when young and now that they have out-grown adolescent rebellion, they are polite to him, but secretive about their thoughts and feelings. Martin is doomed to loneliness even though he is frequently surrounded by people.

The gifted child's need for group activities is particularly intense when school is not in session. Weekends may seem long and sum-mer vacation troublesome unless it is well planned. Whether the child needs help finding ways to pursue a particular passion or ways to broaden or focus his interests, well-planned group ac-tivities can provide satisfaction and stimulation. Here are three places to look for them: (1) activities planned particularly for chil-dren, (2) the world of travel, and (3) the adult world made accessi-ble to children.

Activities planned particularly for children

ATHLETICS

To be a welcome member of an athletic team is to belong! For-tunate indeed is the gifted child who loves baseball, soccer, hockey or lacrosse. And the well-coordinated boy or girl who enjoys sports but dislikes or fears direct physical contact can still be a team player in such cumulative score games as track, swimming, div-ing, or skating. The camaraderie of team practice, the interdepen-dence, the shared suspense of the contest, the victory celebration, or the joint disappointment are powerful group epoxy. Frequently it is unnecessary to belong to an expensive club to play these sports. For local information consult the recreation department of the town where you live as well as the YMCA, YWCA, Boys' Club, or Girls' Club.

SCOUTING

The quality varies from place to place, but scouting is worth investigating. In well-led troups scouts learn skills and facts together, and many young people enjoy the external membership badge of a uniform. Both the Boy Scouts of America and the Girl Scouts of America are making a conscious effort to expand their programs with more contemporary kinds of community outreach than the stereotyped images of helping old ladies across the street and rubbing two sticks together to make a fire. The vigor of the program depends on the local chapter.

COMMUNITY RESOURCES

Here is what the resources in one medium-sized New England community offered on weekends and during the summer for children between the ages of six and fourteen for fees which averaged $2.00 per hour: children's drama, karate, Chinese cooking, birds and snakes, Who Lives in the Marsh?, astronomy, marine biology, macramé, weaving, pottery, woodworking with hand tools, elementary, intermediate, or advanced electronics, and Houses of New England—history and design.

SATURDAY CLUBS FOR GIFTED CHILDREN

As interest in gifted children grows, these clubs are springing up in many places. If there is one near you, investigate it. If there is not, and you are interested in starting one, here are some experiences, philosophies, and activities to consider.

When they are well run, Saturday Clubs provide stimulation, companionship, new opportunities, and new faces. However, those who are trying to administer or establish them find admissions criteria to be a bundle of burrs. An unpleasant atmosphere seems to creep into those clubs whose admissions policies are designed to exclude rather than include: exit sharing, enter upmanship. Sometimes the struggle to establish the criteria is so difficult that adult energies go into codifying rather than into planning for the children. Here is what happens in one club.

Each candidate must take a battery of tests designed to measure IQ, social maturity, creativity, and also achievement tests in reading and mathematics. In order to qualify for the club the child must score a full-scale IQ of over 125 and be at least two years above grade level in achievement scores. In addition to a personal interview, he must present a letter of recommendation from two teachers. Each family is responsible for writing a history of the child's development and paying for the testing, which, at this writing, is $150. If more than one child in a family wishes to apply, each additional child must go through the same procedure and there is no guarantee that siblings will be accepted. With so much time devoted to deciding who may and may not participate, there are lengthy staff meetings and a disproportionately small number of hours left for actual activities.

Another club in a more rural, less affluent community took a different approach. Instead of starting with admissions policies, they began by planning possible programs. They considered available personnel—teachers, parents, mentors—and decided what subjects they could teach in a manner and tempo suitable for gifted children. In the first semester they offered magic, chess, story writing combined with bookbinding, and choral singing.

They printed a small brochure which they distributed locally, inviting applications. Their admissions criteria were:

1. desire of the applicant himself to join
2. parental belief that the child would enjoy and profit from the pace and level of the activities
3. personal interviews with parent and child together
4. evaluation of results of standardized testing already done by the school which would indicate high aptitude

Brothers or sisters of a participant were welcome as long as they themselves wanted to come. Tuition was set by giving each participant a share of the expenses: a small rental fee for the use of a parish house, a modest fee for materials, and the cost of faculty salaries for teachers, who were paid $8.00 per hour. The program bloomed. New courses were added and new families joined, bringing enthusiasm and ideas with them. At the conclusion of the first year there was an exhibit and a party complete with magic show and group singing in which everyone was invited to join. Some of these participants might have scored less than 125 on an IQ test. They came to no harm in the program. Some children left by choice after three or four sessions because the program was too hard for them. Others, by far the greatest number, found companionship, challenge, and new interests.

Here are some activities other groups have used and which have appealed to children of many different ages. I have sorted them into seven categories but not tried to specify any age or grade level for each since so much depends on the size of the group and the expertise of its members. Most of them are inexpensive, reflecting my belief that enrichment and excitement need not depend on a big bank balance.

1. *Games and activities of strategy, probability, and pattern*. These can be learned and played in groups as small as two or as large as a community of interest. Little expense is involved, and there are

great challenge and hours of enjoyment, as well as opportunity for nonphysical competition. Checkers, chess, *Battleship, Mastermind,* and *Othello* are five well-known examples. Gifted children are frequently afraid to compete because losing is so painful. A few tips such as those in the Dover Press chess and checkers strategy books, *Win at Checkers* by Millard Hopper, for example, could provide a needed boost of confidence. Gifted children are frequently good card players. Teach them to play bridge. A book called *Bridge for Bright Beginners,* Dover Publications, will help you get off the ground. A book with clear descriptions of other card games is *Deal Me In* by Margie Golick, W. W. Norton & Co. Some clubs like to organize tournaments as soon as the children have reached an appropriate skill level. Others find that children prefer to choose their own opponents and dislike the ranking within the group that results from tournament play.

Attribute blocks and the games, puzzles, and activities which accompany them are favorites of all ages. They encourage the child to classify and see logical relationships and they can be used cooperatively as opposed to competitively. Activities start with those suitable for preschool children and continue on to very high levels. The blocks and their companion activities can be purchased in many stores. However, I would suggest ordering them from the catalogue of Creative Publications (3977 East Bayshore Rd., P.O. Box 10328, Palo Alto, California, 94303). The catalogue in itself is an excellent source book for teachers, parents, mathematicians, puzzle addicts, thinkers, and questioners. It is arranged in five sections: Arithmetic, Numbers and Operations, Logical Thinking and Problem Solving, Geometry, Measurement, and finally, Resource Books and Materials.

J. Weston Walsh in Portland, Maine, publishes some excellent and inexpensive books of logic puzzles which are arranged in order of difficulty and are appropriate for elementary school children. *Wiff'n Proof* is a challenge to sophisticated mathematicians, as is Martin Gardner's column of mathematical games in each month's issue of *Scientific American*. Two well-written books are *Mathematical Puzzles for Beginners and Enthusiasts* by Geoffrey Mott-Smith (Dover Publications) and *Math Puzzles and Games* by Michael Holt (Walker and Company). This last not only has mathematical games but contains one chapter on Magic and Party Tricks with Numbers, and another on Illusions. The study of illusion is an ideal preamble or companion to the study of magic.

2. *Magic*. Magic is appropriate for pairs or groups to learn together and a strong bond unites the initiates. It can be limited to the kinds of card tricks and illusionary stunts described in *Math Puzzles and Games* or expanded to handkerchiefs and disappearing coins, or top hats and rabbits. This depends partly on what the group is ready to learn but more importantly on how much the magician/teacher knows how to teach—or is willing to share. If you don't know a magic teacher personally, or can't conjure one up, it is possible to locate one by consulting the Yellow Pages for names of practicing magicians and magicians' supply stores. Children enjoy being shown the same trick simultaneously, practicing up on one another, and fanning out into the world to "astonish family and friends."

3. *Visual puzzles*. The Creative Publications catalogue mentioned earlier advertises some beautiful and challenging visual puzzles, many of which are three dimensional. In particular, the Soma puzzle and its companion book by the mathematician and poet Piet Hein can be bought for $4.50. Children from the age of eight on up can spend hours with it. Also offered is a three-dimensional game of Tic Tac Toe; 3D chess and checkers are available in toy and game stores, but not in this catalogue.

Two-dimensional puzzles include jigsaw puzzles, tangrams, mazes, and geoboards. The latter are a favorite with many children. Geoboard activities, which are companionable for two children at a time, offer an opportunity to study a complicated visual pattern, break it down into components, and reproduce it. They are entertaining and challenging for children from the age of four on up. Some children who are highly gifted visually may enjoy them earlier.

4. *Language activities*.

a. *Nonverbal languages*. Languages other than those spoken in human voices are all around us. How many more things we can understand, and how our own store of expressive capabilities expands, as we learn to understand them! Here are three examples.

A group of children can have a wonderful time learning to interpret and use body English. It is a first cousin to pantomime, which all children enjoy. They love finding out supposed meanings of common body positions. Start with a discussion of what emotions they themselves may be expressing with their own bodies. *The Body Language of Children* by Suzanne Szass (W. W. Norton & Co., 500 Fifth Ave., New York, N.Y. 10036) would make a good beginning. The black and white photographs are perfect illustrations of her text and she describes emotions all of us have shared. Continue from there. Does the group agree, for instance, that crossing your legs away from your conversational partner indicates disagreement or aversion? Children who become fascinated with body English may go into a phase of striking poses which will definitely put a damper on spontaneous socializing; however, it will heighten their appreciation of good acting and perhaps improve their performance in charades.

What do animals mean by their various physical poses? Tail-wagging and purring are the idiom of two domestic animals and we all know what skunks and porcupines do to their enemies. But how many know that one wolf shows submission to another by exposing his throat? Adults who are interested in finding out more on this subject can read *The Question of Animal Awareness* by Donald R. Griffin (Rockefeller University Press, 1230 York Ave., New York, N.Y. 10021) and *Look Who's Talking* by Emily Hahn

(T. Y. Crowell, 10 E. 53 St., New York, N.Y. 10022). A card game of matching pose with emotion could go on for hours. Set it up as Old Maid, Rummy, Go Fish, or Concentration. If you want to make such a game order some blank playing cards from Creative Publications. They cost $2.50 for 100 or $8.00 for 400. Make pairs by writing a word naming an emotion on one card, and an illustration of a pose (or verbal description if you cannot draw) on another. To forestall argument make a master card listing possible pairing combinations. Then play the game following the rules of Old Maid, Rummy, or whichever format the group has chosen.

While weather does not actually tell stories, it can be considered a language in that it sends signals we can learn to interpret. For instance, as every sailor and pilot knows, different kinds of clouds herald different weather conditions, as do different winds. Learning to interpret these signals in order to predict what is coming is like being let in on a secret. One Saturday Club for gifted children devoted several months to studying weather— graphing precipitation, wind, temperature, and barometric pressure. As an accompaniment they made a collection of common weather proverbs and tried to discover their probable origins. From "ring around the moon, rain coming soon" to "red sky in the morning, sailors take warning" our folklore is rich with such sayings. It was socially and intellectually entertaining for this group to relate science and old wives' tales.

b. *Foreign languages*. Learning to use and understand a foreign language is a requirement in many schools. A child who is particularly adept may wish to learn additional ones or a child or family going on a trip may want to learn a particular one. But here is a delightful game, not formally academic and not aimed at a specific event, to play with a foreign language and children who are mature enough to understand onomatopoeia.

The person in charge chooses a selection written in another language. He reads it aloud if his pronunciation is good, or plays it from a recording. Each participant listens to it, and from the sounds decides what he thinks it is about and writes out a short translation. Almost always each person has a different interpretation. One teacher read a selection in German to a group of eight students. One thought it was about the moon, one thought it was about a naughty child, one a storm at sea, one a flower garden, and one a hibernating bear. Another thought it was the words to a lullabye and two people thought it had to do with machinery. It turned out to be an insurance policy. Once the truth was revealed the selection was read again and the participants talked about which words and sounds had led them to their various conclusions.

c. *Codes* provide privacy and delight. Use Morse Code, nautical flag code, hieroglyphic code, codes made by substituting numbers for letters or letters for one another. Cryptography appeals to all ages, is available for all levels, and joins the initiates together in a shared secret. A good book for elementary school children to begin with is *Spycraft*, published by Scholastic.

Indian Sign Language by William Tomkins (Dover Publications) provides a clear explanation and illustrations of pictography and sign language and, using short selections, gives simple directions on how to comprehend and transmit words, phrases, and complete sentences. This would be an appropriate companion or extension of code study, a subject likely to have strong appeal for fifth and sixth graders who like to be keepers of hidden mysteries.

d. *Nuances*. One group of gifted eleven- and twelve-year-olds studied the various languages found in newspapers, travel folders, fund-raising appeals, and other printed materials that surround us daily. They learned to distinguish among propaganda, advertising, fact, and opinion. After they had learned to notice these, they practiced using them on one another by inventing new products and deciding what kind of language to use to advertise and sell them. One boy invented a mythical cream called Acni-way, reputed to improve the complexions and social prospects of adolescents afflicted with pimples. He designed a label incorporating before and after caricatures, wrote a jingle using the advertising techniques he had been studying, and promised a free sample to each classmate who would use the cream and write a testimonial. He and his friends never passed a cosmetics counter again with their previous degree of gullibility.

e. *Radio and television.* Remember the caveats in the last chapter on selection and snobbery. Both media offer programs which can teach a great deal to a group, particularly if they are discussed before and after listening to them. Here is one way. Choose a program. Listen to it or watch it together as a group. At the conclusion each group member picks words to describe some element, perhaps the villain. Chart how many words appeared on every person's list. How many appeared only once? Try to think of another person who could be described by these same words. Use the same exercise to describe additional characters, types of plot, different moods, settings, costumes, or subjective evaluations. The opportunities are endless. If each participant tries to choose unusual words instead of obvious ones, the vocabulary will be rich.

Or interpret through crafts instead of words. After a group of seven-year-old children heard a description of different kinds of islands, each child was given a shirt cardboard, some paints, clay, and papier mâché and asked to design his own island. Each child had been given a little booklet in which to write a description of the island's location, climate, vegetation, population, greatest problem, and greatest treasure. Each creation was unique and each child adored seeing what his friends had imagined. The culmination was a reading of *The Bad Island* by William Steig.

Essence, the *Dictionary Game,* and *Botticelli* are old-fashioned parlor games familiar to those of us who grew up in a pretelevision era. Like *Charades* and *The Game* they can be played by

127

young and old together as well as chronologically matched groups.

Essence—a personality-analogy game. Start with four or five public figures whose personalities and occupations are very different from one another. Make a chart or booklet about each one listing such facts as age, birthplace, career, successes, obstacles, failures, favorite sports, hobbies, and favorite foods. Be sure to include some pictures. As the group develops these profiles they will come to know the people well. Then play the game this way. One player chooses one of the five public figures but does not say which one. The others try to figure out the identity by asking such questions as, "If he were a color, what color would he be?" "If he were a plant, what kind of plant would he be?" The point is not to use colors or plants which the character owns, but rather those that express the essence of his personality. One game with ten women characters and ten children went this way:

Q. If she were a color, what color would she be?
A. An orangey-red.
Q. If she were a snack, what would she be?
A. Watercress sandwiches on very thin whole wheat bread, vintage champagne, and fresh strawberries.
Q. If she were a book, what kind of book would she be?
A. A slender volume of poetry, bound in blue leather.
Q. If she were a sport, what sport would she be?
A. Badminton.
Q. If she were a body of water, what kind would she be?
A. Fast-moving stream in the mountains with fish and occasional deep, quiet pools.
A. I know! I know! Katharine Hepburn.

Young children cannot play this game because they get stuck on possessions. When asked what color best represents the character, they will give the color of the dress she is wearing in the picture, or say "blackish" about every man who wears a suit. But once the group catches on to extrapolation and symbolism, there is no end. Continue adding to the central supply of characters, being sure that each member of the group knows who the possibilities are and has some idea what each is like.

For older children or people who share a common knowledge of characters, the preliminary steps are unnecessary. They are suggested to keep an inexperienced player from choosing his grandmother, whom no one else knows. The children may want to use one another, but before allowing it, the teacher must be sure they will be able to carry it off without hurting anyone's feelings by using accurate but unflattering analogies.

The Dictionary Game—a game of definitions. The person who is "it" chooses a word from the dictionary—the more abstruse the better. Other players listen, consider, then write out what sounds to them like a logical definition. "It" writes out the actual definition and adds it to the collection. The person who is "it" reads all the definitions aloud once, then rereads each one aloud and asks for a vote. Players vote for the definition they think is the real one. The player whose bogus definition gets the most points is the winner and either he or the player who guesses the actual definition chooses the next word.

Botticelli—an associative guessing game appropriate for players who share a common cultural knowledge. In general I have found that while this game angers children younger than seventh grade, it is apt to cause an epidemic in high school. The person who is "it" chooses a character, real or fictional, living or dead, and tells the other players the first letter of the character's last name. Other players try to guess the identity of the character by asking indirect identity questions of "it" which he must answer by furnishing the name of still another character with the same initial. Thus, if "it" chooses to be Romeo he would simply say R. Play might proceed thus:

WHAT ELSE THEY NEED

Q. Are you a Russian composer?
A. No, I am not Rachmaninoff.
Q. Are you a baseball player?
A. No, I am not Babe Ruth.
Q. Are you a cowboy?

The questioner must have a specific person in mind before asking his question. In other words he himself must know a cowboy whose last name begins with R. If "it" is stumped by the last question and is unable to come up with Roy Rogers he must give a direct answer to a factual question such as "Are you male or female?" To make the game harder the direct questions can be limited to yes or no questions. To make it more elastic, allow such questions as "Where do you live?" If "it" thinks his interrogator is bluffing and does not, for instance, know a cowboy whose name begins with R he may challenge. He receives one immunity from a direct question for each successful challenge, and must answer one direct question for each unsuccessful challenge. The game ends when Romeo is discovered and the player who discovered the truth is the next "it."

Charades and *The Game* are games of pantomime in which "it" acts out a word by syllables, or acts out whole phrases, titles, or slogans. In *Charades* the goal is to be obscure and make it as hard as possible for the opposition to guess. In *The Game* the goal is to help one's team guess the words as quickly as possible. Though local rules vary as to what hints and how many hints are permissible, there is a common agreement that the actor may not speak.

Scrabble, Boggle, and *Wordsworth*, a verbal cousin to *Mastermind*, are three well-designed games which challenge adults as well as young players. For additional ideas consult *The Mammoth Book of Word Games,* Hart Publishing Co., and *The Book of Think* along with the other titles in the Brown Paper School Book series published by Little, Brown and designed for children and grown-ups to use together.

5. *Brainstorming and simulation*.

Brainstorming. Questions with no known correct answer will delight the divergent thinker. Here are three questions that have been used over and over, and reappear by popular demand.

What if?
Where did?
What will?

"What if the sun never set" can lead to a discussion of:

1. Problems of agriculture and world food supply.
2. People's natural rhythms for working, eating, and sleeping. Is jet lag a myth?
3. How do people behave when they do not have enough sleep?
4. What is the role of nocturnal animals?
5. How diurnal and nocturnal animals share the same territory.
6. The use poets, painters, and philosophers have made of dawn and sunset.
7. Different summer and winter behaviors of people who live in high latitudes.

Other good discussion starters are: "Where did . . . the world get rocks?" and "What will . . . food be in the year 2050?" The participating children themselves will come up with many more.

The answers seem to settle into three categories: probable, possible, and mythical. This can lead the way to finding and reading different cultures' mythical responses to these same questions. Once the children have played with the ideas themselves they will take special delight in other people's thoughts.

Simulation games. One of the most exciting and successful simulation games I have ever seen was invented and led by John Fennell, a gifted teacher in Bedford, New York. Working in school with a group of roughly one hundred fifth and sixth graders, he invented a cross-cultural simulation unit that built group solidarity while teaching the rudiments of anthropology. Although this was done in school it would be entirely suitable for a Saturday Club. He divided the group into three mythical tribal cultures which he named the Mamazons, the Vorichis, and the Urbanians. The children first discussed the component strands all societies have, such as economy, religion, physical environment, technology, and social controls. Then each tribe was told about its own particulars and asked to find ways to chart them. They were asked not to divulge any specific facts about their tribe but to represent them through making artifacts, painting murals, and making dioramas of tribal customs. Each tribe then tried to discover as much as possible about the priorities, prohibitions, and problems of the other two cultures through inference and deduction. More details, and a sample myth and spiritual ritual for each culture is included in the appendix along with the name and address of the originator of the game.

In addition to readily available games such as *Risk*, a world conquest game for two to six players ages ten to adult (Parker Bros.) and *Land Grab* for two to four players ages nine to adult (House of Games, Inc., Elk Grove Village, Chicago, Illinois 60607), the 3M Co. markets the simulation games *Sleuth, Acquire, Stocks and Bonds,* and *Venture*, among others. Similies 11 in LaJolla, California 92037, offers *Explorers I, Explorers II,* and *Roaring Camp*. They will send brochures upon request. There are many others to be sure, but these will give the interested reader a place to begin.

6. *Crafts*. The extent of a craft program depends on available facilities and teachers. If there is elaborate equipment, by all means find out how to use it. If there is a teacher or a mentor with a special skill to teach, build the program around it, or at least incorporate it. If you need help getting started, there are two sources of craft projects for groups which I like. In planning for younger children,

132

roughly up to ten or eleven, consult Scholastic Funcraft Books. They offer such titles as *Magnets and Batteries, Flying Models, Paper Fun, Print and Paint, Action Toys and Action Games*. The books are colorful, the directions are clear, and the topics are appealing. For older children, roughly from ten on up, Dover Publications offers a beautifully varied selection of how-to books covering over fifty topics from dolls and dollmaking to boomerangs. They will send a catalogue on request and there is a catalogue reprint in the backs of their hardcover books. Their address is listed in the appendix.

7. *Music and drama.* Playing music in an ensemble or an orchestra offers social, intellectual, and aesthetic nourishment. If a conductor is available and there are enough skilled performers to make up a group, those blessed with musical gifts can exercise them for their own pleasure as well as the delight of those for whom they play. Depending on the size of a school, a Saturday Club, or a community, such opportunities may abound or be scarce. In a situation which appears to offer scant opportunities there may be chances for gifted children to play with adults. See the final section of this chapter for specifics.

Dramatics provides superb opportunity for imaginative interpretation, cooperation, and use of a wide variety of skills. There are chances for

acting, singing, and dancing
producing and directing
costuming and lighting
designing and building sets
advertising and ticket selling
knowing the dramatic literature and choosing appropriate plays.

Not only is a wide range of skills necessary but each member of the group depends on the others.

"To be or not to be" is merely a famous phrase until it is part of

133

WHAT ELSE THEY NEED

that living whole called a play. When Hamlet has a costume, a stage, lighting, a set, an audience, and other characters around him, his story comes to life. No matter how talented the star, he cannot do it alone. A gifted child needs the experience of being a supporting member of the cast as well as the star.

If opportunities for children's theater do not exist locally, a Saturday Club may wish to provide them. Imagination, energy, one willing director, and a group of children are all that's needed to begin. Start with a small project, and depend on the children to write a script, help with costumes and sets, and make sound effects. Don't feel that each production must be elaborate. One group of twenty imaginative children ages nine and ten with a small budget limited their costumes to tights, turtlenecks, and masks or tunics made from paper bags. They wrote and produced a highly entertaining play about dragons. Rather than preventing expression, the lack of funds for such things as costumes was simply a spur to originality and the challenge of solving a problem.

The World of Travel

Going to a new place is an experience that unites those who share it. Because geographical location, choice of emphasis, budget, and age and number of participants differ in each case I am simply going to list several resources and references for each of four different kinds of travel.

TRAVEL/STUDYING

Many colleges offer alumni weekends or summer sessions for whole families. Room and board are included in the fee. There is a variety of course offerings, athletic and social opportunities are available, and baby-sitting can be arranged if necessary. Different

134

members of the family learn different things and can share their discoveries. For details, consult your own college, or a college or university in the part of the country you would like to visit.

Frequently, museums sponsor special-purpose trips. Some are short, some extensive, but they provide an opportunity to combine an excursion with learning. For information call a nearby museum or write one of the large ones anywhere in the country. The Museum of Natural History in New York City sponsors trips of varying duration and distance. Although some are expensive, they are very well planned.

For a resource book on this subject try *Learning Vacations* by Gerston G. Eisenberg, Acropolis Books. Of course be sure to make a thorough check on any suggestions before setting out.

TRAVEL/CAMPING

Nature is a great teacher and a great leveler. Camping offers the gifted child challenge and companionship. The Sierra Club offers local day hikes and more extended trips for groups at every age and level of experience. They also schedule work trips, which provide an opportunity to contribute to a worthwhile cause while enjoying well-planned camping and beautiful countryside at relatively small cost. Their bulletin has specific details. A hint: bus travel is a relatively inexpensive way to cover large distances with no penalty for stopovers or side trips.

National Outdoor Leadership School in Lander, Wyoming, Outward Bound, whose headquarters are in Andover, Mass., and the American Field Service, with offices all over the country, offer many trips in which members of the group must rely on one another for comfort and safety, and sometimes for survival. These are planned for participants in specific age groups, rarely below the age of fourteen.

There are camps to which whole families go together to share the experience of using an axe, building a fire, climbing or paddling to a destination, relying on one another, and enjoying success and songs around the campfire at the end of the day. Some camps cater only to families and others offer family sessions which precede or follow the camp's regular season. A local YMCA is generally a good source of current information.

If these outings require too much equipment, are too expensive, or too difficult to arrange, a simple day hike can serve many of the same purposes. The point of view matters more than the number of miles covered. An excellent resource book for city and country families who want help planning for young children's summer vacations is *The Sierra Club Summer Book* by Linda Allison (Sierra Club Books, 1050 Mills Tower, San Francisco, Ca. 94104). The fourteen parts cover such topics as Crafts, Games, and The City Naturalist.

TRAVEL/WORKING

For those who are too young to be able to get paying jobs, there are still opportunities to travel to a new place to serve as a volunteer.

These offer a gifted child an opportunity to solve problems, work on programs, and give of himself. In addition to the Sierra Club work trips mentioned earlier, another example is the Quebec Labrador Mission, formerly known as the Grenfell Mission. Under its auspices young men and women from the age of sixteen up are placed in homes in Labrador where they develop and work on community projects for a six- or eight-week period in the summer. For further information contact the main headquarters in Boston (Quebec Labrador Foundation, Mill Rd., Ipswich, Mass. 01938).

For information about other similar opportunities consult American Friends Service Committee. They have offices throughout the country. Their address in New York City is 15 Rutherford Place, New York, N.Y. 10003.

TRAVEL/SEEING A FOREIGN COUNTRY

The gifted child who would like to immerse himself in the living and language of a foreign country should contact the Experiment for International Living in Putney, Vt. 05346. They run programs themselves and know about other existing opportunities.

The reader who wishes to plan a trip in any of the four categories has a resource to consult. This is not intended to be a comprehensive list—that would be a book in itself—but rather to provide a place to begin.

Access to the Adult World

Traditional programs exist and original opportunities can be arranged through a combination of selection, stubbornness, and stamina. A good resource book to stimulate this kind of thinking is *What Color Is Your Parachute* by Richard Bolles (Ten Speed Press, Box 7123, Berkeley, Ca. 94707). Although it was written for an adult audience, many of the points it makes are applicable to a young person interested in doing something out of the ordinary.

Here are some traditional ways a gifted child can join with adults in a group endeavor.

PROGRAMS DESIGNED TO TEACH A SPECIFIC SKILL

A major city's museum education program may offer a course on restoration of furniture or paintings, a craft guild might offer a series of lessons on weaving or decoupage, or a library might offer bookbinding. An interested applicant is usually eligible if he can pay the fee; admission is not decided by age or formal academic degree. If you have a museum, science center, or facility devoted to historical preservation near you, call to see what adult education programs are currently offered and whether they would accept a young applicant. We will consider college courses in the final section of this chapter. While it is difficult to arrange access to them, it is not impossible. Few things are.

VOLUNTEER SERVICE

Every community has needs to be met by those who will volunteer. This is true of individuals and groups. Such activity can be deeply satisfying to a gifted child who would like to give care as well as receive it. The same is true for a group of gifted children working together to meet a need or solve a problem. As a group can build identity through being against other groups or ideas, it can also build it through allegiance to a project or community. For specific details of local needs consult your local Voluntary Association, whose address can generally be found in the telephone book or by writing to the National Center for Voluntary Action, 1215 16th Street, N.W., Washington, D.C. 20036. This is a clearing house for volunteer programs throughout the country.

TEACHING AND TUTORING

Through day-care centers, summer camps, community programs, after-school projects, and children's hospitals there are chances for gifted children to teach or tutor other children. Examples range from a group of fifth, sixth, and seventh graders who worked in a summer remedial reading program, to seventh and eighth grade boys who taught soccer two afternoons a week after school, to Lucia, who financed a winter's worth of theater tickets by giving music lessons when she was fourteen. Just as learning how to be a member of a group is important for a gifted child, learning how to be an effective leader can be a lesson in human nature. Write to the director of whatever local facility appeals to you, or consult a volunteer association.

MUSIC AND DRAMA

The gifted young artist who wants to be part of a musical group without paying the high tuition of formal music schooling can find opportunities through churches, community groups, and those music stores that also arrange music lessons.

Churches usually welcome choir singers and are delighted to have guest instrumentalists. In addition, choir directors are often knowledgeable about choral groups who sing secular music. Frequently there is an overlap in membership of such groups and they may well share the same director.

Information about community orchestras, fife and drum corps, bands, and ensembles can be found through the community newspaper or music store. One such store, which is not unique in its approach, sells instruments, scores, and sheet music. They also sponsor and house a small music school whose faculty is made up of local musicians who are available to give lessons. The store and the music school share a large bulletin board where notices are posted of groups needing a member to play a particular instrument, or individual artists who want to join a group. Young participants are welcome in all the above. Talent is the ticket.

Opportunities for gifted children to gain access to adult theater are difficult but not impossible to arrange, particularly if the young person is willing to do backstage work. Consult a local paper for information about neighborhood amateur groups and apprentice programs for high school and college students. In such a program apprentices work side by side with professionals and though the hours are long, the learning opportunities and the camaraderie are enormous. Many summer theaters offer such programs. Some are more formalized than others. If you are interested, choose several theaters on the basis of their location, their leadership, or the type of play they produce. Get in touch with them. If they do not have programs or opportunities themselves, they may be able to make some suggestions.

Nontraditional Opportunities

Apprenticeship. Some businesses are willing to offer apprenticeships. When these are available they provide unique opportunities to learn and apply newly learned skills. These seem particularly difficult to arrange for children under the age of sixteen who do not yet have working papers, but it can be done. The key word is volunteer. Interest, coupled with the willingness to contribute time without asking for money, will open many doors. Here are four examples of young people aged thirteen, fifteen, seventeen, and nineteen who found unusual opportunities through volunteering.

When Lucia was thirteen, the summer vacation loomed long. She had been to summer camp for two years and did not wish to go again. She cared little for country club athletics and was eager to find an interesting project. She wanted to be a teacher or a camp counselor but it was hard for her to establish her credibility. Too young for the payroll, she volunteered at a day camp for handicapped children. The first few days she was only allowed to tie shoelaces and serve snacks, but then she found a way to start helping in the swimming pool and put on puppet shows. As the children responded to her and she proved herself reliable, the staff came to trust her and genuinely appreciated the imagination she brought to the program. Before two weeks were over she was fully accepted. She was not paid in money, but she earned respect, a place on an adult team, and she received an opportunity to be a giver of care.

Chris, at fifteen, was fascinated by botany and too young for working papers. By volunteering, he wangled his way into an organization that combined a commercial nursery with a research program. At that time the researchers were working to develop a strain of flowering shrub that would be highly resistant to automobile exhaust. Starting with a broom in the laboratory, Chris made himself useful and by the end of his ten-week stay he had a white coat and a name plate. His colleagues seemed to have forgotten he didn't share their extensive training, age, or tax bracket. He was quick to learn, reliable, and interested and those qualities earned him his place on the team.

Susan, highly intellectual and seventeen, ached for a summer opportunity in the New York City publishing world. Jobs were scarce and her chances seemed slim indeed but she was determined. She concentrated on five places she admired and, through diligent searching and help from her family, she found a connection with an editor at one of the five. She wrote him a letter explaining her interest, saying why she had chosen his firm, listing her credentials, describing what she thought she could offer, and saying she would be delighted to work for the experience—she was not asking for a salary. She concluded her articulate letter by volunteering to work in the files. According to the editor, that did it. Today he says, "Anybody who goes to the trouble of finding out that much about your company . . . who likes it that much . . . who has done that much research and is willing to work for no pay has to get a break . . . and after a couple of weeks of watching the files get cleaned out I got a guilty conscience, so I gave her something fun." Susan has had increasingly interesting work given her summer after summer, finally accompanied by a paycheck. She will graduate from college next June with knowledge, training,

141

practical experience, and excellent references from four summers' worth of work.

One young man spent the summer of 1978 as an assistant to a geology professor who is mapping an interior region of a foreign country. The student traveled at his own expense. He could afford it and thought that the opportunity to work side by side with a man whose work he admires was a worthwhile investment in his own future—the equivalent of taking a private course. Those who can afford to volunteer for such positions and would like to do so should put up a notice on a departmental bulletin board of a college or university, or write a letter to the chairman of the department, whose name can be found in the college catalogue.

Not every apprenticeship will or should lead to a permanent career in the same field. That is not their value for the gifted child. Their importance lies in the opportunity they present for a young person of drive and ability to learn new skills and practice them professionally. When looking for similar opportunities keep in mind the three suggestions at the end of this chapter.

Advanced study. To arrange for a gifted child to take advanced courses you again need a combination of selection, stubbornness, and stamina. Most colleges, even those offering extension programs, will not admit students under the age of eighteen or those who do not have a high school diploma or its equivalent. Even though the student may have the prerequisite knowledge, his family is willing and able to pay the tuition, and he is not seeking transferable academic credit, formal college policy usually denies him admission. The head of the continuing education department in a medium-sized private liberal arts college in New England had this advice for anyone who wants to enroll an unusual student: "If the admissions office says no, don't give up. Try the continuing education office, the office of nondegree programs or its equivalent. Try to see the head of one of those offices in person. Know exactly what course or courses you are interested in, what they will cover and what the prerequisites are. You will help your own cause by being well-informed. A college official will be able to plead your cause for you more effectively if you have done your homework. If all the officials say no, go directly to the department head, or the professor who teaches the course. Don't give up!"

Arranging for a gifted child to have access to the adult world is not easy but three things help:

1. Decide on a field.
2. Find a specific person.
3. Volunteer!

Summary

Children's programs, travel, and access to the adult world offer enrichment that need not be solitary. These group activities are appropriate for children who are gifted, children who are quick, or children who are interested.

In writing this chapter I faced a choice—should I speak in generalizations and thus risk superficiality, or should I speak in specifics and risk both omission and giving information that may go out of date? Having chosen the latter, I gave considerable space to ideas and activities I have not seen described in other books or catalogues and simply mentioned by name those that are more in the realm of common knowledge. Consequently, the space devoted to various descriptions is not indicative of their relative importance.

Each combination of people, location, need, and inclination will be different. As the choices are being made, let the children themselves be active agents, not passive recipients. The result will be enthusiasm, excitement, and commitment.

Chapter 8

Stories

Reading aloud to a child is an ideal way to help him enrich his internal language, and this automatically increases his supply of expressive tools. Language is contagious.

Gifted children use receptive and expressive language to manage some of their most powerful intellectual and emotional hungers. The child who is comfortable with words will play with them, will collect them as treasures, and because he can listen to them and comprehend them, he will be able to use them to express his ideas and feelings. The child thus builds a platform of language from which to launch rockets of abstract thinking and is free to venture, risk, learn, and create.

Since you cannot express what you do not have, the gifted child first needs a well-developed, receptive language facility. People, like television sets, are receivers as well as transmitters. Many images and sounds come in from the air. The viewer chooses what appeals to him after consulting the program guide, or by flicking from channel to channel to see what's there. Once the choice is made, the channel receives and transmits only one program at a time. While others still exist in the air, they are not tuned in, so they are not a distraction. The gifted child who absorbs so much, yet struggles to experience the world with inadequate language, is like a television set with all channels receiving simultaneously, no station selector, and no controls for horizontal hold, brightness, and hue.

A child needs to change fantasy from something which controls him to something which he controls in order to grow up. Language bridges fact and fiction. The greater the texture and variety of the gifted child's vocabulary, the more he can master his rich imaginings. Many gifted children automatically apply language to this task but others need help or extra exposure to words.

The gifted child whose personal lexicon is filled with words of texture and strength has many ways of expressing his own thoughts, many of which may be difficult to articulate because they are so original. He also develops many ways to meet the writer when he is reading something new. Real reading is active and energetic. The reader matches an expectation in his head with what his eyes find as they travel along a line of print. Katrina de Hirsch refers to this as "casting a linguistic shadow." With it the reader anticipates what is to come and easily appreciates cadence, rhythm, and humor. The gifted child who is familiar with pattern and theme and is accustomed to hearing the various languages of fairy tales, humor, suspense, journalism, poetry, and commercials, to name but a few, will read these languages with ease and accuracy, distinguishing them from one another.

In addition to enhancing language, reading aloud has at least five other benefits we should consider. These are important to all children, but they are vital nourishment for the gifted child.

1. Expansion of knowledge.
2. Exercise of imagination.

3. Identification with character and the opportunity to share feelings and experiences far beyond his own with a family group or a class.
4. Bibliotherapy, the comfort of finding one's own dilemma described or resolved in stories.
5. Experience of intellectual pleasure and the physical and emotional closeness of sharing a lap or a sofa as well as a story.

Some surprising fears and foibles explain why more adults don't read aloud. The first is a fear that in some way it is "spoiling" the child to read to him once he starts to read by himself. "Shouldn't he be reading to me?" a parent will say. "After all, he's learning to read in school. Shouldn't he practice at home?" Yes, if he wants, but that is no substitute for being read to. We must separate mastery of decoding from enrichment and linguistic pleasure. These are two sides of the language coin. A child can understand things read to him years before he can read them independently, and long before they can read by themselves children love to tell stories. For little children, particularly those with a gift for language, get some books without words. Mercer Mayer has assembled some excellent ones. Among them are *The Great Cat Chase* (Scholastic), *A Boy, a Dog, a Frog and a Friend,* and *Hiccup* (Dial Press) and *Two Moral Tales: Bear's New Clothes and Bird's New Hat* and *Two More Moral Tales: Just a Pig at Heart and Sly Fox's Folly* (Four Winds Press). The illustrations in all of them leave no doubt about the story line but the child tells it in his own words.

Some parents avoid reading aloud because they aren't sure how to pick "the right book." Flanked by this is a horror that, if they once begin, they'll be trapped into reading something boring or demeaning. Some books written for youthful ears are of such thin literary quality that it is humiliating for an intelligent adult to read them aloud. The child detects the distaste immediately, and lacking in experience, attributes it to the activity, not the literary selection. The noble sacrifice is useless and the child is disappointed.

Here's a different way of approaching the problem which may banish the fears and foibles. Let the adult find his or her own favorite kind of story, written on a level appropriate for young listeners.

If you, as an adult, enjoy Jane Austen, read the *Frances* books by Russell Hoban (Harper and Row) to a child. They are filled with parallel puckish profundity, and a tartly accurate view of human relations and social custom. Frances and her little sister Gloria are reminiscent of the Bennett sisters in *Pride and Prejudice*, and the language is delicious!

Are you a comedy-of-manners-and-morals freak? Try *Goops,* and Hilaire Belloc's *Cautionary Verses* on your way to *The Importance of Being Earnest*.

Do you thrill to The Forces of Nature Harnessed and Unharnessed? Try *The Wreck of the Hesperus* and Jack London on the way to Admiral Byrd's *Discovery* and *Alone*, or Charles Lindbergh's *The Spirit of St. Louis*.

If you believe the child is the embodiment of truth and healing and, as an adult, love *Silas Marner*, read *The Emperor's New Clothes,* or Menotti's *Amahl and the Night Visitors* to children.

I once heard a concert of brasses in which the musicians talked about melody and various musical forms: waltzes, marches, scherzos. Then they played *Jingle Bells* in each one. You should hear it as a chorale—it brings tears to the eyes! We, adults and children together, learned to discover the pattern as well as recognize the melody. The same thing can be done with literature.

As linguistic foreshadowing is prerequisite to real reading, so familiarity with a literary theme adds extra dimension to enjoyment of the printed word. Entertaining and important literary themes appear in well-written children's books, as well as in the classics and books written for the adult popular market. Great dreams and stories are found in slender volumes as well as in thick ones. A book is not a sirloin steak that must be two inches thick to merit adult attention or satisfy an adult appetite.

Let's choose five patterns and see on how many levels they appear.

Pattern 1: Psychological Forces at Work in the Community

Pity, greed, passion, sacrifice, love, and death. For a young child? Yes. In this exercise, I'll say that *War and Peace, Gone with the Wind, Middlemarch,* and *Charlotte's Web* are all the same story. They come in different depths and on different levels, to be sure, but they are still the same story. The first three (the so-called adult ones) are laced with social and political history. All kinds of people and many kinds of values are represented. Economics collides with idealism against an agrarian backdrop. The same is true of the fourth!

Try to return these two quotes to their rightful covers.

Although he loved her children and her grandchildren, none of the new ones ever quite took her place in his heart. She was in a class by herself. It is not often that someone comes along who is a true friend and a good writer. _____ was both.[1]

For the growing good of the world is partly dependent on unhistoric acts; and that things are not so ill with you and me as they might have been, is half owing to the number who have lived faithfully a hidden life and rest in unvisited tombs.[2]

[1] E. B. White, *Charlotte's Web* (New York: Harper & Row, 1952), p. 184.
[2] George Eliot, *Middlemarch* (Boston: Houghton Mifflin Co., Riverside Edition, 1956), p. 613.

149

WHAT ELSE THEY NEED

Is this a table of contents for a saga of Russian life, people playing out their lives in the English countryside, or a story of a pig and a spider?

Although in *Charlotte's Web* some of the characters are animals, they act the way people act, and have a human balance of good and bad qualities apiece. Even Templeton, the rat, has moments when the noblest among us must identify with him.

Fern and her father collide early in the story. Mr. Arable is a knowledgeable farmer, well-meaning father, keeper of the Ten Commandments, and also family provider. But he appears to his daughter as a cruel supporter of a double standard. Her vision has

[3]White, Table of Contents.

150

not yet been clouded by worldly compromise between money and morality. Their disagreement involves a choice between practicality and compassion. Should Wilbur be killed? Which should win? What of the leader who makes the cold-blooded choice? How would you feel about him as a father, as a husband, as a town councilor, a tax collector, a minister, or perhaps a doctor? If he were your physician, would you dare to get sick? The arguments on each side are familiar to readers of New Testament parables, Sinclair Lewis, and the Watergate tapes, as well as the four books under discussion.

Charlotte is the practical achiever, as are the team of Arable and Zuckerman. Both are loving, both are sure of right as they see it, but they are on opposite sides. Who will win and how can the author apportion victory without defeating virtue?

In the case of *Charlotte's Web,* the device is just the same as it is in the other stories. By shifting the focus to a newly developing trait in a familiar character, the author changes the balance of the story and a new tack is permissible. Enter love!—a new kind. I'm not going to try to pretend I find Henry Fussy as romantic as Rhett Butler—but don't tell Fern!

England, Russia, and the Old South know the men of affairs whose efforts succeed. So does E. B. White.

A great feeling of happiness swept over the Zuckermans and the Arables. This was the greatest moment in Mr. Zuckerman's life. It is deeply satisfying to win a prize in front of a lot of people.[4]

These 184 pages bring forth tears, laughter, suspense, and transportation into another world. "Salutations," as Charlotte herself might say to all writers who are "humble," "versatile," and "radiant."

One might imagine George Eliot, E. B. White, Margaret

[4]Ibid., p. 160.

151

Mitchell, or Tolstoy saying of their artistic aim, "It is not to resolve a question irrefutably, but to compel one to love life in all its manifestations—and these are inexhaustible."

Which one said:

If I were told that I could write a novel in which I could indisputably establish as true my point of view on all social questions, I would not dedicate two hours to such a work; but if I were told that what I wrote would be read twenty years from now by those who are children today, and that they would weep and laugh over it, and fall in love with the life in it, then I would dedicate all my existence and all my power to it.[5]

I am not advocating that *Charlotte's Web* take the place of *War and Peace,* or either of the other two books, but I am suggesting that the adult who enjoys one will enjoy the others, and the child who is introduced to this kind of book by way of a book like *Charlotte's Web* will find the territory hospitable and familiar, and hence will probably journey there independently in later years.

Here are some books which I have enjoyed reading aloud and which the children to whom I have read them remember vividly. The age suggestions were appropriate to my circumstances but there is nothing sacred about them.

Ages 4–8
   Bedtime for Frances, etc.   Russell Hoban
   A Holiday for Edith and the Bears, etc.   Dare Wright

Ages 8 and up
   Charlie and the Chocolate Factory   Roald Dahl
   Charlotte's Web   E. B. White
   Stuart Little   E. B. White
   A Christmas Carol   Charles Dickens

[5]Leo Tolstoy, *War and Peace*, trans. Rosemary Edmonds (London: Penguin Books Ltd., Society Edition, 1971), p. 10.

STORIES

The Wind in the Willows   Kenneth Grahame
The Lonely Doll Learns a Lesson, etc.   Dare Wright
The Fairy Doll   Rumer Godden
Norse Gods and Giants   Ingri and Edgar d'Aulaire

Ages 10 and up
Danny, Champion of the World   Roald Dahl
Living Free   Joy Adamson
Little Women   Louisa May Alcott
The Doll's House   Rumer Godden
The Snow Goose   Paul Gallico
The Yearling   Marjorie K. Rawlings
Anne and the Sand Dobbies   John Coburn

Judy Blume writes excellent books for the independent reader. Two specific titles are *Are You There God, It's Me, Margaret* and *Tales of a Fourth Grade Nothing.* Children find these both personal and satisfying to read alone, so I would not recommend reading them aloud. Some adults who admired her earlier books strongly disapprove of the sexual content of *Forever.* Follow your personal preference in encouraging or discouraging a child to read it.

An imaginative, humorous, and beautifully written book for readers of all ages is *The Pluperfect of Love* by Dorothy Crayder.

Pattern 2: Human Nature, Good or Evil?

Children and, incidentally, philosophers have wondered about this forever. Is human nature gentle and benevolent, to be encouraged and set free? Is it dangerous, something which must be contained by powerful bonds? The gifted child, whose perception of discrepancy is so acute, may be relieved to discover that this question has troubled wise authors throughout the ages.

The mark of a mature mind is the ability to hold two opposing ideas at once, which is to say to be comfortable with ambiguity. Don't expect this of most children below the age of eleven or twelve, which, as we know from Piaget, is the age when abstract thinking develops as part of formal operations. For children younger than this, the simple process of sorting good from bad is fun, and lays good foundations for later, more complicated thinking. Adults who treasure *The Turn of the Screw, Lord of the Flies, Billy Budd,* and *Song of Myself* may be surprised that there are counterparts in books which theoretically belong to children.

Begin with *The Bad Island* by William Steig. For majestic language it's hard to match. There are huge rumbling words children love to hear long before they can pronounce them or use them independently.

The Start of the Battle

Eventually things really got out of hand, or out of claw and talon. From blaming, and cursing and insulting, and threatening and insulting and hitting, they went on to serious fighting. And all their deepest demons of hate broke loose. Much as they had all loathed and abominated one another before, it was nothing compared to the way they loathed and abominated now. But loathing and abominating no longer gave them enjoyment.[6]

The Battle

It went on and on and on and one day it was finally over. Everyone had succeeded in killing everyone else off. The last ugly ogre had given his last ugly gasp and the last serpent breathed its last flame and the island was a gigantic heap of dead, scaly, thorny, fanged, horned, bug-eyed, barbed, bristling, saw-toothed carcasses, lying in ashes and embers, burning and giving off a dark, horrible smoke. And then there was nothing but hot ashes.[7]

[6] William Steig, *The Bad Island* (New York: Simon & Schuster, Windmill Books, 1969), unpaged.
[7] Ibid.

STORIES

The denouement belongs to Steig and his readers, but there is no ambiguity. His good is as good as his evil is evil. And no, the children won't be scared. You might progress from there to sorting good children from bad children. *A Child's Garden of Verses* works for this, as do *Cautionary Tales, The Bad Child's Book of Beasts, More Beasts for Worse Children,* and *A Moral Alphabet* by Hilaire Belloc, and *The Goop Books* by Gelett Burgess. A child who would otherwise feel too old to be reading "baby-stuff" will enjoy reading children's poetry searching for adult distinctions. And all children will feel a warm rush of superiority reading about other children who are totally bad.

Here are some books from which young gifted listeners have drawn enjoyment and thoughtful perceptions.

Ages 4 and up
    Two books of photographs:
    The Family of Man   Edward Steichen
    Family   Margaret Mead and Ken Heyman
    The Bad Island   William Steig
    Lucy McLockett   Phyllis McGinley

Ages 8 and up
    Pinocchio   Carlo Coloddi
    Trolls   Ingri and Edgar d'Aulaire
    Nora's Tale   Edith Vonnegut Rivera
    Fables   Aesop
    A Child's Garden of Verses   Robert Louis Stevenson
    Poems Every Child Should Know   Eugene Field
    Goops and How to Be Them   Gelett W. Burgess
    Goops and How Not To Be Them   Gelett W. Burgess
    Cautionary Verses   Hilaire Belloc
    Manners Can Be Fun   Munro Leaf

155

WHAT ELSE THEY NEED

Ages 10 and up
  Miracle in the Wilderness   Paul Gallico
  The Call of the Wild   Jack London
  The Velveteen Rabbit   Margery Williams
  The Little Mermaid   Hans Christian Andersen
  Julie of the Wolves   Jean George

Pattern 3: Time and Space: Science Fiction

We count on time and space to give shape to our lives. They make boundaries which we interpret as safety. Some people are uncomfortable when these concepts are bent or distorted, which may explain why we have made a separate category for such stories: science fiction. It's as though this gives us a safe way to play with potentially dangerous ideas. For adults who are devotees of Jules Verne or Isaac Asimov here are some suggested stories for gifted children.

The story of *Peter Pan* can be both soothing and liberating to a gifted child who may feel like a Ping-Pong ball traveling between paddles of omnipotence and dependence. Personally, I find a story version more manageable than trying to read the actual play aloud.

With reality in one hand, hold Ann Lindbergh's volume of poems, *The Unicorn,* in the other. Read the section on Sky and the Winds of Time. Who better to lead you through the stars, and give a whole new dimension to your reality than this explorer-poet? Once you have stepped into this amplified world, the list of people with more secrets to tell is endless. Miraculously, their stories are for all ages. Here are a few specific suggestions from an enormous number of possibilities: *The Little Prince* by Antoine de Saint-Exupéry, *A Wrinkle in Time* by Madeleine L'Engle, *The Wonderful Adventures of Nils* by Selma Lagerlof, and *The Phantom Tollbooth* by Norton Juster.

Special mention must be made of *The Lion, The Witch and The Wardrobe*, the first book in the series *The Chronicles of Narnia* by the British philosopher and theologian C. S. Lewis. Through an entertaining, seemingly simple story, this book makes profound observations on time, space, and human nature.

Books by Ray Bradbury are popular with old and young enthusiasts alike. Science fiction stories do not separate into age categories in the same way other types of narratives do. But a word of caution: save *Alice in Wonderland* for much older children. An adolescent meeting it for the first time has had an appropriate treat preserved for an appropriate time.

Pattern 4: Hero Stories

Hero stories frequently have powerful appeal for a gifted child. A story of dream and conquest can match wishes he may be unable to articulate. The wishes may be ones he cannot or dare not put into words and the dreams may be so grandiose he would fear mockery if they were known.

If you, as an adult, love reading *Sailing Alone Around the World, The Odyssey, Jason and the Golden Fleece,* and other myths and fairy tales, read Maurice Sendak's thirty-seven-page picture book, *Where the Wild Things Are,* to a gifted child. Sendak and Homer? Yes. To see how beautifully they fit together, first remember the components of a traditional hero story and then look at Sendak's plot. The fact jumps out that each has the ingredients and story line of a classic hero tale: the task, the journey, the confrontation, and the return. The task is defined in terms of obstacles that are frequently ferocious, uncontrolled or uncontrollable beasts which must be outwitted or tamed as Theseus vanquished the Minotaur and Odysseus tricked the Cyclops. Both of these are classical heroes. Psychoanalysis introduced us to the story of man trying to

157

tame himself, a tricky adversary, as we know from *Equus* or *I Never Promised You a Rose Garden,* and the modern hero's task is to vanquish alienation.

The journey takes the hero away from familiar surroundings, out of sight of those who might protect or help him, into a different country where the language and customs are probably unfamiliar. Although he may travel through a deep forest or through the air, the main journey is frequently over water. Water symbolizes many different things and represents comfort and danger simultaneously.

Next comes a confrontation, with a cunning, powerful, or seductive adversary. Usually something tempts the hero to join the opposition and to abandon his quest, but then he finds a way to resist and return home, having accomplished his deed. The passing of time will usually have been marked by the changing of seasons, or, if it is a story in a dream, day will have changed to night and back again within the dream, regardless of externals. This is the storyteller's device for indicating the making and closing of a circle. We meet the hero, learn his charge, see him off, and wait for his return, knowing he will be beyond our sight—on the dark side of the moon—until his reappearance.

Odysseus and Jason each make circular journeys and so, in *Where the Wild Things Are,* does Max, whose task is to tame himself —the first three pages leave no doubt about that. Then swiftly comes the setting for the voyage, complete with forest, ocean, and boat. No picture of Jason in the *Argo* could show more lust for adventure and pride in captaincy than does the picture of Max as he sets out to sail "through night and day, and in and out of weeks and almost over a year to where the wild things are." First he tamed them. Then he joined them with his glorious hymn to bacchanalia. "And now," cried Max, "let the wild rumpus start!" Seduction reigns. Medea, Circe, and the Sirens, as rendered by Sendak, are irresistible. The quest is abandoned—but not for good. Homesickness and the need for tempered love claim our hero and he turns his back on the wild things. He acknowledges them, but they cannot devour him, even though they threaten to. He is able to turn his back on them and wave goodbye. He is ready for the return. The ocean is ready, so is his boat, and he returns to his familiar surroundings—mission accomplished. The language in this story is a beautiful blend of realistic and fanciful, and the artwork is superb. It is a favorite among all the children I know. In psychological terms, it describes a journey all children—and all grown-ups—make repeatedly.

Are there only male heroes and voyagers? No, indeed. Listen to Phyllis McGinley.

Girl's Eye View of Relatives
The thing to remember about fathers is, they're men.
A girl has to keep it in mind.
They are dragon-seekers, bent on improbable rescues.
Scratch any father, and you find
Someone chock full of qualms and romantic terrors,
Believing change is a threat—
Like your first shoes with heels on, like your first bicycle
It took such months to get.

Walk in strange woods, they warn you about the snakes there.
Climb and they fear you'll fall.
Books, angular boys or swimming in deep water—
Fathers mistrust them all.
Men are worriers. It is difficult for them
To learn what they must learn:
How you have a journey to take and very likely,
For a while, will not return.[8]

[8]Phyllis McGinley, *Times Three* (New York, The Viking Press, 1960), p. 42.

159

WHAT ELSE THEY NEED

Here are a few other suggestions which are personal favorites of mine and the children to whom I have read them.

Ages 4 and up
  Where the Wild Things Are   Maurice Sendak

Ages 8 and up
  Greek Myths   Ingri and Edgar d'Aulaire
  James and the Giant Peach   Roald Dahl
  Lona, a Fairy Tale   Dare Wright

Ages 10 and up
  King Arthur and the Knights of the Round Table   Golden
    Illustrated Classic
  The Boy Who Sailed Around the World   Robin Graham
  White Fang   Jack London
  Kon Tiki   Thor Heyerdahl

Pattern 5: Magic and Wish Fulfillment

Gifted children need fantasies of power in order to feel some sense of control in their lives. If they can be strong and big, they can lead their lives by decision, not by default. If they are always small, while their parents (and siblings) and the world are always big, they cannot. Passivity is the product of ineffectiveness, and of course this perpetuates itself. However, growing up is an aggressive activity. All children need to be able to try on the mantle of power without being mocked. This kind of story provides opportunities for pretending without risk of guilt.

With guilt out the window, and fantasy permissible, consider the glory of such wish-fulfillment–dream-come-true stories as *Jane Eyre*. The frail young governess, poor but noble, meets the person and the life she wants. Just when everything seems within her grasp, it is snatched away by cruel intervening forces. What

160

happens, subsequently, to those forces? One by one they die or are removed to dreadful ends. How delicious! For little girls there can be no more satisfying example of a wish-fulfillment story than *A Little Princess*. Sara Crewe is by turns rich and kind, impoverished and noble, and rescued and forgiving—but dreadful fates befall those who were cruel to her along the way. Shudder to consider the final days of Miss Minchin.

It is important to distinguish between wish-fulfillment stories with happy endings and those with tragic endings, which is to say, the difference between fairy tales and myths. Fairy tales have happy endings. Myths have tragic endings because they usually describe human attempts to usurp godly powers, which must, of course, be punished. This is the difference between Cinderella and King Midas and why Sara Crewe can be set free and Icarus must fall.

It is a comfortable step from *Huckleberry Finn,* the adult book, to the child's book, *How Tom Fooled Captain Najork and His Hired Sportsmen* by Russell Hoban. A part of every one of us is set free each time Tom, surely a gifted child and a quintessential divergent thinker, outwits Aunt Fidget Wonkham-Strong, scrupulous keeper of convergent codes and wearer of an iron hat. He scores a run for imagination and independence when, spurning his dinner of greasy bloaters, he defeats the well-rehearsed uniformed opposition in successive games of Sneed-ball, Muck, and Womble. Enjoy life, Tom, with Aunt Bundle-Joy-Cozy-Sweet, the companion you finally find. Mark Twain would applaud your success and your taste.

Some wish-fulfillment stories depend on magic and the supernatural rather than on circumstance or coincidence. Surely therein lies the appeal of that classic pair in American folklore: Clark Kent, mild-mannered reporter for a major metropolitan daily, and second, silhouetted behind him—faster than a speeding bullet, more powerful than a locomotive, able to leap tall buildings at a single bound—synthesis of dreams come true—Superman.

161

WHAT ELSE THEY NEED

In *Puss 'n Boots,* the seemingly worthless cat brings wealth and the hand of the Princess to his master. In *The Bad Island,* one little flower conquers all. And in *The Brave Cowboy* by Joan Walsh Anglund, the small boy wearing a cowboy hat, playing near his front door, is in fact intrepid explorer, successful hunter of vicious beasts, and champion of the right through relentless war against outlaws. The gifted child who feels surges of intellectual strength in the confines of a childish body can forestall frustration through imagining.

Here are some suggestions:

Ages 4 and up
   Behold Man   Lennart Nilsson
      a book of photographs which provide endless trompe l'oeil surprises.
   The Brave Cowboy   Joan Walsh Anglund
   And to Think That I Saw It on Mulberry St.   Dr. Seuss

Ages 8 and up
   The Story of the Bad Little Boy Who Didn't Come to Grief
   Mark Twain
   How Tom Fooled Captain Najork and His Hired Sportsmen
   Russell Hoban
   The Wizard of Oz, etc.   L. Frank Baum
   Great Swedish Fairy Tales   selected by Elsa Olenius
   The Happy Prince and Other Tales   Oscar Wilde
   Fairy Tales   Hans Christian Andersen
   Fairy Tales   Grimm
   Norse Gods and Giants   Ingri and Edgar d'Aulaire
   The Red Fairy Book   Andrew Lang
   The Blue Fairy Book   Andrew Lang
   Wishes, Lies and Dreams   Kenneth Koch
   Mary Poppins   P. L. Travers

STORIES

Ages 10 and up

    Mrs. 'arris Goes to Paris, etc.   Paul Gallico
    Thomasina   Paul Gallico
    The Man Who Was Magic   Paul Gallico
    A Little Princess   Frances Hodgson Burnett
    The Secret Garden   Frances Hodgson Burnett
    Harriet, the Spy   Louise Fitzhugh
    Pippi Longstocking, etc.   Astrid Lundgren
    Freaky Friday   Mary Rodgers

The patterns and titles I have mentioned are intended to be representative, not encyclopedic. You will find others you prefer or want to add. Gifted children, particularly, need to feel at home with rich vocabulary, narrative, explanations, imagery, rhythm, and metaphor. They need to absorb many different kinds of language both for pure enjoyment and as a way of increasing their own expressive capabilities.

Pick the kind of book *you* as an adult enjoy reading and find it on a level appropriate to the child, or children, you want to read to. Do not fear forcing your taste on them. Enthusiasm is contagious. You may well introduce the child to something you enjoy at a level satisfying to him. Chances are this alone will produce a lifelong convert. You are, in effect, taking him on a trip to a country always accessible to re-exploration. At the least, the child will enjoy your willingness, physical closeness, and attention as well as the words he hears. Let him catch language from you through literature.

For those who would enjoy studying this topic further, here are some books I, personally, enjoy and from which I have learned a great deal.

    The Uses of Enchantment   Bruno Bettelheim
    The Green and Burning Tree   Eleanor Cameron
    The Hero with a Thousand Faces   Joseph Campbell

WHAT ELSE THEY NEED

The Masks of God   Joseph Campbell
Language and Myth   Ernst Cassirer
Language and the Discovery of Reality   Joseph Church
Myth and Reality   Mircea Eliade
Myths, Dreams and Mysteries   Mircea Eliade
Childhood and Society   Erik H. Erikson
The Magic Years   Selma Fraiberg
The Birth of Language   Shulamith Kastein and B. Trace
The Miracle of Language   Charlton Laird
Thought and Language   L. S. Vygotsky

PART IV

What They Say

Chapter 9

The Gifted Speak

Biographies allow us to see what well-known people have done with their lives. Some, like Alexander Calder, build success and find fulfillment and enjoyment in work well into old age Some, like Ernest Hemingway, create, struggle, and rage. Others, like John Keats or Edna St. Vincent Millay, sing a brief song of piercing beauty and die.

Looking back on a completed life is very different from predicting what course a life will take. It is impossible to say in advance which gifted people will fulfill their promise, which will dilute or scatter their treasure, or which will make outstanding contributions starting from seemingly modest beginnings.

The people in this chapter are intellectually outstanding. While they are different in talent, background, schooling, and age (they range from six to seventy-five), they are alike in seeming to be gifted. Each has dilemmas and goals, and each was asked the question, "If you had three wishes what would they be?"

WHAT THEY SAY

Eddie, Age 6

Eddie is six years old and has been identified as a gifted child by a California public school which honors intellectual achievement and has a new program for gifted children. He is one of three children in a bright, enterprising family. His parents say that Eddie's brothers do well in school, they are lively and quick to understand, but Eddie is different. His brothers think so too. His reading and mathematics are two or three years beyond grade level. He reads music, plays the piano, and is eager to learn a foreign language. He has an enormous store of general knowledge gathered from the media and absorbed from general conversation. Furthermore, he can play with his knowledge, extrapolate from it, and reapply it to different situations. This distinguishes him from a pseudo-gifted child who has been overtaught and simply trained to recite.

Eddie is a busy, happy child who is content to dig to China at the beach along with other six-year-old excavators. He does not have a special dilemma at the moment, but his parents do.

They waver between wanting to treat him like everyone else and wanting different things for him. They want to share their pride with the world, proclaim him gifted, yet they don't want to separate him from other children. They want to recognize his difference, but they do not want him to have to pay a social price for it. They are caught in a conflict between acknowledgment and secrecy. They must choose among acceleration, segregation, or enrichment in his schooling. If he stays in his present school, he will be moved into a program for children identified as gifted. His parents ask two questions. Is the labeling itself a healthy thing? Is the curriculum designed for expressing and training or is it merely an express train?

If his parents move Eddie to the independent school half an hour away, he will be separated from his brothers and his neighborhood friends. If he stays in a regular section of his public school, will his intellectual curiosity be stimulated and satisfied by whatever extracurricular enrichment activities are available? Must there be an inevitable choice between boasting and blooming, or hiding and hurting?

Eddie's three wishes are:

to have as many more wishes as I want;
to burp louder than anyone else in the world;
to be able to fly.

Peter, Age 13

Peter has just turned thirteen. He is one of two children of professional parents, both of whom work at a high level in demanding careers. In addition, each makes a strong commitment to local and national social issues. Peter attends an academically challenging coeducational country day school outside New York City where he is the outstanding scholar of the 150 children in his division. He is a fine athlete. For many years he was a handsome, shy boy with a secret.

Starting at age eight he traveled into New York three or four afternoons a week to attend the School of American Ballet, directed by George Balanchine. He studied, practiced, and performed—telling no one outside his immediate family.

As a little child he had struggled to overcome social timidity and he had worked hard to make a place for himself among his classmates. Friendly, scrupulously fair and compassionate, with a highly developed sense of justice, he had seen other children suffer pain from ridicule or exclusion. Each community has its own customs and codes. Peter's community does not emphasize artistic enlightenment. Peter was not going to invite difficulty by admitting that he was a ballet dancer. Nor was he willing to run the risk that something as pure to him as his love of dancing might be soiled by mockery.

He led a double life, dreading discovery. Each winter brought panic. The students in his ballet school make up the company which performs *The Nutcracker* at Lincoln Center. For several years he was simply one of the cast. His name was printed in tiny letters in the back of the program and he hid whenever a VIP tour came backstage in case someone from his school might be in the group.

But his gifts insisted on living, and demanded exercise. His heart was with them, although his mind required the safety of camouflage. Once again an element of hiding and hurting was an inevitable part of a gifted child's life.

Each year Peter grew bolder, as though the kind of strength he was developing in his dancer's muscles was growing, too, in his emotional and intellectual fiber. When he was eleven he confided his secret to a selected number of trusted friends. He felt strong enough to risk having to hear and answer:

"Ballet? Ballet? What are you? Some kind of a sissy?"

"Dancing's for girls."

"Dancers are queers."

He and his family knew that such remarks might come from unenlightened people—students in his school, or their parents.

When Peter turned twelve he was cast in the leading role of the Prince. He was interviewed by CBS for the evening news; his name was in large letters in the program; he was totally visible, totally identifiable. His secret belonged to the world.

His performances were exquisite. Audiences gave themselves willingly to him as they do when they know they are safely in the hands of an artist.

During the run of *The Nutcracker*, Peter commuted to New York. Each day he would go to school, travel into the city, dance (sometimes two performances), receive waves of applause, return to the country, and appear the following day in school—homework done, ready to learn, maintaining academic excellence and locker room camaraderie.

At thirteen he will dance the role of the Prince again, knowing that the moment of decision is coming. He must choose whether or not dance will be his career. An affirmative decision would mean a nearly total commitment of time, physical presence, and emotional energy with no guarantee that his success will continue past the bodily changes of adolescence. Thirteen is very young to make a decision which is a gamble and which will have such a far-reaching effect. There are many family footsteps he could follow in other directions. The keenness of his intellect puts any profession within his grasp. He could aim to be a lawyer, a physicist, a philosopher, a physician—or a ballet dancer.

In the concluding scene of *The Nutcracker*, the child Prince and child Princess fly slowly into the sky in a beautiful, glistening sleigh decorated with candy—quintessential wish-fulfillment.

When Peter climbs into the sleigh and rides off into the sky for the last time will he be saying goodbye to his childhood and the dance which has been such a cherished part of it, or will he be flying into the demands and uncertainties of an artistic career?

When asked for his three wishes Peter was boyishly, appropriately fresh and said, "The first one is not to have to be in that book." Since that was not granted, he continued:

to be a principal dancer with the New York City Ballet Company and then go to college and get a good job;

to be able to stay at school for the whole day without having to leave in the middle;

to enjoy life.

WHAT THEY SAY

Meg, Age 20

Meg, nearly twenty, is one of four children. Her father commutes daily to New York City. Her mother is busy and happy in their exurban community. Meg attended an academically demanding country day school where her performance was adequate but not outstanding. She went on to boarding school where she was very active in such student affairs as the magazine, the glee club, and varsity athletics. She seemed the definition of "an all-around good kid." She is now doing breathtaking work in science in her sophomore year at Yale. She said, "It feels so good not to have to hide how much you know. I've always had to do that before. I always thought I had to pretend I was trying to figure things out like everybody else. Now I feel as if I'm standing in a big strong wind. It feels good."

Meg wishes:

to be able to draw and paint;
to be able to wish myself to any place in the world whenever I want;
to know what I want to be.

Andrew, Age 26

Andrew is one of three sons of parents who each have busy professional lives. He attended an independent school in a large northeastern city, went off to a highly competitive boarding school, Ivy League college, and business school.

He completed his education without seeming to give it much thought—prowling, effortlessly absorbing what was presented, and consistently showing an uncanny ability to solve problems. As an amusing example, although Andrew overflows with ideas, he has never enjoyed putting words on paper. In order to complete ninth grade, his school required each member of the class to write a poem. Prose would have been bad enough but poetry produced panic and procrastination. Finally, at the last minute, his back against the wall, he wrote an amusing parody of "I must go down to the sea again." To his amazement the faculty thought it so good they required him to stand up and read it at the final assembly. The audience loved it and one parent came to him afterwards saying, "You certainly have a wonderful way with words." "Shot with luck, more like it," Andrew laughed to himself. His laugh is big, deep, and frequent.

Everything about Andrew is big. He seems to overflow most rooms. Walls seem inappropriate and boundaries Lilliputian. When his Graduate Record Exam scores came, for instance, he thought there had been an error because he received 812, although the published perfect score is 800. The score was correct, explained the testing service. They expect everyone to make one or two mistakes so they call 800 perfect. Actually it is possible, though very rare, to score over that number.

Andrew has always had a gigantic supply of physical energy. Throughout his youth he ran, batted, bounced, kicked, dove, chinned, and played team sports and individual sports with equal energy and enthusiasm.

He strides toward challenge in seven-league boots, taking issues seriously but seldom himself. He has not been burdened by hiding and hurting. In a naive, unself-conscious way he has not yet realized how extraordinary he is.

As he moves from business school, where quick, aggressive thinking is acceptable, to real-life business situations in which tact and political reality may require the youngest, most junior team player to hide his light under a bushel, he meets a dilemma. He must discover how to use his brain, and what it generates, without mowing down other people. Having finally decided to choose business over architecture, he must find ways to satisfy his enormous aesthetic appetite. These present two hefty challenges to his problem-solving ability!

When asked his three wishes he laughed, put his arm around the diminutive law school student with whom he has lived for the past five years, and said, "The first thing would be a rich girl friend!" Then, turning uncharacteristically shy, he said he'd like to be able to speak three or four other languages. After that he thought and said, "I don't really have a whole lot of wishes. If I want something I guess I just go out and do it if it matters to me. That sounds arrogant—I don't mean it to. I guess I just trust in my own strength. Oh, here's one: I'd like to do reasonably well in the Boston Marathon. I don't want to win it—I don't want to spend that much time working out, but I'd like to just go in cold, and do reasonably well."

Stephen, Age 25

Stephen comes from a family in which aesthetic sensitivity and intellectual achievement are highly valued. Their life and his schooling reflect these priorities. As a young child his scholastic achievement was superior in all respects. He knew things other children had never heard of, he saw connections other people missed, and he has always been highly articulate. He is now a professional musician. He sings and is the director of a new, exciting opera workshop. He said, "I was relieved to settle on music. I can't 'con' music. I was so used to bullshitting my way through everything else. I always got A's but I wasn't doing anything. You can't get away with that in singing."

Stephen's dilemma, which music resolved for him, was how to stay intellectually honest when he continually received high grades for work he knew was superficial. Cynicism is frequently

174

born of undeserved praise and effortless success. Stephen has given himself, completely, to the discipline of his art and finds joy in its rigor. In addition to singing and directing, he writes. He was an editor of *Opera News Magazine*, to which he contributed regularly. He assembled programs and materials for teachers to use in regular classrooms, and in cooperation with the Metropolitan Opera is writing a book for young people. He wants so much to share his perceptions, bursting the dowager-like balloon of pomposity many people associate with opera, and bringing it close to an audience and age group traditionally antagonistic.

From early childhood an obligation to share and teach has accompanied his awareness of his own gifts. In his own words, "I need to make public the insane passion I have for opera and all that it can be."

Stephen's three wishes:

to be able to communicate the full joy of the things with which I'm gifted;

to have enough money to be able to stay tan all year;

to end up doing what uses my talents, is fulfilling, and gives me the spectrum of excitement I need as a person.

Talbert, Age 47

Controversial, articulate, in love with challenge and surprise, Talbert is finding personal fulfillment after resigning from a job which was a pinnacle of worldly success. Academic honors and positions of leadership have always been his. It seems that he needed to accumulate them in order to flesh out a required personal and family portrait. Then, having done so, he needed to discard their trappings in order to commit himself completely to his own life and to realize his particular potential. So many times successful people become prisoners of their own positions. Fear of losing supremacy leads to a timidity and rigidity which contradict the qualities behind the original success. Talbert has not been netted.

His early scholastic performance in no way predicted his subsequent brilliance. From first through fourth grade he had little idea what he was meant to be doing or what schooling was supposed to accomplish. For example, he remembers sitting in an arithmetic lesson in a prestigious New York City boys' school doing an addition problem made up of several rows of five-digit numbers. To his eye they made a beautiful design. With no regard for mathematical process he enthusiastically invented some glamorous-looking totals. His teacher, in exasperation, showed the paper to the headmaster, who interpreted it as final evidence that Talbert should pursue learning somewhere else.

So it was he found himself headed off to boarding school to repeat the fourth grade. He was there for five years, joyously throwing himself into the artistic and athletic as well as the academic life of the school. Participating in their work program, he discovered for the first time how much he liked being the foreman. He not only enjoyed being in control, but learned very early that a boss's dedication to a job is usually far greater than other people's, and therefore realistic expectations must be set accordingly. He learned this lesson young and has never forgotten it. He loved the freedom of earning his wage and spending it as he wished at the local bubble gum emporium. Looking back on those years, he describes the warmth, structure, and opportunity for artistic expression of a school which helped many troubled and gifted students.

Having deservedly won a reputation for intellectual prowess, Talbert went to a large boarding school that offered more freedom than he could handle. When he was expelled his father was furious: "steely and cold." He was accepted at another boarding school whose headmaster saw promise in the boy. Once there, he lived as much as possible on his own resources, consciously separating himself from the other students. He felt different from them and wanted to show it. His years there were marked by solitude but not loneliness and provided the external discipline he needed. Of course his pride required him to fight the rules. He accomplished this not by shirking his studies but by devouring them. Since dormitory lights, controlled by a master switch, were extinguished at an hour deemed suitable for growing boys, Talbert bribed the maid for a key to her room where he would go after lights out to study late and illegally.

He went to college and after some recurrent difficulty in handling freedom, discovered his area of intellectual passion quite by chance in a course he took to balance his degree requirements. From the first lecture he was hooked. After graduating summa cum laude, he continued through graduate school and at the age of twenty-eight was filled with knowledge, vigor, and sharp memory of what it was like to be the foreman.

He became foreman many times in the ensuing twenty years, each time being known as the youngest, most audacious, and frequently most controversial person to have held each of the varying positions. But the more renowned the organizations he headed, the more restricted Talbert felt. It seems that his period of hiding and hurting came simultaneously with high visibility and professional acclaim.

Several years ago he resigned from a secure, rather glamorous position, leaving himself with no salary and an unknown future. Today he says that was one of the best decisions he has ever made. He has started his own enterprise and finally has found something which can absorb all that bubbles up from within him. He is alive, awake, and filled with zest. Once again, he is the foreman, but this time there are no restrictions of tradition and no limits to scope. He seems to have outgrown his need for externally imposed discipline and to be ready to manage the obligations of freedom. Of his wishes Talbert says:

> I wish that the joy I have in writing really translates into professionalism.
> I wish that someday I could really tell the truth.
> I wish that I may never lose the sense of controversy.

Pamela, Age 51

Pamela describes herself as "a scientist turned generalist." She was born abroad and came to this country at the age of three when her father, a distinguished scientist and professor, was appointed department chairman at an outstanding American university. She says her mother and father always assumed that their only child would be a gifted student and a high achiever. They wanted to identify with democratic American practice and ideals; consequently they sent their daughter to the public school near the university. Schoolwork came easily to Pamela and she accelerated, completing the eighth grade when she was only eleven. The plan for her to return to England for further schooling was changed by World War II. She recrossed the ocean and ended up adoring the sociability of her Canadian boarding school from which she graduated in glory. She entered Radcliffe as a sophomore at age sixteen. She went from Radcliffe to MIT and by the age of twenty-three had earned her Ph.D. She laughs now and says it seemed easier to get a Ph.D. than to learn to type. She continued her scientific work in the early years of her marriage and, having given birth to three children, changed from science to independent education, which offered her an opportunity to have the same hours and calendar year as her children. She became headmistress and served in that capacity for thirteen years. From there she went to be head of a

THE GIFTED SPEAK

national organization devoted to young people, and was the first woman elected to the board of directors of two major corporations. Later, for a brief period, she was president of a company working on energy problems. In retrospect she says she never felt like a driven career woman. Rather she thinks she always took the path of least resistance.

At fifty-one she is looking for her next path. She is no longer married and her children are independent. She says she adores playing with ideas. She leans toward science, saying, "A scientist is a creative entrepreneur." Her interests are widespread and she has many theoretical options open to her. She enjoys playing with the question of choices—who has them? How many are real, how many mirage?

Pamela's is different from the classic mid-life dilemma of a woman trying to decide what to do next. Her intellectual capacity must be used and her previous level of achievement matched. Not for her the reentry-level job in sportswear at Lord and Taylor. What is the next thing this generalist will generate?

Pamela wishes:

to have contributed ideas to society and have them put into action;
to see her children find inner peace and emotional as well as intellectual satisfaction through wise and careful choice of lifelong partners;
to follow their example and do the same.

Linda, Age 54

Linda grew up in the outskirts of a large midwestern industrial city. She received her education in a nationally famous public school system, where she was an outstanding student in science, mathematics, foreign languages, and English, including both

179

literary criticism and composition. She was raised by a divorced mother and had one sister, much older than she, who became an alcoholic. Linda attended a university near her home where she continued to be an outstanding student, graduating summa cum laude. Her thesis on interactions of poetry and philosophy in eighteenth-century England was published and received favorable reviews. Although she majored in English literature, she continued her studies in mathematics and history.

After graduating from college, Linda took a job with a publishing company. She stayed there for six years, finally leaving because she felt restricted. She changed to a job which offered opportunities for scientific research. She enjoyed it initially, but soon outgrew it. Her mother died, and her sister was frequently hospitalized for alcoholism.

Linda moved to California where she took a job teaching history and English to high school students. She enrolled in a doctoral program at a nearby university. After several years, she lost her enthusiasm for teaching and decided to pursue her studies full time. She married a wealthy man who longed for her companionship. They had not known each other well before the marriage, and they subsequently proved incompatible. Their passionless divorce left Linda financially secure for the first time in her life.

That was eleven years ago. Linda never finished her doctoral work. She has volunteered in some political campaigns and helped out with a few ecological projects. She tried her hand at writing, and has published two articles in a local newspaper. She has acquired a small white dog and rents an attractive house.

She wishes:

to have a garden without weeds;
to have E.S.P.;
to go into space.

Jean, Age 75

Jean was the oldest in a family of seven children born to a successful industrialist and his southern wife. She contracted poliomyelitis in her girlhood and was crippled as a result. Walking required supreme effort and her hands were badly twisted. After graduating from school with highest academic honors, she tried to adjust to her family's expectations that she would be content to stay at home, but she could not. She was sensitive and scientifically gifted with wide-ranging curiosity and an imperative need to experience life. Tea on the terrace, lovely and warm though it was, did not fill her up. In her late twenties she went to Barnard College, where she was an unusual student. Her age and her physical disability made her noticeable. So did the outstanding quality of her work. (The story of her being accepted at Barnard is in Chapter Four.)

To the astonishment of her family, she applied and was admitted to the College of Physicians and Surgeons of Columbia University. She finished medical school and completed a residency, not shirking any duties. She rode the ambulances and climbed staircases in tenement buildings alongside her classmates in spite of the physical difficulties these jobs presented. Then she was trained to be a psychoanalyst. She had an active psychiatric practice in New York City for more than twenty-five years, working well into her seventies.

A common bond among her many dilemmas was forged by her need to make peace between two very different sides of her own nature: the gentle, reflective, domestic side, and the intellectually aggressive, scientific, inquisitive side. She had to first acknowledge and then channel her powerful drives when she realized she could not spend her life docilely at home. In order to be the gracious young woman her mother's southern tradition and contemporary custom required, she had to conceal the quickness and power of her mind. Once again, a gifted person was hiding and hurting.

After her career decisions had been made and she had begun her studies and work, it was difficult to maintain warm, strong relationships with some of her relatives and family friends. In spite of being proud of her determination and success, some did not understand her need to be independent, and others were surprised and shocked by the branch of medicine she chose. In the 1940s many people considered psychiatry unscientific and unclean. She faced further dilemmas of studying and working while shackled by severe physical limitations and the difficulties of moving ahead in her profession, being disabled, a woman, and single.

Tapping her deepest reservoirs of will power and warmth, she was able to separate her professional life from her life as a willing member of a large, extended family with powerful traditions and taboos. She learned how to be the receiver of human nature's darkest secrets during the day, and in the evening, a gracious southern hostess, appreciative of assistance, sharing in gentle desultory conversation. She made those around her—little children, awkward adolescents, tired young mothers, the middle-aged and the elderly—feel warm, interesting, and capable. Thoughtless people referred to her as sweet. She was not sweet.

She preserved her gentle, empathetic, generous qualities by stubbornly refusing to let bitterness taint them. This was a monumental task, requiring perpetual vigilance. She tempered the steel of her spirit with intellect, energy, and determination. She managed thus to convert her anguish for the things she could not have (a husband, children, physical well-being) into profound understanding of others' needs and fears.

She wished:

to figure skate;

to know all Shakespeare's plays by heart without ever having to
   memorize them;
not to need to waste the long night hours in sleep.

She died in 1976. Virginia Woolf wrote a tribute to George
Eliot, another gifted woman who struggled against both physical
weakness and the prejudice of her society against women writers.
It is a fitting epitaph for Jean.

For her too the burden and complexity of womanhood were not
enough; she must reach beyond the sanctuary and pluck for herself the
strange bright fruits of art and knowledge. Clasping them as few women
have ever clasped them, she would not renounce her own inheritance—
the difference of view, the difference of standard—not accept an inappropriate reward . . . reaching out with "a fastidious yet hungry ambition" for all that life could offer the free and inquiring mind, and con-
fronting her feminine aspirations with the real world of men. Trium-
phant was the issue for her, whatever it may have been for her creations,
and as we recollect all that she dared and achieved, how with every obstacle against her—sex and health and convention—she sought more
knowledge and more freedom till the body, weighted with its double
burden, sank worn out, we must lay upon her grave whatever we have it
in our power to bestow of laurel and rose.[1]

[1]Virginia Woolf, *The Common Reader* (New York, Harcourt Brace Jovanovich,
Inc., 1955), p. 176.

Epilogue

Treat gifted children as real people. Look into their eyes as well as their IQs. They are not freaks unless we make them so.

Help them develop powerful bonds to their world and other people. Do not separate them from humanity, join them to it.

Nurture them with honesty, humor, and common sense that they may grow into whole people and, bright to brilliant, shine among us.

P. L. V.
August 1978

Appendix

1. A Book

The papers presented at the first World Conference on Gifted Children, which was held in London in September 1975, are collected in *Gifted Children, Looking to Their Future,* edited by Joy Gibson and Prue Chennells, published in 1976 by Latimer New Dimensions Ltd., 14 West Central Street, London WCIAI JH, England.

2. Some Organizations

AMERICAN ASSOCIATION FOR GIFTED CHILDREN
15 Gramercy Park South
New York, N. Y. 10003
Marjorie Craig, Executive Director
COUNCIL OF STATE DIRECTORS OF PROGRAMS FOR GIFTED
California State Department of Education
721 Capital Mall
Sacramento, California 95814
Paul D. Plowman, President

ERIC Clearing House on G/T
Council for Exceptional Children
1920 Association Drive
Reston, Va. 22091

METROPOLITAN COUNCIL FOR GIFTED
40 Seventh Avenue South
New York, N.Y. 10014
Virginia Z. Ehrlich, President

NATIONAL ASSOCIATION FOR GIFTED CHILDREN
8080 Springvalley Drive
Cincinnati, Ohio 45236
John Curtis Gowan, President

THE NATIONAL ASSOCIATION FOR GIFTED CHILDREN
1 S. Audley Street
London W1Y 5DA, England
Henry Collis, Director

THE NATIONAL ASSOCIATION OF INDEPENDENT
SCHOOLS
4 Liberty Square
Boston, Massachusetts

OFFICE OF GIFTED AND TALENTED EDUCATION
U.S. Office of Education
Room 2100, ROB-3, 7th and D Streets, S.W.
Washington, D.C. 20202
Director, Harold Lyon; Deputy Director, Jane Case Williams

THE ASSOCIATION FOR THE GIFTED (TAG)
A division of the Council for Exceptional Children
1411 South Jefferson Davis Highway
Arlington, Virginia 22202
Joseph Renzulli, President

3. Some Publications

THE GIFTED CHILD QUARTERLY
Route 5, P.O. Box 630A
Hot Springs, Arkansas 71901
This is available to members of the National Association for
Gifted Children.

THE ROEPER REVIEW: A Journal on Gifted Child Education
2190 N. Woodward Avenue
Bloomfield Hills, Michigan 48013

4. Some Publishers

CREATIVE PUBLICATIONS
P.O. Box 10328
Palo Alto, California 94303

DOVER PUBLICATIONS
180 Varick Street
New York, N.Y. 10014

DRAKE HOME CRAFTSMEN'S BOOKS
801 Second Avenue
New York, N.Y. 10017

GOLDEN PRESS PUBLISHERS
850 Third Avenue
New York, N.Y. 10022

McCALL'S
230 Park Avenue
New York, N.Y. 10017

SCHOLASTIC MAGAZINES AND BOOK SERVICES
906 Sylvan Avenue
Englewood Cliffs, N.J. 07632

189

SUNSET HOBBY AND CRAFT BOOKS
Lane Publishing Co.
Menlo Park, California 94025

TIME/LIFE BOOKS
1271 Avenue of the Americas
New York, N.Y. 10020

WALKER AND CO.
720 Fifth Avenue
New York, N.Y. 10019

5. Simulation Game

Here is some further information on the simulation game described briefly in Chapter Seven. To contact the originator write to:

Mr. John P. Fennell
Head of the Middle School
The Rippowam-Cisqua School
Bedford, New York 10506

Reprinted here, with Mr. Fennell's permission, are a sample ritual and myth for each of his three tribes.

SPIRITUAL RITUAL OF THE MAMAZONS

Each year, at the end of the rainy season, the Mamazons make their annual pilgrimage to Mama, a sacred volcanic mountain located at the very heart of their territory. To reach this high place of worship, the Mamazons must first traverse the Great Falls, whose thundering roar and violent spume make the swaying, cantilevered, vine supported cat-walks seem fragile indeed. Arriving at the foot of Mama, the younger and stronger of the venerable Clan-Mother's husbands secure her firmly to a bamboo lifter and, hoisting her carefully on their broad shoulders, begin the long, treacherous assent over the jagged lava flows to the summit. In accordance with long-standing tradition the Clan-Mother is followed in solemn procession by blood relatives: mothers and daughters in the lead, husbands and sons trailing respectfully behind. Upon reaching the summit, the members of the tribe arrange themselves along the lip of the volcanic opening and begin the Flame Dance, a strictly prescribed series of undulating body movements which slowly gather in intensity as the drums increase in tempo. By nightfall the fires have been lit and the dancers are nearing frenzy. Six male infants, born within the last year, are brought forth and prepared for the sacrifice. Chanting sacred incantations, the She-Doctor smears the tiny bodies with berry juice and snake oil. Finally, as the dancers moan and cry out in exhausted euphoria, the six infants are fed to the waiting mouth of Mama; for a time the smouldering and ravenous force within shall be propitiated.

MAMAZON MYTH

Mama is all powerful, the great force that occupies the land and water and sky. Mama can bring good luck to people, and she who possesses more of Mama shall be the She-Doctor. Mama can also bring bad luck. Mama can become very angry. When Mama is angry the whole earth shakes. Mama can destroy all. Mama can bury all. Mama can burn all. Mama can swallow all. Mama is always hungry. Mama is always seething. Mama's energy is always there, ready to burst forth. Mama must be respected above all. Mama must be fed and chanted to. If Mama is not happy, Mama will bring bad, bad luck. May Mama never be unhappy.

SPIRITUAL BELIEFS AND RITUAL OF THE VORICHIS

The Vorichis believe in one great spirit, Puritani Vorichi. Upon coming of age, each Vorichi is initiated into the society by receiving a wooden disk, cut from a sacred tamarand or hemlock, the grain and markings of which indicate his life path, his fate—everything from his mate to his material success.

Four times a year they hold gigantic feasts. All Vorichis gather and bring the best of their flocks. They are seated in concentric circles around a large wooden totem, with those who bring more woven blankets, dried scrod, and wild corn forming the Inner Circle. Everyone partakes and sacrifices, with the Inner Circle chanting a prayer vouching for the diligent work which the tribe has performed.

VORICHI MYTH

And Puritani looked with favor upon the Vorichis and he multiplied their flocks and the food of the sea. And each Vorichi waxed great in his goods for the toil he undertook, so that none was withdrawn from the Inner Circle, but all had grace and favor.

And it came to pass that the old Vorichis became lax and forgot Puritani's commands. They no longer labored but spoke to one another, saying, "Why should we toil when slight effort increases our goods a hundredfold?" They took after vanity, forgetting the sacred feasts.

Puritani became exceedingly angry and hid his face from the Vorichis. "Thou hast not called upon me, O Vorichis, nor wearied yourselves for me. Nor hast thou honored me with thy paintings and carvings." In his wrath he turned to the Warlike Ones and caused them to wax mighty.

Therefore the Warlike Ones swept as the raging blizzard from the North. As a shark within a net did they destroy all in their path, burning cabins and boats alike. The remnant of the tribe of Vorichi fled to the forests, each family unto itself.

And the remnant saw the smoking, barren ruins that had been their home and portion. Our fathers were ashamed and knew that they had done evil. They worked and sweated, and Puritani forgave them, setting them apart from their ancestors by calling them the New Vorichi.

Hence, it has been from that time forth, that Puritani has looked with favor upon those that toil and gives sustenance for their labor, but withholds his hand from those that seek to ease their burdens and casts them to the outermost circle. It is for us of the New Vorichi to abide by his command, lest we are again afflicted by the Warlike Ones.

Significant Urbanian Ceremonies

Urbanian religious life is organized by the High Priests around ceremonies of various types and importance. Just before the swelling of the Great River, the High Priests have spent many evenings on the tall walls of the city calculating the precise moment when the ceremony should begin.

Accompanied by a vicious guard dog, younger less important Priests have already collected assorted grains, stoneware, and jewelry from the lesser classes, for use in the Harvest Ceremony. Most of this tax is laid at the foot of the Golden Statue of the Great Dog God, while the remainder goes to satisfy lesser deities.

Smaller ceremonies are held whenever necessary to divine and assure the success of Urbanian conquests in foreign lands. The Emperor picks from all the guard dogs the one he deems the most strong and fierce. The High Priests then administer a secret sleeping potion, lay the unconscious dog upon a layer of carefully leveled, red river mud, and cut it open. The Emperor, in a trance, makes his interpretation from the dog's entrails and the cracks in the now dried mud. He assigns his Generals to their tasks and retreats once again into the Temple.

URBANIAN MYTH

There was once a very old priest who chanted the first coming of the Great Dog God. His story, long since put down in clay by the High Priests, told of a red tinge, shaped like a dog's face, surrounding the bright cross in the evening sky. The very next day at dusk there appeared a brown and black dog—as tall as the combined height of two men—who ended the conquest by invaders seeking the rich farming soil of Urbania. Ever since that day the people, who live in this land fringed by yellow sand, have been in awe of their Emperor, who has in him the blood of the Great Dog God.

In more recent years, however, the Emperor has grown listless and full of worry; his guard dogs have dwindled in number and the Emperor feels that the lower classes will soon try to take over his Palace. He prays nightly to the Great Dog God to help him find more dogs with which to protect his palace and his priests.

The Emperor is also bothered terribly by the fact that the High Priests have not yet been able to choose a suitable heir to his kingdom from all the sons of his many fair wives. The son who seems to be the most capable warrior and teller of the future will follow in his father's footsteps as the next blood descendent of the fearless Dog God.

Index

195

INDEX

INDEX

INDEX

INDEX

199

INDEX

INDEX

INDEX

OXFORD ASSESS AND PROGRESS

Series Editors

Katharine Boursicot
Director, Health Professional Assessment Consultancy (HPAC)
Honorary Reader in Medical Education St George's,
University of London

David Sales
Consultant in Medical Assessment

OXFORD ASSESS AND PROGRESS

Clinical Specialties

Fourth Edition

EDITED BY

Luci Etheridge

Consultant Paediatrician and Honorary Senior Lecturer in Clinical
Education, St George's University Hospitals NHS Foundation Trust and
St George's, University of London

Henry Collier

Specialty Trainee in Anaesthesia, Lancashire Teaching Hospitals NHS
Foundation Trust and Clinical Fellow, Health Education England

CONSULTANT EDITOR

Alex Bonner

Consultant Anaesthetist, Lancashire Teaching Hospitals NHS
Foundation Trust

UNIVERSITY PRESS

OXFORD
UNIVERSITY PRESS

Great Clarendon Street, Oxford, OX2 6DP,
United Kingdom

Oxford University Press is a department of the University of Oxford.
It furthers the University's objective of excellence in research, scholarship,
and education by publishing worldwide. Oxford is a registered trade mark of
Oxford University Press in the UK and in certain other countries

First Edition published in 2010
Second Edition published in 2013
Third Edition published in 2018
Fourth Edition published in 2021

Published in the United States of America by Oxford University Press
198 Madison Avenue, New York, NY 10016, United States of America

British Library Cataloguing in Publication Data
Data available

Library of Congress Control Number: 2020950909

ISBN 978–0–19–886255–0

DOI: 10.1093/oso/9780198862550.001.0001

Printed in Great Britain by
Ashford Colour Press Ltd, Gosport, Hampshire

Series editor preface

The *Oxford Assess and Progress* series is a groundbreaking development in the extensive area of self-assessment texts available for medical students. The questions were specifically commissioned for the series, written by practising clinicians, extensively peer-reviewed by students and their teachers, and quality-assured to ensure that the material is up-to-date, accurate, and in line with modern testing formats.

The series has a number of unique features and is designed to be as much a formative learning resource as a self-assessment one. The questions are constructed to test the same clinical problem-solving skills that we use as practising clinicians, rather than only to test theoretical knowledge. These skills include:

• gathering and using data required for clinical judgement
• choosing the appropriate examination and investigations, and interpretation of the findings
• applying knowledge
• demonstrating diagnostic skills
• ability to evaluate undifferentiated material
• ability to prioritize
• making decisions and demonstrating a structured approach to decision-making.

Each question is bedded in reality and is typically presented as a clinical scenario, the content of which has been chosen to reflect the common and important conditions that most doctors are likely to encounter both during their training and in exams! The aim of the series is to build the reader's confidence in recognizing important symptoms and signs and suggesting the most appropriate investigations and management, and in so doing to aid the development of a clear approach to patient management which can be transferred to the wards.

The content of the series has deliberately been pinned to the relevant *Oxford Handbook* but, in addition, has been guided by a blueprint which reflects the themes identified in *Tomorrow's Doctors* and *Good Medical Practice* to include novel areas such as history taking, recognition of signs (including red flags), and professionalism.

Particular attention has been paid to giving learning points and constructive feedback on each question, using clear fact- or evidence-based explanations as to why the correct response is right and why the incorrect responses are less appropriate. The question editorials are clearly referenced to the relevant sections of the accompanying *Oxford Handbook* and/or more widely to medical literature or guidelines. They are designed to guide and motivate the reader, being multi-purpose in nature and covering, for example, exam technique, approaches to difficult subjects, and links between subjects.

Another unique aspect of the series is the element of competency progression from being a relatively inexperienced student to being a more experienced junior doctor. We have suggested the following four degrees of difficulty to reflect the level of training, so that the reader can monitor their own progress over time:

- graduate should know ★
- graduate nice to know ★★
- foundation doctor should know ★★★
- foundation doctor nice to know ★★★★

We advise the reader to attempt the questions in blocks as a way of testing their knowledge in a clinical context. The series can be treated as a dress rehearsal for life on the ward by using the material to hone clinical acumen and build confidence by encouraging a clear, consistent, and rational approach, proficiency in recognizing and evaluating symptoms and signs, making a rational differential diagnosis, and suggesting appropriate investigations and management.

Adopting such an approach can aid not only success in examinations, which really are designed to confirm learning, but also—more importantly—being a good doctor. In this way, we can deliver high-quality and safe patient care by recognizing, understanding, and treating common problems, but at the same time remaining alert to the possibility of less likely, but potentially catastrophic, conditions.

David Sales and Kathy Boursicot
Series Editors

A note on single best answer questions

Single best answer questions are currently the format of choice being widely used by most undergraduate and postgraduate knowledge tests, and therefore all the assessment questions in this book follow this format.

Single best answer questions have many advantages over other machine-markable formats, such as extended matching questions (EMQs), notably the breadth of sampling or content coverage that they afford.

Briefly, the single best answer or 'best of five' question presents a problem, usually a clinical scenario, before presenting the question itself and a list of five options. These consist of one correct answer and four incorrect options or 'distractors', from which the reader has to choose a response.

All of the questions in this book, which are typically based on an evaluation of symptoms, signs, or results of investigations, either as single entities or in combination, are designed to test *reasoning* skills, rather than straightforward recall of facts, and utilize cognitive processes similar to those used in clinical practice.

The peer-reviewed questions are written and edited in accordance with contemporary best assessment practice, and their content has been guided by a blueprint pinned to all areas of *Good Medical Practice*, which ensures comprehensive coverage.

The answers and their rationales are evidence-based and have been reviewed to ensure that they are absolutely correct. Incorrect options are selected as being plausible, and indeed they may appear correct to the less knowledgeable reader. When answering questions, the reader may wish to use the 'cover' test in which they read the scenario and the question but cover the options.

Kathy Boursicot and David Sales
Series Editors

A note on single best answer questions

Editor preface to the fourth edition

During the journey through medical school as a student, you experience medicine in a range of settings, from the rural general practice to the inner-city teaching hospital. You encounter doctors working in a wide range of specialties, many of which will be appealing future career choices and many of which will seem daunting. Specialty attachments may be the first time that you encounter people with mental illness, or children, or pregnant women. Trying to absorb all these new experiences while also continuing to work towards final examinations can seem like a roller-coaster ride to some!

In partnership with the well-established *Oxford Handbook of Clinical Specialties*, the *Oxford Assess and Progress: Clinical Specialties* volume seeks to tie together the clinical specialties and to provide a grounding in knowledge that may get pushed to the back burner when medicine and surgery have to be revised. This fourth edition has been produced in line with the new edition of the *Oxford Handbook of Clinical Specialties* and builds on the success of the first three books, bringing you questions on the latest hot topics, current issues, and core material. As in the third edition, there are chapters ranging from primary care and pre-hospital care through to medical and surgical specialties, anaesthesia and intensive care, and eponymous syndromes. This ensures the full spectrum of specialty practice is considered and covered.

The questions in each chapter have been written by experienced doctors working within the specialty, who are familiar with the common presentations, pathologies, and dilemmas that are encountered. Their knowledge of teaching medical students about their specialty, often within the confines of very short attachments, has been transferred to these pages. All the questions map on to medical school curricula and are rooted in real-life clinical encounters. The grading system allows you to judge for yourself which knowledge is core and which might require some further reading. We have added many new guidelines and key websites to guide this reading, and we hope that you will find these useful. The strong focus on clinical experiences also allows you to look forward to, and prepare for, your time as a foundation doctor.

We hope that, as a result of working through these questions, your interest in, and appreciation and understanding of, the different clinical specialties will grow, and you will have a useful tool for judging your own learning needs.

Luci Etheridge and Henry Collier

Acknowledgements

The editors would like to thank all the contributors from all editions for their hard work in combining their specialist knowledge with clinical experience to provide this resource of stimulating, realistic questions with considered explanations. Sadly, one of our much valued contributors Dr Gill McGauley passed away in 2016. Gill was a well-known and respected psychiatrist and educationalist, and we are grateful to her for being one of the original contributors to this Series. Thank you also to all of the reviewers—students and specialists—for your much valued feedback. We hope that we have managed to address your suggestions in this new edition. Finally, Luci would like to thank her ever patient children, who are a constant source of inspiration and joy. Henry would like to thank his parents for their support and encouragement throughout his training, Dr Alex Bonner for his support in starting in an editorial role, and his two cats Lyro and Rosie for their attempts to interfere with the editorial process whenever possible.

Acknowledgements

Contents

Contents

About the editors

Volume editors

Luci Etheridge is a Consultant Paediatrician and Honorary Senior Lecturer in Clinical Education at St George's University Hospitals NHS Foundation Trust in London. She previously worked for four years with UCL Medical School and was involved with the development of Fitness to Practise assessments for the General Medical Council and item writing for the Professional and Linguistics Assessments Board Part 1 and the Royal College of Paediatrics and Child Health. She has a doctorate in education from the Institute of Education, University of London, and plays an active role in undergraduate and postgraduate education, regionally and nationally, in the UK.

Henry Collier is a Speciality Trainee in Anaesthesia in the North West Deanery. He studied medicine at the Royal Free and University College Medical School from 2006 to 2012 (now UCL Medical School) and has returned to work in the North West. Following successful completion of the FRCA examinations, he has become more involved with NHS improvement and activity redesign with the Clinically Led Workforce and Activity Redesign Programme (CLEAR). He has also begun work as a Cochrane Clinical Dissemination Fellow, and begun working towards a Postgraduate Certificate in Medical Education. Throughout his training, he has been actively involved in teaching and training of medical students, foundation doctors, and junior anaesthetic trainees.

Alex Bonner is a Consultant Anaesthetist at Lancashire Teaching Hospitals NHS Foundation Trust, with subspecialty interests in vascular anaesthesia and medical education. He is regularly involved in the teaching of medical students, foundation doctors, and anaesthetic trainees who are preparing for their FRCA examinations. He is an instructor for Adult and Paediatric Advanced Life Support courses and has experience of practising anaesthesia and teaching in sub-Saharan Africa. He has also contributed to the development of Fitness to Practise assessments for the General Medical Council.

Series editors

Katharine Boursicot BSc MBBS MRCOG MAHPE NTF SFHEA FRSM is a consultant in health professions education, with special expertise in assessment. Previously, she was Head of Assessment at St George's, University of London, Barts and The London School of Medicine and Dentistry, and Associate Dean for Assessment at Cambridge University

School of Clinical Medicine. She is a consultant on assessment to several UK medical schools, medical Royal Colleges, and international institutions, as well as an assessment advisor to the General Medical Council.

David Sales is a general practitioner by training who has been involved in medical assessment for over 20 years, having previously been convenor of the MRCGP knowledge test. He has run item-writing workshops for a number of undergraduate medical schools and medical Royal Colleges, and internationally. He has chaired the Professional and Linguistic Assessments Board Part 1 panel for the General Medical Council and is their consultant on Fitness to Practise knowledge testing.

Contributors

Erica Allason-Jones
NHS Consultant in Genitourinary
Medicine, Mortimer Market
Centre (Camden PCT),
London, UK

Dinesh Bhugra
Professor of Mental Health
and Cultural Diversity, Institute
of Psychiatry, King's College,
London, and Honorary
Consultant, Maudsley Hospital,
London, UK

Jennifer Birch
Consultant in Neonatal Medicine,
Luton and Dunstable NHS
Foundation Hospital Trust,
Luton, UK

Alex Bonner
Consultant Anaesthetist,
Lancashire Teaching Hospitals
NHS Foundation Trust

Ruth Brown
Consultant in Emergency
Medicine, St Mary's Hospital,
Imperial College NHS Trust,
and Honorary Senior Lecturer,
Imperial College London, UK

Will Coppola
Clinical Lecturer and Sub-Dean
E-learning, UCL Medical School,
London, UK, and salaried General
Practitioner

Jonathan Darling
Senior Lecturer in Paediatrics
and Child Health, University of
Leeds, and Honorary Consultant
Paediatrician, Leeds Teaching
Hospitals NHS Trust, Leeds, UK

Nev Davies
Consultant in Trauma and
Orthopaedics, Royal Berkshire
Hospital, Reading, UK

James Dawson
Registrar in Anaesthesia and
Intensive Care, Trent Region, UK

Philippa Edwards
Salaried General Practitioner,
Portsmouth, UK

Luci Etheridge
Consultant Paediatrician,
St George's University Hospital,
London, UK

Oliver Harrison
Consultant Anaesthetist,
Department of Anaesthesia,
Royal Preston Hospital and North
West Air Ambulance

Kamila Hawthorne
General Practice Principal in
Cardiff, and Sub Dean for
Assessment, School of Medicine,
Cardiff University, Cardiff, UK

Kevin Hayes
Senior Lecturer and Consultant
in Obstetrics and Gynaecology,
St George's University Hospital,
London, UK

Virginia Hubbard
Consultant Dermatologist,
Homerton University Hospital,
and Clinical Senior Lecturer,
Barts and The London School of
Medicine and Dentistry, UK

Vikram Jha
Senior Lecturer in Medical
Education, Leeds Institute of
Medical Education, University of
Leeds, and Honorary Consultant
Obstetrician, Bradford Teaching
Hospitals NHS Trust, UK

Matthew Mathai
Consultant Paediatrician,
Bradford Royal Infirmary, and
Honorary Lecturer in Paediatrics
and Child Health, University of
Leeds, UK

Gill McGauley
Reader in Forensic
Psychotherapy, St George's
University of London, and
Consultant in Forensic
Psychotherapy, Broadmoor
Hospital, West London Mental
Health NHS Trust, UK

Isabel McMullen
Consultant Liaison Psychiatrist,
Department of Psychological
Medicine, South London and
Maudsley NHS Foundation Trust,
King's College Hospital, UK

Catherine Roberts
Consultant in Emergency
Medicine, Emergency Medicine
Department, Royal Preston
Hospital, Lancashire Teaching
Hospitals NHS Foundation
Trust, UK

Zeryab Setna
Consultant Obstetrician, Lady
Dufferin Hospital, Karachi,
Pakistan

Gemma Simcox
Salaried General Practitioner with
Special Interest in Dermatology,
West Yorkshire, UK

Venki Sundaram
Consultant Ophthalmologist,
Department of Ophthalmology,
Luton and Dunstable NHS
University Hospital, UK

Philippa Tostevin
Senior Lecturer in Surgical
Education, St George's University
of London, and Honorary
Consultant Otolaryngologist,
St George's Hospital, London, UK

Anuhya Vusirikala
Core Surgical Trainee, Oxford
Deanery, UK

Normal and average values

Biochemistry: reference intervals

All laboratory discourse is probabilistic. Drugs may interfere with any chemical method; as these effects may be method-dependent, it is difficult for us to be aware of all of the possibilities. If in doubt, discuss the issue with the laboratory.

Substance	Specimen	Normal value
Adrenocorticotrophic hormone	P	<80 ng/L
Alanine aminotransferase	P	5–35 IU/L
Albumin	P†	35–50 g/L
Aldosterone	P*	100–500 pmol/L
Alkaline phosphatase	P†	30–150 IU/L (adults)
α-fetoprotein	S	<10 kU/L
α-amylase	P	0–180 Somogyi units/dL
Angiotensin II	P*	5–35 pmol/L
Antidiuretic hormone	P	0.9–4.6 pmol/L
Aspartate transaminase	P	5–35 IU/L
β-HCG	S	M: <10 mIU/mL; F (non-pregnant): <25 mIU/mL; F (4 weeks pregnant): >1000 mIU/mL
Bicarbonate	P†	24–30 mmol/L
Bilirubin	P	3–17 μmol/L (0.25–1.5 mg/100 mL)
Calcitonin	P	<0.1 micrograms/L
Calcium (ionized)	P	1.0–1.25 mmol/L
Calcium (total)	P†	2.12–2.65 mmol/L
Chloride	P	95–105 mmol/L
Cholesterol‡	P	3.9–7.8 mmol/L
VLDL	P	0.128–0.645 mmol/L
LDL	P	1.55–4.4 mmol/L
HDL	P	0.9–1.93 mmol/L

Substance	Specimen	Normal value
Cortisol	P	a.m.: 450–700 nmol/L; midnight: 80–280 nmol/L
C-reactive protein (CRP)	S	<10 mg/L
Creatine kinase	P	M: 25–195 IU/L; F: 25–170 IU/L
Creatinine (related to lean body mass)	P†	70–≤150 µmol/L
CSF glucose	CSF	>2/3 of blood range
CSF protein	CSF	<40 mg/dL
CSF white cells	CSF	<5/mm³
Ferritin	P	12–200 micrograms/L
Folate	S	2.1 micrograms/L
Follicle-stimulating hormone (FSH)	P/S	Luteal: 2–8 U/L Ovulatory peak: 8–15 U/L Follicular phase, and M: 0.5–5 U/L Post-menopausal: >30 U/L
Gamma-glutamyl transpeptidase	P	M: 11–51 IU/L; F: 7–33 IU/L
Glucose (fasting)	P	3.5–5 mmol/L
Glycated (glycosylated) haemoglobin	B	<48 mmol/mol
Growth hormone	P	<20 mU/L
Iron	S	M: 14–31 µmol/L; F: 11–30 µmol/L
Lactate dehydrogenase (LDH)	P	70–250 IU/L
Lead	B	<1.8 mmol/L
Luteinizing hormone	P/S	Pre-menopausal: 3–13 U/L Follicular: 3–12 U/L Ovulatory peak: 20–80 U/L Luteal: 3–16 U/L Post-menopausal: >30 U/L
Magnesium	P	0.75–1.05 mmol/L
Osmolality	P	278–305 mOsmol/kg
Parathyroid hormone (PTH)	P	<0.8–8.5 pmol/L
Phosphate (inorganic)	P	0.8–1.45 mmol/L
Potassium	P	3.5–5.0 mmol/L
Prolactin	P	M: <450 U/L; F: <600 U/L

Substance	Specimen	Normal value
Prostate-specific antigen	P	0–4 ng/mL
Protein (total)	P	60–80 g/L
Red cell folate	B	0.36–1.44 μmol/L (160–640 micrograms/L)
Renin (erect/recumbent)	P*	2.8–4.5/1.1–2.7 pmol/mL/hour
Sodium	P†	135–145 mmol/L
Thyroid-binding globulin (TBG)	P	7–17 mg/L
Thyroid-stimulating hormone (TSH) (normal range widens with age)	P	0.5–5.7 mU/L
Thyroxine (T4)	P	70–140 nmol/L
Thyroxine (free)	P	9–22 pmol/L
Total iron-binding capacity	S	54–75 μmol/L
Triglyceride	P	0.55–1.90 mmol/L
Tri-iodothyronine	P	1.2–3.0 nmol/L
Urea	P†	2.5–6.7 mmol/L
Urate	P†	M: 210–480 μmol/L; F: 150–390 μmol/L
Vitamin B$_{12}$	S	0.13–0.68 nmol/L (<150 ng/L)

* The sample requires special handling. Contact the laboratory.
† Range is significantly different in pregnancy (see table in later text).
‡ Desired upper limit of cholesterol level would be <5 mmol/L.
Abbreviations: P, plasma (heparin bottle); S, serum (clotted; no anticoagulant); B, whole blood (edetic acid (EDTA) bottle); CSF, cerebrospinal fluid specimen; IU, international unit; M, males; F, females; HDL, high-density lipoprotein; LDL, low-density lipoprotein; VLDL, very-low-density lipoprotein.

Arterial blood gases

pH	7.35–7.45
PaCO$_2$	4.7–6.0 kPa
PaO$_2$	<10.6 kPa
Base excess	± 2 mmol/L

Note: 7.6 mmHg = 1 kPa (atmospheric pressure ≈ 100 kPa).

Haematology: reference intervals

Measurement	Reference interval
White cell count (WCC)	$4.0–11.0 \times 10^9$/L
Red cell count	M: $4.5–6.5 \times 10^{12}$/L; F: $3.9–5.6 \times 10^{12}$/L
Haemoglobin	M: 13.5–18.0 g/dL; F: 11.5–16.0 g/dL
Packed red cell volume (PCV) or haematocrit	M: 0.4–0.54 I/L; F: 0.37–0.47 I/L
Mean cell volume (MCV)	76–96 fL
Mean cell haemoglobin (MCH)	27–32 pg
Mean cell haemoglobin concentration (MCHC)	30–36 g/dL
Neutrophil count	$2.0–7.5 \times 10^9$/L; 40–75% WCC
Lymphocyte count	$1.3–3.5 \times 10^9$/L; 20–45% WCC
Eosinophil count	$0.04–0.44 \times 10^9$/L; 1–6% WCC
Basophil count	$0.0–0.1 \times 10^9$/L; 0–1% WCC
Monocyte count	$0.2–0.8 \times 10^9$/L; 2–10% WCC
Platelet count	$150–400 \times 10^9$/L
Reticulocyte count	$25–100 \times 10^9$/L; 0.8–2.0%
Erythrocyte sedimentation rate	<20 mm/hour (but depends on age; see OHCM 10th edn, p. 372)
Activated partial thromboplastin time (VIII, IX, XI, XII)	35–45 seconds
Prothrombin time	10–14 seconds

International normalized ratio (INR)	Clinical state (see OHCM 10th edn, p. 351)
2.0–3.0	Treatment of deep vein thrombosis (DVT), pulmonary emboli (treat for 3–6 months)
2.5–3.5	Embolism prophylaxis in atrial fibrillation (see OHCM 10th edn, p. 351)
3.0–4.5	Recurrent DVT and pulmonary embolism; arterial disease, including myocardial infarction; arterial grafts; cardiac prosthetic valves (if caged ball, aim for 4–4.9) and grafts

Plasma chemistry in pregnancy

	Non-pregnant		Trimester 1		Trimester 2		Trimester 3	
Centile	2.5	97.5	2.5	97.5	2.5	97.5	2.5	97.5
Na⁺ (mmol/L)	138	146	135	141	132	140	133	141
Ca²⁺ (mmol/L)	2	2.6	2.3	2.5	2.2	2.2	2.2	2.5
Corrected*	2.3	2.6	2.25	2.57	2.3	2.5	2.3	2.59
Albumin (g/L)	44	50	39	49	36	44	33	41
Free T4 (pmol/L)	9	23	10	24	9	19	7	17
Free T3 (pmol/L)	4	9	4	8	4	7	3	5
TSH	0	4	0	1.6	1	1.8	7	7.3

* Calcium corrected for plasma albumin (see OHCM 10th edn, p. 676).

Other plasma reference intervals (not analysed by trimester)

	Non-pregnant	Pregnant
Alkaline phosphatase (IU/L)	3–300	Up to 450*
Bicarbonate (mmol/L)	24–30	20–25
Creatinine (µmol/L)	70–150	24–68
Urea (mmol/L)	2.5–6.7	2–4.2
Urate (µmol/L)	150–390	100–270

* Occasionally very much higher in apparently normal pregnancies.

- C-reactive protein levels do not change much during pregnancy.
- TSH levels may be low in the first half of a normal pregnancy (suppressed by HCG). For other thyroid changes, see earlier text and OHCS 10th edn, p. 25.
- Protein S levels fall during pregnancy, so protein S deficiency is difficult to diagnose.
- Activated protein C (APC) resistance is found in 40% of pregnancies, so special tests are required when looking for this. Genotyping for factor V Leiden and prothrombin G20210A is unaffected by pregnancy.

Paediatric reference intervals

Laboratories vary, so it is important to consult your own.

	Specimen	Normal value
Biochemistry (1 mmol = 1 mEq/L)		
Albumin	P	36–48 g/dL
Alkaline phosphatase	P	Depends on age*
α1-antitrypsin	P	1.3–3.4 g/dL
Ammonium	P	2–25 μmol/L; 3–35 micrograms/dL
Amylase	P	70–300 U/L
Aspartate aminotransferase	P	<40 U/L
Bilirubin	P	2–16 μmol/L; 0.1–0.8 mg/dL
Bicarbonate	P	21–25 mmol/L
Calcium	P	2.25–2.75 mmol/L; 9–11 mg/dL
Neonates		1.72–2.47 mmol/L; 6.9–9.9 mg/dL
Chloride	P	98–105 mmol/L
Cholesterol	P, F	≤5.7 mmol/L; 100–200 mg/dL
Creatine kinase	P	<80 U/L
Creatinine	P	25–115 μmol/L; 0.3–1.3 mg/dL
Glucose	F	2.5–5.3 mmol/L; 45–95 mg/dL (lower in newborn; fluoride tube)
IgA	S	0.8–4.5 g/L (low at birth, rising to adult level slowly)
IgG	S	5–18 g/L (high at birth, then falls, and finally rises slowly to adult level)
IgM	S	0.2–2.0 g/L (low at birth, rising to adult level by 1 year)
IgE	S	<500 U/mL
Iron	S	9–36 μmol/L; 50–200 micrograms/dL
Lead	EDTA	<1.75 μmol/L; <36 micrograms/dL
Mg^{2+}	P	0.6–1.0 mmol/L
Osmolality	P	275–295 mosmol/L
Phenylalanine	P	0.04–0.21 mmol/L
Potassium (mean)	P	3.5–5.5 mmol/L
Protein	P	63–81 g/L; 6.3–8.1 g/dL
Sodium	P	136–145 mmol/L
Transferrin	S	2.5–4.5 g/L

	Specimen	Normal value
Triglycerides	F, S	0.34–1.92 mmol/L (30–170 mg/dL)
Urate	P	0.12–0.36 mmol/L; 2–6 mg/dL
Urea	P	2.5–6.6 mmol/L; 15–40 mg/dL
Gamma-glutamyl transferase	P	<20 U/L
Hormones: a guide (consult laboratory)		
Cortisol	P	9 a.m.: 200–700 nmol/L; midnight: <140 nmol/L (mean)
Dehydroepiandrosterone sulfate	P	Days 5–11 of life: 0.8–2.8 μmol/L (range); 5–11 years: 0.1–3.6 μmol/L
17α-hydroxyprogesterone	P	Days 5–11 of life: 1.6–7.5 nmol/L (range); 4–11 years: 0.4–4.2 nmol/L
T4	P	60–135 nmol/L (not neonates)
TSH	P	<5 mU/L (higher on days 1–4)

* Alkaline phosphatase (U/L): 0–0.5 years: 150–600; 0.5–2 years: 250–1000; 2–5 years: 250–850; 6–7 years: 250–1000; 8–9 years: 250–750; 10–11 years: G = 259–950, B = ≤730; 12–13 years: G = 200–750, B = ≤785; 14–15 years: G = 170–460, B = 170–970; 16–17 years: G = 75–270, B = 125–720; <18 years: G = 60–250, B = 50–200.
Abbreviations: B, boys; EDTA, edetic acid; F, fasting; G, girls; P, plasma; S, serum.

Haematology (mean ± ~1 standard deviation; range × 10⁹/L (median in parentheses))

	Hb (g/dL)	MCV (fL)	MCHC (%)	Reticulocyte count (%)	White cell count	Neutrophil count	Eosinophil count	Lymphocyte count	Monocyte count
Days									
1	19.0 ± 2	119 ± 9	31.6 ± 2	3.2 ± 1	9–30	6–26 (11)	0.02–0.8	2–11	0.4–3.1
4	18.6 ± 2	114 ± 7	32.6 ± 2	1.8 ± 1	9–40				
5	17.6 ± 1	114 ± 9	30.9 ± 2	1.2 ± 0.2					
Weeks									
1–2	17.3 ± 2	112 ± 19	32.1 ± 3	0.5 ± 0.03	5–21	1.5–10 (5)	0.07–0.1	2–17	0.3–2.7
2–3	15.6 ± 3	111 ± 8	33.9 ± 2	0.8 ± 0.6	6–15	1–9.5 (4)	0.07–0.1	2–17	0.2–2.4
4–5	12.7 ± 2	101 ± 8	34.9 ± 2	0.9 ± 0.8	6–15	(4)		(6)	
6–7	12.0 ± 2	105 ± 12	33.8 ± 2	1.2 ± 0.7	6–15	(4)		(6)	
8–9	10.7 ± 1	93 ± 12	34.1 ± 2	1.8 ± 1	6–15	(4)		(6)	
Months (all the following Hb values are medians/lower limit for normal)									
3	11.5/9	88/88			6–15	(3)		(6)	
6	11.5/9	77/70			6–15	(3)		(6)	
12	11.5/9	78/72			6–15	(3)		(6)	

	Hb (g/dL)	MCV (fL)	MCHC (%)	Reticulocyte count (%)	White cell count	Neutrophil count	Eosinophil count	Lymphocyte count	Monocyte count
Years									
2	11.5/9	78/74			6–15	(3)		(5)	
4	12/10	80/75			6–15	(4)		(4)	
6	13/10.4	82/75			5–15	(4.2)		(3.8)	
12	13.8/11	83/76			4–13	(4.9)		(3.1)	
14B	14.2/12	84/77			4–13	(5)		(3)	
14G	14/11.5								
16B	14.8/12	85/78	30–36	0.8–2	4–13	2–7.5 (5)	0.04–0.4	1.3–3.5	0.2–0.8
16G	14/11.5								
18B	15/13								

Note:
Basophil range: 0–0.1 × 10^9/L; vitamin B_{12} (serum): ≥150 ng/L.
Red cell folate (EDTA): 100–640 ng/mL.
Platelet counts do not vary with age: 150–400 × 10^9/L.
Abbreviations: B, boys; G, girls.

Abbreviations

ABC	Airway, breathing, and circulation
ABCDE	Airway, breathing, circulation, disability, and exposure
ADHD	Attention-deficit/hyperactivity disorder
AIN	Anterior interosseous branch of the median nerve
AION	Anterior ischaemic optic neuropathy
ALS	Advanced Life Support
ASA	American Society of Anesthesiologists
ATLS	Advanced Trauma Life Support
AUDIT	Alcohol Use Disorders Identification Test
BCC	Basal cell carcinoma
BD	Twice daily
BMI	Body mass index
BNF	British National Formulary
BP	Blood pressure
bpm	Beats per minute
BPPV	Benign paroxysmal positional vertigo
BSA	Body surface area
C	Celsius
CD4+	Cluster of differentiation 4
CHC	Combined hormonal contraceptive
CIN	Cervical intraepithelial neoplasia
CKD	Chronic kidney disease
cm	Centimetre
CMV	Cytomegalovirus
CNS	Central nervous system
CO	Carbon monoxide
CO2	Carbon dioxide
COPD	Chronic obstructive pulmonary disease
CPAP	Continuous positive airway pressure
CPR	Cardiopulmonary resuscitation
CRP	C-reactive protein
CSF	Cerebrospinal fluid
CT	Computed tomography
CTG	Cardiotocography

CVD	Cardiovascular disease
CVP	Central venous pressure
dB	Decibel
DDH	Developmental dysplasia of the hip
DEXA	Dual-energy X-ray absorptiometry
DKA	Diabetic ketoacidosis
dL	Decilitre
DMSA	Dimercaptosuccinic acid
DNA	Deoxyribonucleic acid
DVLA	Driver and Vehicle Licensing Agency
EAS	External anal sphincter
ECG	Electrocardiogram
ECV	External cephalic version
EEG	Electroencephalogram
ENT	Ear, nose, and throat
ERCP	Endoscopic retrograde cholangiopancreatography
ESR	Erythrocyte sedimentation rate
FBC	Full blood count
fL	Fluid ounce
FSH	Follicle-stimulating hormone
FTA-ABS	Fluorescent treponemal antibody absorption test
FU	Fluorouracil
g	Gram
G	Gauge
GABA	Gamma-aminobutyric acid
GAG	Glycosaminoglycan
GCS	Glasgow Coma Scale
GFR	Glomerular filtration rate
GGT	Gamma-glutamyl transpeptidase
GI	Gastrointestinal
GMC	General Medical Council
GP	General practitioner; general practice
HART	Hazardous Area Response Team
Hb	Haemoglobin
HBcAb	Hepatitis B virus core antibody
HBeAg	Hepatitis B virus e antigen
HBsAb	Hepatitis B virus surface antibody
HBsAg	Hepatitis B virus surface antigen
HBV	Hepatitis B virus

HCG	Human chorionic gonadotrophin
HCO$_3$	Bicarbonate
Hg	Mercury
HIV	Human immunodeficiency virus
HPV	Human papillomavirus
HRT	Hormone replacement therapy
IAS	Internal anal sphincter
Ig	Immunoglobulin
IM	Intramuscular
INR	International normalized ratio
IQ	Intelligence quotient
IU	International unit
IUD	Intrauterine device
IUS	Intrauterine system
IV	Intravenous
IVF	*In-vitro* fertilization
kg	Kilogram
kPa	Kilopascal
KTD	Kendrick traction device
kU	Kilo-unit
L	Litre
LFT	Liver function test
LH	Luteinizing hormone
LPA	Lasting Power of Attorney
m	Metre
MAOI	Monoamine oxidase inhibitor
MAST	Military anti-shock trousers
MCHC	Mean corpuscular haemoglobin concentration
MCNS	Minimal change nephrotic syndrome
MCV	Mean corpuscular volume
mEq	Milli-equivalent
MEWS	Modified Early Warning Score
mg	Milligram
MI	Myocardial infarction
min	Minute
mIU	Milli-international unit
mL	Millilitre
mm	Millimetre
mmHg	Millimetre of mercury

µmol	Micromole
mmol	Millimole
MMSE	Mini-Mental State Examination
mol	Mole
mosmol	Milliosmole
mph	Miles per hour
MPS	mucopolysaccharidosis
MRI	Magnetic resonance imaging
mU	Milli-unit
NEB	By nebulizer
ng	Nanogram
NICE	National Institute for Health and Care Excellence
NIPT	Non-invasive prenatal testing
NIV	Non-invasive ventilation
nmol	Nanomole
NSAID	Non-steroidal anti-inflammatory drug
O_2	Oxygen
OAV	oculo-auriculo-vertebral
OD	Once daily
OHCM	*Oxford Handbook of Clinical Medicine*
OHCS	*Oxford Handbook of Clinical Specialties*
OP	Occiput posterior
ORT	Oral rehydration therapy
$PaCO_2$	Partial pressure of carbon dioxide in arterial blood
PaO_2	Partial pressure of oxygen in arterial blood
PCI	Percutaneous coronary intervention
pCO_2	Partial pressure of carbon dioxide
PCOS	Polycystic ovary syndrome
PCP	*Pneumocystis carinii* pneumonia
PEP	Post-exposure prophylaxis
pg	Picogram
PHEM	Pre-hospital emergency medicine
pmol	Picomole
PO	Per os (by mouth)
pO_2	Partial pressure of oxygen
RPR	Rapid plasma reagin
SCC	Squamous cell carcinoma
SGLT2	sodium–glucose co-transporter-2
SLE	Systemic lupus erythematosus

SSRI	Selective serotonin reuptake inhibitor
TB	Tuberculosis
TDS	Three times daily
TENS	Transcutaneous electrical nerve stimulation
THR	Total hip replacement
TIA	Transient ischaemic attack
TPPA	*Treponema pallidum* particle agglutination
TURP	Transurethral resection of the prostate
U	Unit
UK	United Kingdom
UTI	Urinary tract infection
VBAC	Vaginal birth after Caesarean section
VDRL	Venereal Disease Research Laboratory
VF	Ventricular fibrillation
VT	Ventricular tachycardia
WHO	World Health Organization
ZIG	Zoster immunoglobulin

How to use this book

Oxford Assess and Progress: Clinical Specialties has been carefully designed to ensure you get the most out of your revision and are prepared for your exams. Here is a brief guide to some of the features and learning tools.

Organization of content

Chapter editorials will help you unpick tricky subjects, and when it is late at night and you need something to remind you why you are doing this, you will find words of encouragement!

Answers can be found at the end of each chapter, in order.

How to read an answer

Unlike other revision guides on the market, this one is crammed full of feedback, so you should understand exactly why each answer is correct, and gain an insight into the common pitfalls. With every answer, there is an explanation of why that particular choice is the most appropriate. For some questions, there is additional explanation of why the distractors are less suitable. Where relevant, you will also be directed to sources of further information such as the *Oxford Handbook of Clinical Specialties*, websites, and journal articles.

→ http://www.bmj.com/cgi/content/full/334/7583/35

Progression points

The questions in every chapter are ordered by level of difficulty and competence, indicated by the following symbols:

★   *Graduate 'should know'*—you should be aiming to get most of these correct.

★★   *Graduate 'nice to know'*—these are a bit tougher but not above your capabilities.

★★★   *Foundation doctor 'should know'*—these will really test your understanding.

★★★★   *Foundation doctor 'nice to know'*—give these a go when you are ready to challenge yourself.

Oxford Handbook of Clinical Specialties

The OHCS page references are given with the answers to some questions (e.g. OHCS 11th edn → p. 340). Please note that this reference is the **eleventh edition** of the OHCS, and that subsequent or previous editions are unlikely to have the same material in exactly the same place.

Chapter 1

Obstetrics

Zeryab Setna

This chapter will be of interest and help to all those studying the healthcare of women. Obstetrics, like all fields of medicine, continues to evolve at a rapid pace, and keeping up-to-date with the latest literature, guidelines, and protocols can be a daunting task. In the following questions, we have tried to encompass all of the important areas of this subject.

Pregnancy can be a joyful experience for both the mother and her family. However, it can occasionally be associated with complications, resulting in severe short- and long-term harm to both the mother and her baby. This chapter covers the most important aspects of pregnancy and its commonly associated problems, drawing on important guidelines to highlight the core knowledge and skill practitioners in the field are expected to have.

Zeryab Setna, *Obstetrics* In: *Oxford Assess and Progress: Clinical Specialties.*
Edited by: Luci Etheridge and Henry Collier, Oxford University Press.
© Oxford University Press 2021. DOI:10.1093/oso/9780198862550.003.0001

QUESTIONS

1. An 18-year-old woman who is 34 weeks pregnant has abdominal pain and moderate fresh vaginal bleeding. The symphysio-fundal height measures 41 cm and the uterus feels tense and tender. The patient's pulse rate is 98 bpm and her blood pressure is 90/50 mmHg. Which is the single most likely diagnosis? ★

A Cervical ectropion

B Placental abruption

C Placenta praevia

D Pre-term labour

E Vasa praevia

2. A 22-year-old woman comes to the antenatal booking clinic at 12 weeks' gestation. Which is the single most appropriate group of booking investigations? ★

A Full blood count, blood group, and hepatitis C serology

B Full blood count, blood group, and Venereal Disease Research Laboratory (VDRL) test

C Full blood count, thalassaemia screen, and thyroid function test

D Full blood count, thalassaemia screen, and urea and electrolytes

E Full blood count, thyroid function test, and VDRL test

3. A 34-year-old primiparous woman is having generalized tonic–clonic convulsions. She is 32 weeks pregnant. Her blood pressure on arrival is 150/110 mmHg; she has 3+ proteinuria and she is still having convulsions. The fetal heart rate is reassuring. Which is the single most appropriate management? ★

A Diazepam and plan delivery

B Diazepam plus antihypertensive drug, and plan delivery

C Magnesium sulfate

D Magnesium sulfate plus antihypertensive drug

E Magnesium sulfate plus antihypertensive drug, and plan delivery

4. A 23-year-old woman is 34 weeks pregnant and has raised blood pressure. She is on 200 mg labetalol twice daily. Her blood pressure is 160/105 mmHg and she has 3+ proteinuria. She feels well, with no headaches or epigastric pain. The cardiotocograph (CTG) is reassuring. All blood tests are normal. Which is the single most appropriate management? ★

A Admit her to hospital for urgent delivery

B Admit her to hospital to stabilize her blood pressure

C Arrange for her to attend the day unit for twice-daily CTG

D Increase the labetalol dose, and follow up with the community midwife

E Increase the labetalol dose, and follow up in the day unit

5. A 32-year-old primipara is seen at 42 weeks' gestation. She is keen to go into labour naturally and refuses an induction of labour. Which is the single best reason to give for allowing induction of labour when counselling her? ★

A There is an increased risk of Caesarean section beyond 42 weeks' gestation

B There is an increased risk of intrauterine growth restriction beyond 42 weeks' gestation

C There is an increased risk of placental abruption beyond 42 weeks' gestation

D There is an increased risk of shoulder dystocia beyond 42 weeks' gestation

E There is an increased risk of unexplained fetal death beyond 42 weeks' gestation

6. The midwife on the delivery suite calls for help. A woman who has just had a normal delivery with active management of the third stage of labour is bleeding heavily. The bleeding started 15 minutes after delivery of the placenta. Her estimated blood loss is 900 mL. Her pulse rate is 95 bpm and her blood pressure is 100/55 mmHg. Which is the single most appropriate first-line management? ★

A Massage the uterus and give intramuscular (IM) carboprost (Haemabate®)

B Massage the uterus and give IM Syntocinon®

C Massage the uterus and start a Syntocinon® infusion

D Massage the uterus and start a blood transfusion

E Take the woman to theatre immediately for examination under anaesthesia

7. A 24-year-old woman has regular painful uterine contractions at 26 weeks' gestation. She is 2 cm dilated. Her membranes are intact. The cardiotocograph (CTG) is reassuring. Which is the single most appropriate management plan? ★

A Admit her, and administer analgesics and Syntocinon®

B Admit her, and administer antibiotics and intramuscular (IM) steroids

C Admit her, and administer antibiotics and tocolytic drugs

D Admit her, and administer tocolytic drugs and IM steroids

E Reassure her, and send her home

8. A para 4 is referred at 34 weeks' gestation to the antenatal day unit for parenteral iron therapy. Her haemoglobin is 6.9 mg/dL, with a ferritin of 3 micrograms/L. Her serum haemoglobin electrophoresis is normal. During administration of the parenteral iron, she develops headache, hypertension, and wheeze. What is the single most important medication to give immediately after stopping the infusion? ★

A Adrenaline intramuscularly (IM) 1:1000 0.5 mL

B Chlorphenamine intravenously (IV) 10 mg

C Hydrocortisone IV 200 mg

D Paracetamol by mouth (PO) 1 g

E Salbutamol by nebulizer (NEB) 5 mL

9. A 26-year-old primigravida is in advanced labour. Her labour has been augmented using Syntocinon®, so a cardiotocograph (CTG) is performed. This is shown in Figure 1.1 (see Colour Plate section). Which is the single most appropriate management? ★ ★

A Perform urgent fetal blood sampling

B Perform an emergency Caesarean section

C Reassure the woman

D Stop the CTG recording

E Stop the Syntocinon® infusion

10. A 36-year-old woman who is human immunodeficiency virus (HIV)-positive discovers that she is pregnant. She is uncertain whether to continue the pregnancy, in particular because of the risk of the child acquiring her HIV infection. Her health is good and she has not yet needed to take antiretroviral therapy. If the pregnancy is managed appropriately, which is the single probability of her baby acquiring HIV infection? ★ ★

A 0% (i.e. no risk)

B Approximately 1%

C Approximately 15%

D Approximately 25%

E Approximately 40%

11. A 32-year-old primiparous woman is 'small for dates' at 34 weeks' gestation. An ultrasound scan shows a singleton fetus with an abdominal circumference at the tenth centile. The amniotic fluid volume and umbilical artery Dopplers are normal. Which is the single most appropriate management? ★ ★

A CTG monitoring on alternate days

B Reassure her that the baby is growing appropriately

C Repeat the ultrasound scan in 2 weeks' time

D Repeat the ultrasound scan in 4 weeks' time

E Urgent delivery by Caesarean section

12. A 42-year-old woman is 15 weeks pregnant and requests a quadruple test to rule out Down's syndrome. Which is the single most appropriate advice to give her? ★ ★

A It is too early in pregnancy to have the quadruple test

B It is too late in pregnancy to have the quadruple test

C She could have the quadruple test arranged today

D She must first agree to have an amniocentesis if the test is screen-positive

E The quadruple test will definitely be screen-positive because of her age

13. A 33-year-old woman has severe headache, blurred vision, abdominal pain, and bleeding per vaginum at 33 weeks' gestation. The fetal heartbeat is absent. Which is the single most important associated clinical sign that may help in the diagnosis? ★★

A Brisk tendon reflexes

B Enlarged thyroid gland

C Oedema

D Raised jugular venous pressure

E Tachycardia

14. A 29-year-old gravid 2 + 1 woman is 35 + 6 weeks pregnant. She has a history of a previous Caesarean section. She has had regular uterine contractions for 4 hours and a per vaginum 'show'. Following speculum examination, which is the single most appropriate management? ★★

A Cardiotocograph (CTG) monitoring

B Fibronectin test

C Intramuscular (IM) steroid

D Rescue cerclage

E Tocolysis

15. A primigravida presents to the delivery suite at 39 weeks' gestation with a history of regular contractions and rupture of membranes more than 8 hours ago. On examination, she is 6 cm dilated. The cardiotocograph (CTG) is abnormal; therefore, a fetal blood sample is collected. The pH is 7.018 and lactate 5.0 mmol/L. What is the single most appropriate management plan? ★★

A Deliver within 30 minutes

B Deliver within 60 minutes

C No action required

D Repeat sample after 30 minutes

E Repeat sample after 60 minutes

16. A 31-year-old para 1, with a history of a previous Caesarean section, is requesting a vaginal birth after Caesarean section (VBAC). She asks about the risk of problems. What single figure most accurately reflects the risk of scar dehiscence during labour? ★★★

A 0.5%

B 0.75%

C 1%

D 1.5%

E 2%

17. The midwife on the delivery suite calls for help. The fetal head has been delivered 2 minutes earlier and there is difficulty with delivery of the fetal shoulders. What is the single most effective manoeuvre to overcome this situation? ★★★

A Episiotomy

B Fundal pressure

C McRoberts' manoeuvre

D Suprapubic pressure

E Zavenelli manoeuvre

18. A 31-year-old primigravida, 29⁺³ weeks, presents to the antenatal clinic with reduced fetal movement for the last 6 hours. What is the single most appropriate initial investigation to confirm fetal viability? ★★★

A Biophysical profile

B Cardiotocography

C Doppler of umbilical artery

D Fetal movement chart

E Handheld Doppler

19. A 41-year-old primigravida presents to the antenatal clinic at 11⁺³ weeks' gestation, requesting a screening test for trisomy 21. Which is the single most sensitive and specific test available to her? ★★★

A Biophysical profile

B Cell free deoxyribonucleic acid (DNA) analysis

C Nuchal translucency test

D Triple test

E Quadruple test

20. A 27-year-old primigravida is seen in the antenatal clinic at term^{+14}. The pregnancy has been uneventful and she is declining induction of labour. What is the single most appropriate management plan to ensure fetal well-being? ★★★

A Daily fetal kick chart monitoring

B Weekly biophysical profile

C Weekly amniotic fluid index and umbilical artery Doppler

D Twice-weekly cardiotocography (CTG) and amniotic fluid index

E Twice-weekly CTG and umbilical artery Doppler

21. A 19-year-old woman is taking carbamazepine as treatment for her epilepsy. She is 16 weeks pregnant. She had been fit-free for 5 years before becoming pregnant but has had two episodes of absence seizures in the past month. She has not informed the Driver and Vehicle Licensing Agency (DVLA) of her recent seizures. Which is the single most appropriate action to take at this stage? ★★★★

A Advise her to inform the DVLA immediately of her recent seizures

B Advise her to seek a second opinion about the safety of driving

C Inform the DVLA medical adviser immediately about the recent seizures

D Inform the patient's general practitioner (GP) about the recent seizures

E Reassure the patient that there is no need to inform the DVLA

22. A 22-year-old primigravida undergoes a Neville–Barnes forceps delivery. The fetal head is delivered in the occiput posterior (OP) position. On examination, the woman has a tear involving approximately one-third of the external anal sphincter thickness. What is the single most appropriate classification of this tear? ★★★★

A Second-degree tear

B Third-degree 3a tear

C Third-degree 3b tear

D Third-degree 3c tear

E Fourth-degree tear

23. A 21-year-old primigravida presents to the antenatal clinic with a breech presentation at 37⁺⁴ weeks' gestation. She is requesting an external cephalic version (ECV). What single drug treatment, given prior to ECV, is most effective at increasing the success rate? ★ ★ ★ ★

A Atosiban

B Glyceryl trinitrate

C Indomethacin

D Nifedipine

E Salbutamol

24. A 31-year-old primigravida presents to the labour ward at 31 weeks with a history of regular contractions. On vaginal examination, she is 2 cm dilated and the cervix is partially effaced. What is the single most cost-effective tocolytic treatment to give her? ★ ★ ★ ★

A Atosiban

B Indomethacin

C Magnesium sulfate

D Nifedipine

E Ritodrine

25. A 29-year-old, 31⁺⁴ weeks pregnant primigravida presents to the Emergency Department with a history of travel to rural India. On examination, her pulse is 118 bpm and blood pressure (BP) 90/60 mmHg, and her Glasgow Coma Scale (GCS) score is 11/15. She is diagnosed with falciparum malaria. What is the single most effective treatment option? ★ ★ ★ ★

A Artesunate

B Chloroquine

C Clindamycin

D Primaquine

E Quinine

26. A para 1⁺³ is reviewed in the high-risk antenatal clinic at 32⁺² weeks' gestation. She has an uncomplicated triplet pregnancy. What is the single most appropriate time to deliver this pregnancy? ★ ★ ★ ★

A 32 weeks' gestation

B 33 weeks' gestation

C 34 weeks' gestation

D 35 weeks' gestation

E 36 weeks' gestation

ANSWERS

1. B ★   OHCS 11th edn → p. 42

This woman is shocked. The abdominal pain and tense uterus suggest abruption. Blood loss may be concealed, so do not expect large amounts of visible bleeding. Placenta praevia is usually painless and the blood loss is greater, so it is often noticed earlier. There are no contractions, so labour has not started, although delivery will be expedited as the patient is unwell. A cervical ectropion may bleed but will not cause pain and shock.

2. B ★   OHCS 11th edn → p. 10

There are clear guidelines for antenatal care.
→ http://www.nice.org.uk/guidance/CG62

3. E ★   OHCS 11th edn → p. 90

Magnesium sulfate is the evidence-based treatment for eclamptic seizures. This patient also needs to have her blood pressure controlled carefully and delivery expedited.
→ https://www.nice.org.uk/guidance/ng133

4. B ★   OHCS 11th edn → p. 35

Although the patient is currently asymptomatic, her blood pressure is above 160/100 mmHg and she has significant proteinuria, despite labetalol treatment. She needs admission for careful monitoring and controlled management with antihypertensives, and consideration of delivery if there is no improvement.
→ https://www.nice.org.uk/guidance/ng133

5. E ★   OHCS 11th edn → p. 60

The reason why inductions are booked at 42 weeks is that the risk of intrauterine death increases significantly thereafter.

6. B ★   OHCS 11th edn → p. 96

Massaging the uterus helps to stimulate a contraction; the commonest cause is uterine atony. Syntocinon® IM is the first-line treatment. It is a synthetic version of oxytocin and stimulates contractions. If bleeding does not stop, Syntocinon® infusion and carboprost can be used, along with other approaches within a major haemorrhage protocol such as blood transfusion and fresh frozen plasma. Blood loss of over 1000 mL or clinical signs of shock are considered to represent a major incident.

7. D ★   OHCS 11th edn → p. 52

This woman has gone into premature labour, but this is at an early stage, so there is a possibility that it can be stopped with tocolytic drugs. However, steroids should still be given to mature the fetal lungs in case delivery goes ahead. There is no indication of infection, so antibiotics are not routinely given.

→ http://www.nice.org.uk/guidance/ng25

8. A ★   OHCS 11th edn → p. 609

Patients having an anaphylactic reaction should be identified early and help sought immediately. The initial assessment and treatment should be based on the ABCDE (airway, breathing, circulation, disability, and exposure) approach. Pregnant women should be placed in the left lateral position to prevent aorto-caval compression. Stop any drug/trigger suspected of causing the reaction, then give adrenaline (epinephrine), administered as IM 1:1000 in a dose of 0.5 mL. The other medications will be needed after this, but adrenaline is lifesaving and should be given without delay.

→ https://www.resus.org.uk/anaphylaxis/emergency-treatment-of-anaphylactic-reactions/

9. C ★★   OHCS 11th edn → pp. 47–9

This is a normal CTG, with a baseline of 110–160 bpm, a variability of more than 5 bpm, and accelerations seen.

→ http://www.nice.org.uk/guidance/cg190/resources/interpretation-of-cardiotocograph-traces-248732173

10. B ★★   OHCS 11th edn → p. 24

The risks associated with modern management using antiretroviral drugs and elective Caesarean section are very low, although they are not eliminated completely.

11. C ★★   OHCS 11th edn → p. 54

Serial ultrasound scans to detect changes in abdominal circumference are accurate in diagnosing growth restriction. As this baby's abdominal circumference is less than the tenth centile, it may be growth-restricted and a scan should be repeated after 2 weeks.

→ https://www.rcog.org.uk/globalassets/documents/guidelines/gtg_31.pdf

12. C ★★   OHCS 11th edn → p. 16

The quadruple test measures maternal serum levels of α-fetoprotein, human chorionic gonadotrophin, and unconjugated oestriol, interpreted along with a dating scan. It uses these values, together with maternal age, to calculate the risk of certain conditions. It is a screening tool and is not diagnostic. If the risk is high, the mother can, if she wishes, choose further diagnostic tests.

→ https://www.nice.org.uk/guidance/cg62/ifp/chapter/Screening-and-tests#screening-tests-for-downs-syndrome

13. A ★★   OHCS 11th edn → p. 50

These symptoms indicate severe pre-eclampsia. Brisk reflexes are commonly associated with pre-eclampsia. The others are just general clinical signs.

14. A ★★   OHCS 11th edn → p. 58

This woman may be in labour, and the single most appropriate plan of management in her case will involve a speculum examination and CTG to assess this. It is inappropriate to insert a cerclage at this gestation. A fibronectin test is contraindicated if there is bleeding per vaginum. A single course of antenatal corticosteroids is administered to women between 24^{+0} and 34^{+6} weeks' gestation.

→ http://www.nice.org.uk/guidance/ng25

15. A ★★   OHCS 11th edn → p. 48

Fetal blood sampling is done to give a sign of how distressed a fetus is. An acidotic sample with a high lactate indicates a high level of distress and should be acted upon. The recommended intervention cut-off value for lactate is 4.8 mmol/L.

Above this, the fetus should be delivered immediately, either by instrument or by an urgent Caesarean section.

→ http://www.nice.org.uk/guidance/cg190/resources/intrapartum-care- for-healthy-women-and-babies-35109866447557

16. A ★★★   OHCS 11th edn → p. 95

Women should be informed that a planned VBAC is associated with an approximately 1:200 (0.5%) risk of uterine rupture. The success rate for a VBAC is 72–76%.

→ https://www.rcog.org.uk/en/guidelines-research-services/guide-lines/gtg45/

17. C ★★★   OHCS 11th edn → p. 94

An episiotomy is not always necessary, and maternal pushing should be discouraged as this may impact fetal shoulders further. Fundal pressure should not be used and is associated with high fetal and maternal complication rates, including uterine rupture. The McRoberts' manoeuvre consists of flexion and abduction of the mother's hips, with her thighs placed onto her abdomen. The reported success rates for this manoeuvre is 90%, and therefore, it should be employed first. If this fails to correct the problem, other manoeuvres can be used—applying pressure to the posterior aspect of the anterior shoulder (suprapubic pressure) or internal manipulations. In the Zavenelli manoeuvre, the fetal head is re-placed into the birth canal and the fetus is rescued abdominally, but this has a high mortality rate, so it is a last resort.

→ https://www.rcog.org.uk/en/guidelines-research-services/guide-lines/gtg42/

18. E ★★★ OHCS 11th edn → p. 70

A handheld Doppler will, in most cases, confirm the presence of a fetal heartbeat. This is widely available in most settings. If the fetal heartbeat is not confirmed, then immediate referral for an ultrasound scan to assess fetal cardiac activity is required.

After viability has been confirmed, if the woman still complains of reduced fetal movement, then a CTG should be performed. If she continues to complain of reduced fetal movements, and despite having a normal CTG, then a detailed ultrasound scan should be undertaken.

→ https://www.rcog.org.uk/en/guidelines-research-services/guidelines/gtg57/

19. B ★★★ OHCS 11th edn → p. 17

Cell free DNA analysis works by analysing, counting, and mapping the DNA fragments that are present in maternal plasma during pregnancy and can be performed from about 10 weeks. It has a less than 0.1% false positive rate for trisomies 21, 18, and 13. Fewer than 1 in 1000 non-invasive prenatal testing (NIPT) tests yield a false positive result. The detection rate for conventional screening tests, including quadruple screen, is 81%. A first-trimester screen with a nuchal translucency scan is 85%. Integrated screening gives a 95% detection rate. The biophysical profile is not a screening test.

→ Grace M, Hardisty E, Dotters-Katz S, Vora N, Kuller J. Cell-free DNA screening: complexities and challenges of clinical implementation. *Obstet Gynecol Surv.* 2016;**71**:477–87.

20. D ★★★ OHCS 11th edn → p. 60

Women with uncomplicated pregnancies should be offered induction of labour at 41 weeks. After 42 weeks, if a woman declines induction, then the health of the fetus should be monitored. She should be offered at least twice-weekly CTG and ultrasound estimation of the maximum amniotic pool depth. These best monitor fetal distress and placental function.

→ https://www.nice.org.uk/guidance/cg62/

21. A ★★★★

Patients who have had a seizure should refrain from driving for 1 year. It is the patient's responsibility to inform the DVLA, which may then seek information from the doctor. However, the doctor should inform the patient of this requirement, as they may be unaware of it.

→ http://www.epilepsysociety.org.uk/driving-regulations

22. B ★★★★   OHCS 11th edn → pp. 84–5

It is important to recognize and appropriately treat perineal tears in order to prevent future morbidity, particularly anal incontinence. Risk factors for tears include primiparity, large babies (>4 kg), occiput posterior (OP) position, induction, epidural use, prolonged second stage, forceps use, and midline episiotomy.

Classification is as follows:*

• first degree: injury to the perineal skin only
• second degree: injury to the perineum involving the perineal muscles, but not the anal sphincter
• third degree: injury to the perineum involving the anal sphincter complex, consisting of the external anal sphincter (EAS) and internal anal sphincter (IAS):
  • 3a: less than 50% of EAS thickness torn
  • 3b: more than 50% of EAS thickness torn
  • 3c: both EAS and IAS torn
• fourth degree: injury to the perineum involving the anal sphincter complex (EAS and IAS) and anal epithelium.

→ https://www.rcog.org.uk/en/guidelines-research-services/guidelines/gtg29/

23. E ★★★★   OHCS 11th edn → p. 68

Women should be counselled that, with a trained operator, about 50% of ECV attempts will be successful. ECV success rates are increased by the use of tocolysis. The drugs shown to be effective include ritodrine, salbutamol, and terbutaline.

→ https://www.rcog.org.uk/en/guidelines-research-services/guidelines/gtg20a/

24. D ★★★★   OHCS 11th edn → p. 52

Nifedipine and atosiban have comparable effectiveness in delaying birth up to 7 days. Atosiban, an oxytocin receptor antagonist, is licensed in the United Kingdom (UK) for treatment of pre-term labour. Although the use of nifedipine for pre-term labour is an unlicensed indication, it is associated with improved neonatal outcomes and is therefore in use and recommended first line, with oxytocin receptor antagonists used if nifedipine is contraindicated. It is also orally administered, and the cost for a standard 48-hour treatment with nifedipine is £1, as compared with £494 with atosiban.

→ https://www.nice.org.uk/guidance/ng25

---

*Adapted from: Royal College of Obstetricians and Gynaecologists. *The Management of Third- and Fourth-Degree Perineal Tears.* Green-top Guideline No. 29. London: RCOG; 2015, with the permission of the Royal College of Obstetricians and Gynaecologists.

25. A ★★★★　OHCS 11th edn → p. 30

Admit women with complicated malaria and treat it as an emergency. Intravenous artesunate is the treatment of choice for severe falciparum malaria, including in pregnant women. Intravenous quinine can be used if artesunate is not available. Primaquine should not be used in pregnancy. Quinine and clindamycin can be used to treat uncomplicated *Plasmodium falciparum* or *Plasmodium vivax*.

→ https://www.rcog.org.uk/en/guidelines-research-services/guide-lines/gtg54b/

26. B ★★★★　OHCS 11th edn → p. 66

Triplet pregnancies should be offered elective delivery by Caesarean section from 35 weeks' gestation, after a course of antenatal corticosteroids. Seventy-five per cent of triplet pregnancies will result in spontaneous labour before 35 weeks 0 days. Delivery too early puts the infants at more risk of complications so should be avoided.

→ https://www.nice.org.uk/guidance/ng137

Gynaecology and genitourinary medicine

Kevin Hayes

Gynaecological practices are changing constantly, with more emphasis on management in primary care, conservative, rather than surgical, management of conditions, and an increase in sub-specialization such as gynaecological oncology and urogynaecology. This chapter reflects these changes and covers the commonest areas in this interesting field.

Sexual health is a specialty in its own right. The number of cases of sexually transmitted infections are rising in the UK, despite efforts to raise awareness of safe sex, so knowledge of their presentations is important. The UK also has the highest rate of teenage pregnancy in Europe, and the Government has set targets to improve access to contraceptive advice for women. In recent years, astounding advances have been made in the treatment of human immunodeficiency virus (HIV) infection, and people with HIV can now expect to have a much better quality of life.

Although this chapter primarily focuses on diseases affecting women, we have included questions on the sexual health of men to represent the full spectrum of sexual health practice.

Kevin Hayes, *Gynaecology and genitourinary medicine* In: *Oxford Assess and Progress: Clinical Specialties.* Edited by: Luci Etheridge and Henry Collier, Oxford University Press.
© Oxford University Press 2021. DOI:10.1093/oso/9780198862550.003.0002

QUESTIONS

1. A 20-year-old woman and her 23-year-old male partner have been trying to conceive for 6 months, without success. Her periods are regular. Which is the single most appropriate management at this stage? ★

A Arrange a semen analysis for the man

B Arrange a laparoscopy and dye test for the woman

C Arrange luteal-phase progesterone levels for the woman

D Arrange referral to the assisted conception unit for *in-vitro* fertilization (IVF)

E Reassure the couple and suggest that they keep trying

2. A 55-year-old woman has hot flushes. Her last period was 2 years ago. She is keen to start hormone replacement therapy (HRT). In terms of safety of prescribing, what is the single most appropriate question to ask her before commencing HRT? ★

A Do any of your relatives have Alzheimer's disease?

B Do you know whether you have osteoporosis?

C Have any of your relatives suffered from premature menopause?

D Have you ever suffered from deep vein thrombosis?

E Have you ever suffered from depression?

3. A 14-year-old girl requests emergency contraception. She had unprotected intercourse with her 14-year-old boyfriend 2 days ago. She appears to understand the nature of emergency contraception. Which is the single most appropriate management? ★

A Advise her that she cannot have emergency contraception, as it is too long since intercourse took place

B Advise her that she is too young to be legally prescribed emergency contraception

C Prescribe emergency hormonal contraception and advise her about future contraception

D Prescribe emergency hormonal contraception only after informing her parents

E Prescribe emergency hormonal contraception only after informing social services

4. A 31-year-old woman has vulval soreness and recurrent white vaginal discharge. Microscopy shows the presence of hyphae. Which is the single most appropriate treatment option? ★

A Clindamycin

B Clotrimazole

C Doxycycline

D Erythromycin

E Metronidazole

5. A 35-year-old woman who is taking Cerazette® (a progestogen-only contraceptive pill) has a chest infection and is prescribed amoxicillin. Which single piece of advice should be given about her contraception? ★

A No additional contraceptive precautions are required

B Use additional precautions for the duration of the antibiotic course

C Use additional precautions for the duration of the antibiotic course and for 2 days after the end of the course

D Use additional precautions for the duration of the antibiotic course and for 7 days after the end of the course

E Use additional precautions for the remainder of the current packet of Cerazette®

6. A 32-year-old woman has increasing white vaginal discharge. She is 7 weeks pregnant. Her *Chlamydia* swab is positive. All other tests are normal. Which is the single most appropriate treatment? ★

A Amoxicillin

B Azithromycin

C Clindamycin

D Doxycycline

E Metronidazole

7. A 42-year-old woman has frequency, urgency, and urge incontinence. Examination is unremarkable and a midstream specimen of urine is sterile. She is treated empirically for detrusor overactivity with oxybutynin. What is the principal mechanism of action for this drug? ★

A Anti-adrenergic

B Anti-GABAergic

C Anti-muscarinic

D Anti-nicotinic

E Anti-serotonergic

8. A 60-year-old woman is recovering post-operatively following a vaginal hysterectomy and anterior vaginal repair. She has had voiding difficulty and has been catheterized for 3 days. A catheter specimen of urine is taken due to low-grade pyrexia, and it confirms the presence of a urinary tract infection (UTI). Which single organism is most likely to be causative? ★

A *Escherichia coli*

B *Klebsiella pneumoniae*

C *Proteus* species

D *Pseudomonas* species

E *Staphylococcus epidermidis*

9. A 24-year-old woman has had an abnormal vaginal discharge for the past week. It is off-white and non-itchy, with an offensive odour. She has had one sexual partner in the last 8 months, and he has no symptoms. There is an off-white vaginal discharge pooling in the posterior fornix, with no inflammation of the vulva or vagina. Which is the single most likely finding on a Gram-stained sample of the vaginal discharge? ★

A Gram-negative intracellular diplococci

B Gram-positive and Gram-negative mixed bacteria

C Numerous lactobacilli

D Polymorphonuclear leucocytes

E Yeast cells with hyphae

10. A 14-year-old girl has been sexually active for 6 months and seeks sexual health advice. She has a regular partner and has no symptoms. She is very anxious that her mother does not find out that she is sexually active, and she wants reassurance that her confidentiality will be maintained. In which single situation might breaching her confidentiality be justified? ★

A She is found to have a sexually transmitted infection

B She is in a sexually abusive relationship

C She requests a prescription for the oral contraceptive pill

D She requests a termination of pregnancy

E None of the above, as she has an absolute right to confidentiality

11. A 25-year-old woman has her first routine cervical cytology test as part of the NHS Cervical Screening Programme. This shows 'mild dyskaryosis' and her high-risk human papillomavirus (HPV) test is positive. She attends the colposcopy clinic and has a biopsy-proven diagnosis of cervical intraepithelial neoplasia (CIN) 1. She has a body mass index (BMI) of 30 kg/m² and uses a progestogen-only oral contraceptive pill. She smokes 15 cigarettes daily and drinks approximately 25 units of alcohol per week. She wants to know if there is anything she can do that might help to reverse the abnormality. Which single action that she can be advised about is most likely to increase the chances of spontaneous resolution of her cervical abnormality? ★

A Get vaccinated against HPV infection

B Give up smoking cigarettes

C Reduce alcohol consumption

D Reduce the BMI

E Switch to an alternative contraceptive pill

12. A 24-year-old woman requests post-coital contraception. Her condom broke 36 hours ago, on day 7 of a regular 29-day cycle. She is undecided about future contraceptive use. A pregnancy test is negative. Which is the single most effective form of post-coital contraception for her? ★

A A combined oral oestrogen/progestogen pill

B A progestogen-only pill

C Insertion of a copper-containing intrauterine device (IUD)

D Insertion of a progestogen-containing intrauterine system (IUS)

E No post-coital contraception is required

13. A 27-year-old man has had mild dysuria for 1 week. He has been having sex with his current girlfriend for 4 weeks, occasionally using condoms. She has no symptoms. He last had sex with his previous female partner 3 months ago. There is a slight mucoid discharge at the urethral meatus. Which single organism is the most likely cause? ★

A *Chlamydia trachomatis*

B *Mycoplasma hominis*

C *Neisseria gonorrhoeae*

D *Trichomonas vaginalis*

E *Ureaplasma urealyticum*

14. A 32-year-old man has a history of weight loss and general malaise. He takes a human immunodeficiency virus (HIV) test. The result is positive and his CD4+ count is $180 \times 10^6/L$ (12%) (normal range is $450–1600 \times 10^6/L$). He is otherwise well. He does not feel ready to start antiretroviral therapy straightaway but is keen to stay well in the interim. For which single organism should he be offered primary prophylaxis? ★

A Cryptococcus neoformans

B Mycobacterium avium intracellulare

C Mycobacterium tuberculosis

D Pneumocystis jirovecii

E Toxoplasma gondii

15. A 19-year-old woman has had pain in her vulval area for 4 days. A photograph of the vulval lesion is shown in Figure 2.1 (see Colour Plate section). Which is the single most likely diagnosis? ★

A Behçet's disease

B Genital herpes

C Lichen sclerosis

D Syphilitic ulcer

E Vulval cancer

16. A 19-year-old woman has had pain in her vulval area for 4 days. A photograph of the vulval lesion is shown in Figure 2.1 (see Colour Plate section). Which is the single most appropriate initial management? ★ ★

A Perform a vulval biopsy

B Prescribe oral aciclovir

C Prescribe oral azithromycin

D Prescribe oral prednisolone

E Prescribe topical clobetasol (Dermovate®)

17. A 29-year-old man from South Africa has collapsed at work. An eyewitness gives a clear description of a convulsion. The man is drowsy, barely rousable, and unable to communicate. His wife states that she fears he may be human immunodeficiency virus (HIV)-positive. His breathing becomes erratic, and artificial ventilation is being considered. In which single situation should an HIV test be carried out, given that he is unable to give informed consent? ★★

A At the request of his wife as next of kin

B If knowledge of his HIV status would benefit his care

C Prior to admitting him to the intensive therapy unit

D Prior to any invasive procedure being performed

E Prior to making the decision to ventilate

18. A 23-year-old woman has a large, 20-week-sized cystic mass on her ovary. She undergoes laparotomy and oophorectomy, and histology confirms that this is a benign mucinous cystadenoma. Which is the single most likely ovarian tissue of origin for this type of cyst? ★★

A Epithelial

B Follicular

C Germ cell

D Sex cord

E Stromal

19. A 22-year-old woman who is struggling to conceive has the following hormone profile, taken on day 6 of her cycle:

• luteinizing hormone (LH): 12 IU/mL (normal pre-menopausal range, 3–13 IU/mL)
• follicle-stimulating hormone (FSH): 4 IU/mL (normal range, 3–20 IU/mL)
• testosterone: 18 ng/dL (normal range, 6–86 ng/dL).

An ultrasound scan shows numerous peripheral ovarian follicles. Which single set of symptoms is she most likely to have? ★★

A Amenorrhoea and infertility

B Amenorrhoea and pelvic pain

C Oligomenorrhoea and facial hair

D Oligomenorrhoea and pelvic pain

E Oligomenorrhoea and temporal headaches

20. A 24-year-old man who has sex with men has read on the Internet that his sexual orientation puts him at risk of hepatitis B virus (HBV) infection. He is interested in being immunized. His hepatitis status results are as follows:

- hepatitis B virus surface antigen (HBsAg) negative
- hepatitis B virus core antibody (HBcAb) positive
- hepatitis B virus surface antibody (HBsAb) negative
- hepatitis B virus e antigen (HBeAg) negative.

Which is the single most appropriate advice regarding his results and proposed immunization? ★★

A He has evidence of previous exposure to HBV and is a 'high-risk' carrier; immunization will not help

B He has evidence of previous exposure to HBV and is a 'low-risk' carrier; immunization will not help

C He has evidence of previous exposure to HBV, with a partial immune response; immunization is unlikely to help

D He has evidence of previous exposure to HBV, with an appropriate immune response; immunization is unnecessary

E He has no evidence of previous exposure to HBV and should proceed with immunization as planned

21. A 16-year-old girl has had painful periods for 6 months. Her periods are regular and last 3 days. She misses a couple of days of school every month due to the pain. She is not sexually active. Which is the single most appropriate initial management? ★★

A Gonadotrophin-releasing hormone analogues

B Intrauterine system (Mirena®)

C Mefenamic acid

D Progesterone-only oral contraceptive pill

E Tranexamic acid

22. A 26-year-old woman with no children has had amenorrhoea for 6 weeks and has some pelvic discomfort. Her pregnancy test is positive. Her pulse rate is 68 bpm, and her blood pressure is 110/80 mmHg. An ultrasound scan shows an empty uterus, with normal adnexae. Her serum β-human chorionic gonadotrophin (β-HCG) level is 950 mIU/mL. Which is the single most appropriate next step in management? ★★

A Arrange for a laparoscopy

B Arrange for a laparotomy

C Repeat the β-HCG test after 48 hours

D Repeat the ultrasound scan and β-HCG test after 48 hours

E Repeat the ultrasound scan after 48 hours

23. A 30-year-old nurse sustained a significant needle-stick injury during her last shift, 36 hours ago. The patient (i.e. 'donor') involved is human immunodeficiency virus (HIV)-positive. He is taking anti-retroviral therapy, and his last viral load was 1000 copies/mL (acceptable load is <5000 copies/mL). He is hepatitis B virus-immune and negative for hepatitis C virus. The nurse also had unprotected sex earlier in her current menstrual cycle, and there is a possibility that she may be pregnant. Which is the single most appropriate advice regarding HIV post-exposure prophylaxis (PEP)? ★ ★

A It is already too late for her to start taking PEP

B PEP is contraindicated because of the possibility that she is pregnant

C She does not need PEP, as the patient's viral load is so low

D She should start PEP without further delay

E The risks associated with PEP are higher than the risk of acquiring HIV

24. A 42-year-old man attends a genitourinary medicine clinic and asks for a routine check for sexually transmitted infections. He has no symptoms and no abnormal clinical findings. Serological tests for syphilis show:

• rapid plasma reagin (RPR) positive at a titre of 1:64
• *Treponema pallidum* particle agglutination (TPPA) assay positive
• fluorescent treponemal antibody absorption test (FTA-ABS) positive.

The same tests were negative 18 months ago. Which single stage of syphilis can be diagnosed? ★ ★

A Early latent

B Late latent

C Primary

D Secondary

E Tertiary

25. A 22-year-old woman is 6–8 weeks pregnant and is brought into the Emergency Department in cardiac arrest. No other medical information about her is available. Which is the single most likely cause of her cardiac arrest in early pregnancy? ★ ★

A Miscarriage bleeding

B Pre-existing cardiac disease

C Pulmonary embolus

D Ruptured ectopic pregnancy

E Sepsis following termination of pregnancy

26. A 22-year-old woman has an acute onset of right iliac fossa pain, but no vomiting. She has marked tenderness to palpation in the right iliac fossa. There is no rebound tenderness and some voluntary guarding. Her temperature is 37.2°C, her pulse rate 80 bpm, and her blood pressure 115/80 mmHg. Her pregnancy test is negative. An ultrasound scan shows a 7-cm right-sided haemorrhagic ovarian cyst with no free fluid. Which is the single most appropriate initial management? ★★★

A Admit her with a view to conservative management

B Allow her to go home, with advice to come back if the pain worsens

C Perform an immediate laparoscopy in case the diagnosis is torsion

D Refer to the surgeons to rule out appendicitis

E Request a computed tomography (CT) scan to confirm the diagnosis

27. A 70-year-old woman has had vulval itching and discomfort for 12 months. There is widespread erythema on both labia minora, extending onto the majora and involving the fourchette. There are no ulcers and there is no inguinal lymphadenopathy. Which is the single most appropriate initial management? ★★★

A Empirical treatment with potent corticosteroid ointment

B Immediate punch biopsy to exclude cancer

C Referral to the sexual health clinic to rule out a sexually transmitted infection

D Treatment with oestrogen cream for atrophy

E Vulval excision to treat the affected area

28. A 24-year-old woman has dysmenorrhoea and deep dyspareunia. A transvaginal ultrasound scan shows a 4-cm endometrioma on the left ovary. The patient wants relief of her pain symptoms. She has also been trying to conceive for over 12 months. Which is the single most appropriate treatment to use? ★★★

A Combined oral contraceptive pill

B Danazol

C Gonadotrophin-releasing hormone analogues

D Laparoscopic surgery

E Medroxyprogesterone acetate (Provera®)

29. A previously well 67-year-old woman has abdominal distension, a large irregular pelvic mass, and ascites. An ultrasound scan, a computed tomography (CT) scan, and a raised CA125 confirm a likely ovarian carcinoma. Which is the single most appropriate first-line management? ★★★

A External beam radiotherapy

B High-dose progestogen therapy

C Hysterectomy, bilateral oophorectomy, omentectomy, and debulking

D Symptomatic palliative care

E Vincristine-containing chemotherapy

ANSWERS

1. E ★   OHCS 11th edn → p. 142

Normal healthy couples can take up to a year to conceive, so investigations are not normally started until after 1 year of regular attempts to conceive.

2. D ★   OHCS 11th edn → p. 120

Overall, HRT doubles the risk of venous thromboembolism, so other risk factors need to be considered. HRT helps to reduce the risk of fractures in osteoporosis. There is no association with Alzheimer's disease; in fact, HRT may be protective. In some women, symptoms of depression may occur with some forms of HRT, but this would not be a contraindication.

→ https://www.nice.org.uk/guidance/ng23

3. C ★   OHCS 11th edn → p. 149

The girl appears to be Gillick-competent, as she understands the nature of the treatment. Therefore, she should be prescribed emergency contraception, like any other patient. Emergency contraception can be given up to 72 hours after unprotected sex. Thought must be given to ongoing contraception to avoid further incidents.

→ https://www.nhs.uk/live-well/sexual-health/confidentiality-at-sexual-health-services/

4. B ★   OHCS 11th edn → p. 132

Hyphae indicate the presence of *Candida* or 'thrush'. Antibiotics are not an appropriate treatment for a fungal infection. Clotrimazole is an antifungal topical treatment.

5. A ★   OHCS 11th edn → pp. 154–6

Most people remember that there is some interaction between the combined oral contraceptive pill and antibiotics. In truth, the evidence is slight, but the official advice to women taking the combined oral contraceptive pill is to use additional contraceptive methods for the duration of the course and for 7 oral contraceptive pill-taking days afterwards (i.e. the pill-free week does not 'count', so if a pill-free week is coming up, the woman might want to run two packets together). However, this rule does not apply to progestogen-only contraceptive pills, such as Cerazette®, and the woman should continue to take this continuously at the same time every day.

→ https://www.nhs.uk/conditions/contraception/combined-contraceptive-pill/

6. B ★   OHCS 11th edn → p. 133

Amoxicillin, clindamycin, and metronidazole are ineffective against *Chlamydia*, and doxycycline is contraindicated in pregnancy.

→ https://www.nhs.uk/conditions/chlamydia/treatment/

7. C ★   OHCS 11th edn → pp. 158–9

Detrusor contraction is activated via muscarinic cholinergic receptors, and oxybutynin is a direct anti-muscarinic agent. Serotonin and nor-adrenaline (norepinephrine) are important for sympathetic activation, which reduces detrusor activity intrinsically. There are no nicotinic or GABAergic receptors in the bladder.

8. A ★

E. coli is by far the commonest cause of sporadic or catheter-related urinary tract infection. *Pseudomonas* species are usually only associated with pro-longed catheterization, and *S. epidermidis* is usually a contaminant.

9. B ★   OHCS 11th edn → p. 132

This is a description of bacterial vaginosis, which is caused by an altered vaginal flora and overgrowth of a number of different microorganisms, which may show up on Gram staining.

10. B ★   OHCS 11th edn → p. 149

The doctor has to judge whether the girl is Gillick-competent, and if she is, she can consent to treatment herself. However, if she is thought to be the victim of any kind of abuse and/or coercion, safeguarding her trumps her right of confidentiality, and the doctor has a duty of care to at least seek advice—for example, from the local named doctor for safeguarding children. The General Medical Council (GMC) gives guidance on this, which should be read.

→ https://www.gmc-uk.org/ethical-guidance/ethical-guidance-for-doctors/0-18-years/principles-of-confidentiality

11. B ★   OHCS 11th edn → pp. 164–5

All of these are protective against cervical changes. HPV vaccination has now been introduced into the UK and will help to prevent changes from occurring. However, in this case, in which the changes are already pre-sent, it will not be effective. The evidence shows that smoking is the most important risk factor in women who show mild change.

→ https://www.nhs.uk/conditions/cervical-cancer/causes/

12. C ★   OHCS 11th edn → p. 151

Combined oral contraceptive pills are no longer used for post-coital contraception. There is no efficacy advantage, and they have more side effects than Levonelle® (a progestogen-only pill). Levonelle® may be an option. However, it does not offer the additional benefit of an ongoing method of contraception, and there is also a recognized failure rate. An IUD is always the most effective form of post-coital contraception for anyone, but in this case, it has the added advantage of providing ongoing contraception. Mirena® coils are not used for post-coital contraception.

→ https://www.nhs.uk/conditions/contraception/emergency-contraception/

13. A ★

Chlamydia is the commonest sexually transmitted infection in the UK. Around 50% of men have no symptoms, but those who do may have dysuria, epididymo-orchitis, clear penile discharge, and low-grade fever.

→ https://www.nhs.uk/conditions/chlamydia/symptoms/

14. D ★

P. jirovecii (previously known as *Pneumocystis carinii*) can cause severe pneumonia (*P. carinii* pneumonia or PCP) in immunocompromised individuals. The risk increases when the CD4+ count falls below 200×10^6/L, especially if the viral load is detectable. Therefore, measures are taken to try to prevent this with antibiotic prophylaxis. It has been standard practice for many years to offer HIV patients with a CD4+ count of $<200 \times 10^6$/L primary prophylaxis against *Pneumocystis*. Without prophylactic therapy, *Pneumocystis* is the single most likely serious or life-threatening opportunistic infection they will develop. Patients can develop *C. neoformans* infection, but it is much less common and primary prophylaxis is not given, although secondary prophylaxis would be continued in those who do develop it until their CD4+ count rises in response to therapy. *M. avium intracellulare* is unlikely to be a problem with a CD4+ count of >100/μL and primary prophylaxis is not routinely given. *M. tuberculosis* can, of course, affect any patient, regardless of the CD4+ count, but primary prophylaxis is not given. *T. gondii* is unlikely to be a problem with a CD4+ count of >50/μL, so primary prophylaxis would not be given in this case.

15. B ★   OHCS 11th edn → pp. 162–3

Genital herpes causes multiple painful sores on the vulva and may also cause lymphadenopathy and flu-like symptoms. It is the only common cause of genital ulceration in this age group. Behçet's syndrome can cause genital ulceration but is rare. Lichen sclerosus causes white, atrophic-looking areas and usually occurs in older women. Syphilitic chancres are usually single and ulcerated.

→ https://www.nhs.uk/conditions/genital-herpes/

16. B ★★   OHCS 11th edn → pp. 162–3

This is herpes simplex virus infection, so antiviral treatment is required.

17. B ★★

General principles of consent mean that the patient is the only person capable of giving consent for any investigation or treatment. If the medical information may guide his treatment (e.g. determining which drugs to start), investigations can be performed when he is unable to give consent. This would be acting in the patient's best interests. However, this is rarely straightforward and the General Medical Council (GMC) guidance on consent should be read. Universal precautions mean that full infection control precautions should be taken for *all* patients, regardless of whether they are known to be HIV-positive or not.

→ https://www.gmc-uk.org/ethical-guidance/ethical-guidance-for-doctors/consent/part-3-capacity-issues#paragraph-75

18. A ★★   OHCS 11th edn → p. 173

Adenomata, by definition, are derived from the ovarian glandular epithelium. They can produce serous or mucinous cystadenomas.

19. C ★★   OHCS 11th edn → p. 116

A reversed LH:FSH ratio of around 3:1 and numerous small peripheral follicles in the ovaries are characteristic of polycystic ovary syndrome (PCOS). This is sometimes seen, but the most sensitive biochemical test for PCOS is a high free androgen index (testosterone:sex hormone-binding globulin ratio). The symptoms of this include reduced periods, reduced fertility, hirsutism, acne, and weight gain.

20. C ★★

This patient has detectable HBcAb. The only way that an individual can develop core antibody is in response to HBV infection. There is no core antigen in the vaccine. However, the patient is HBsAg-negative and HBeAg-negative, so he is not a chronic virus carrier. Unfortunately, he has not developed any HBsAb, which is the antibody that confers protective immunity (and what the vaccine aims to produce). There is some controversy as to whether vaccinating patients with a blunted response to previous HBV infection achieves anything (if the infection did not result in immunity, the vaccine is unlikely to do any better). However, there is no evidence base for it.

21. C ★★   OHCS 11th edn → p. 114

Mefenamic acid is effective for the management of period pain and can be taken around the time of the period only. Tranexamic acid has some pain-relieving properties but is more effective for the treatment of heavy periods. An intrauterine system (IUS) would be one option, but as the patient is not sexually active, this would not be the first-line management. The progesterone-only pill may well lighten periods but does not necessarily relieve the pain. Gonadotrophin-releasing hormone analogues have no role.

22. C ★★   OHCS 11th edn → pp. 126–7

This is a pregnancy of unknown location. The β-HCG level is only slightly lower than 1000 mIU/mL, and we need to know what is happening with the trophoblastic activity. The woman is clinically well and not shocked, so urgent treatment is not needed. β-HCG levels normally double over 48 hours, so a repeat test will help to decide if this is likely to be a normal pregnancy, a possible ectopic pregnancy, or a failing one.

23. D ★★

If the donor in a needle-stick injury is at high risk of blood-borne viruses, PEP should be started straightaway until confirmatory testing can be done. Delays reduce the effectiveness. Many antiretroviral drugs are safe in pregnancy. Indeed, pregnant HIV-positive women are advised to take antiretroviral drugs to reduce the risk of HIV transmission to the fetus.

→ http://www.patient.info/doctor/hiv-post-exposure-prophylaxis

→ https://www.who.int/occupational_health/activities/5pepguid.pdf

24. A ★★

There are four stages of syphilis:

• primary: characterized by painless ulcers, called chancres, at the site of infection. They may not be noticed. Chancres occur about 3 weeks after infection
• secondary: occurs 2–10 weeks after the chancres appear. Symptoms include a rash, mouth ulcers, lymphadenopathy, fever, and myalgia
• latent: occurs months to years after the initial infection if it goes untreated and it is usually asymptomatic, but the infection remains in the body
• tertiary: occurs years after the initial infection in a minority of people and can affect almost any part of the body.

Testing for syphilis can be complex because of the different stages. However, in an individual who is asymptomatic but has positive serological tests, this implies that the infection is latent. If the patient is known to have acquired the infection within the last 2 years, it is early latent. In this case, we can be completely confident that the infection is less than 2 years old, because we are told that the syphilis serology was negative 18 months ago.

25. D ★★   OHCS 11th edn → pp. 126–7

The commonest cause of arrest and death in early pregnancy is hypo-volaemia due to a ruptured ectopic pregnancy, and it is the first consideration in a collapsed patient in early pregnancy. Heavy vaginal bleeding rarely presents in an arrest, as help tends to be sought early for visible bleeding. The risk of a pulmonary embolus is raised throughout pregnancy, but the most severe morbidity and mortality occur in later trimesters or postpartum, and both sepsis due to termination and pre-existing cardiac conditions are fortunately rare.

→ https://www.npeu.ox.ac.uk/mbrrace-uk/reports/confidential-enquiry-into-maternal-deaths

26. A ★★★ OHCS 11th edn → p. 172

A patient with marked tenderness should not be allowed home. The history, examination, and ultrasound scan findings are highly suggestive and commensurate with a haemorrhagic cyst accident, which should be managed conservatively. The absence of vomiting, peritonism, and pyrexia makes torsion and appendicitis unlikely, and there is no need to refer the patient to the surgeons at this stage, as the diagnosis is basically straightforward. Therefore, no further imaging is required at this stage.

27. A ★★★ OHCS 11th edn → p. 130

This is likely to be lichen sclerosus et atrophicus, a poorly understood inflammatory condition. It responds well to potent corticosteroid ointment, and a biopsy is indicated if there is no response to treatment or if an actual suspicious lesion, such as an ulcer, is present. Oestrogen cream is only effective for pure atrophy, and the likelihood of a sexually transmitted infection in a 70-year old is very small. Excision is reserved for neoplastic conditions.

→ https://patient.info/womens-health/vulval-problems-leaflet/lichen-sclerosus

28. D ★★★ OHCS 11th edn → p. 140

All of the medical treatments listed are effective for pain, although there is increasing evidence that surgery gives the best results overall. Endometriomata tend to respond poorly to medical treatment and usually require excision. Only surgical treatment has been demonstrated to improve subsequent fertility which is relevant to this case.

→ https://www.nice.org.uk/guidance/ng73/chapter/Recommendations#surgical-management

29. C ★★★ OHCS 11th edn → pp. 174–5

Primary pelvic clearance and tumour debulking are the mainstays of ovarian cancer treatment initially. Neoadjuvant chemotherapy is a reasonable option in some women but involves the use of carboplatin and paclitaxel, not vincristine. Hormonal treatment and radiotherapy have little or no place in ovarian cancer treatment, and palliative care is for women with terminal disease who have not responded to surgery and chemotherapy.

→ https://www.nice.org.uk/guidance/cg122/chapter/1-Guidance#management-of-suspected-early-stage-i-ovarian-cancer

Paediatrics

Luci Etheridge

Children are not merely small adults. To be a good paediatrician requires as much knowledge about health as about disease. The normal patterns of growth and development can be a mystery to many, and paediatricians are often called upon to help to interpret these for confused parents. There is a unique need to be aware of the range of congenital disorders that may present before, at, or shortly after birth. Younger children cannot tell us their symptoms. Therefore, paediatricians have to learn to pick up on non-verbal clues and often subtle signs, when the answer may lie in something unexpected and far removed from the traditional history and examination format. At the other end of the spectrum, adolescents have their own range of health issues and are traditionally an under-represented and often forgotten group. In this chapter, we aim to cover many of the key presentations and issues in children of all ages, from neonates to teenagers.

Even in this modern age, children are susceptible to infection. Respiratory and gastrointestinal infections are the commonest presentations in both general practice and paediatric hospital practice. Fortunately, most of these infections are self-limiting, but serious infections do occur and must be recognized. However, the leading cause of death in all children over 1 year of age is accidents. Recognizing risk factors for accidental and non-accidental harm is a major responsibility for all those working with children.

The questions in this chapter will test not only the common areas that present to paediatricians, but also relevant issues such as knowledge of disease factors, ethics, and risk management in relation to children and their families. However, the best way to learn about children is to get out there and meet them—play with them, talk to their parents and carers, and see them when they are ill and well. You will learn the most this way and be able to apply that knowledge and experience to answer questions such as these.

Luci Etheridge, *Paediatrics* In: *Oxford Assess and Progress: Clinical Specialties.*
Edited by: Luci Etheridge and Henry Collier, Oxford University Press.
© Oxford University Press 2021. DOI:10.1093/oso/9780198862550.003.0003

QUESTIONS

1. A 1-day-old girl has a harsh systolic cardiac murmur all over the precordium, with a thrill at the left sternal edge. Femoral pulses are palpable. A chest X-ray shows an enlarged heart, and an electrocardiogram (ECG) shows left ventricular hypertrophy. Which is the single most likely diagnosis? ★

A Aortic stenosis

B Coarctation of the aorta

C Patent ductus arteriosus

D Pulmonary stenosis

E Ventricular septal defect

2. A 4-month-old boy is due to have his routine immunization. After the last set of immunizations, he had a 2-cm red area on his thigh around the injection site and seemed irritable for several hours. He has had a runny nose for the last 2 days, but no fever. His mother asks whether it is all right to proceed with his immunizations. Which is the single most appropriate piece of advice to give? ★

A Postpone immunization until his runny nose has settled

B Immunize him in hospital

C Omit pertussis, but proceed with the other immunizations

D Omit this set of immunizations

E Reassure the mother and proceed with the planned immunizations now

3. A 7-year-old girl is drowsy and panting, and has a capillary blood glucose level of 25 mmol/L and ketones and protein in her urine. Initial blood results show:

- sodium 145 mmol/L
- potassium 3.8 mmol/L
- creatinine 100 μmol/L
- urea 12 mmol/L
- calcium 2.6 mmol/L
- glucose 26 mmol/L.

She is given two fluid boluses of 10 mL/kg 0.9% saline and is then started on a 0.9% saline infusion to deliver a total of maintenance plus 10% over 48 hours. Intravenous (IV) insulin is also started. Two hours later, she has improved, has passed urine, and is more alert. Her blood results show:

- sodium 143 mmol/L
- potassium 3.8 mmol/L
- creatinine 82 μmol/L
- urea 10 mmol/L
- calcium 2.2 mmol/L
- glucose 20 mmol/L.

Which single fluid should she now be given IV? ★

A 0.45% saline and 5% dextrose

B 0.45% saline and 5% dextrose with added calcium

C 0.45% saline and 5% dextrose with added potassium

D 0.9% saline

E 0.9% saline with added potassium

4. A 5-year-old girl had been passing hard stools once every 5 to 7 days for 6 months. She was started on two Movicol® Paediatric sachets daily. She continued this treatment for 1 month and started passing a stool every day, so her parents stopped it. For the last month, she has been soiling her pants, with intermittent runny stools. She opens her bowels on the toilet most days and passes pellet-like stools and an occasional large, hard stool. Which is the single main deficiency in her management so far? ★

A Colonoscopy should have been performed

B Glycerol suppositories should have been added

C Movicol® should have been continued for several more months

D She should have had an enema when she was first seen

E Stimulant laxatives should have been used

5. A 7-year-old boy wets the bed most nights and has never been reliably dry. He is a heavy sleeper. He has kept a star chart for 4 weeks and his parents have been supportive. His chart shows one dry night each week, with no particular pattern. He has a cub camp in 4 months' time. Urinalysis is negative. Which is the single most appropriate management? ★

A Star chart

B Enuresis alarm

C Desmopressin melts at night

D Imipramine tablets at night

E Oxybutynin tablets at night

6. A 1-year-old boy has had diarrhoea for the past 12 hours. At the beginning of the illness, he vomited twice. He has not passed urine for the past 6 hours. He is thirsty and restless, and his eyes are sunken; the mucous membranes are dry, and skin turgor has decreased. His pulse rate is 160 bpm, and his capillary refill time is 2 seconds. Which is the single best description of his degree of dehydration and the appropriate initial fluid to give? ★

A Mild; oral rehydration solution

B Mild; 0.9% saline intravenously (IV)

C Moderate; oral rehydration solution

D Moderate; 0.9% saline IV

E Severe; 0.9% saline IV

7. A 20-hour-old term newborn boy has a short soft early systolic murmur on his baby check. He is pink, with no signs of respiratory distress, and has normally palpable femoral pulses and a normal apex beat. The murmur is heard at the upper left sternal edge and radiates through the chest. There are no associated heaves or thrills. Which is the single most likely diagnosis? ★

A Atrial septal defect

B Innocent heart murmur

C Patent ductus arteriosus

D Pulmonary stenosis

E Ventricular septal defect

8. A 12-year-old girl, who recently arrived in the United Kingdom from South Asia, has had pain and swelling of both knees, ankles, and wrists for 5 days, and these symptoms come and go. Five weeks ago, she had a cold and a sore throat. For the last day, she has had a rash on her trunk, which has a pink border and is fading centrally. Both knees have an effusion and limited flexion to 70 degrees. The girl's temperature is 39.2°C and her pulse rate is 160 bpm. Which single organism is likely to be responsible for this illness? ★

A *Corynebacterium diphtheriae*

B Human cytomegalovirus

C Epstein–Barr virus

D Group A β-haemolytic *Streptococcus*

E *Staphylococcus aureus*

9. A 6-year-old boy has had vomiting for 24 hours and has been unable to keep any liquids down, although he has not wanted to eat any food. Today he has central abdominal pain, which was coming and going but is now constant and sharp. He has pain when he tries to pass urine and gets very upset if he is moved. He has opened his bowels once today and passed a loose stool. Which is the single most likely diagnosis? ★

A Appendicitis

B Gastro-oesophageal reflux

C Mesenteric adenitis

D Viral gastroenteritis

E Volvulus

10. A 39-week-gestation baby girl, who weighs 3.4 kg, is due for her baby check. She is lying supine. The examiner's left hand is stabilizing the pelvis and his right hand is grasping the left leg, flexed at the hip and knee, with his thumb over the lesser trochanter and the tip of his middle finger over the greater trochanter. He wants first to check whether the right hip is dislocatable with Barlow's manoeuvre. Which is the single most accurate description of how the examination should be performed? ★

A Adduct the leg to the midline and apply gentle anterior pressure over the greater trochanter

B Adduct the leg to the midline and apply gentle posterior pressure over the lesser trochanter

C Fully abduct the leg and apply gentle posterior pressure over the lesser trochanter

D Fully abduct the leg and apply gentle anterior pressure over the greater trochanter

E Partially abduct the leg and apply gentle anterior pressure over the greater trochanter

11. A 24-month-old girl enjoys 'feeding' her dolls. She does not like taking turns. She is able to walk upstairs with help but is unable to stand on one leg. She is able to scribble but is unable to draw a circle. She can say 'mama' and 'dada' with meaning, but no other recognizable words. In which single developmental area is she showing delay? ★

A Fine motor skills

B Gross motor skills

C Social skills

D Speech and language skills

E Play skills

12. A 14-year-old girl has chronic kidney disease. Her nephrologist advises that dialysis is the only option while she is awaiting renal transplant. She refuses to have dialysis and appears to understand the consequence of not having treatment. She was in and out of local authority care between the ages of 1 and 6 years but has been living with her parents for the last 8 years. Her mother, who has sole parental responsibility, wants her to have dialysis, but her father feels that she should decide for herself. The family have been through extensive counselling with the team but have not been able to reach a consensus. Which single decision takes precedence when deciding further management? ★

A That of the father

B That of the local authority

C That of the mother

D That of the nephrologist

E That of the patient

13. A 2-month-old boy has faltering growth. He is a sweaty baby, particularly during breastfeeding. He has a palpable 4-cm liver edge. He is pale and has a respiratory rate of 60 breaths/minute, a heart rate of 180 bpm, and a blood pressure of 80/40 mmHg, and his oxygen saturation is 96% in air. His capillary refill time is 3 seconds, and his capillary blood glucose concentration is 5 mmol/L. Which single system of the body is most likely to be affected? ★

A Cardiovascular system

B Gastrointestinal system

C Metabolic system

D Neurological system

E Respiratory system

14. A 37-week-gestation baby who weighed 2.7 kg at birth is now 4 days old. He is being breastfed. During the first 24 hours of life, he did not latch on to the breast well and fed for approximately 5 minutes at a time every 4 to 5 hours. He is now feeding for 15–20 minutes every 2 to 3 hours. His weight today is 2.55 kg. His mother is worried about his weight loss. Which is the single most appropriate advice to give her? ★

A Any weight loss in the first week is worrying, and he should have supplementary feeds

B He has lost less than 10% of his birthweight, which is acceptable in the first week, and she should continue breastfeeding

C He has lost less than 10% of his birthweight, which is acceptable in the first week, but he should have supplementary feeds until he gains weight

D He has lost more than 10% of his birthweight, which is acceptable in the first week, and she should continue breastfeeding

E He has lost more than 10% of his birthweight, which is more than is normal in the first week, so he should have supplementary feeds

15. A 14-year-old Caucasian boy has had raised temperatures with drenching night sweats and malaise for 8 weeks. He has lost 4 kg in weight. He had a ventricular septal defect repaired in infancy. He looks pale, has extensive dental decay, and has small, linear areas of bleeding under his nail beds. He has a three-finger-breadth splenomegaly and a grade 2 systolic murmur, heard best on the lower left sternal edge. His temperature is 38°C. Which is the single most appropriate treatment? ★

A Antibiotics

B Chemotherapy

C Diuretics

D High-dose steroids

E Surgery

16. An 18-month-old girl from a black Caribbean background is not yet walking. She was breastfed for 9 months and is thriving along the 25th centile for weight. She has bow legs, Harrison's sulci, and swollen wrists. Which single vitamin deficiency is she most likely to have? ★

A Vitamin A

B Vitamin B_{12}

C Vitamin C

D Vitamin D

E Vitamin E

17. A mother brings her 7-month-old boy to the Emergency Department. She says he is always 'on the go', and that morning he fell out of his cot onto the laminate flooring, from a height of approximately 3 feet. He is now not moving his right leg. He has a spiral fracture of the right femur on X-ray. Which single part of the history will help most in deciding further management? ★

A Birth history

B Family medical history

C Developmental history

D Social history

E Systems review questioning

18. A 4-year-old boy from a white British background has poorly controlled asthma, despite being on a high-dose steroid inhaler and a leukotriene receptor antagonist and compliant with his medication. He has recurrent chest infections and has significant nasal discharge. He also has poor growth, Harrison's sulci, and finger clubbing. Which is the single most appropriate next investigation? ★

A Bronchial brush biopsy

B Bronchoalveolar lavage

C Computed tomography (CT) scan of the chest

D Lung function tests

E Sweat test

19. A 4-year-old boy has periorbital oedema, central abdominal discomfort, and decreased urine output. His urine dipstick shows 3+ proteinuria and no blood. He is asthmatic and recently had a bad 'cold'. Which is the single most likely diagnosis? ★

A Angio-oedema

B Nephrotic syndrome

C Post-streptococcal glomerulonephritis

D Postural proteinuria

E Systemic lupus erythematosus (SLE)

20. A 7-year-old boy with asthma has had a 'cold' and a temperature of 37.7°C for 24 hours. He has severe respiratory distress and requires 15 L/minute of oxygen to maintain his oxygen saturation above 95%. He is started on nebulized salbutamol therapy, which causes an initial improvement in his symptoms. He then suddenly deteriorates, with marked respiratory distress, hypoxia, and hypotension. Which is the single most likely diagnosis? ★

A Anaphylaxis

B Pleural effusion

C Pneumonia

D Pulmonary embolus

E Tension pneumothorax

21. A 6-year-old girl has had vomiting and central abdominal pain for 3 days. She has eczema and poorly controlled asthma. She looks pale and has a Glasgow Coma Scale score of 11/15. Her abdomen is generally tender, but there is no rigidity, rebound, or guarding. Bowel sounds are present and normal. Her respiratory rate is 36 breaths/minute, with no recession. Her heart rate is 160 bpm and her capillary refill time is 4 seconds. She is given a 20 mL/kg bolus of fluid. Blood tests show:

- haemoglobin 13 g/dL
- white cell count 22 × 10^9/L
- C-reactive protein 25 mg/L
- sodium 120 mmol/L
- potassium 6.8 mmol/L
- urea 9.3 mmol/L
- creatinine 110 μmol/L.

Which is the single most important next investigation? ★

A Abdominal ultrasound scan

B Blood glucose

C Computed tomography (CT) scan of the head

D Serum ammonia

E Urine osmolality

22. A 3-year-old boy is in acute respiratory distress. There is no past history of note, except that he has not been immunized. He has a temperature of 40°C, looks flushed and unwell, is drooling, and has an inspiratory stridor. His cough is muffled. A colleague asks for help examining the boy's throat. Which is the single most appropriate advice to give? ★

A Do not disturb the child, and call for senior help urgently

B Give nebulized budesonide, and then examine the throat

C Go ahead and examine the throat, but have a laryngoscope and an endotracheal tube to hand

D Go ahead and examine the throat straightaway to help to make a diagnosis

E Site an intravenous line and give a dose of cefotaxime first, and then examine the throat

23. A 9-month-old boy has had a generalized seizure, which lasted for 5 minutes, during which he stared straight ahead and his arms and legs shook. He had been unwell for 12 hours with fever, a runny nose, and cough. He has never had any fits before, and there is no family history of epilepsy. His development had been appropriate for his age, but in the last 6 weeks he has stopped pulling to stand or cruising round furniture. His temperature is 39°C and he has pharyngitis. A diagnosis of febrile convulsion is made. Which single feature in the history is least consistent with a diagnosis of febrile convulsion? ★

A The absence of previous febrile fits

B The age of the child

C The description of the seizure

D The developmental history

E The duration of the seizure

24. A 3-month-old baby girl has dry skin on her scalp, as shown in Figure 3.1 (see Colour Plate section). It has been present for the past 5 weeks and is getting progressively worse. Which is the single most likely diagnosis? ★

A Atopic eczema

B Impetigo

C Psoriasis

D Seborrhoeic dermatitis

E Tinea capitis

25. A 2.8-kg, 37-week-gestation baby girl has been treated briefly with phototherapy for jaundice. She is now 7 days old, breast-feeding well, and starting to regain weight. She has been off photo-therapy for over 48 hours, and her bilirubin chart is shown in Figure 3.2 (see Colour Plate section). Her mother has heard someone mention that her baby has 'breast milk jaundice' and wants to know how she should continue to feed her baby. Which is the single most appropriate advice to give the mother? ★★

A She should continue to breastfeed, but also give some extra formula feeds to ensure a good milk intake to help to reduce the jaundice

B She should continue to breastfeed exclusively, as this is still the best milk for her baby, regardless of the jaundice, which is already improving

C She should give mainly formula milk for the next 3 weeks, with the occasional breastfeed to ensure an ongoing breast milk supply

D She should stop breastfeeding completely and change to a term formula to prevent the jaundice from worsening again

E She should stop breastfeeding for 48 hours to allow the jaundice level to fall further, and then restart

26. A 20-month-old boy of South Asian background has bow legs. He was breastfed until the age of 6 months. The family live in a sixth-floor, two-bedroom flat, and his mother wears the hijab. He has mild genu varum bilaterally. His wrist X-ray is shown in Figure 3.3 (see Colour Plate section). Which single area of the X-ray shows the bony abnormalities that indicate the likely diagnosis? ★★

A Carpal bones

B Diaphyses of long bones

C Epiphyses of long bones

D Metacarpal bones

E Metaphyses of long bones

27. A 7-year-old girl has had general malaise and pallor for the past 3 days. She is passing small amounts of urine infrequently. She was unwell the previous week with bloody diarrhoea, but this has now settled. Blood results show:

- haemoglobin 8.2 g/dL
- platelets 400 × 10^9/L
- white cell count 10.4 × 10^9/L
- sodium 135 mmol/L
- potassium 4.2 mmol/L
- urea 22 mmol/L
- creatinine 230 μmol/L
- C-reactive protein 11 mg/L.

Which single organism is the most likely cause of her illness? ★★

A *Clostridium difficile*

B *Escherichia coli*

C *Salmonella typhi*

D *Shigella sonnei*

E *Streptococcus pneumoniae*

28. An 8-year-old boy has had headaches for 12 months. They are usually left-sided and throbbing and are made worse by noise and light. They last for around 12 hours, during which time he is nauseated but does not vomit. There are no obvious triggers. Treatment with paracetamol during attacks is of some benefit. He has one bad attack every 3 weeks on average, missing 1 to 2 days of school each time. Which is the single most appropriate next step in management? ★★

A Anti-emetic during attacks

B Computed tomography (CT) scan of the head

C Oral propranolol

D Psychology referral

E Sumatriptan nasal spray

29. A 15-year-old boy is worried that he is shorter than all his friends and that he has not yet started puberty. He is otherwise well. His father started puberty at around the age of 14 years. The boy's parental heights are both on the 25th centile. His growth chart is shown in Figure 3.4 (see Colour Plate section). Which single aspect of his growth and pubertal development will be most likely to assist with diagnosis? ★★

A Axillary hair stage

B Height centile

C Height velocity centile

D Pubic hair stage

E Testicular size

30. A 5-year-old boy returned from visiting relatives in Bangladesh a week ago. He has had a temperature of 39°C, lower abdominal pain, and loose stool for 5 days. Blood tests show:

- haemoglobin 10.6 g/dL
- white cell count 17 × 10⁹/L
- lymphocyte count 13 × 10⁹/L
- platelet count 400 × 10⁹/L
- Gram-negative bacilli on blood culture.

Which is the single most likely diagnosis? ★★

A Dengue fever

B Leishmaniasis

C Leptospirosis

D Malaria

E Typhoid

31. A 4-month-old baby girl has had a temperature of 38°C for 2 days and is consuming less than half of her usual amount during feeding. She has had an irritable cry and has been very unsettled for the last 24 hours. She has had three loose stools and two vomiting episodes in the last 12 hours. A lumbar puncture is performed which shows:

- clear, colourless cerebrospinal fluid (CSF)
- glucose 2.9 mmol/L (blood glucose 5.4 mmol/L)
- protein 32 mg/dL
- white cell count 60/mm³ (90% mononuclear cells)
- red cell count 10/mm³
- Gram-negative staining.

Intravenous (IV) access is established and she is started on IV ceftriaxone. Which is the single most appropriate medication to add? ★★

A IV aciclovir

B IV metronidazole

C Oral dexamethasone

D Oral isoniazid

E Oral rifampicin

32. A 25-week-gestation infant has just been delivered by spontaneous vaginal delivery. The full neonatal resuscitation team is present and the Resuscitaire® has been pre-warmed. The baby is handed to the team and they have started the clock. Which is the single most important action to take next? ★★★

A Assess the baby's initial Apgar score

B Dry the baby thoroughly and check the heart rate

C Intubate immediately and start ventilation breaths

D Put a hat on the baby's head and a plastic bag over his body

E Suction the mouth under direct vision using a laryngoscope

33. A 14-year-old girl has an osteosarcoma of her tibia. She has worsening pain in her leg. She is on regular oral paracetamol and ibuprofen. Which is the single most appropriate next treatment? ★★★

A Codeine phosphate

B Diazepam

C Diclofenac

D Hyoscine bromide

E Morphine sulfate

34. A newborn baby boy has a urethral meatus that emerges on the dorsum of the penis, as shown in Figure 3.5 (see Colour Plate section). He is able to pass a good stream of urine. Which single piece of advice should be given to his parents before discharge? ★ ★ ★

A He should not be circumcised

B He should not wear disposable nappies

C The foreskin should be retracted gently every day

D The penis should be cleaned with mild soapy water daily

E This is entirely normal and no further measures are needed

35. A 4-year-old boy was accidentally given intravenous (IV) cefuroxime 30 minutes ago, which was prescribed on the wrong drug chart. He has no relevant allergies and does not seem to have suffered any ill effects. The antibiotic has been crossed off his chart. His parents have now returned to the ward after being at home. Which is the single most appropriate course of action? ★ ★ ★

A Discuss the error at handover later in the day and write a reflective portfolio entry

B Do nothing further until the error has been discussed with a medical defence organization

C Explain the error and apologize to the parents and notify a senior colleague promptly

D Notify a senior colleague with a view to explaining the error to the parents later in the day

E Shred the incorrect prescription chart and write a new one

36. A 4-month-old girl has been irritable, with a temperature of 38°C for 2 days. She is diagnosed with a coliform urinary tract infection (UTI). Blood and cerebrospinal fluid cultures are negative. She responds to oral antibiotics and is afebrile after 24 hours. Which single set of investigations should be performed (Table 3.1)? ★ ★ ★

Table 3.1 Investigation options

	Ultrasound of kidneys, ureters, and bladder	Dimercaptosuccinic acid (DMSA) renal isotope scan	Micturating cystourethrogram
A	No	No	No
B	Yes	No	No
C	Yes	Yes	No
D	Yes	No	Yes
E	Yes	Yes	Yes

37. A 14-year-old girl of Pakistani ethnic background has had polyuria and polydipsia for 4 months. She has a body mass index of 28 kg/m² and dark, velvety pigmentation of the skin in her axillae. She has a random serum glucose concentration of 12 mmol/L and no blood ketones. Which is the single most likely diagnosis? ★★★

A Cushing's syndrome

B Diabetes insipidus

C Simple obesity

D Type 1 diabetes mellitus

E Type 2 diabetes mellitus

38. A 30-week-gestation infant is now 12 hours old. She was in good condition at birth and did not require resuscitation, although she did have some mild subcostal recession and needed 25% incubator oxygen. Over the past few hours, she has developed increasing respiratory distress, with grunting, intercostal and subcostal recession, and an increasing oxygen requirement to 45%. Her blood gas analysis shows a respiratory acidosis, and her chest X-ray has a homogeneous ground-glass appearance with air bronchograms. She has just been intubated. Which is the single most appropriate medication to give immediately? ★★★

A Amoxicillin intravenously (IV)

B Dexamethasone IV

C Gentamicin IV

D Morphine infusion IV

E Surfactant via an endotracheal tube

39. A 6-year-old boy is 'always on the go' and finds it difficult to take turns. He is easily distracted and finds it difficult to focus on any task. His father says that he has no sense of danger and often runs across the main road without any care. He has difficulty following a series of simple instructions and is 1 year behind his peers in his numeracy and literacy skills. Which is the single most likely diagnosis? ★★★

A Attention-deficit/hyperactivity disorder (ADHD)

B Autistic spectrum disorder

C Dyspraxia

D Global developmental delay

E Oppositional defiant disorder

40. A 38-week-gestation, 3.1-kg baby is delivered by spontaneous vaginal delivery. The pregnancy has been complicated by polyhydramnios. At birth, there are copious oral secretions and respiratory distress. The baby requires intubation and ventilation for respiratory distress and continues to drool. It is not possible to pass a nasogastric tube to the estimated length required, and no acid reaction is obtained. Chest X-ray shows the nasogastric tube coiled in the oesophagus, a moderately large stomach bubble, and a normal gas pattern in the bowel. Which is the single most likely diagnosis? ★ ★ ★ ★

A H-type tracheo-oesophageal fistula

B Isolated oesophageal atresia

C Oesophageal atresia and tracheo-oesophageal fistula

D Oesophageal stenosis

E Oesophageal stricture

41. An 8-year-old boy had a throat infection and was given penicillin 2 days ago. He now has a peeling red rash on his trunk and sore red eyes, and has developed lesions on his mouth, shown in Figure 3.6 (see Colour Plate section). He looks unwell and has a temperature of 39°C and a heart rate of 175 bpm. Which is the single most likely diagnosis? ★ ★ ★ ★

A Bullous impetigo

B Chickenpox

C Hand, foot, and mouth disease

D Measles

E Stevens–Johnson syndrome

42. A 9-week-old girl has had brief seizures for the last day, during which she stares straight ahead, her body shakes for a few seconds, and her right hand twitches. Pregnancy was normal, but delivery was difficult due to shoulder dystocia. Her Apgar scores were 7 at 1 minute and 9 at 5 minutes. She has some pale areas of skin over her right thigh. She is afebrile. Urea and electrolytes, calcium, magnesium, and glucose are all normal. Lumbar puncture is bloodstained, with a protein concentration of 0.97 g/L (normal range is up to 0.4 g/L). Her electro-encephalogram (EEG) is normal. Her magnetic resonance imaging (MRI) brain scan is shown in Figure 3.7 (see Colour Plate section). Which is the single most likely diagnosis? ★ ★ ★ ★

A Benign neonatal seizures

B Hypoxic–ischaemic birth injury

C Infantile spasms

D Subdural haematoma

E Tuberous sclerosis

43. Five boys attend the same nursery. They are all aged 2 years 0 months and, by chance, they all have the same weight of 12.5 kg (50th centile). Their parents compare their birthweights and gestations, which are listed in Table 3.2. Which single child is most at risk of later obesity? ★★★★

Table 3.2 Birthweights and gestations

	Birthweight (centile)	Gestation (weeks)
A	1.5 kg (<0.4th)	40
B	1.5 kg (50th)	30
C	2.0 kg (98th)	30
D	3.5 kg (50th)	40
E	5.0 kg (99.6th)	40

44. A 48-hour-old, 2.8-kg term baby girl has pallor, poor perfusion, cyanosis, and respiratory distress. She was born in good condition and was well for the first few hours of life. She has been intubated and ventilated, but her oxygen saturations remain in the range of 70–80%, despite 100% oxygen and good chest movement. Her femoral pulses are not palpable. Which is the single most appropriate medication to commence next? ★★★★

A Dobutamine

B Dopamine

C Indomethacin

D Prostaglandin E2

E Surfactant

45. A 4-year-old boy has had generalized oedema for 2 days and has 3+ proteinuria on dipstick testing of his urine. His blood pressure is 73/36 mmHg. His plasma albumin level is 18 g/L. All other blood tests, including his urea and electrolytes, are normal. He is started on high-dose daily oral prednisolone. Which single likelihood is there that he will respond to the treatment and not have any further relapses? ★★★★

A 3%

B 30%

C 50%

D 70%

E 90%

ANSWERS

1. E ★ OHCS 11th edn → p. 239

Heart murmurs are heard in many neonates. It is important to know the characteristics that signify congenital heart disease. Significant murmurs are usually harsh-sounding and may be associated with thrills. In this case, the systolic murmur indicates a lesion where turbulent flow occurs in systole (i.e. aortic stenosis, pulmonary stenosis, ventricular septal defect, and atrial septal defect). The thrill at the left sternal edge indicates turbulent flow in the area of the septum. A patent ductus has a continuous murmur as blood flows across the ductus in both systole and diastole. Normal femoral pulses argue against a severe aortic stenosis or coarctation.

For an excellent learning resource on congenital heart disease that explains the anatomy of different congenital defects, see:

→ https://www.cardiosmart.org/topics/congenital-heart-disease/

2. E ★ OHCS 11th edn → p. 257

The mild upper respiratory symptoms are not a reason for delaying immunization. The red area and irritability after the previous immunization are normal, and the mother should have been counselled to expect this.

→ http://immunisation.dh.gov.uk/gb-complete-current-edition/ ('The Green Book'; see Chapter 6. This is a key UK resource for immunization.)

3. E ★ OHCS 11th edn → pp. 248–9

This child has diabetic ketoacidosis (DKA). Fluid management has been appropriate so far, but now that she has passed urine, potassium needs to be added to her maintenance fluid; otherwise she will rapidly become hypokalaemic. Her glucose level is falling at a rate of 2.5 mmol/hour, which is about right. It should not be allowed to fall faster than 5 mmol/hour. Once her blood glucose concentration reaches 14–17 mmol/L, you would change her IV fluid to one containing dextrose and potassium. The slight fall in her calcium level is not significant. The British Society for Paediatric Endocrinology and Diabetes has published guidelines on the management of DKA in children:

→ https://www.bsped.org.uk/clinical-resources/guidelines/

4. C ★ OHCS 11th edn → p. 268

A common mistake in the management of constipation is to discontinue the laxative too quickly. It should have been continued for about 6 months to allow time for the distended 'baggy' colon to return to normal, and this needs to be explained to the parents at the outset. This girl's constipation has relapsed, and her soiling is due to overflow. The use of suppositories in young children should be avoided, if at all possible. Movicol® is an osmotic laxative (containing ethylene glycol particles).

→ https://www.nice.org.uk/guidance/cg99

5. B ★   OHCS 11th edn → p. 269

This is primary monosymptomatic nocturnal enuresis, and the boy should do well with an enuresis alarm. He should be followed up every few weeks while using it. He has not made progress after keeping a star chart for 4 weeks, so it is best not to persist with this on its own, but it could be combined with alarm treatment. Desmopressin could be used in the short term if he is not dry by the time of the cub camp. Imipramine is a second-line drug treatment because of the higher incidence of side effects. Oxybutynin would only be appropriate if there were symptoms of detrusor instability (e.g. daytime urgency and frequency). Enuresis is common.

→ http://www.nice.org.uk/guidance/CG111

6. C ★   OHCS 11th edn → p. 218

This child is moderately dehydrated due to gastroenteritis. According to the National Institute for Health and Care Excellence (NICE) traffic light system, he should have an initial trial of oral rehydration therapy (ORT), especially as he is not vomiting. The aim should be for him to drink 50 mL/kg over 4 hours. If he is not managing to drink this amount, change to nasogastric ORT. If he is vomiting, use IV fluid. If he was severely dehydrated, you would initially give 20 mL/kg IV 0.9% saline.

→ http://www.nice.org.uk/CG84

7. B ★   OHCS 11th edn → p. 282

Up to 60% of newborn infants have audible, but benign, heart murmurs in the first 24 hours of life. These are due to the increase in pulmonary blood flow that occurs after birth in association with relatively high pulmonary vascular resistance. As the pulmonary vascular resistance drops, the murmur disappears.

8. D ★

This child has signs of a flitting polyarthritis—that is, arthritis affecting more than four joints that comes and goes. She also has the rash of erythema marginatum. Coupled with the recent history of a sore throat, this fits the criteria for rheumatic fever. Either two major criteria (which both of these fit) or one major and two minor criteria (fever is a minor criterion) are needed. Rheumatic fever is now less common in the UK, possibly due to the use of antibiotics to treat streptococcal throat infections. However, it is still seen in other parts of the world. It is caused by a cross-sensitivity reaction to group A Streptococcus in susceptible individuals.

→ https://www.cdc.gov/groupastrep/diseases-public/rheumatic-fever.html

9. **A** ★   OHCS 11th edn → p. 220

Appendicitis is the commonest cause of acute abdomen and should not be forgotten in children. It is rare in children under 5 years and becomes commoner with increasing age thereafter. The classic presentation is with central, colicky abdominal pain, which then spreads to the right iliac fossa and becomes constant in nature. However, the pain may not always be in a classic position, so other clues need to be looked for. Vomiting is almost universal, together with associated anorexia. Loose stool and dysuria may occur as a result of irritation from the inflamed appendix, so in a child with other symptoms, one should not automatically assume that these are due to simple gastroenteritis or a urinary tract infection.

10. **B** ★   OHCS 11th edn → p. 492

Barlow's test and Ortolani's test are used to check for developmental dysplasia of the hip. Barlow's test should be performed first (Barlow's = Back). Hold the thigh in one hand while stabilizing the pelvis with the other. With the leg in the midline, push back gently. If the hip is dislocatable, the femoral head will pop out of the acetabulum. Then perform Ortolani's test (Ortolani's = Out). Holding the leg in the same way, gently and steadily abduct the leg as far as you can, pushing up gently with your fingers on the greater trochanter. If the hip is dislocated, you will feel the femoral head pop back into the acetabulum, or the hip will simply not abduct fully.

11. **D** ★   OHCS 11th edn → pp. 260–1

It is important to know some of the common developmental milestones for children aged 0–5 years in all four developmental areas. In this case, development is normal, apart from the lack of language.

→ https://gpnotebook.com/simplepage.cfm?ID=-623902671

12. **C** ★   OHCS 11th edn → p. 149

As the law stands, children under the age of 16 years can consent to treatment if they are judged to be Gillick-competent, but they cannot refuse treatment. A person with parental responsibility gives consent on behalf of a child under 16 years of age. As the mother is the only person with parental responsibility, it is she who should decide future treatment. However, in practice, every effort is made to help all of the parties to reach a decision together.

→ https://www.gmc-uk.org/ethical-guidance/ethical-guidance-for-doctors/0-18-years

13. **A** ★   OHCS 11th edn → p. 238

These are symptoms of heart failure—shortness of breath and sweating, which are worse on effort (e.g. during feeding), tachypnoea, tachycardia, and hepatomegaly. This baby is also showing signs of shock. Heart failure often presents in neonates at about 4–6 weeks of age, when the pulmonary vascular resistance falls.

14. B ★ OHCS 11th edn → p. 293

Babies can lose up to 10% of their birthweight in the first week but should have regained their birthweight by 2 weeks of age. This baby has lost 150 g, which is 5.5% of 2.7 kg. Although breastfeeding was slow initially, it is now going well and should be encouraged due to the benefits of exclusive breastfeeding.

15. A ★ OHCS 11th edn → p. 288

Children who have congenital heart lesions are at risk of infective endocarditis. Poor dental hygiene is a risk factor.

→ https://www.nice.org.uk/guidance/cg64/ifp/chapter/infective-endocarditis

16. D ★

These features point to a diagnosis of rickets. This is especially common in children from a black or Asian ethnic background in the UK who are breastfed for a prolonged period. This is because dark-skinned people absorb less sunlight and there is less conversion of 7-dehydrocholesterol to previtamin D3. This results in even lower levels of vitamin D in breast milk.

→ https://patient.info/doctor/vitamin-d-deficiency-including-osteomalacia-and-rickets-pro

17. C ★ OHCS 11th edn → p. 196

The concern here is the possibility of non-accidental injury. When thinking about the mechanism of an injury, it is vital always to take into account the child's developmental stage. In this case, consider whether a 7-month-old child is capable of climbing out of a cot.

★ https://www.nice.org.uk/guidance/cg89

18. E ★ OHCS 11th edn → p. 214

It is important always to reconsider a diagnosis of 'asthma' in children who do not respond to treatment and to consider referral for specialist opinion. In this case, the recurrent infections, nasal discharge, poor growth, and clubbing suggest cystic fibrosis. Defects in the *CFTR* gene involved in cystic fibrosis are more common in white ethnic populations. A sweat test is diagnostic for this and should be done. Lung function and a CT scan of the chest may be performed following diagnosis in order to obtain additional information, but the important step is making the diagnosis.

→ https://patient.info/doctor/cystic-fibrosis-pro

19. B ★ OHCS 11th edn → p. 226

Nephrotic syndrome is a triad of hypoalbuminaemia, proteinuria, and oedema. It often presents with periorbital oedema just after a viral infection, and it is important to dip a urine sample to look for the proteinuria; otherwise it may be dismissed as an allergic reaction, of which angio-oedema may be a variety. The lack of blood in the urine rules out glomerulonephritis, and systemic lupus erythematosus (SLE) is rare. The presence of oedema rules out benign postural proteinuria.

→ https://gpnotebook.com/simplepage.cfm?ID=-1167392767

20. E ★

Tension pneumothorax must always be considered in acutely ill asthmatic patients who deteriorate suddenly.

21. B ★   OHCS 11th edn → pp. 248–9

With any sick child, remember ABCDEFG—Airway, Breathing, Circulation, and Don't Ever Forget Glucose. This girl is shocked and dehydrated, and has altered consciousness and a relative hyponatraemia and hyperkalaemia caused by hyperglycaemia. The diagnosis is diabetic ketoacidosis, and a capillary blood glucose test will confirm this.

22. A ★   OHCS 11th edn → p. 208

This child is very likely to have epiglottitis. He has not been immunized so is not protected against Haemophilus influenzae type B, and he shows signs of upper airway obstruction. Any disturbance may cause deterioration, and an attempt to examine the throat may cause fatal respiratory arrest. Intubation is difficult due to the swollen epiglottis, and occasionally emergency tracheostomy is required. Senior anaesthetic and ear, nose, and throat (ENT) help should be summoned urgently.

23. D ★   OHCS 11th edn → p. 232

There seems to be developmental regression (at least for gross motor skills), which would not be consistent with a febrile convulsion. Other more serious diagnoses should be considered.

→ https://gpnotebook.com/simplepage.cfm?ID=x20161230 152848191130

24. D ★   OHCS 11th edn → p. 292

This is a severe case of seborrhoeic dermatitis affecting the scalp (also known as 'cradle cap' in young children). Note the thick yellow scale and crust.

25. B ★★   OHCS 11th edn → p. 295

The benefits of breast milk far outweigh any disadvantages related to mild jaundice. Although it is not entirely clear why breastfed babies develop persistent jaundice, these babies rarely, if ever, have levels of unconjugated bilirubin high enough to cause kernicterus.

26. E ★★

The wrist X-ray shows widened, frayed, and cupped metaphyses of the radius and ulna. These changes are typical of rickets and are usually combined with osteopenia. The metaphysis is the growth plate, and it lies between the diaphysis (the shaft of the long bone) and the epiphysis (the end of the bone). This area fails to mineralize normally in the growing child, due to low vitamin D levels. The aetiology is most probably a combination of initial low vitamin D stores, secondary to maternal deficiency, and ongoing low sunlight exposure.

→ http://www.bmj.com/content/340/bmj.b5664

27. B ★★   OHCS 11th edn → pp. 230–1

This is haemolytic uraemic syndrome—low haemoglobin (anaemia), with raised urea and creatinine (uraemia). A blood film would show evidence of haemolysis. This is usually caused by verocytotoxin-producing E. coli, which causes an acute colitis with bloody diarrhoea. It is usually contracted after contact with animals or contaminated vegetables. After recovery from the diarrhoeal illness, the child begins to get symptoms consistent with acute kidney injury (oliguria) and anaemia (lethargy and pallor).

→ https://www.gov.uk/government/publications/verocytotoxin-producing-e-coli-o157-pt-34

28. C ★★   OHCS 11th edn → p. 236

The headache is typical of migraine. The long history and lack of any suggestive features effectively rule out a space-occupying lesion. For this reason, and because there is a clear clinical diagnosis, a CT scan is not indicated. The frequency of bad attacks (more than once a month) interfering with school justifies prophylactic treatment, and propranolol is probably most commonly used in the UK. However, it is not of proven benefit. This boy is too young to be treated with sumatriptan nasal spray (although sumatriptan can be given orally, there is no good evidence for its benefit). Simple analgesia should continue to be used for headache when it occurs.

→ https://www.nice.org.uk/guidance/cg150

→ https://www.ichd-3.org (International Headache Society)

29. E ★★   OHCS 11th edn → pp. 254–5

This boy is most likely to have constitutional delay in growth and puberty. As testicular enlargement is the first sign of puberty in boys, measurement of testicular volume (using an orchidometer, consisting of a string of testicle-shaped beads of different volumes) will indicate whether he has started puberty, even in the absence of other signs. If his testicular size is greater than 4 mL, you can reassure him that he has entered puberty and that the other signs and a growth spurt will follow. The pubertal growth spurt is a late event in boys. All of the other items are relevant and should be recorded.

30. E ★★

All of these are tropical infections that can occur in South Asia and cause high fever. Typhoid is caused by Salmonella enterica serotype typhi, a Gram-negative bacillus. It is transmitted from human to human through water or food contaminated with faeces. The incubation period is usually 7–14 days, and the first phase of the illness causes increasing fever, headache, malaise, anorexia, abdominal pain, and usually diarrhoea in children. Classic features of the disease, such as rose spots, generally do not appear until the second week. Diagnosis is based on finding the bacteria on blood culture. Dengue fever is a viral infection that is transmitted via mosquito bites. The incubation period is about 4–7 days, and infection causes an acute febrile illness with headache, myalgia, and joint pain. There is a risk of developing a haemorrhagic illness as the fever subsides. Leishmaniasis is a parasitic disease that is spread by the bite of infected sandflies. It can have a very long incubation period and an abrupt or gradual onset of symptoms, which typically include fever, weight loss, and hepatosplenomegaly. Malaria is a common illness in travellers returning to the UK. It is a mosquito-borne parasitic infection caused by Plasmodium species. After an incubation period of 1 to 2 weeks, symptoms of fever, rigors, myalgia, headache, cough, and diarrhoea develop. Malaria is diagnosed by seeing the parasites on thick and thin blood films or by a rapid antigen test. Leptospirosis has a long incubation period of 2 to 3 weeks and is typically contracted from water that has been contaminated with the urine of animals, such as rats. The acute phase is similar to that of typhoid. However, Leptospira species are spirochaete bacteria.

31. A ★★ OHCS 11th edn → pp. 198–9

This baby's presentation raises concern about the possibility of meningoencephalitis, and ceftriaxone is a broad-spectrum antibiotic that should be started if this is suspected. The CSF picture confirms this with a raised white cell count. However, it indicates that a viral cause is likely, with a near-normal glucose level, normal protein, and mostly mononuclear cells seen. Aciclovir is an antiviral medication that can be used to treat herpes simplex, which is the most likely cause of viral encephalitis in this age group. It should be started alongside broad-spectrum antibiotics whenever viral encephalitis is thought to be a possibility. Infection with anaerobes is very unlikely in an otherwise well child, so metronidazole will offer no benefit. IV dexamethasone is used at the time of giving antibiotics in bacterial meningitis, to reduce the incidence of neurological complications. Isoniazid is used to treat tuberculosis (TB). Rifampicin is sometimes used as chemoprophylaxis in cases of meningococcal meningitis.

32. D ★★★ OHCS 11th edn → p. 184

Pre- term babies lose heat very easily. Placing them immediately into a plastic bag has been shown to be most effective in conserving heat. Hypothermia is associated with a worse outcome and should be avoided.

→ https://www.resus.org.uk/library/2015-resuscitation-guidelines/resuscitation-and-support-transition-babies-birth

33. A ★★→

Analgesia should not be forgotten in children who are in pain. There is well-published guidance on a step-wise approach to analgesia, starting with simple treatments and adding in further treatment. However, different analgesics are effective for different types of pain. Bony pain responds well to non-steroidal anti-inflammatory drugs (NSAIDs), and this girl is already on one of these, so another is not appropriate. In malignancy, opioids are often needed, and simple opioids such as codeine should be tried first. Diazepam and hyoscine may be adjunctive treatments in symptom control in palliative care but are not analgesics.

→ https://www.who.int/ncds/management/palliative-care/cancer-pain-guidelines/en/

34. A ★★★   OHCS 11th edn → p. 228

This shows epispadias where the urethral meatus comes out on the dorsum of the penis. More common is hypospadias where the urethral meatus comes out on the ventral aspect of the penis and is often narrowed. In reconstruction of both, the foreskin may be needed, so it is vital to warn the parents not to have the child circumcised until the surgeon has made an operative assessment. Otherwise there is no increased risk of infection, and it is always better not to retract the foreskin of babies.

35. C ★★★

Drug errors are one of the commonest types of error in paediatric practice. Anyone can make an error, and the best way to improve patient safety is to improve systems and training. The parents should receive an early explanation and apology. Any such incident is serious, and you should promptly involve a senior colleague. You may think that no harm has been done, but there may be wider issues to consider, in particular the Trust's obligation under Duty of Candour guidance. Reflective portfolio entries and notification of your defence society are often appropriate but are not the most important actions.

→ http://www.gmc-uk.org/guidance/ethical_guidance/27233.asp

36. B ★★★   OHCS 11th edn → pp. 224–5

Investigation of UTIs in children is guided by the National Institute for Health and Care Excellence (NICE) guidelines. This child is under 6 months of age, but her UTI was typical and not recurrent, and she responded to treatment within 48 hours. Therefore, she needs a renal ultrasound scan, which should be performed within 6 weeks, to look for anatomical abnormalities, but she does not require any other imaging.

→ http://www.nice.org.uk/guidance/CG54

37. E ★★★   OHCS 11th edn → p. 246

The incidence of type 2 diabetes in children is rising, although it is still far less common than type 1 diabetes. The risk is increased in children who are overweight, who have a family history of type 2 diabetes, and who are of South Asian ethnic background. The velvety skin in this girl's axillae is characteristic of acanthosis nigricans, a finding in insulin resistance and obesity.

38. E ★★★   OHCS 11th edn → p. 304

Surfactant treatment via an endotracheal tube is the most important treatment for respiratory distress syndrome and should be given as rescue treatment as soon as the baby has been intubated. Antibiotics should also be commenced (if this has not already been done) after blood cultures have been taken, and morphine may be needed for sedation on the ventilator.

39. A ★★★

ADHD is part of a spectrum of hyperactive behaviour. It is characterized by lack of concentration and impulsivity, with or without hyperactivity, that pervades all areas of the child's life. It is commoner in children with learning difficulties. Autism is also part of a spectrum, characterized by persistent difficulties with social communication and restricted and repetitive patterns of behaviour and interests that limit everyday functioning. Dyspraxia is a developmental coordination disorder. Oppositional defiant disorder is a pattern of defiant, disobedient, and hostile behaviour.

→ http://www.nice.org.uk/guidance/CG72

40. C ★★★★   OHCS 11th edn → p. 222

This is a typical picture of oesophageal atresia, with polyhydramnios, 'blowing bubbles', respiratory distress, and inability to pass a nasogastric tube. Approximately 92% of oesophageal atresias are also associated with a tracheo-oesophageal fistula. The H-type, in which both the oesophagus and the trachea are patent but with a small connection between them, is rare and often diagnosed later.

41. E ★★★★   OHCS 11th edn → p. 451

The combination of a sick child, an erythematous rash with exfoliation, and severe mucous membrane involvement indicates Stevens–Johnson syndrome. This is associated with some viral infections and certain drugs, including penicillins.

→ https://dermnetnz.org/topics/stevens-johnson-syndrome-toxic-epidermal-necrolysis/

42. E ★★★★

The MRI scan shows subependymal nodules in the left ventricle. This, combined with seizures and hypopigmented skin lesions, is strongly suggestive of tuberous sclerosis.

→ https://www.nhs.uk/conditions/tuberous-sclerosis/symptoms/

43. A ★★★★   OHCS 11th edn → p. 264

In 1990, Barker proposed that intrauterine growth retardation was a risk factor for later metabolic syndrome in developed countries. It has since been discovered that catch-up growth for weight in early childhood is a risk factor for future obesity. Babies who are born small-for-gestational age are advised to gain weight at a slower rate than babies born at a 'normal' weight—no more than 100 g per week for the first few months, rather than 180–200 g per week.

44. D ★★★★   OHCS 11th edn → p. 238

Prostaglandin E2 should be commenced because the clinical presentation is consistent with a duct-dependent congenital cardiac lesion where the duct has just closed. This means that blood can no longer flow around the body. It should cause the duct to reopen until something definitive can be done. The duct typically closes at around 48 hours of age, so a duct-dependent lesion should always be considered in babies who collapse at this age.

45. B ★★★★   OHCS 11th edn → p. 226

This boy almost certainly has minimal change nephrotic syndrome (MCNS), given his age, normal blood pressure, lack of haematuria, and normal renal function and other blood tests. Around 95% of children with MCNS will respond to steroids, although most relapse at some point. The long-term outlook is good.

→ https://www.nhs.uk/conditions/nephrotic-syndrome/

Ophthalmology

Venki Sundaram

Ophthalmology principally aims to prevent visual loss, restore visual function, and relieve ocular discomfort. The majority of the pathology can be directly visualized and thus requires proficient ocular examination techniques and visual recognition skills.

Another distinguishing aspect of ophthalmology is the overlap between medical and surgical conditions. Common systemic diseases such as diabetes and hypertension have ocular features, and diseases involving every organ of the body can have ocular manifestations. A thorough medical knowledge is paramount, as is the ability to collaborate with other medical teams. Intraocular surgery for conditions such as cataract is technically challenging, as ocular tissues are so delicate. It therefore requires high levels of fine hand–eye coordination.

As an ophthalmologist, you will be faced both with acute eye conditions, some of which are sight-threatening and require prompt diagnosis and management, and with chronic conditions, which require monitoring and treatment for many years. You will be exposed to patients of all ages, from premature babies to the elderly, so good communication with a wide range of patient groups and their families is essential. Patients often say that what they fear most is losing their sight. Therefore, empathy and support for patients with debilitating visual impairment are imperative.

The questions in this chapter will test your knowledge of acute emergency ophthalmic presentations and the understanding and interpretation of ophthalmic examination, as well as ocular conditions that have systemic associations. In addition, questions relating to ophthalmic risk factors, communication, and probity are included. Eye problems can be daunting to many medical students and doctors. Through practice in examining patients and recognizing key conditions, confidence can be gained in how best to manage these patients and, importantly, when to refer them to other specialties. Ophthalmology incorporates a unique and appealing mix of medical and surgical conditions. It is a rapidly advancing specialty with recent significant advances in diagnostic and therapeutic options. It also provides an opportunity for a good work–life balance.

Venki Sundaram, *Ophthalmology* In: *Oxford Assess and Progress: Clinical Specialties.*
Edited by: Luci Etheridge and Henry Collier, Oxford University Press.
© Oxford University Press 2021. DOI:10.1093/oso/9780198862550.003.0004

QUESTIONS

1. A 72-year-old man has painless, sudden of loss of vision in his right eye. Twenty-four hours later, visual acuity in his right eye is limited to counting fingers, and there is a carotid bruit on the right side. His blood pressure (BP) is 155/100 mmHg. His fundus appearance is shown in Figure 4.1 (see Colour Plate section). Which is the single most likely diagnosis? ★

A Central retinal artery occlusion

B Central retinal vein occlusion

C Papilloedema

D Rhegmatogenous retinal detachment

E Transient ischaemic attack

2. A 69-year-old woman with hypermetropia has had increasing left ocular pain, redness, and blurring of vision for 6 hours. She is seeing haloes around bright lights, and she feels nauseated. Her left eye is shown in Figure 4.2 (see Colour Plate section). Which is the single most likely diagnosis? ★

A Acute angle closure

B Anterior scleritis

C Bacterial conjunctivitis

D Iritis

E Subconjunctival haemorrhage

3. A 72-year-old woman has sudden loss of vision in her right eye. She has been experiencing temporal headache, jaw ache, and shoulder pain for the last 2 weeks. Her visual acuity in the right eye is limited to seeing hand movements. The appearance of her fundus is shown in Figure 4.3 (see Colour Plate section). Which single investigation would be most likely to support the diagnosis? ★

A Blood cultures

B Computed tomography (CT) scan of the head

C Erythrocyte sedimentation rate (ESR)

D Fluorescein angiography

E Full blood count

QUESTIONS 65

4. A 54-year-old woman has had increasing severe right ocular pain for 3 days, which is now affecting her sleep. Her vision is unaffected, but she has considerable ocular tenderness. Her right eye is shown in Figure 4.4 (see Colour Plate section). Which single systemic condition is most commonly associated with her ocular condition? ★

A Acute lymphocytic leukaemia

B Bacterial endocarditis

C Malignant carcinoma of the colon

D Multiple sclerosis

E Rheumatoid arthritis

5. A 6-year-old boy has had increasing fever, malaise, and right lid swelling over the last 48 hours. His eyelid is shown in Figure 4.5 (see Colour Plate section). When the eyelid is opened with difficulty, he has conjunctival chemosis and mild proptosis, with limitation of upgaze. His temperature is 38.6°C. Which is the single most appropriate treatment? ★

A Intravenous broad-spectrum antibiotics

B Oral antihistamines

C Oral broad-spectrum antibiotics

D Systemic steroids

E Topical antibiotics

6. A 22-year-old man is hit in his right eye with a glass bottle. His vision is 6/24 unaided, and his eye is shown in Figure 4.6 (see Colour Plate section). Which is the single most serious complication of this injury? ★

A Cataract

B Endophthalmitis

C Hyphaema

D Iridodialysis

E Lens subluxation

7. A 27-year-old woman has accidentally splashed an alkaline detergent in both eyes. She is in considerable discomfort and has marked diffuse bilateral conjunctival injection and hazy corneas. Which is the single most appropriate immediate management? ★

A Application of eye pads

B Irrigation with normal saline

C Limbal stem cell transplant

D Topical antibiotic

E Topical vitamin C

8. A 33-year-old man has had increasing diplopia, drooping of the left upper lid, and headache over the last 2 days. There is a complete left ptosis and the left pupil is dilated. The left eye is depressed and abducted, and eye movements are limited in all directions, except downgaze and abduction. Which single condition must be investigated for immediately? ★

A Aponeurotic ptosis

B Myasthenia gravis

C Orbital myositis

D Posterior communicating artery aneurysm

E Thyroid eye disease

9. A 77-year-old woman had uneventful right cataract surgery 3 days ago. She now has increasing pain, redness, and reduced vision in this eye. Her vision is 6/60, and there is marked conjunctival injection and anterior chamber inflammation with a 1-mm hypopyon. The fundal view is hazy. Which is the single most likely diagnosis? ★

A Acute angle-closure glaucoma

B Bacterial conjunctivitis

C Bacterial endophthalmitis

D Iritis

E Scleritis

10. A 45-year-old woman complains of irritable eyes and double vision when she looks to her side. She is concerned that her facial appearance has changed in recent months and that she has had some weight loss despite an increased appetite. There is moderate conjunctival vessel injection, and the sclera is visible between her upper lids and cornea. There is proptosis of both eyes. On extreme lateral gaze, there is limitation of eye movement and diplopia. Which is the single most likely cause of her eye problems? ★

A Carotid–cavernous fistula

B Optic nerve glioma

C Orbital haemangioma

D Orbital myositis

E Thyroid eye disease

11. A 66-year-old man who smokes 15 cigarettes a day has unequal pupil size. His visual acuity is unaffected and his right pupil is smaller, becoming more apparent in darker conditions. His pupils react normally to light and there is mild right upper lid ptosis. Which is the single most appropriate test to confirm the diagnosis of his pupil abnormality? ★ ★

A Chest X-ray

B Erythrocyte sedimentation rate (ESR)

C Magnetic resonance imaging (MRI) scan of the head

D Topical cocaine eye drops

E Topical phenylephrine eye drops

12. A 47-year-old man is referred after being found on annual check-up by his optician to have raised intraocular pressures. He has type 2 diabetes and his uncle receives treatment for glaucoma. His visual acuity is 6/6 in both eyes, with glasses for myopia, and his intraocular pressures are 34 mmHg in the right eye and 36 mmHg in the left eye. Which single risk factor is most important for the development of glaucoma? ★ ★

A Age

B Diabetes

C Family history of glaucoma

D Myopia

E Raised intraocular pressure level

13. A 41-year-old woman has had gradual visual loss in her left eye over the last few years. Her optician initially commented that she had an early cataract that was too 'immature' for surgery to be considered, but this has now progressed. Her visual acuity is 6/60 in the left eye and 6/6 in the right eye. There is a mild left cortical cataract, and fundal examination reveals a total rhegmatogenous retinal detachment. Which is the single most appropriate course of action? ★ ★

A Explain in detail the pathological processes involved in developing a retinal detachment

B Explain that she has developed a retinal detachment, and discuss the surgical options for reattaching the retina and the likely visual prognosis

C Explore why she did not suspect that something more serious was causing her visual loss

D Recommend that she pursues legal action against her optician for delay in diagnosis of a retinal detachment

E Tell her that she has a retinal detachment and is likely to go blind in the left eye, but that she still has the sight in her other eye

14. A 68-year-old woman with hypertension has had gradually decreasing vision in her left eye. Her visual acuity is 6/36, improving to 6/9 with pinhole testing, in this eye. Which is the single most likely diagnosis? ★ ★ ★

A Cataract

B Central retinal artery occlusion

C Central retinal vein occlusion

D Dry age-related degeneration

E Glaucoma

15. A 58-year-old man with hypertension who has previously undergone a renal transplant complains of floaters and blurring of vision in his right eye. He is highly myopic, and his visual acuity is 6/18. Fundoscopy shows peripheral areas of a yellow-white retina, surrounded by haemorrhage. Which is the single most likely diagnosis? ★ ★ ★

A Central retinal vein occlusion

B Choroidal melanoma

C Cytomegalovirus (CMV) retinitis

D Hypertensive retinopathy

E Retinal detachment

16. A 65-year-old woman with multiple sclerosis has reduced right visual acuity. She has type 2 diabetes and underwent squint surgery to her right eye as a child. Her right visual acuity is 6/36 with glasses, and there is no pinhole improvement. A swinging flashlight test shows a right relative afferent pupillary defect. Which is the single most likely diagnosis? ★ ★ ★ ★

A Amblyopia

B Background diabetic retinopathy

C Cataract

D Diabetic macular oedema

E Optic neuritis

17. A 73-year-old man had routine right cataract surgery 2 weeks ago. At his post-operative visit, it was found that his vision is not as clear as he was expecting. Refraction and review of the operation notes reveal a significant (4 dioptre) refractive error due to an intraocular lens of the wrong power being inserted during surgery. Which is the single most appropriate course of action? ★ ★ ★ ★

A Advise the patient that things will settle and that it can take time for the brain to adjust to the new vision

B Apologize and explain that an error has occurred, and involve a senior colleague who can discuss the various management options

C Apologize and explain that the wrong lens was inserted during the operation because the surgeon was handed a lens of the wrong power

D Apologize and explain that some natural lens fragments have unfortunately been retained in the eye and that a further operation is needed to remove these and replace the lens

E Do not mention that an error has occurred, and advise the patient to visit his optician, who can 'fine-tune' his vision

ANSWERS

1. A ★   OHCS 11th edn → p. 345

A pale fundus with a 'cherry-red' spot at the macula is classically found in central retinal artery occlusions. Hypertension and sources of potential emboli (e.g. carotid artery disease) are risk factors for developing this condition.

2. A ★   OHCS 11th edn → p. 331

Ocular pain and nausea are due to the acute rise in intraocular pressure. This also causes corneal oedema, with reduced vision and glare symptoms. Examination findings are typically ciliary vessel injection, mid-dilated pupil, shallow anterior chamber depth, and high intraocular pressure (>40 mmHg). Increasing age and hypermetropia are risk factors for developing acute angle closure.

3. C ★   OHCS 11th edn → p. 344

This woman has a left anterior ischaemic optic neuropathy (AION), secondary to giant cell arteritis (temporal arteritis). A very raised ESR is typically found in patients with *arteritic* AION, and patients can experience temporal headache, jaw pain, and myalgia. The posterior ciliary arteries may be affected by the arteritis, resulting in an AION causing dramatic visual loss and a swollen disc with flame-shaped haemorrhages. ESR may be normal in *non-arteritic* AION.

4. E ★   OHCS 11th edn → p. 333

This woman has a right diffuse anterior scleritis. This is associated with an underlying autoimmune condition in nearly 50% of cases, of which rheumatoid arthritis is the most common.

5. A ★   OHCS 11th edn → p. 342

This boy has a right-sided orbital cellulitis, which usually arises from bacterial spread from adjacent sinuses. This differs from preseptal cellulitis, as congestion from orbital spread results in chemosis, proptosis, and restriction of eye movement, in addition to eyelid involvement. This is an emergency, requiring urgent intravenous antibiotics and possible drainage of any sinus abscess. A delay in treatment can result in complications such as optic nerve compression and meningeal spread.

6. B ★   OHCS 11th edn → p. 548

This man has a penetrating eye injury. This requires urgent closure of the corneoscleral laceration, with appropriate antibiotic cover. A delay in management can increase the risk of developing endophthalmitis and can result in severe, permanent visual loss.

7. B ★   OHCS 11th edn → p. 548

Alkali-induced eye injuries are potentially sight-threatening, as they can cause liquefactive necrosis of ocular tissue. Immediate copious irrigation with normal saline until a neutral pH is reached can prevent further alkali penetration and destruction.

8. D ★   OHCS 11th edn → p. 366

This man has a left-sided third nerve palsy. Pupil involvement implies a compressive cause, and the rapid, painful onset suggests an expanding lesion such as a posterior communicating artery aneurysm. This needs to be investigated immediately in order to prevent a potentially fatal sub-arachnoid haemorrhage.

9. C ★   OHCS 11th edn → p. 351

Post-operative bacterial endophthalmitis is a rare, but serious, complication of cataract surgery. Patients typically present with poor vision, pain, and significant intraocular inflammation within 2 weeks of surgery. The fundal view can be obscured by significant vitritis. Prompt recognition and management can help to prevent irreversible visual loss.

10. E ★   OHCS 11th edn → p. 342

This woman has thyroid eye disease, which can cause ocular irritation, conjunctival vessel injection, and lid retraction. Proptosis and restriction of eye movements are secondary to enlargement of the extraocular muscles. The other conditions typically result in unilateral proptosis and are not associated with systemic symptoms.

11. D ★★   OHCS 11th edn → p. 366

This man has right-sided Horner's syndrome. This occurs because of interrupted sympathetic innervation to the eye. Topical 4% cocaine drops instilled into both eyes will only cause dilatation of the normal pupil. This is because cocaine blocks the reuptake of noradrenaline (norepinephrine) at nerve endings, causing pupil dilatation. In Horner's syndrome, no noradrenaline is secreted, so cocaine has no effect. Horner's syndrome has many causes, including Pancoast tumour of the lung.

12. E ★★   OHCS 11th edn → p. 348

Raised intraocular pressure is the strongest risk factor for the development and progression of glaucoma. Lowering of intraocular pressure is currently the only method of preventing visual field loss.

→ https://www.nice.org.uk/guidance/NG81 (National Institute for Health and Care Excellence (2009). *Glaucoma: diagnosis and management of chronic open angle glaucoma and ocular hypertension*)

13. B ★★★ OHCS 11th edn → p. 356

The news that this woman's visual loss is the result of retinal detachment, rather than cataract, is likely to come as a shock and be anxiety-provoking. Therefore, this information needs to be conveyed in a sensitive manner without placing the blame on either the patient or other professionals. Attention can then be focused on the management options available, including what possible surgery would be involved and the likely visual outcome.

14. A ★★★ OHCS 11th edn → p. 350

Pinhole use focuses light entering the eye, so it can compensate for refractive errors (up to several dioptres) or conditions that cause glare such as cataract. Visual acuity improvement with pinhole testing therefore implies a refractive problem, rather than an organic problem.

15. C ★★★ OHCS 11th edn → p. 368

CMV retinitis usually only affects immunocompromised individuals—in this case following transplant, although this is a common cause of visual loss in patients with human immunodeficiency virus (HIV). It results in areas of yellow-white retinal necrosis and haemorrhage ('pizza-pie' appearance), which can spread if not recognized and promptly treated. A raised brown fundal mass is usually evident with choroidal melanoma. Although central retinal vein occlusion can also cause retinal haemorrhage, retinal necrosis is not a feature. Significant retinal haemorrhage and retinal necrosis do not occur with retinal detachment or hypertensive retinopathy.

16. E ★★★★ OHCS 11th edn → p. 344

A relative afferent pupillary defect occurs when light shone into the affected eye causes initial dilatation of both pupils. The pupils initially dilate because the stimulus from light being shone into the affected eye is less than the stimulus of withdrawing light from the unaffected eye. This most commonly occurs in optic nerve lesions but can also be due to other gross pathology of the anterior visual pathway (e.g. total retinal detachment, optic tract lesions).

17. B ★★★★

For a variety of reasons, insertion of an intraocular lens of the wrong power during cataract surgery can unfortunately occur. Patients have a right to know about this and need to be appropriately informed of such errors and the various management options, so that they can make an informed decision on how best to rectify any visual difficulties. It is important to be open and honest, as all clinicians have a professional duty of candour.

The surgeon who performs the operation is ultimately responsible for the power of the intraocular lens that is inserted, even if they are handed the wrong one by a scrub nurse or assistant.

Careful preoperative selection, double-checking of all prostheses, and a safety-orientated culture in operating theatres (e.g. using the World Health Organization's Safer Surgery Checklist) can reduce the risks of such errors occurring.

→ http://www.who.int/patientsafety/safesurgery/en/

→ https://www.gmc-uk.org/ethical-guidance/ethical-guidance-for-doctors/candour---openness-and-honesty-when-things-go-wrong/

ENT

Philippa Tostevin

Ear, nose, and throat (ENT) surgery is a fascinating specialty. It is involved in the diagnosis and management of a vast range of diseases presenting from birth through to all ages. The pathologies covered range from congenital airway obstruction in the neonate to head and neck malignancies in the elderly. Systemic diseases can also manifest for the first time in the ENT area. The creation of a surgical airway in the form of a tracheostomy can be lifesaving, but some ENT surgery is performed to improve quality of life, so it is particularly important to understand the indications for surgical interventions. In contrast to other surgical specialties, many of the patients who are seen in the outpatient setting do not need surgery and medical management is required.

For those interested in ENT surgery as a career, there are different areas within this diverse field that can be followed to a specialist level. These include rhinology, otology, and neuro-otology, in addition to the specialist areas of paediatric ENT, head and neck cancer surgery, voice, and facial plastic surgery.

A thorough knowledge and understanding of the diagnosis and management of common ENT conditions is vital for those who wish to work in general practice, paediatrics, or emergency medicine. ENT conditions in children represent a very large proportion of the workload in any general practice setting. Various foreign bodies can be swallowed, inhaled, or inserted into the nose or ear, so an understanding of how and when these need to be removed is essential for any junior doctor working in the Emergency Department.

In this chapter, the questions are based on the important knowledge that needs to be accrued as an undergraduate or a recently qualified doctor, as many readers may not have the opportunity to work as a junior doctor in an ENT team before treating ENT patients in the Emergency Department or in a general practice setting.

Philippa Tostevin, *ENT* In: *Oxford Assess and Progress: Clinical Specialties.*
Edited by: Luci Etheridge and Henry Collier, Oxford University Press.
© Oxford University Press 2021. DOI:10.1093/oso/9780198862550.003.0005

QUESTIONS

1. A 78-year-old man has sudden onset of hoarse voice. He has a weak cough and he coughs when eating. He has been a smoker since the age of 18 years. He has a right-sided vocal cord palsy. Which is the single most likely anatomical site for his primary malignancy? ★

A Bronchus

B Larynx

C Oesophagus

D Oral cavity

E Parotid

2. A 32-year-old lorry driver has had a painless, discharging left ear for 10 years. His Weber's test lateralizes to the left. His Rinne's test is negative on the left and positive on the right. The external auditory meatus is filled with mucopurulent debris. Which is the single most likely diagnosis? ★

A Chronic otitis externa

B Chronic secretory otitis media

C Chronic suppurative otitis media

D Malignant otitis externa

E Middle ear effusion

3. A 66-year-old man has unilateral, non-pulsatile tinnitus that is keeping him awake at night. His pure-tone audiogram shows asymmetrical sensorineural hearing loss. Which single benign tumour may be responsible for these findings? ★

A Astrocytoma

B Glioma

C Meningioma

D Pleomorphic adenoma

E Vestibular schwannoma

4. A 76-year-old woman has right-sided otalgia and vertigo. Her Rinne's test is positive in both ears, and her Weber's test lateralizes to the left ear. There are vesicles present on the superior aspect of her right pinna and drooping of her face on the right side. Which single virus is most likely to have caused this clinical presentation? ★

A Adenovirus

B Cytomegalovirus

C Epstein–Barr virus

D Herpes simplex virus

E Varicella-zoster virus

5. A 23-year-old man has a 2-cm ulcer in his oral cavity. He has lost 3 kg in weight over the last 3 months. The edge of the ulcer is biopsied, and the histopathology result shows non-caseating granulomata. Which is the single most likely diagnosis? ★

A Actinomycosis

B Crohn's disease

C Tuberculosis

D Ulcerative colitis

E Vitamin B_{12} deficiency

6. A 23-year-old woman has had a fall at the gym. She now has a transient sensation of movement when she turns her head to the right. There is no hearing loss or tinnitus. Which is the single most likely diagnosis? ★

A Benign paroxysmal positional vertigo

B Labyrinthitis

C Ménière's disease

D Temporal bone fracture

E Vestibular neuronitis

7. A 17-year-old boy has sudden-onset hearing loss after standing near an exploding firework. He has a central perforation of the tympanic membrane and a conductive hearing loss. Which is the single most appropriate acute management? ★

A Emergency myringoplasty

B Grommet insertion

C Intravenous antibiotics

D Keep the ear dry and review

E Topical antibiotic and steroid drops

8. A 26-year-old man has had a foul-smelling, painless otorrhoea and a conductive hearing loss for 3 years. There is moist white debris in the attic of the right tympanic membrane. Which is the single most appropriate next intervention? ★

A Daily suction toilet

B Intravenous antibiotics

C Mastoid exploration

D Myringoplasty

E Ventilation tube insertion

9. A 63-year-old man has otalgia and a hard, craggy mass on the right tonsil. He has been a smoker for the last 40 years. Which is the single most likely histological type of tumour? ★

A Adenocarcinoma

B Lymphoma

C Rhabdomyosarcoma

D Small-cell carcinoma

E Squamous cell carcinoma

10. A 75-year-old woman has had a hoarse voice, lethargy, and weight gain for 8 weeks. On examination, her vocal cords appear thickened. Which single blood test is most likely to be helpful in making a diagnosis? ★

A Full blood count

B Liver function test

C Serum calcium level

D Thyroid function test

E Urea and electrolytes

11. A 3-year-old girl is snoring so loudly that she is keeping the family awake. She has never had tonsillitis, but an overnight sleep study has shown desaturations to 80% in room air when she is asleep. The oropharyngeal examination is shown in Figure 5.1 (see Colour Plate section). Which is the single most appropriate management strategy? ★

A Adenotonsillectomy

B Continuous home oxygen at night

C Continuous positive airway pressure (CPAP) via a face mask at night

D Palatal stiffening procedure

E Tonsillectomy

12. A 63-year-old diabetic man has an intensely itchy and painful right ear. Spores are seen in the external auditory meatus, which are cleared with microsuction. Which is the single most appropriate management? ★

A Aluminium acetate ear drops

B Glycerine and ichthammol

C Intravenous voriconazole

D Oral ketoconazole

E Topical clotrimazole

13. A 2-year-old boy has a temperature of 39°C and purulent otorrhoea. His pinna is laterally and inferiorly displaced, but the post-auricular sulcus is maintained. Which is the single most appropriate first-line emergency management strategy? ★

A Admit the patient for analgesia and observation

B Admit the patient for intravenous antibiotics

C Emergency grommet insertion

D Give antibiotic ear drops

E Give oral antibiotics

14. A 70-year-old man has had an intermittently discharging ear for 5 years. He has come for review. Which single new clinical finding would indicate that he may have developed a malignancy? ★

A Black spores in the external auditory meatus

B Circumferential oedema of the external auditory meatus

C Offensive-smelling discharge

D Purulent discharge

E Sanguineous discharge

15. A 20-year-old man has chronic facial pain and rhinorrhoea. He has had multiple courses of antibiotics, with little improvement in his symptoms. A coronal computed tomography (CT) scan of his paranasal sinuses shows a round opacity with mixed density within the right maxillary sinus. Which is the single most likely explanation for these findings? ★ ★

A Allergic polyp

B Angiofibroma

C Antrochoanal polyp

D Fungal ball

E Foreign body within the sinus

16. A 4-year-old boy with Down's syndrome has a proven middle ear effusion bilaterally that has been present for 6 months. His pure-tone hearing thresholds are 40 dB bilaterally. Which is the single most appropriate management? ★★

A Adenoidectomy

B Bilateral mastoidectomy

C Bilateral ventilation tube insertion

D Cochlea implantation

E Watch and wait for 3 months

17. A 68-year-old woman has otalgia and dysphagia. She has angular cheilitis and pale conjunctivae. Her oropharyngeal examination is normal. In which single anatomical site is this patient likely to have a tumour? ★★

A Lower oesophagus

B Nasopharynx

C Post-cricoid

D Thyroid

E Tonsil

18. A 47-year-old woman has pulsatile tinnitus in her right ear. Her hearing is normal. There is a red lesion visible on the promontory in the middle ear behind the tympanic membrane. Which is the single most likely diagnosis? ★★

A Arteriovenous malformation

B Carotid body tumour

C Glomus tumour

D Middle ear polyp

E Otosclerosis

19. A 72-year-old woman with rheumatoid arthritis has hoarseness of her voice. There is a left vocal cord palsy. Which single joint is likely to be involved? ★★

A Atlanto-occipital

B Cricoarytenoid

C Cricothyroid

D Costochondral

E Sternoclavicular

20. A 32-year-old woman is having intermittent episodes of vertigo. Each episode lasts for up to 12 hours, with associated tinnitus and hearing loss. Which single medication may be of help in reducing the frequency of her vertiginous episodes? ★★

A Amitriptyline

B Betahistine

C Cyclizine

D Paroxetine

E Prochlorperazine

21. A 2-year-old girl had an episode of acute otitis media 3 weeks ago. She now has no pain or temperature but has a residual hearing loss. A type B tympanometry trace is found, with a normal canal volume measurement. Which is the single most likely explanation for this result? ★★

A Cholesteatoma

B Chronic suppurative otitis media

C Perforation of the tympanic membrane

D Persistent acute otitis media

E Serous middle ear effusion

22. You are on a mountaineering expedition, far from medical help, and your colleague develops difficulty breathing, with cyanosis. You are unable to resuscitate him with rescue breaths and realize that a surgical airway is required to save his life. Which single anatomical structure would you locate and enter to access his airway in this situation? ★★

A Cricoid ring

B Cricothyroid membrane

C Third tracheal ring

D Thyrohyoid membrane

E Thyroid cartilage

23. A 5-year-old boy has a submandibular lump. It is non-tender, with a light purplish discoloration of the overlying skin. He is apyrexial and otherwise well. His general practitioner (GP) has tried several courses of antibiotics, but the lump has continued to grow. Which is the single most likely diagnosis? ★★

A Atypical mycobacterial infection

B Brucellosis

C Infectious mononucleosis

D Lymphoma

E Toxoplasmosis

24. A 76-year-old man has acute disabling vertigo, with nausea and vomiting. He has no tinnitus and has normal hearing. He has an intention tremor. Which single test would be most helpful in establishing a diagnosis? ★★

A Audiogram

B Brainstem-evoked response testing

C Caloric testing

D Computed tomography (CT) scan of the brain

E Otoacoustic emissions

25. A 47-year-old opera singer presented to the ear, nose, and throat (ENT) clinic with loss of vocal range. Nasendoscopic examination revealed bilateral vocal cord nodules. Which single initial treatment option should be offered to this patient? ★★

A Laser ablation of the nodule

B Microdebridement of the nodule

C Propranolol

D Sharp dissection of the nodule

E Voice therapy

26. A 3-year-old child presents with periorbital oedema and chemosis. Her right eye is proptosed and the eye movement is restricted. Which is the single most appropriate imaging technique to reveal any subperiosteal abscess formation in the orbit? ★★★

A Computed tomography (CT) angiogram

B CT scan

C Magnetic resonance imaging (MRI) scan

D Ultrasound scan

E Sinus X-ray

27. A 2-year-old boy was playing with a small plastic toy and then began coughing for 2 minutes. His mother called 999. He is now completely well and eating and drinking normally, but the toy is nowhere to be found. Which is the single most appropriate initial management? ★ ★ ★

A Computed tomography (CT) scan of the chest

B Flexible oesophagogastroduodenoscopy

C Microlaryngoscopy and bronchoscopy

D Nasendoscopy in the Emergency Department

E Rigid oesophagoscopy

28. A 23-year-old woman has fallen from a tree onto her face. She has a nasal fracture and clear rhinorrhoea. The nasal discharge is positive for glucose. Which single test would you ask for to confirm the nature of the nasal fluid? ★ ★ ★

A Albumin

B β-galactosidase

C β-2 transferrin

D Ferritin

E Myoglobin

29. A 16-year-old boy sustains a nasal fracture during a game of football. He feels that his nose is obstructed. Both nasal bones are in the midline, and both nasal airways are obscured by red swollen mucosa, which is soft when palpated. Which is the single most appropriate initial management? ★ ★ ★

A Incision and drainage

B Manipulation of the nasal fracture

C Oral antibiotics and review

D Rhinoplasty

E Septoplasty

30. At 7 p.m., a 3-year-old girl is brought to the Emergency Department, having pushed a lithium battery up her nose earlier in the afternoon. It cannot be removed in the department. She last ate at 4 p.m. Which is the single most appropriate time to list her for removal of the battery under general anaesthetic? ★★★

A After a course of steroids to decrease the inflammation

B After waiting a few days for the inflammation to subside

C On the next available elective list

D This evening, as soon as possible

E Tomorrow morning once adequately fasted

31. A 47-year-old man presents to the general practitioner (GP) with a left-sided lower motor neurone facial palsy and an insidiously developing dysphagia. On oral examination, the doctor notices that the uvula is deviated to the right. The patient is apyrexial and otherwise appears well and is not in pain. What is the single most likely diagnosis? ★★★

A Deep lobe of a parotid tumour

B Glomus tumour

C Lymphoma of the tonsil

D Retropharyngeal abscess

E Quinsy

32. Following his laryngectomy operation, a 74-year-old man has his speech restored using a valve in a tracheo-oesophageal fistula. The speech therapist wishes to explain to him the mechanism whereby he is able to communicate again. Which is the single best description of the mechanism for his post-laryngectomy speech restoration? ★★★★

A A hand-held resonating device is used in conjunction with the valve to create speech

B A fenestrated tracheostomy tube is fitted to enable speech restoration

C Air from the lungs is diverted through the valve and up to the pharynx, which vibrates to create sound

D Air from the lungs is diverted through the valve, which vibrates to create sound

E Air is taken into the oesophagus, and this causes the valve to vibrate

33. A 37-year-old man has an epistaxis that has not been controlled with 24 hours of nasal packing and bed rest. His blood pressure is 120/72 mmHg. A decision to perform arterial ligation is made. Which single artery is most commonly ligated first in this situation? ★ ★ ★ ★

A External carotid

B Greater palatine

C Maxillary

D Posterior ethmoid

E Sphenopalatine

ANSWERS

1. B ★

About one-third of recurrent laryngeal nerve palsies are caused by cancers, and 40% of these are in the larynx. The risk is increased in smokers. The left recurrent laryngeal nerve has a long course and loops down under the arch of the aorta in the chest, so it may be affected in malignant tumours of the mediastinum. This is less common on the right side. Oesophageal cancers can have pressure effects, but dysphagia would be more prominent.

2. C ★   OHCS 11th edn → p. 394

There is a long history of suppuration here. Chronic suppurative otitis media causes a conductive hearing loss, demonstrated by the tuning fork tests. Otitis externa does not cause mucoid discharge, as the external ear canal does not produce mucus.

3. E ★   OHCS 11th edn → p. 403

A schwannoma, or acoustic neuroma, is a slow-growing benign tumour that causes problems by exerting local pressure on the eighth cranial nerve, which can result in tinnitus and hearing loss. The main differential diagnosis is a meningioma. However, in this location, vestibular schwannomas are commoner, although magnetic resonance imaging is needed to distinguish them.

4. E ★   OHCS 11th edn → p. 856

This is Ramsay Hunt syndrome, caused by reactivation of varicella-zoster virus in a patient who has had chickenpox in the past. The combination of otalgia, hearing impairment, vertigo, a lower motor neurone facial nerve palsy, and visible vesicles gives the diagnosis.

5. B ★

Crohn's disease causes non-caseating granulomata in the gastrointestinal (GI) tract anywhere from the mouth to the anus. It should always be a differential diagnosis in any patient with unusual or persistent mouth ulceration, especially when coupled with other GI signs or symptoms. Tuberculosis causes caseating granulomata. Ulcerative colitis affects only the colon, not the upper GI tract.

6. A ★   OHCS 11th edn → pp. 404–5

Benign positional vertigo is common after a head injury. Attacks are provoked by head movement. Labyrinthitis usually follows a viral illness. In Ménière's disease, there is associated with tinnitus. Temporal bone fracture causes severe dizziness, often associated with facial nerve palsy and hearing loss.

7. D ★

Perforations may heal on their own, but while the drum is perforated, there is an increased risk of ear infection, so it is best to keep water out. Sudden loud noises may cause perforations, and surgical closure by means of a myringoplasty operation may be needed later.

8. C ★   OHCS 11th edn → p. 395

This man has a cholesteatoma—an area of skin in the middle ear that is locally destructive. It can be secondary to a tear in the tympanic membrane, followed by skin growing through. It should be considered if a patient has chronic discharge. On examination, a cottage cheese-like discharge is seen. If left untreated, it can invade intracranially, so surgical treatment is needed to remove the sac. A mastoidectomy may be required.

9. E ★   OHCS 11th edn → p. 422

Around 85% of pharyngeal cancers are squamous. Risk factors are smoking or chewing tobacco and older age. Human papillomavirus infection is an increasingly common cause.

10. D ★   OHCS 11th edn → p. 418

Hypothyroidism can cause oedema of the vocal cords, and therefore hoarseness. The history of lethargy and weight gain adds further clues. Thyroid dysfunction can also cause hoarseness due to pressure from a goitre. The list of causes of hoarseness is long, and therefore you need to look for other clues in the history and examination.

11. A ★

Airway obstruction due to tonsillar hypertrophy is an indication for tonsillectomy. This child's saturations are dipping to 80% during sleep, which indicates significant obstruction. Adenoid and tonsil tissue can be large in young children, and in this situation, both need to be removed. Although a Cochrane review has highlighted the fact that there are no good-quality trial data on efficacy, this is still the gold standard treatment when obstruction is demonstrated. If this fails and there are other problems such as significant obesity or neuromuscular disease, oxygen and CPAP may become necessary, but they are not first-line approaches to management. Similarly, palatal stiffening procedures, such as the insertion of implants, may be used in adults but are not appropriate in growing children.

→ https://www.cochrane.org/CD011165/ENT_tonsillectomy-or-without-adenoidectomy-versus-no-surgery-obstructive-sleep-disordered-breathing

12. E ★

Spores indicate a fungal infection, so an antifungal medication is needed. People who are immunocompromised are at increased risk of such infections. However, oral and intravenous treatments are not usually necessary as a first-line treatment, and topical treatment should be given in healthy patients. Aluminium acetate can be used as an astringent for otitis externa, but antifungal agents would be better in this proven fungal case.

13. B ★   OHCS 11th edn → p. 395

The high fever, thick purulent discharge, and distorted ear suggest mastoiditis. The ear is typically displaced laterally and inferiorly, and there may be swelling seen over the mastoid process behind the ear. This is a serious infection, and the child should be admitted and given intravenous antibiotics while surgical treatment is considered. Depending on the degree of damage, different surgical procedures are used to drain the pus.

14. E ★

Bloody discharge indicates a squamous cell carcinoma. The tumour tissue is friable and can bleed easily on contact.

15. D ★★   OHCS 11th edn → pp. 406–7

In any patient with chronic recurrent sinus problems, unusual infections or causes need to be considered. An overgrowth of fungi, usually *Aspergillus* species, can form a ball in the sinuses, usually the maxillary sinus. This will look like a mass filling the sinus on scanning. Polyps look like swellings coming from the lining of the sinus on a CT scan. Allergic polyps commonly occur in the ethmoid sinuses. Angiofibromas are rare and usually cause some distortion of the sinus on a CT scan; they often cause bleeding. Foreign bodies in the sinuses are rare; they sometimes occur as a result of facial trauma.

16. C ★★   OHCS 11th edn → p. 396

Ventilation tubes, or grommets, are the treatment for glue ear which is commoner in Down's syndrome. Glue ear refers to otitis media with effusion and is the main cause of hearing loss in young children. This boy has evidence of hearing impairment on his audiograms. If left untreated, this may seriously affect his learning and development.

17. C ★★   OHCS 11th edn → pp. 420–1

Post-cricoid tumours in the hypopharynx often cause the sensation of a lump in the throat before they interfere with swallowing. As they grow, they cause local pain. They can also cause referred pain to the ear along the sensory fibres of the vagus nerve. This is an ominous sign. Clinical anaemia also indicates that the tumour is advanced.

18. C ★★   OHCS 11th edn → p. 402

A glomus tumour, or non-chromaffin paraganglioma, is a rare vascular
benign tumour that arises from the glomus body (a small collection of
paraganglionic tissue). These tumours often occur in the middle ear.
Because of blood flow, the tinnitus is pulsatile. A mass may also be felt in
the ear. Glomus tumours can also occur in the carotid body but would
not give these symptoms.

19. B ★★   OHCS 11th edn → p. 418

The cricoarytenoid joints rotate with the vocal cords, so arthritis here
causing stiffness can affect the pitch and tone of the voice. This has been
reported in 17–70% of patients with rheumatoid arthritis, and airway
obstruction by swelling is a rare, but serious, complication.

20. B ★★   OHCS 11th edn → p. 404

This is a description of Mé   nière's disease, which involves attacks
of disabling vertigo with unilateral tinnitus and progressive sensorineural
hearing loss. Treatment is symptomatic initially. Anti-emetics, such as
cyclizine or prochlorperazine, may help to relieve the symptoms but will
not reduce the frequency of attacks. Betahistine may be helpful and can
be tried, although trial results are equivocal.

21. E ★★   OHCS 11th edn → pp. 390, 396

Fluid in the middle ear causes dampening of the tympanic membrane
movement and results in hearing impairment and a flat trace on tympanometry. Serous effusion can occur during the resolution of an acute
otitis media, probably due to Eustachian tube dysfunction. It will usually resolve within 3 months. Recurrent infections can lead to a cycle of
inflammation and can cause chronic suppurative otitis media.

22. B ★★

In this emergency situation, the cricothyroid membrane should be identified in the midline, as it is the safest way to approach the airway prior to
a formal tracheostomy. When performing a surgical tracheostomy under
anaesthesia, a fenestration would be made into the trachea itself, usually
at the level of the second or third ring. A cricoid split procedure is very
occasionally performed in neonates, and never in an adult. The thyroid
cartilage and thyrohyoid membrane should not be entered, as there may
be damage to the vocal cords.

23. A ★★   OHCS 11th edn → p. 426

The characteristic appearance of this infection is an enlarging, non-
tender, violaceous mass. It does not disappear following antibiotic use. It
is rare but should be considered.

24. D ★★   OHCS 11th edn → p. 404

The unusual feature here is the intention tremor, which should raise suspicion of a brain lesion. Vertigo caused by central lesions is rare, but features in the history may lead you to suspect these. The other tests assess hearing or assess each labyrinth in turn.

25. E ★★

Voice therapy may be all that is required. Surgical approaches employing sharp dissection or laser should only be used if the nodule is resistant to voice therapy. Hypothyroidism is a cause of hoarseness, but not of nodules. Propranolol is used to treat haemangiomata of the larynx, but not nodules.

Surgical versus non-surgical interventions for vocal cord nodules:

→ https://www.cochranelibrary.com/cdsr/doi/10.1002/14651858. CD001934.pub2/full

26. B ★★★

The orbital abscess would be seen on CT scan, and any bony defect would be seen on the CT scan, but not on the MRI scan. A sinus X-ray is very rarely performed and would not show details of abscess formation. An ultrasound probe could not be used for an abscess in this location, as it is medial to the orbit and the probe could not be accommodated in the available anatomical space.

→ Rahbar R, Robson C, Petersen RA, et al. Management of orbital subperiosteal abscess in children. Arch Otolaryngol Head Neck Surg. 2001;**127**:281–6.

27. C ★★★

Children often choke on small foreign bodies, which may become lodged in the airway. If left, they can cause erosion, obstruction, or infection and collapse. Larger objects tend to get stuck in the larynx and may cause airway obstruction or hoarseness. The majority of foreign bodies get stuck in the bronchus and cause unilateral wheeze and breath sounds, and may cause cough. Without the classic history, these may be missed or mistaken for asthma. Although inspiratory and expiratory chest X-rays may be helpful, very young children cannot cooperate with these and a single chest film may miss the diagnosis. To look for the foreign body, the upper and lower airway must be carefully examined with bronchoscopy.

28. C ★★★   OHCS 11th edn → p. 410

Clear fluid that is positive for glucose on a dipstick test suggests a basal skull fracture and leakage of cerebrospinal fluid (CSF). β-2 transferrin is a protein found only in the CSF and perilymph, so it can be used to confirm CSF rhinorrhoea in a suspected basal skull fracture.

29. A ★★★   OHCS 11th edn → p. 410

This boy has a septal haematoma causing the obstruction. The condition is rare but serious and, if left untreated, can cause septal necrosis and collapse. Treatment involves draining it under general anaesthesia and packing the nose. Septoplasty or rhinoplasty may be needed later after fractures if the nose sets abnormally and causes deviation of the septum and blockage or deformity.

30. D ★★★   OHCS 11th edn → p. 410

Batteries are corrosive and require urgent removal.

31. A ★★★   OHCS 11th edn → p. 426

A tumour of the deep lobe of the parotid will medialize the tonsil, and the uvula will be deviated away from the lesion. The facial nerve palsy suggests malignant infiltration of the nerve which lies between the deep and superficial lobes. A lymphoma of the tonsil can medialize the tonsil but would not develop a facial palsy. A retropharyngeal abscess is unusual in this age group and would always be associated with signs of toxicity and a raised temperature. Similarly, a patient with a quinsy or abscess around the tonsil would be in pain. A glomus tumour could produce lower cranial nerve palsies but would not deviate the uvula, as it tends to present lower in the neck.

32. C ★★★★

Following laryngectomy, the potency of the upper airway is lost, and therefore the ability to phonate is lost. There are a variety of ways to restore speech following laryngectomy, and this is a specialist area managed by speech and language therapists.

→ https://www.cancerresearchuk.org/about-cancer/laryngeal-cancer/living-with/speaking-after-laryngectomy

33. E ★★★★   OHCS 11th edn → p. 412

Ongoing epistaxis despite nasal packing is an emergency, and the nose needs to be examined under anaesthesia. The sphenopalatine artery is a branch of the external carotid artery. It passes through the sphenopalatine foramen into the back of the nose. It is distal, so ligation usually controls bleeding, with few complications. Older techniques involving ligation of the external carotid or maxillary artery have higher complication rates.

Dermatology

Gemma Simcox

Skin disease has a serious impact on an individual's quality of life. It is well recognized that conditions such as psoriasis may have a similar impact on a patient's quality of life to chronic diseases such as diabetes, hypertension, and depression.

Skin problems account for approximately 20% of all patient consultations in primary care in the UK. It is important that clinicians are able to diagnose common skin diseases such as acne, eczema, psoriasis, and cutaneous malignancies and initiate an appropriate management plan. This requires the ability to take a full history and conduct a complete examination. A complete dermatological examination involves examination of the entire skin, mucous membranes, hair, and nails. The description of cutaneous pathologies should include the location and distribution of lesions. The morphology of a lesion or each component of a generalized eruption should be noted. Other organ systems may also need to be examined.

The questions in this chapter will test your knowledge of the skin problems that are frequently encountered in non-specialist clinical practice. Other more rare skin disorders are also covered, either because they are potentially life-threatening or because they are a sign of systemic disease. The questions are designed to improve your ability to recognize the morphology and distribution of cutaneous physical signs.

Hopefully you will find these questions stimulating and an aid to improving your knowledge of skin disease.

Gemma Simcox, *Dermatology* In: *Oxford Assess and Progress: Clinical Specialties*.
Edited by: Luci Etheridge and Henry Collier, Oxford University Press.
© Oxford University Press 2021. DOI:10.1093/oso/9780198862550.003.0006

QUESTIONS

1. A 42-year-old man with type 2 diabetes has hyperpigmented skin in his axillae, as shown in Figure 6.1 (see Colour Plate section). Which is the single most likely diagnosis? ★

A Acanthosis nigricans

B Atopic eczema

C Erythrasma

D Seborrhoeic dermatitis

E Tinea corporis

2. A 28-year-old man has had red, scaly patches over his cheeks, as shown in Figure 6.2 (see Colour Plate section), for 2 years. He also has scaling of the skin around his eyebrows. Which is the single most likely diagnosis? ★

A Atopic eczema

B Candidiasis

C Psoriasis

D Seborrhoeic dermatitis

E Tinea faciei

3. A 14-year-old girl has lesions on her fingers, as shown in Figure 6.3 (see Colour Plate section). They have been present for 5 months. Which is the single most likely causative organism? ★

A Adenovirus

B Coxsackie virus

C Herpes simplex virus

D Human papillomavirus

E Molluscum contagiosum virus

4. A 23-year-old woman has a rash affecting her forehead, cheeks, and chin, as shown in Figure 6.4 (see Colour Plate section). Which is the single predominant lesion shown here? ★

A Comedone

B Macule

C Nodule

D Papule

E Pustule

5. A 30-year-old woman has had itchy skin for most of her life. Her face is shown in Figure 6.5 (see Colour Plate section). Which is the single most likely diagnosis? ★

A Acne rosacea

B Atopic eczema

C Impetigo

D Psoriasis

E Seborrhoeic dermatitis

6. A 38-year-old woman with lifelong atopic eczema has noticed that her eczema has been getting worse over the past 7 days. She has been taking flucloxacillin for 4 days, but her condition is worsening, as shown in Figure 6.6 (see Colour Plate section), and is becoming painful. Which single treatment should be given? ★

A Betamethasone valerate ointment

B Emulsifying ointment

C Intravenous (IV) aciclovir

D IV benzylpenicillin

E Oral metronidazole

7. A 36-year-old man has had a skin rash, as shown in Figure 6.7 (see Colour Plate section), for 20 years. He noticed his nails have become pitted and his scalp scaly. Which is the single most likely diagnosis? ★

A Atopic eczema

B Lichen planus

C Pityriasis versicolor

D Psoriasis

E Seborrhoeic dermatitis

8. A 40-year-old woman attends her general practice (GP) surgery for a Well Woman check-up. She has multiple skin lesions, as shown in Figure 6.8 (see Colour Plate section), that have been present since she was a child and are slowly increasing in number. Which is the single most likely diagnosis? ★

A Epidermoid cysts

B Ganglions

C Neurofibromatosis

D Tuberous sclerosis

E Viral warts

9. A 56-year-old man presents with a thumb that appears as shown in Figure 6.9 (see Colour Plate section). He jammed the thumb in a door a few months ago. The rest of his skin examination is normal. Which is the single most likely diagnosis? ★

A Haematoma

B Lichen planus

C Malignant melanoma

D Onychomycosis

E Psoriasis

10. A 37-year-old woman has painful, swollen distal interphalangeal joints. She has the nail changes shown in Figure 6.10 (see Colour Plate section) and says that her nails have been like this for 10 years. Which is the single most likely diagnosis? ★

A Atopic eczema

B Lichen planus

C Psoriasis

D Systemic lupus erythematosus

E Tinea manuum

11. A 40-year-old woman has had a swollen leg for 6 days, as shown in Figure 6.11 (see Colour Plate section). Her temperature is 38.6°C, and her full blood count shows a neutrophil count of 11×10^9/L. Which is the single most likely diagnosis? ★

A Cellulitis

B Deep vein thrombosis

C Psoriasis

D Tinea corporis

E Venous eczema

12. A 40-year-old man has skin between his toes, as shown in Figure 6.12 (see Colour Plate section). Which is the single most likely diagnosis? ★

A Atopic eczema

B Candidiasis

C Psoriasis

D Tinea pedis

E Viral wart

13. A 5-year-old girl has had blisters on her left thigh, as shown in Figure 6.13 (see Colour Plate section), for 2 days. The condition started with a yellow crusted area 5 days ago, which spread, and then the blisters appeared. The girl is otherwise well. Which is the single most likely diagnosis? ★

A Bullous impetigo
B Bullous pemphigoid
C Chronic bullous disease of childhood
D Insect bites
E Scabies

14. A 35-year-old woman has had a skin problem for a number of years. She had a Caesarean section last year, and her scar is shown in Figure 6.14 (see Colour Plate section). Which is the single best description of the appearance? ★

A Auspitz sign
B Impetiginization
C Keloid scar
D Köebner phenomenon
E Striae

15. A 34-year-old man has a lesion on his leg, as shown in Figure 6.15 (see Colour Plate section). He first noticed it about 2 months ago. Which is the single most likely diagnosis? ★

A Actinic keratosis
B Benign naevus
C Bowen's disease
D Malignant melanoma
E Seborrhoeic keratosis

16. A 10-month-old baby has had skin lesions, as shown in Figure 6.16 (see Colour Plate section), for 2 days. He had an upper respiratory tract infection last week but seems to be well in himself now. The lesions appear to be in a different place from the ones he had yesterday. Which is the single most likely diagnosis? ★

A Acute urticaria
B Atopic eczema
C Erythema multiforme
D Meningococcal septicaemia
E Urticaria pigmentosa

17. A 28-year-old woman developed a rash on her body 1 week ago. Today it has spread to her hands, as shown in Figure 6.17 (see Colour Plate section). Three weeks ago, she had a 3-day course of trimethoprim to treat a urinary tract infection. Which is the single most likely diagnosis? ★

A Acute urticaria

B Allergic contact eczema

C Erythema multiforme

D Erythema nodosum

E Psoriasis

18. A 64-year-old man has had a sore back and mouth for 2 months. These are shown in Figure 6.18 (a, b) (see Colour Plate section). Which is the single most likely diagnosis? ★

A Bullous pemphigoid

B Erythema multiforme

C Herpes simplex virus infection

D Lichen planus

E Pemphigus vulgaris

19. A 30-year-old man with ulcerative colitis has lesions on his anterior shins. The lesions started to develop 7 months ago and are getting bigger. They are shown in Figure 6.19 (see Colour Plate section). Which is the single most likely diagnosis? ★

A Erythema nodosum

B Leukocytoclastic vasculitis

C Necrobiosis lipoidica

D Pyoderma gangrenosum

E Venous ulcers

20. A 60-year-old man has a lesion on his arm that has grown rapidly over the past 3 weeks and is not painful. It is shown in Figure 6.20 (see Colour Plate section). Which is the single most likely diagnosis? ★

A Actinic keratosis

B Basal cell carcinoma

C Keratoacanthoma

D Malignant melanoma

E Seborrhoeic keratosis

21. A 22-year-old man has a lesion on his lower abdomen that is increasing in size and which is shown in Figure 6.21 (see Colour Plate section). He has tried 1% hydrocortisone cream, to no avail. Which is the single most appropriate treatment? ★

A Betamethasone valerate cream

B Ketoconazole shampoo

C Oral flucloxacillin

D Oral prednisolone

E Oral terbinafine

22. A 45-year-old man had a cardiac transplant 8 years ago. He has developed a painful lesion on his forehead that is irregular in shape with a thick crust. The lesion has grown rapidly over the past 3 months. Which is the single most likely diagnosis? ★

A Actinic keratosis

B Bowen's disease

C Malignant melanoma

D Seborrhoeic keratosis

E Squamous cell carcinoma

23. An 18-year-old man has severe scarring acne with multiple nodules and cysts on his face, which has been getting progressively worse over the past 5 years. Treatment with oxytetracycline for 8 months has not helped. He is otherwise well. Which is the single most appropriate treatment? ★

A 5% benzoyl peroxide cream

B Clobetasone butyrate cream

C Oral erythromycin

D Oral isotretinoin

E Oral prednisolone

24. A 3-month-old baby has a rash on his groin. He is otherwise well. The rash is shown in Figure 6.22 (see Colour Plate section). Which is the single most appropriate treatment to prescribe? ★

A 1% hydrocortisone cream

B Aqueous cream

C Fucidin cream

D No treatment

E Nystatin cream

25. A 56-year-old woman has a sore, red, dry, itchy rash that is confined to her face. It has developed over the past month. The rest of her skin is normal. She is otherwise well and is taking no medication. Which is the single most likely diagnosis? ★

A Acne rosacea

B Allergic contact dermatitis

C Atopic eczema

D Seborrhoeic dermatitis

E Systemic lupus erythematosus

26. The nose of a 69-year-old man has the appearance shown in Figure 6.23 (see Colour Plate section). It has looked like this for 9 years. Which is the single best term to describe the appearance? ★★

A Acne vulgaris

B Lupus pernio

C Lupus vulgaris

D Rhinophyma

E Wegener's granulomatosis

27. A 26-year-old man with atopic eczema has lesions on his palms, as shown in Figure 6.24 (see Colour Plate section), which are very itchy. They come and go, and seem to flare up when the rest of his eczema is bad. He has not yet tried any treatments, as he is unsure which of them to use. Which is the single most appropriate treatment? ★★

A 1% hydrocortisone ointment

B 5% permethrin cream

C Aciclovir cream

D Betamethasone valerate ointment

E Ketoconazole cream

28. A 12-year-old boy has had atopic eczema for many years. He is concerned about paler patches on his face, shown in Figure 6.25 (see Colour Plate section), which have been present for the past 6 months. He has changes consistent with eczema over the rest of his skin, but no pigmentary change. Which is the single most likely diagnosis? ★★

A Cutaneous T-cell lymphoma

B Pityriasis alba

C Seborrhoeic dermatitis

D Tinea faciei

E Vitiligo

29. A 78-year-old woman has an itchy rash over her trunk and limbs, as shown in Figure 6.26 (see Colour Plate section). She has been itchy for several weeks, and blisters appeared last week. She is not taking any regular medication. Which is the single most likely diagnosis? ★★

A Bullous pemphigoid

B Erythema multiforme

C Pemphigus vulgaris

D Psoriasis

E Scabies

30. A 47-year-old man has had a rash over both lower legs for 2 days, as shown in Figure 6.27 (see Colour Plate section). He was treated with amoxicillin for a throat infection last week. Which is the single most likely diagnosis? ★★

A Cellulitis

B Erythema multiforme

C Erythema nodosum

D Leukocytoclastic vasculitis

E Streptococcal septicaemia

31. A 36-year-old woman is concerned about the pigmentation on her cheeks, shown in Figure 6.28 (see Colour Plate section), which is spreading. She is not taking any medication. Which is the single most appropriate treatment? ★★

A Betamethasone valerate cream

B High-factor sunblock

C Hydroquinone cream

D Hydroxychloroquine

E Oral prednisolone for 6 weeks

32. A 30-year-old woman gave birth 7 weeks ago. She has had a lesion on her breast for 2 weeks. It bleeds profusely and interferes with breastfeeding of her baby. Which is the single most likely diagnosis? ★★

A Bacillary angiomatosis

B Granuloma annulare

C Pyoderma gangrenosum

D Pyogenic granuloma

E Viral wart

33. A 30-year-old man has been on a walking holiday in Spain and now has blisters, shown in Figure 6.29 (see Colour Plate section). The remainder of his skin is normal. Which is the single most likely diagnosis? ★★

A Allergic contact eczema

B Bullous pemphigoid

C Impetigo

D Insect bite reaction

E Linear immunoglobulin A (IgA) disease

34. A 38-year-old man with coeliac disease has a very itchy rash over his buttocks and a similar rash over the elbows and knees, shown in Figure 6.30 (see Colour Plate section). Which is the single most likely diagnosis? ★★

A Atopic eczema

B Dermatitis herpetiformis

C Lichen planus

D Psoriasis

E Scabies

35. An 18-month-old girl has a widespread rash on her trunk. It started to develop 2 weeks ago with a single round red plaque, 2 cm in diameter, on her left flank. This was treated with a topical antifungal cream, with no effect. During the last 3 days, several more scaly plaques have appeared over the trunk. These are 1 cm in diameter and pink in the centre, with a dark red ring around the outside. They are itchy. The girl is well in herself and is thriving. Which is the single most likely diagnosis? ★★★

A Guttate psoriasis

B Pityriasis rosea

C Seborrhoeic dermatitis

D Tinea corporis

E Viral exanthema

36. A 63-year-old man is referred for treatment of the lesion shown in Figure 6.31 (see Colour Plate section). Which single treatment modality should be offered? ★ ★ ★

A Cryotherapy

B Direct excision and primary closure

C Mohs micrographic surgery

D Radiotherapy

E Topical 5-fluorouracil (5FU)

37. A 55-year-old woman has a patch of hair loss over the parietal region of the scalp, as well as an atrophic lesion over her ear, as shown in Figure 6.32 (see Colour Plate section). Which is the single most likely diagnosis? ★ ★ ★ ★

A Alopecia areata

B Discoid lupus

C Lichen planopilaris

D Psoriasis

E Tinea capitis

ANSWERS

1. A ★   OHCS 11th edn → p. 438

This condition is commoner in patients with type 2 diabetes and obesity.
It causes velvety, hyperpigmented plaques in the axillae, groin, and neck
folds. It can be associated with other underlying causes such as polycystic ovaries, Cushing's syndrome, and acromegaly and can also be
drug-induced. As such, it is advised to take a full history from the patient.
Acanthosis nigricans itself is harmless; weight loss and treatment of any
underlying conditions *may* improve the appearance of the lesions. There
is an association with internal malignancy (mostly gastrointestinal); however, this is very rare and the onset of symptoms is usually more rapid.

→ http://www.nhs.uk/conditions/acanthosis-nigricans/Pages/
Introduction.aspx

2. D ★   OHCS 11th edn → p. 446

This common dermatosis causes scaling and erythema in the nasolabial
folds, eyebrows, and hairline. There may be associated fine scale on the
scalp and within the ears. This distribution rather than in the flexures
(eczema), extensors (psoriasis) or an asymmetrical distribution is typical
of tinea or candida, both of which favour warm, moist sites. Seborrhoeic
dermatitis is often associated with yeast infections and, as such, treatment is aimed to target this, as well as the eczematous inflammatory
response, with emollients and mild topical steroids. The treatments will
need to be specific to the area affected, e.g. shampoo for scalp.

→ https://cks.nice.org.uk/seborrhoeic-dermatitis

3. D ★   OHCS 11th edn → p. 449

These are viral warts, caused by human papillomavirus. This is a very
common presentation in general practice and, in most cases, requires no
treatment but can cause pain and distress. There are several options for
therapy, including topical cytotoxic agents, cryotherapy, and duct tape,
all of which require perseverance. Fifty per cent of warts resolve within
6 months without treatment.

→ http://patient.info/doctor/viral-warts-excluding-verrucae

→ http://www.nhs.uk/Conditions/Warts/Pages/Introduction.aspx

4. E ★   OHCS 11th edn → p. 450

A comedone can be open (blackhead) or closed (whitehead). A macule
is a flat, distinct lesion/area of skin, up to 1 cm in diameter (plaque
greater than 1 cm). A nodule is a solid, palpable lesion, up to 10 mm in
diameter. A papule is a solid, palpable lesion, up to 5 mm in diameter.
A pustule is a papule or nodule containing purulent material.

5. B ★ OHCS 11th edn → p. 446

Atopic eczema is classically itchy and typically affects flexural sites. It is common for there to be facial involvement, as seen here.

Acne rosacea would not be expected to be itchy. Impetigo again would not itch and would be of a short duration, rather than lifelong. Impetigo may affect a patient with eczema, as the skin barrier is not as effective. However, the picture would note well-defined patches of yellow, crusting plaques or blistering, which are not seen here. The final two conditions given as options are psoriasis and seborrhoeic dermatitis. Psoriasis is also not itchy (although it can be sore at times), and the latter tends to be confined to the nasolabial folds and eyebrows, which are not noted in the illustration.

→ http://www.dermnetnz.org/topics/atopic-eczema/

→ http://www.eczema.org/basic-treatment

6. C ★

This is eczema herpeticum (eczema infected with herpes simplex virus). Note the characteristic monomorphic vesicles. The history of the eczema getting worse despite antibiotic treatment is a clue. This infection spreads very quickly and requires IV treatment. The patient will present feeling unwell with a fever and the characteristic rash, as illustrated in Figure 6.6 (although initially there may be fewer vesicles). This is a dermatological emergency and requires admission and often IV antiviral treatment.

→ https://dermnetnz.org/topics/eczema-herpeticum/

7. D ★ OHCS 11th edn → p. 444

Note the symmetrical distribution of plaques with a silvery scale on the surface. The extensor aspects of the elbows are involved—a classic site for psoriasis. The additional information o the nails and scalp gives the final clue of psoriasis and should always form part of the examination of the dermatology patient. Lichen planus (LP) can affect the nails, from dystrophy to total nail destruction, which is different from pitting. LP can, in addition, also affect the scalp with a form of scarring alopecia, which is quite different from the thick scale of scalp psoriasis. LP and psoriasis both koebnerize, but LP classically affects the volar aspect of the wrist and can also affect mucosal surfaces. Pityriasis versicolor causes altered skin pigmentation secondary to a yeast infection, rather than thickened plaques. Atopic eczema and seborrhoeic dermatitis have been noted in previous questions.

→ https://www.nice.org.uk/guidance/cg153

→ http://patient.info/doctor/chronic-plaque-psoriasis

8. C ★

This is neurofibromatosis type 1. It is an autosomal dominant condition. The multiple dome-shaped tumours are neurofibromas. There may also be café-au-lait macules and axillary freckling of the skin. Epidermoid cysts tend to occur in isolation, certainly not in the numbers shown in the illustration. Ganglions are also solitary and should be found on the limbs. The skin manifestation of tuberous sclerosis are numerous and include café-au-lait spots, shagreen patches, and skin tags.

→ https://nervetumours.org.uk/ (Nerve Tumours UK)

→ http://www.tuberous-sclerosis.org/about-tsc.html

9. C ★   OHCS 11th edn → p. 442

This is an acral subungual melanoma. Note the pigmentation of the skin around the nail (Hutchinson's sign). The nail has been distorted by the growth of the melanoma under the nail bed. As noted in previous questions, psoriasis causes nail pitting; lichen planus causes nail dystrophy and destruction. Fungal nail infection is known as onychomycosis and requires nail clippings for laboratory analysis prior to treatment.

→ http://www.dermnetnz.org/topics/nail-terminology/

→ http://www.pcds.org.uk/clinical-guidance/nails

10. C ★   OHCS 11th edn → p. 444

The severe nail dystrophy, swollen distal interphalangeal joints, and fine scaling over the fingertips are suggestive of psoriasis. Approximately 5% of patients with psoriasis develop arthropathy. Joint involvement would not be expected with atopic eczema or tinea manuum (the history is also a little too prolonged for tinea). The nail changes associated with lichen planus have been noted previously. Systemic lupus erythematosus does have dermatological sequelae, in particular discoid lupus erythematosus which mainly affects the scalp and sun-bearing areas. There can be nail changes, but those tend to be limited.

→ http://www.jabfm.org/content/22/2/206.full

→ http://www.dermnetnz.org/topics/discoid-lupus-erythematosus/

11. A ★

A patient with a hot, red, swollen leg may have cellulitis or deep vein thrombosis. In this case, the raised temperature, the sharp demarcation of the erythema at the ankle, and the neutrophilia support the diagnosis of cellulitis. A common cause for cellulitis and recurrent cellulitis is tinea pedis, and this should be treated to prevent recurrence. Treatment should include the commonest pathogens, i.e. streptococci and *Staphylococcus*.

→ http://bestpractice.bmj.com/best-practice/monograph/63.html

12. D ★   OHCS 11th edn → p. 448

This is 'athlete's foot'. Note the macerated and scaled appearance of the skin in the web space.

13. A ★   OHCS 11th edn → p. 448

Impetigo can cause tense blisters, as shown here. Note the yellow, crusted patches which are more typical of impetigo seen in children. Bullous pemphigoid would not be seen at this age, and scabies would present with a more widespread, intensely pruritic rash. The lesions may have started as simple insect bites which have become secondarily infected.

→ http://patient.info/doctor/impetigo-pro

14. D ★   OHCS 11th edn → p. 434

The Köebner phenomenon describes the occurrence of skin lesions in areas of trauma or surgery. It occurs with psoriasis (as seen here), warts, vitiligo, and lichen planus.

The Auspitz sign is small areas of bleeding when removing scale from plaques, which may indicate psoriasis. Impetiginization merely describes a lesion that has become secondarily infected. Striae are stretch marks, and a keloid scar is a specific type of scarring characterized by raised, red scar.

→ http://www.dermnetnz.org/topics/the-koebner-phenomenon/

15. D ★   OHCS 11th edn → p. 442

Note the irregular colour of, and edge to, this lesion. Remember the ABCDE for pigmented lesions:

- asymmetry
- border
- colour
- diameter >7 mm
- evolution.

There is a movement towards a 7-point checklist for the identification of a suspected malignant melanoma. However, the ABCDE rules are helpful to use with patient self-monitoring. Lesions scoring 3 or more should be referred. This is based on major features scoring 2 each and minor features scoring 1. A lesion that stands out from the others is always cause for concern.

→ https://cks.nice.org.uk/melanoma-and-pigmented-lesions#!topic Summary

16. A ★   OHCS 11th edn → p. 453

These are wheals. The history of them being present for less than 24 hours is typical. Acute urticaria can result from infection, drugs, or a food allergy, but often no cause is found. The lesions of erythema multiforme are targetoid, and these lesions are also not typical of meningococcal septicaemia, which has palpable, dark purple plaques. Urticaria pigmentosa tends to have a more prolonged course and the lesions are lighter brown.

→ http://patient.info/doctor/urticaria-pro

17. C ★   OHCS 11th edn → pp. 436, 451

The targetoid lesions are typical of erythema multiforme. This usually starts on the trunk and spreads acrally (to the hands, feet, and head). Common causes are drugs and infection (typically herpes simplex virus or *Mycoplasma* infection). Lesions of erythema nodosum would usually be found on the anterior shins and without the typical targetoid pattern.

→ http://www.dermnetnz.org/topics/erythema-multiforme/

→ http://www.pcds.org.uk/clinical-guidance/erythema-nodosum

18. E ★   OHCS 11th edn → p. 452

Note the eroded areas from superficial blisters that have burst. This is typical of pemphigus vulgaris. The skin around the eroded areas is normal (in contrast, in bullous pemphigoid, it is erythematous). The erosions on the lip further support the diagnosis of pemphigus vulgaris.

→ http://www.pemphigus.org.uk

19. D ★   OHCS 11th edn → p. 438

This condition is commoner in patients with inflammatory bowel disease. Note the ulcers with a purple-red border. The ulcers often appear undermined at the edge. Surgical intervention will make this condition worse and may lead to limb amputation, so do not cut these lesions out! Treatment options include topical, intralesional, and oral steroids and biological therapy. Erythema nodosum presents as subcutaneous nodules; these lesions are not vasculitic in nature which would exclude answer B. They can often mistakenly be treated as venous ulcers over some time, but attention must be given to the site (not in the gaiter area), the age of the patient, and the characteristics of the lesions themselves. Necrobiosis lipoidica are distinct yellow/brown patches on the shins.

→ http://www.pcds.org.uk/clinical-guidance/pyoderma-gangrenosum

→ http://www.dermnetnz.org/topics/necrobiosis-lipoidica/

20. C ★   OHCS 11th edn → p. 440

This nodule is growing rapidly and has a symmetrical dome shape with a central plug of keratin. These lesions are usually excised in order to differentiate them from a squamous cell carcinoma. This is very typical of this type of lesion.

→ http://patient.info/doctor/keratoacanthoma-pro

21. E ★   OHCS 11th edn → p. 448

This is tinea corporis (incognita). It has been exacerbated by the topical steroid that this patient has used. An oral antifungal agent is needed. Once a topical steroid has been used on tinea corporis/pedis/manuum, the symptoms will reduce, but the rash itself will spread (tinea incognita). Oral antifungal agents are indicated. This can be the case for some time and, as such, it is important to take a thorough history of the start of the symptoms.

→ http://www.dermnetnz.org/topics/tinea-incognita/

22. E ★ OHCS 11th edn → p. 440

This describes an exophytic tumour with a hyperkeratotic crust on a sun-exposed site. Squamous cell carcinoma is commoner in organ transplant recipients as a result of immunosuppressive medication, so it must always be considered.

→ https://dermnetnz.org/topics/cutaneous-squamous-cell-carcinoma/

23. D ★ OHCS 11th edn → p. 450

For severe acne, isotretinoin for 16 weeks is the drug of choice. However, close supervision is required, as it has significant side-effects. Up to 80% of patients have side-effects and the potential list is long. Significant ones to note are depression, dry lips and skin, effects on the liver and lipids, and an association with birth defects. Oral and topical steroids should be avoided in acne.

→ https://cks.nice.org.uk/acne-vulgaris

24. E ★ OHCS 11th edn → p. 448

The satellite pustules that are visible are characteristic of candidiasis. The folds are involved (which makes an extrinsic dermatitis, such as irritant dermatitis, unlikely). This infection is treated with an antifungal cream such as nystatin. Aqueous cream should be avoided, as it can itself cause irritation.

→ http://www.dermnetnz.org/topics/candida/

25. B ★ OHCS 11th edn → p. 447

The distribution of this eruption gives the clue that this is allergic contact eczema—the eczema is limited to one body site. The face is a common site to be affected by allergic contact dermatitis (common allergens are make-up and hair dye). As noted in previous questions, seborrhoeic dermatitis does not tend to be itchy, nor does rosacea. The cutaneous manifestations of systemic lupus erythematosus can affect the face and are classically described as a malar rash (butterfly distribution) over the cheeks, with a sore mouth and sun sensitivity.

→ http://www.pcds.org.uk/clinical-guidance/eczema-contact-allergic-dermatitis-including-latex-and-rubber-allergy

26. D ★★ OHCS 11th edn → p. 450

This bulbous swelling of the nose has occurred as a result of long-standing rosacea. The tissues have been infiltrated by granulomatous inflammation. This is very distinctive. Lupus pernio is cutaneous sarcoid and is characterized by bluish red nodules over the nose. Lupus vulgaris is cutaneous tuberculosis and again has a very distinctive appearance.

→ http://patient.info/doctor/rosacea-and-rhinophyma

27. D ★★

This is pompholyx hand eczema. It consists of very itchy vesicles and papules on the palms. Scabies is less likely in this patient, because the papules come and go together with the rest of his eczema. This form of eczema requires treatment with a potent topical corticosteroid such as betamethasone valerate. There is no evidence of an infection—an infection, whether viral, bacterial, or fungal, would tend to produce an asymmetrical rash or an asymmetrical exacerbation of an existing inflammatory dermatosis.

→ http://www.dermnetnz.org/topics/pompholyx/

28. B ★★   OHCS 11th edn → p. 436

The patches here have an indistinct border and are hypopigmented (not sharp-edged and depigmented, as would be seen in vitiligo). This is pityriasis alba, which occurs on the faces of children with atopic eczema. It improves with treatment with emollients and mild topical corticosteroid creams. Seborrhoeic dermatitis may cause changes in skin pigmentation, but this is far less common. Tinea faciei is a fungal infection on the face and presents in the same manner as on the body/feet. This would be a very unusual age for cutaneous T-cell lymphoma.

→ http://www.dermnetnz.org/topics/pityriasis-alba

29. A ★★   OHCS 11th edn → p. 452

Note the tense blisters on an erythematous, urticated base. Bullous pemphigoid does not usually affect the mucosal membranes. The lesions in the illustration are very typical for this condition.

→ http://www.dermnetnz.org/topics/bullous-pemphigoid/

30. D ★★   OHCS 11th edn → p. 438

This is a small-vessel vasculitis causing palpable purpura of the skin. This was the result of a hypersensitivity reaction to amoxicillin. Whenever purpura is seen, it is important to think of systemic sepsis. However, this man is well and has too long a history for this to be the diagnosis.

→ http://www.dermnetnz.org/topics/leukocytoclastic-vasculitis-pathology/

31. B ★★

This is melasma. The safest treatment is to advise the daily use of a sunblock. Sunshine makes this condition worse. Some women develop melasma while pregnant or when taking the oral contraceptive pill. Hydroquinone can be damaging to the skin, especially at high strength.

→ http://patient.info/doctor/melasma-chloasma-pro

32. D ★★   OHCS 11th edn → p. 452

This is a benign vascular tumour that is commoner in pregnancy. Lesions are often triggered by trauma. They can be easily removed with minor surgery or cryotherapy for smaller lesions. Some may resolve spontaneously. Granuloma annulare is a distinctive annular collection of smooth papules.

→ http://www.dermnetnz.org/topics/pyogenic-granuloma/

33. D ★★

Note the tense blisters in this case. The surrounding skin is normal, which makes bullous pemphigoid, linear IgA disease, and allergic contact eczema unlikely. There is no evidence of impetigo here. Linear IgA disease can present in childhood and adulthood with grouped lesions and, as noted earlier, the surrounding skin is often affected. IgA autoantibodies are directed against the basement membrane.

→ http://patient.info/doctor/linear-iga-dermatosis

34. B ★★   OHCS 11th edn → p. 438

The key is the relationship to coeliac disease. This can be considered a dermatological manifestation of the disease and is treated with strict adherence to a gluten-free diet plus dapsone.

→ https://www.dermnetnz.org/topics/dermatitis-herpetiformis/

35. B ★★★   OHCS 11th edn → p. 452

This is a fairly typical description of pityriasis rosea. The condition starts with a herald patch, which is the key to diagnosis. This is a round plaque, 1–2 cm in diameter, with a pink centre separated from a dark red edge by a fine, scaly area. One to two weeks later, a secondary rash appears, which is usually on the trunk in a symmetrical distribution. These lesions look like smaller versions of the herald patch, and the rash is usually itchy. Guttate psoriasis is very unusual in young children and tends to form drop-like salmon-pink lesions with a fine scale. Seborrhoeic dermatitis causes dry, flaky skin, often on the scalp, but it can occur in folds and flexural areas. Tinea is a fungal infection, and it usually responds to antifungal agents. A single red, inflamed patch tends to keep growing, with the outer edge more inflamed like a ring. Viral exanthemata are typically erythematous, maculopapular rashes that occur with a viral upper respiratory infection.

→ http://www.dermnetnz.org/topics/pityriasis-rosea/

36. C ★★★

Mohs micrographic surgery is now routinely offered to patients with basal cell carcinoma (BCC), as in this case, and squamous cell carcinoma (SCC) on high-risk sites on the face where it is important to preserve as much healthy tissue as possible. Direct excision and closure would not be the preferred option at this site, due to unknown margins and also poor cosmetic result. Cryotherapy, topical therapy such as 5FU, or radiotherapy would not be appropriate, as it would not expect to achieve either a tissue diagnosis or a curative resection, although they do all have roles in the treatment of skin malignancy.

→ https://www.nice.org.uk/guidance/csg8

37. B ★★★★   OHCS 11th edn → p. 439

The diagnosis can be very difficult if the symptoms are confined only to the scalp, but in this case, there is the addition of atrophic lesions in the ears which is typical of discoid lupus. Lichen planopilaris would typically present with frontal loss of hair and scarring alopecia; however, the skin may look slightly scaly or merely scarred, with few visible hair follicles. Alopecia areata is a non-scarring form of hair loss. Psoriatic patients have very thick, adherent scale, particularly around the nape of the neck.

→ http://www.dermnetnz.org/topics/discoid-lupus-erythematosus/

Orthopaedics

Nev Davies and Anuhya Vusirikala

Over the years, orthopaedic surgery has evolved into a vast specialty that is ever growing, with new technology, techniques, and implants. Computer-assisted surgery and minimally invasive approaches are current hot topics that are pushing the boundaries of what constitutes gold standard care for patients.

This specialty touches people of all ages from all walks of life. The practicality and logic in decision-making and management appeal to today's modern 'orthopods'.

Common paediatric orthopaedic conditions, such as developmental dysplasia of the hip and septic arthritis, can have serious consequences for the rest of a child's life if unrecognized and so are represented in this chapter.

Arthroplasty has been one of the true successes of the twenty-first century, and now over 160 000 knee and hip replacements are performed each year in the UK, revolutionizing the quality of life of patients with painful, disabling arthritis.

To be a good orthopaedic surgeon requires not only a wide knowledge base, but also common sense, logic, and practical skills. 'A good surgeon knows how to operate; a great surgeon knows when to operate' is a classic saying that was drilled into me as a young houseman. In this specialty, there are often several management options facing the surgeon and the patient, and through careful discussion and the process of informed consent, a joint plan can be formulated and executed.

The questions in this chapter will help you to prepare both for your exams and for a future career as a doctor.

Nev Davies and Anuhya Vusirikala, *Orthopaedics* In: *Oxford Assess and Progress: Clinical Specialties*. Edited by: Luci Etheridge and Henry Collier, Oxford University Press.
© Oxford University Press 2021. DOI:10.1093/oso/9780198862550.003.0007

QUESTIONS

1. A 6-week-old baby with a 'clicky' hip is referred by the health visitor. She has had an ultrasound scan that confirms a dislocated right hip and a dysplastic acetabulum. Which single clinical finding best supports the diagnosis of a dislocated right hip? ★

A Asymmetrical skin creases on the thighs

B Clicking on abduction of the hip

C A dimple at the base of the spine

D Leg length discrepancy

E Limited abduction of the hip on the right

2. An 83-year-old man has had intermittent pain in the base of his spine for 4 months. It has become constant in nature and is not responding to simple analgesics. Which single factor in the history should alert you to the possibility of a serious pathology? ★

A Night pain

B Past history of malignancy

C Sciatic pain radiating down the leg from the buttock to the foot

D Scoliosis

E Temperature of 38°C or more

3. A 30-year-old woman who is usually fit and well has had intermittent urinary incontinence and loss of sensation around her bottom for the last 24 hours. Which is the single most appropriate next step in management? ★

A Blood tests, spinal X-rays, and a urine dipstick

B History and examination, including a rectal examination

C Mobilization of the theatre team, as she needs to go straight to theatre

D Opiate analgesia and review by senior colleagues

E Urgent magnetic resonance imaging (MRI) scan of the spine

4. A 7-year-old boy has had intermittent pain in his left hip for the past month. He walks with a slight limp and has decreased abduction at the hip joint. Which is the single most likely diagnosis? ★

A Juvenile idiopathic arthritis

B Missed developmental dysplasia of the hip

C Perthes' disease

D Slipped upper femoral epiphysis

E Transient synovitis

5. A 4-year-old boy has had pain and tenderness in his lower leg for 1 week. He is refusing to weight-bear. There is an area of swelling and warmth at the upper tibia which is tender. He has a temperature of 39°C. His blood tests show:

- white cell count 30 × 10⁹/L
- erythrocyte sedimentation rate (ESR) 110 mm/hour
- C-reactive protein (CRP) 200 mg/L.

Which is the single most likely causative microorganism? ★

A *Kingella kingae*

B *Pseudomonas aeruginosa*

C *Salmonella paratyphi*

D *Staphylococcus aureus*

E *Staphylococcus epidermidis*

6. A 70-year-old woman with rheumatoid arthritis is having a total knee replacement. Which is the single most important preoperative investigation? ★

A Anteroposterior and lateral radiographs of the cervical spine

B Arterial blood gas analysis

C Dual-energy X-ray absorptiometry (DEXA) scanning

D Inflammatory markers

E Up-to-date anteroposterior and lateral X-rays of the knee

7. A newborn baby has 'clicky' hips at birth. Which single feature is a risk factor for developmental dysplasia of the hip (DDH)? ★

A Family history of DDH

B Low birthweight

C Male gender

D Polyhydramnios

E Second sibling

8. A 45-year-old builder has pins and needles down the medial border of his forearm and weakness in the small muscles in his hand, causing him to drop things. Which are the single name and location of the nerve that is being compressed? ★

A Anterior interosseous nerve under the fibres of the flexor digitorum sublimis

B Median nerve in the carpal tunnel

C Posterior interosseous nerve under the proximal edge of the supinator muscle

D Ulnar nerve at the cubital tunnel

E Ulnar nerve in Guyon's canal

9. A 65-year-old man sustained a fracture of the femoral neck 4 years ago. He is undergoing a total hip replacement for collapse of the head and secondary osteoarthritis. He walks with a stick and has an antalgic gait and a significant leg length discrepancy. Which is the single most likely benefit of the procedure? ★

A Equalization of the leg length discrepancy

B Improvement of walking distance

C Improvement of range of motion

D Pain relief

E Prevention of compensatory osteoarthritis in other joints

10. A 60-year-old man has a deformed, painless right ankle and foot. He has had blistering and ulceration of his foot in the past. X-rays show a destructive Charcot-type arthropathy of the ankle and subtalar joints. Which is the single most likely underlying diagnosis? ★

A Alcohol-induced peripheral neuropathy

B Diabetes mellitus

C Hereditary motor and sensory neuropathy

D Leprosy

E Tertiary syphilis

11. A 75-year-old man attends his 6-week follow-up appointment after a primary right total hip replacement for osteoarthritis. He walks in with the aid of one stick and as he walks, his upper body sways to the right when he stands on his operated leg. Which is the single best description of his altered gait? ★

A Antalgic

B Normal for this stage in his post-operative recovery

C Short leg

D Trendelenburg positive

E Varus thrust

12. A 36-year-old computer programmer has a painful lump on the volar aspect of his wrist. The lump is well defined, fluctuant, and pulsatile, but it does not transilluminate. Which is the single most appropriate next step in management? ★

A Aspirate the lump in the clinic under local anaesthesia, and inject steroid

B Explain the benign nature of the lump and that it is likely to resolve spontaneously with time

C Organize an ultrasound scan to confirm the diagnosis

D Put the patient on the waiting list for excision of the lump under general anaesthesia

E Put the patient on the waiting list for excision of the lump under local anaesthesia

13. A 60-year-old woman has sustained a low-energy fracture of the distal radius. Last year, she fell and sustained a proximal femoral fracture, which was fixed with a dynamic hip screw. A recent dual-energy X-ray absorptiometry (DEXA) scan has shown a T score of −3. Which is the single most likely diagnosis? ★★

A Oligodystrophy

B Osteomalacia

C Osteopenia

D Osteopetrosis

E Osteoporosis

14. A patient is concerned about the risk of deep infection following a primary total hip replacement. Which single factor has had the greatest impact on reducing joint replacement infection? ★★

A Antibiotic-loaded cement

B Body-exhaust suits for the surgeons

C Disposable gowns

D Laminar air flow systems

E Peri-operative prophylactic systemic antibiotics

15. A 60-year-old woman has had neck pain for several years. She now has an acute prolapse of the C5/6 disc, causing nerve root compression on the right side. Which single set of symptoms and signs is she most likely to have? ★★

A Dysaesthesia in the thumb and index finger, and weakness of elbow extension

B Increased tone and hyper-reflexia in the right arm

C None of these

D Pain and numbness in the medial forearm

E Weakness of elbow flexion and loss of triceps reflex

16. A 2-year-old girl has had multiple bony fractures since birth. She has discoloured teeth, poor growth, and blue sclera. Which is the single most likely diagnosis? ★★

A Achondroplasia

B Craniocleidodysostosis

C Hypophosphatasia

D Osteogenesis imperfecta

E Osteopetrosis

17. A 50-year-old man has increasing pain in his right knee. The pain is not controlled by daily ibuprofen and paracetamol, and he is particularly troubled by it when going up and down stairs. He experiences pain even when at rest. He had a total meniscectomy 30 years ago after a football injury when he also ruptured his anterior cruciate ligament. His X-ray is shown in Figure 7.1 (see Colour Plate section). Which is the single most appropriate management? ★★

A Increase his pain medications and advise him to use a stick

B Medial unicompartmental knee replacement

C Referral for physiotherapy

D Steroid injection and review

E Total knee replacement

18. A baby has been born with a foot deformity, as shown in Figure 7.2 (see Colour Plate section). Which is the single best description of this foot deformity? ★★

A Calcaneus, abductus, valgus

B Cavus, adductus, varus, equinus

C Cavus, calcaneus, adductus, varus

D Cavus, valgus, equinus

E Pes planus

19. A 26-year-old man who plays squash socially presents with a 4-month history of unilateral heel pain. He has circumferential thickening of the Achilles tendon, 2 cm proximal to its insertion at the os calcis, and is unable to perform a tiptoe test. Which is the single most likely diagnosis? ★★

A Achilles insertional tendonitis

B Chronic Achilles tendon rupture

C Hagland's deformity of the os calcis

D Retrocalcaneal bursitis

E Tibialis posterior tendonitis

20. A 15-year old boy presents to the orthopaedic paediatric clinic with a 3-month history of pain and swelling in his right thigh. He has also reported night sweats and recent weight loss. An X-ray of his right thigh shows a large lesion in the diaphysis of his femur with an onion skin appearance. A needle biopsy is performed, and the histological evaluation shows small, round blue cells. Which is the single most likely diagnosis? ★★★★

A Chrondrosarcoma

B Ewing's sarcoma

C Osteochondroma

D Osteosarcoma

E Osteoid osteoma

21. A 60-year-old man has an acutely painful, swollen knee. In total, 100 mL of synovial fluid is aspirated. The fluid is straw-coloured and viscous. Analysis shows no crystals and a white cell count of 4000/mm³ with neutrophils <25%. The patient reports that his pain is much improved after aspiration. Which is the single most likely diagnosis? ★ ★ ★ ★

A Gout

B Pseudogout

C Reactive arthritis

D Rheumatoid arthritis

E Septic arthritis

22. A 65-year-old man has undergone a primary total hip replace-ment for osteoarthritis. Post-operatively, he has developed a foot drop, with numbness in his foot and weakness of ankle dorsi-flexion to 2/5 power. Which is the single most likely cause of the foot drop? ★ ★ ★ ★

A Axonotmesis of the common peroneal nerve at the head of the fibula due to pressure from positioning during the procedure

B Axonotmesis of the sciatic nerve due to intra-operative traction injury secondary to misplaced retractors

C Neuropraxia of the common peroneal nerve at the head of the fibula due to pressure from positioning during the procedure

D Neuropraxia of the sciatic nerve due to intra-operative traction injury secondary to misplaced retractors

E Neurotmesis of the sciatic nerve during surgery

23. A 13-year-old boy has had repeated ankle sprains, mid-foot pain, and problems walking on uneven ground. He has a flat foot that does not correct into varus when he stands on tiptoe. He also has a stiff subtalar joint. Which is the single most likely diagnosis? ★ ★ ★ ★

A Charcot–Marie–Tooth disease

B Lateral ligament insufficiency (ankle)

C Physiological flexible flat foot

D Sever's disease

E Tarsal coalition

24. A 50-year-old diabetic man has recurrent triggering of the ring finger. The finger is stuck in flexion. It was injected 2 years ago, with good results. Which is the single most appropriate management? ★ ★ ★ ★

A Operative release under general anaesthesia

B Operative release under local anaesthesia

C Repeat of the injection

D Stretching and a night splint with physiotherapy

E Ultrasound scan to confirm the diagnosis

ANSWERS

1. E ★ OHCS 11th edn → pp. 492–3

Clicking and asymmetry of skin creases are 'soft' signs of hip dislocation. The limitation of abduction of the hip suggests a positive Ortolani's test, which means that the hip is out of joint posteriorly.

2. B ★ OHCS 11th edn → p. 486

This suggests that spinal metastases may be the cause. The other features may also be present with metastatic lesions but can be features of other diagnoses. Night pain can indicate significant pathology and should be taken seriously.

3. B ★ OHCS 11th edn → p. 487

This history suggests cauda equina syndrome, of which there are many causes. However, the young age makes a sinister cause unlikely. The first step is always a thorough history and examination, and a rectal examination must always be performed to assess anal tone.

4. C ★ OHCS 11th edn → p. 490

In this age group, the most important cause of persistent limp is Perthes' disease, which is an avascular necrosis of the femoral head. Slipped upper femoral epiphysis tends to occur in older overweight children. Transient synovitis should not last for a month. Dysplasia of the hip would have been seen at an earlier age than 7 years. All children in the UK have their hips checked at birth, at 6 weeks, at 8 months, and at 2 years. Juvenile idiopathic arthritis is possible, but less likely.

5. D ★ OHCS 11th edn → p. 502

This is a picture of osteomyelitis, commonly caused by *Staphylococcus aureus*.

6. A ★ OHCS 11th edn → pp. 658–9

Guidelines exist that recommend which preoperative investigations should be performed. However, patients with rheumatoid arthritis are at risk of cervical involvement, which can make anaesthetic management of the neck and airway difficult. If in doubt, always discuss the case with an anaesthetist.

→ https://www.nice.org.uk/guidance/NG45 (routine preoperative tests for elective surgery)

7. A ★ OHCS 11th edn → pp. 492–3

The risk factors for DDH are as follows:

• female gender
• first born

- foot first (breech)
- family history
- further bony abnormalities (e.g. talipes equinovarus).

8. D ★   OHCS 11th edn → p. 475

The ulnar nerve is responsible for the sensory and motor presentation of this problem. The ulnar nerve passes through the cubital tunnel at the elbow, whereas Guyon's canal is at the wrist. Compression at Guyon's canal could not account for the symptoms.

9. D ★   OHCS 11th edn → p. 510

The main benefit of hip replacement is pain control. It is much less successful in improving mobility.

10. B ★

This patient's age makes hereditary motor and sensory neuropathy unlikely. Diabetes is the commonest cause of neuropathy, leading to arthropathy.

11. D ★   OHCS 11th edn → p. 488

The Trendelenburg test assesses the stability of the hip. When the patient stands on the affected leg, the pelvis falls on the opposite side, causing the upper body to lurch to the affected side in order to compensate. This is a positive test. It is caused by weak abductor muscles, a dislocated hip, or the absence of a stable fulcrum.

12. C ★   OHCS 11th edn → p. 476

This is the classic location and description of a ganglion, i.e. a benign bulge of the synovium. It may resolve spontaneously, but if it is painful, it can be aspirated or excised. However, diagnosis should be confirmed first with soft tissue imaging.

13. E ★★

DEXA stands for dual-energy X-ray absorptiometry and is considered to be the most accurate test for bone density. Although standard X-rays show changes in bone density after about 40% bone loss, a DEXA scan can detect changes after about a 1% change. The results of a DEXA scan are reported in two ways—as T scores and as Z scores. A T score compares the bone density with the optimal peak bone density for gender. It is reported as the number of standard deviations below the mean. A T score of greater than −1 is considered to be normal. A T score of −1 to −2.5 is considered to be osteopenia and the patient is at risk of developing osteoporosis. A T score of less than −2.5 is diagnostic of osteoporosis. A Z score compares the patient's bone density with that of someone of the same age.

14. E ★★

To prevent surgical site infections, antibiotic prophylaxis should be given before:

- clean surgery involving the placement of a prosthesis or implant
- clean-contaminated surgery
- contaminated surgery.

→ https://www.nice.org.uk/guidance/cg74 (surgical site infections: prevention and treatment)

15. A ★★   OHCS 11th edn → pp. 466, 522–3

Knowledge of the specific patterns of nerve damage is useful in diagnosis (see the tables and pictures in OHCS 11th edn).

16. D ★★

These are the features of some types of osteogenesis imperfecta, a rare cause of multiple fractures. These signs may help to raise suspicion of the diagnosis.

17. E ★★   OHCS 11th edn → p. 510

For this patient, non-operative measures for the management of his osteo-arthritis have been exhausted, and surgical treatment is warranted. His X-ray shows medial compartment osteoarthritis. However, he requires a total knee replacement because a unicompartmental knee replacement is contraindicated in a patient without an anterior cruciate ligament.

18. B ★★   OHCS 11th edn → p. 492

This is an image of club foot, or talipes equinovarus. A full club foot involves the ankle (talus) and foot (pes), and is equinus (the heel is elevated like that of a horse) and cavus (with an exaggerated arch). It is varus (turned inward) and adducted (moved towards the midline). It cannot be moved through the normal range of movements, and the Achilles tendon is tight and the calf muscle shortened.

19. B ★★

This question requires you to correctly identify the Achilles tendon as the source of the pathology. Patients with tibialis posterior tendonitis also find it difficult to stand on tiptoe. Circumferential thickening could be due to chronic rupture or tendonitis. Retrocalcaneal bursitis tenderness tends to be located more distally, behind the tendon.

20. B ★★★★   OHCS 11th edn → p. 504

Ewing's sarcoma is the second commonest primary malignant bone tumour in children. These tumours are found in the diaphysis of long bones. Based on the history, radiological appearance (periosteal reaction may give an onion skin or sunburst appearance), and histology, the patient has Ewing's sarcoma.

21. C ★★★★ OHCS 11th edn → pp. 512–13

Analysis of the colour, viscosity, and composition of the synovial fluid is important. In this patient, the straw colour and high viscosity, but low number of neutrophils point to a non-inflammatory cause. In patients with inflammation or infection, the fluid is yellow with a high number of neutrophils.

22. D ★★★★ OHCS 11th edn → pp. 510–11

Neuropraxia (physiological conduction block) is the commonest type of nerve injury encountered, usually due to compression on the nerve. In total hip replacement, misplaced retractors are the usual cause of this, and the sciatic nerve is the most commonly involved nerve. Neuropraxia is often explained to patients as 'bruising to the nerve'. Nerve function usually returns to normal, although this can take many months.

23. E ★★★★

Tarsal coalition—an abnormal connection between the tarsal bones—commonly presents in adolescence as the connection ossifies with growth of the child. Often there is a history of repeated ankle sprains and difficulty walking on uneven ground.

24. B ★★★★ OHCS 11th edn → p. 476

Diabetics are renowned for having recurrent resistant triggering digits. Operative release under local anaesthesia avoids the complications of general anaesthesia (which are increased in a diabetic patient) and allows the surgeon to check the release by asking the patient to move the finger intra-operatively.

Trauma

Nev Davies and Anuhya Vusirikala

Trauma is a major public health problem and it is the commonest cause of death in those under the age of 40. Trauma care is a multidisciplinary specialty, and orthopaedic surgeons play an essential role in the initial and definitive management of patients with musculoskeletal injuries—saving lives and saving limb.

The care provided to seriously injured trauma patients has improved significantly for a variety of reasons, including enhanced pre-hospital input, provision of care within a network of Major Trauma Units, and the availability of specialist rehabilitation services in hospital and in the community. The primary aim of the trauma team is to rapidly assess, resuscitate, and stabilize trauma patients and determine the extent of injuries sustained, so that the most appropriate immediate treatment can be administered.

The questions in this chapter will highlight the important principles of trauma care and help you better comprehend the management of a seriously injured trauma patient.

Nev Davies and Anuhya Vusirikala, *Trauma* In: *Oxford Assess and Progress: Clinical Specialties.* Edited by: Luci Etheridge and Henry Collier, Oxford University Press. © Oxford University Press 2021. DOI:10.1093/oso/9780198862550.003.0008

QUESTIONS

1. A 17-year-old man is knocked off his moped. He is wearing a helmet, and witnesses thought that he was travelling at 30 mph before impact. Which is the single most appropriate immediate management? ★

A Advanced Trauma Life Support (ATLS) assessment following guidelines

B Computed tomography (CT) scan of his head

C Glasgow Coma Scale assessment and pupil reaction

D Thorough mechanism of injury history and full examination

E X-rays of his chest, pelvis, and cervical spine

2. A motorcyclist has been involved in a motor vehicle collision. He is talking and has bruising on the right side of his chest, but normal breath sounds; his pulse rate is 120 bpm, and his blood pressure is 60/40 mmHg. His Glasgow Coma Scale score is 15/15. He has bruising around his flanks and an obvious open fracture of his right tibia. He has blood at the urethral meatus. His chest X-ray shows some fractured ribs on the right, and his pelvic film is shown in Figure 8.1 (see Colour Plate section). Which is the single most appropriate next step in his management? ★

A Betadine-soaked dressing, intravenous (IV) antibiotics, and washout of his tibial fracture

B Chest drain for his rib fractures and potential haemothorax

C IV access, IV fluids, and blood replacement

D Pelvic external fixation

E Securing of a definitive airway with the anaesthetist

3. A 6-year-old boy is brought to the Emergency Department with a painful swollen arm. His mother is unsure what happened and gives a story of an unwitnessed fall off a bunk bed the day before. The boy has a lot of bruising all over his arm and upper body. Which is the single most appropriate management? ★

A Admit the child to the ward and contact your consultant

B Contact the duty social worker

C Discuss your concerns with the paediatrician on call

D Probe the mother about the cause of the bruises

E Send off a full blood count and clotting screen

4. A 9-year-old boy has put his arm through a glass door. There is significant bleeding from a 5-cm deep wound in his forearm. Which is the single most appropriate immediate management? ★

A Apply a high arm tourniquet

B Apply direct pressure over the axillary artery

C Apply direct pressure over the wound

D Give intravenous (IV) antibiotics and tetanus prophylaxis

E Give local anaesthetic and clip the bleeding vessel

5. A 25-year-old man has been involved in a drunken brawl and has been stabbed in the chest. His respiratory rate is 25 breaths/minute, heart rate 110 bpm, and blood pressure 85/60 mmHg. He has two wounds in the left thorax. Which is the single most appropriate immediate management? ★

A Apply direct pressure over the stab wounds to stem the bleeding

B Fast bleep the cardiothoracic surgeons

C Obtain intravenous (IV) access and cross-match 6 units of blood

D Open the airway and give high-flow oxygen

E Open the chest (thoracotomy) and begin internal cardiac massage

6. A 7-year-old boy has an open fracture of his forearm. He is on a scout trip away from home and attends the hospital with his scout leader. You need to take him to theatre immediately but are unable to contact his parents who are away on holiday. Which is the single most appropriate course of action? ★

A Ask a duty social worker to sign the consent form

B Ask another doctor to sign the consent form

C Ask the boy to sign the consent form

D Ask the scout leader to sign the consent form

E Written consent is not required as this is an emergency

7. A 25-year-old man has been knocked off his motorcycle. He has an open fracture of his femur. His leg X-ray is shown in Figure 8.2 (see Colour Plate section). Which is the single most appropriate definitive management? ★★

A External fixator with washout and debridement of the wound and delayed primary closure

B Intramedullary nail with washout and debridement of the wound and delayed primary closure

C Open reduction and plate fixation with washout and debridement of the wound and primary closure

D Washout and debridement of the wound and application of a Thomas splint

E Washout and debridement of the wound and a long leg cast with a window for a vacuum suction pump

8. A 79-year-old woman has fallen at home. She has hip pain and a short, externally rotated left leg. Radiographs show a displaced intracapsular fracture of her left neck of femur. Previously she walked outdoors independently with the aid of a stick. She is otherwise medically fit. Which is the single most appropriate surgical management? ★★

A Cemented hemiarthroplasty

B Dynamic hip screw and plate

C Total hip replacement

D Uncemented hemiarthroplasty

E Three divergent cannulated screws

9. A 35-year-old man, who was injured in a road traffic accident, is admitted to the Emergency Department. His eyes open to painful stimuli and he moans periodically. His left arm is deformed and does not respond to painful stimuli, but his right arm purposefully moves towards the painful stimulus. Which is the single most appropriate Glasgow Coma Scale (GCS) score for this patient? ★★★

A 4

B 5

C 8

D 9

E 13

10. A 75-year-old man sustained a head injury following a fall, sustaining a 3-cm scalp laceration. In the Emergency Department, he appears mildly confused, with a Glasgow Coma Scale (GCS) score of 14. His heart rate is 85 bpm and his blood pressure is 135/70 mmHg. He has had one episode of vomiting in hospital. He is currently on warfarin for atrial fibrillation but is otherwise well. Which is the single most appropriate initial management? ★★★

A Admit for head injury observations

B Check ethanol levels

C Perform a computed tomography (CT) scan of his head

D Skull X-ray

E Suture the scalp laceration

11. A 20-year-old man falls off his motorbike and fractures his tibial shaft. The management options are discussed with him and he opts for an intramedullary nail. He is put into a backslab cast and listed for surgery the next day. His leg is kept strictly elevated. At 3.30 a.m., he develops increasing pain despite morphine treatment. Which is the single most appropriate next step in management? ★★★

A Add a non-steroidal anti-inflammatory drug to his pain relief, and review in 30 minutes

B Call the anaesthetist to set up a patient-controlled morphine analgesia system

C Call your senior colleague, as the patient needs to go to theatre immediately

D List the patient for theatre at 6 a.m., when his stomach will be empty and it will be safe to give him an anaesthetic

E Split his cast to skin, continue elevation, and review him with a senior colleague in 15 minutes

12. A 93-year-old woman is bed-bound in a nursing home and has severe dementia. She has fallen out of bed. Her right hip is stiff but painless, and an X-ray reveals a dislocated total hip replacement (THR). She also has a large 10 × 5 cm open pre-tibial laceration. She has a respiratory rate of 23 breaths/minute, with evidence of ischaemic changes on the electrocardiogram (ECG). Which is the single most appropriate specialty to call for help with the management of this patient? ★★★

A Anaesthetist, to give a general anaesthetic to reduce the THR

B Cardiologist, to help to interpret the ECG changes

C General medical team, to optimize medical care prior to any intervention

D Plastic surgeon, to help to manage the open pre-tibial laceration

E Psychiatrist, to assess whether the patient can consent to treatment

13. A 6-year-old boy has a fall onto his left outstretched hand. He now has difficulty in pronating his forearm, flexing his wrist and thumb. He also complains about loss of sensation in the lateral palm and radial three-and-a-half digits. His X-ray shows a supracondylar fracture of the left humerus. Which is the single most likely nerve that is damaged? ★★★

A Anterior interosseous branch of the median nerve

B Deep branch of the radial nerve

C Palmar cutaneous branch of the median nerve

D Superficial branch of the radial nerve

E Ulnar nerve

14. A 35-year-old man was playing five-a-side football when he thought he had been kicked in the back of the leg. The next day, he is hobbling and has pain and swelling around his Achilles tendon. Simmonds' test is equivocal. Which is the single most appropriate investigation to confirm the diagnosis and plan further management? ★★★★

A Computed tomography (CT) scan

B Examination under anaesthesia

C Magnetic resonance imaging (MRI) scan

D Plain X-ray

E Ultrasound scan

15. A 25-year-old man with epilepsy has a painful swollen shoulder after having a fit earlier that day. X-rays are taken and shown in Figure 8.3 (see Colour Plate section). Which is the single most appropriate management? ★★★★

A Arrange for a computed tomography (CT) scan to help to plan operative management

B Arrange for the patient to go to theatre for a closed reduction

C Arrange for the patient to go to theatre for an open reduction

D Perform reduction using the Hippocratic method under sedation

E Perform reduction using Kocher's method under sedation

16. A 45-year-old woman has an oblique fracture of her distal fibula. Which is the single best technique to compress the two fragments of bone? ★ ★ ★ ★

A Dynamic compression plate and cancellous screws

B Elastic titanium intramedullary nails

C External fixation with supplementary K-wire fixation

D Lag screw and neutralization plate

E Locking plate with locking screws

17. A 45-year-old man has fallen 20 feet off a ladder. As he fell, his right leg became caught in the rungs of the ladder and he felt his knee 'pop in and pop out'. He has a very swollen, tender knee, with a cool, white limb and a very faint dorsalis pedis pulse. Which is the single most appropriate immediate management? ★ ★ ★ ★

A Anteroposterior and lateral lower limb radiographs

B Mobilize the theatre team immediately, as the patient needs to undergo an open exploration of the popliteal vessels

C Magnetic resonance imaging (MRI) of the patient's knee to determine which ligaments are damaged

D Organize an arteriogram and contact the vascular surgeons for an urgent review

E Organize an urgent fasciotomy to prevent compartment syndrome

18. A 15-year-old boy has fractured his humerus. His X-ray is shown in Figure 8.4 (see Colour Plate section). Which is the single most likely mechanism of injury? ★ ★ ★ ★

A Bending force

B Bending force with axial compression

C Direct impact from the lateral aspect

D Direct impact from the medial aspect

E Torsional force

19. A 22-year-old footballer ruptures his anterior cruciate ligament and tears his medial meniscus after twisting his knee in training. Which single group of clinical findings is most likely 2 weeks after the initial injury? ★ ★ ★ ★

A Effusion, hyperextension, and generalized joint line tenderness

B Effusion, medial joint line tenderness, and positive Lachman's test

C Increased opening on valgus stress, and tenderness medially

D Increased posterior sag, positive anterior draw, and negative Lachman's test

E Quadriceps wasting, extensor lag, and positive Lachman's test

ANSWERS

1. A ★   OHCS 11th edn → pp. 576, 587

The ATLS guidelines are regarded as the international gold standard for the initial management of the traumatized patient.

→ https://www.rcseng.ac.uk/education-and-exams/courses/search/advanced-trauma-life-support-atls-provider-programme/

2. C ★

In keeping with any significant injury, as per the Advanced Trauma Life Support (ATLS) principles, the immediate priority is to ensure that airway, breathing, and circulation are not compromised. This man's airway and breathing seem to be secure, as determined by a normal Glasgow Coma Scale score and the ability to phonate, so you should go on to treat the potential blood loss from the pelvic fracture by securing circulation.

3. C ★   OHCS 11th edn → p. 196

Any doctor who sees children needs to be aware of the possibility of non-accidental injury. However, although it is important to document exactly what you have found, specialist paediatric doctors should be involved in these cases. They can work with the parent specialty team to gather further information and plan appropriate management.

4. C ★

Following the ABC (airway, breathing, and circulation) guidelines, the first step in controlling bleeding is the application of direct pressure. Once the bleeding is under control, this patient may need further surgical intervention, and antibiotics and tetanus prophylaxis may be indicated, but these are not the priorities.

5. D ★

Following the Advanced Trauma Life Support (ATLS) guidelines, securing an airway is always the first priority.

6. E ★

Only a person with parental responsibility can give valid consent on behalf of a child who is not Gillick-competent. In some cases, the parent may sign over parental responsibility to another adult, but usually this does not happen. In an emergency, the doctor should document the need for an emergency procedure clearly and state why it is needed, but can proceed to save life or limb without formal written consent.

→ http://www.gmc-uk.org/guidance/ethical_guidance/children_guidance_index.asp (*Good medical practice: 0–18 years: guidance for all doctors*)

7. B ★★   OHCS 11th edn → pp. 540–1

Intramedullary nails align and stabilize the bone and share the load with the bone. They allow early mobilization. Because the fracture is open, it requires careful washing out. Delayed primary closure refers to the initial debridement and then closing of the wound at a later stage. This allows better healing of contaminated wounds.

→ https://www.boa.ac.uk/resources/boa-standards-for-trauma-and-orthopaedics/boast-4-pdf.html (*BOAST 4 guideline: the management of severe open lower limb fractures*)

8. C ★★

Intracapsular fractures require either a total hip replacement or a hemiarthroplasty. Patients who were able to walk independently outside with the aid of no more than a stick, who are not cognitively impaired, and who are medically fit for anaesthesia and surgery should be offered a total hip replacement.

→ http://guidance.nice.org.uk/CG124 (National Institute for Health and Care Excellence (2011). *Hip fracture: management*. NICE clinical guideline, CG124)

9. D ★★★

It is important to be able to calculate the Glasgow Coma Scale score in critically ill patients. This patient has a score of 9:

• eye opening—2
• best verbal response—2
• best motor response—5. An abbreviated coma scale—AVPU—can be used for a quick initial assessment of a patient:[*]
• A—alert
• V—responds to voice
• P—responds to pain
• U—unresponsive.

→ http://www.glasgowcomascale.org/

10. C ★★★

As per the National Institute for Health and Care Excellence (NICE) guidelines on head injury, a CT head would be the priority in this patient because of the following reasons:

• mildly confused with a GCS score of 14 since injury
• one episode of vomiting
• on warfarin therapy for atrial fibrillation.

[*]Source data from *Annals of Emergency Medicine*, 44, 2, Kelly CA, Upex A, Bateman DN, Comparison of consciousness level assessment in the poisoned patient using the alert/verbal/painful/unresponsive scale and the Glasgow Coma Scale, pp. 108–113.

11. E ★★★   OHCS 11th edn → p. 528

Patients with leg fractures are at risk of developing compartment syndrome, inflammation, and swelling within a closed fascial compartment, leading to an impaired blood supply. However, this man is in a cast, so simple relief of the external pressure and elevation may alleviate the pain and swelling. If the pain continues, he may be developing compartment syndrome and require fasciotomy, so a close review is essential.

12. C ★★★

This situation is not uncommon. The patient is more likely to suffer harm as a result of her medical illness than in relation to her dislocated THR, and medical problems should be co-managed with medical teams in the interest of best outcome for the patient.

Ortho-geriatricians are medically trained doctors who work closely with orthopaedic doctors to provide exactly this kind of input.

13. A ★★★   OHCS 11th edn → p. 533

The anterior interosseous branch (AIN) of the median nerve is the most commonly damaged nerve in supracondylar fractures. The AIN supplies the deep muscles of the forearm (flexor pollicis longus, lateral half of the flexor digitorum profundus, pronator quadratus). Damage to the AIN results in loss of pronation of the forearm, weakness in wrist flexion, and inability to flex the thumb. As his fracture is above the origin of the palmar cutaneous branch, there is loss of sensation in the lateral palm and the radial three-and-a-half digits.

14. E ★★★★   OHCS 11th edn → p. 518

A ruptured Achilles tendon causes sudden pain when running or jumping, and the heel cannot be raised from the floor when the patient is standing on the affected leg. In Simmonds' test, the patient kneels on a chair and the calf is squeezed; there will be less plantar flexion of the foot on the affected side. An ultrasound scan is the easiest and most discriminatory test for soft tissue injuries, although it is operator-dependent.

15. A ★★★★   OHCS 11th edn → p. 530

The radiographs show a locked posterior dislocation of the glenohumeral joint. This injury is often missed, as the signs (positive 'light-bulb' sign) are subtle in the anteroposterior view. The diagnosis is obvious in the axillary view. This is a difficult problem, and often further imaging is necessary to plan surgical management.

16. D ★★★★   OHCS 11th edn → p. 544

A lag screw is the best technique for producing interfragmentary compression in the context of absolute stability. This allows the fracture to heal by primary bone healing without the formation of a callus.

17. D ★★★★ OHCS 11th edn → p. 543

The history and examination findings should alert you to a possible knee dislocation that has self-reduced. This poses a significant risk to the neurovascular bundle. An arteriogram is the gold standard investigation, with an urgent review by the vascular surgeons.

18. E ★★★★

This is a spiral fracture, which is caused by a twisting force.

19. B ★★★★ OHCS 11th edn → pp. 549–50

This patient is likely to have a residual effusion 2 weeks after a significant knee injury. Joint line tenderness is a non-specific examination finding in a knee with intra-articular damage. Lachman's test, performed with the knee in 30° of flexion, is the most sensitive clinical test for diagnosing an anterior cruciate ligament injury. Important points are to compare with the other knee and the presence or absence of an end point.

Emergency medicine

Catherine Roberts

Emergency medicine is not all 'ER'—glamour and fast-moving action; much of it requires caring for relatively minor problems or complex elderly patients. Emergency Departments are busy, high-intensity work environments with a high turnover of patients. In order to make time-critical decisions effectively, it is necessary to have a good breadth and depth of knowledge underpinning a sensible and safe approach to dealing with clinical uncertainty. Patients will present with acute and chronic conditions from all specialties.

Gathering information rapidly is important. Gaining clues from the patient and their relative(s) is useful, as is obtaining information on events at the scene from the ambulance paramedics. Hospital notes are often not available and neither is the general practitioner (GP), so decisions are made on the basis of limited information. Rather than making definitive diagnoses confirmed by expensive tests, the role of the emergency physician is to determine the immediate threat to life or limb and to treat that threat, while gathering information to make a 'most likely' diagnosis so that treatment can be started. Observing the patient in a Clinical Decision Unit can often help to confirm your suspicions, give you further information on how severe a condition is, or eliminate a possible diagnosis.

Ultimately, emergency medicine requires the assessment of risk, evaluation of the added benefit of admission over discharge, and excellent communication. The only way to learn emergency medicine is to practice, to discuss patients, and to develop your analytical and decision-making skills. The following questions are designed to develop some of these skills, by showing you an approach to solving the clinical problems that are commonly encountered in the Emergency Department, how to use tests efficiently and effectively, and some of the options for treatment that are available other than admission under inpatient teams.

Catherine Roberts, *Emergency medicine* In: *Oxford Assess and Progress: Clinical Specialties.*
Edited by: Luci Etheridge and Henry Collier, Oxford University Press.
© Oxford University Press 2021. DOI:10.1093/oso/9780198862550.003.0009

QUESTIONS

1. A 24-year-old man is hit by a car travelling at 50 mph. He is unconscious at the scene and there are only two rescuers. He has an obvious fracture of his right leg and swelling of his abdomen. Which is the single most appropriate immediate management of this patient's assumed cervical spine injury at the scene? ★

A Halo traction

B Manual in-line immobilization

C Manual in-line traction

D Semi-rigid cervical collar, blocks, and tape

E Soft sponge collar

2. A 46-year-old woman is in a coma. Her partner tells you that she has had abdominal pain and vomiting for 3 days. She is clinically dehydrated. Her blood sugar level is 48 mmol/L and her arterial pH is 7.0. An anaesthetist is present and managing her airway. Which is the single most appropriate immediate management? ★

A A 500 mL bolus of 0.9% saline

B Infusion of short-acting insulin at 10 U/hour

C Intravenous (IV) cyclizine

D IV piperacillin/tazobactam (Tazocin®)

E Normal saline 2 L with potassium 40 mmol/L over 4 hours

3. A 45-year-old man has a 2-cm laceration to the radial border of the middle and distal phalanges of his right index finger. Which is the single most appropriate local anaesthetic to use while closing the wound? ★

A 0.5% bupivacaine without adrenaline (epinephrine)

B 1% lidocaine with adrenaline (epinephrine) 1:1000

C 1% lidocaine without adrenaline (epinephrine)

D 2% lidocaine with adrenaline (epinephrine) 1:1000

E 5% prilocaine without adrenaline (epinephrine)

4. A 40-year-old woman has pain and discharge from her right ear, a temperature of 38.3°C, a blocked nose, and a mild cough. She had slight pain and deafness in her right ear 1 week ago, which she treated with warm olive oil dripped into her ear. She is a tele-banking operator who uses a headset with an earpiece in her right ear. Which is the single most likely diagnosis? ★

A Extensive wax in the ear

B Foreign body in the ear

C Otitis externa

D Otitis media

E Perforated eardrum

5. A 56-year-old man has had a fall. He has a fracture of the radial head, which is non-displaced. Which is the single most appropriate method of immobilizing this fracture? ★

A Above-arm back slab

B Broad arm sling

C Collar and cuff

D Futura splint

E High arm sling

6. An 85-year-old man has an epistaxis. He is on warfarin for atrial fibrillation and his international normalized ratio (INR) is 6. Which single drug that he has recently been started on is most likely to be related to the cause of the epistaxis? ★

A Aspirin

B Bendroflumethiazide

C Clopidogrel

D Erythromycin

E Penicillin

7. An 89-year-old woman has had multiple falls. She has been to the Emergency Department 30 times in the last 6 months but has only been admitted once. You assess her and can find little acutely wrong with her, but are concerned about sending her home. She appears to be unsteady on her feet. Which single service would be most helpful in contributing to a management plan? ★

A General practitioner (GP)

B Hospital chiropody

C Hospital optician

D Medical registrar

E Occupational therapy

8. A 72-year-old man is brought to the Emergency Department in shock. His systolic blood pressure is 76 mmHg, with a pulse rate of 120 bpm. He has a history of 'coffee ground' vomiting and has melaena on rectal examination. Which is the single most appropriate immediate management? ★

A Application of a military anti-shock trouser (MAST) suit

B Intravenous (IV) bolus of gelofusine

C IV bolus of 5% dextrose

D IV infusion of noradrenaline (norepinephrine)

E Transfusion of packed red blood cells

9. A 27-year-old man has a sudden onset of severe occipital headache. Which single clinical sign is of greatest concern? ★

A Loss of consciousness

B Neck stiffness

C Photophobia

D Unilateral pain

E Vomiting

10. A 45-year-old man has a systolic blood pressure of 50 mmHg and a pulse rate of 120 bpm. Which single vascular access line would be the best to use? ★

A Green Venflon (18G)

B Grey Venflon (16G)

C Intraosseus needle

D Single-lumen central line

E Triple-lumen central line

11. A 45-year-old scaffolder has fallen 30 feet from a scaffold. He is unconscious and brought in on a spinal board. You wish to 'log roll' him off the spinal board. Which single instruction to the team about a log roll should be given? ★

A A rectal examination must be performed first

B Five members of staff are required in total

C One staff member should take the patient's shoulders and pelvis

D The patient's head must be held slightly flexed on the body

E The staff member who examines the patient's back is in charge

12. A 23-year-old woman has been tackled during a football match and has a fracture of the tibial plateau, which is non-displaced. Which is the single most appropriate method of immobilizing this fracture? ★

A Above-knee back slab

B Below-knee back slab

C Cast brace

D Cricket bat splint

E Wool and crêpe bandage

13. A 2-year-old boy is brought to the Emergency Department from his nursery. The nursery staff are concerned because he has multiple bruises on his arms and legs. Which single injury is the most likely to be non-accidental? ★

A Bruising to the anterior shins

B Dislocation of the radial head (a 'pulled elbow')

C Greenstick fracture of the distal radius

D Hot water splash burns to the arm and face

E Small, round bruises on the sides of the chest

14. A 75-year-old man has an acutely red left eye and is vomiting. His visual acuity is 6/24 and he appears very unwell. The eye is red, the cornea is hazy, and the pupil is irregular and unreactive. Which is the single most likely diagnosis? ★

A Acute closed-angle glaucoma

B Central retinal vein thrombosis

C Conjunctivitis

D Episcleritis

E Herpetic ulcer

15. A 34-year-old man is crushed against a wall by a reversing car. He is distressed and has difficulty breathing. Which is the single most reliable sign of a right-sided tension pneumothorax? ★

A Absent breath sounds on the right side

B Dullness of the chest to percussion

C Hyper-resonance to percussion

D The presence of circulatory shock

E Tracheal deviation to the left

16. A 25-year-old man has had a generalized seizure that lasted for 5 minutes. He remains post-ictal and his breathing is noisy. Which single piece of equipment is the most appropriate to use to maintain a patent airway? ★

A Endotracheal tube

B Guedel airway

C Nasopharyngeal airway

D Suction

E Tracheostomy tube

17. A 6-week-old boy has been vomiting immediately after every feed for the last 5 days. He vomits large quantities of non-bilious vomitus, which shoots out all over his mother while she is feeding him. He is screaming hungrily and has sunken eyes and dry mucous membranes. Which is the single most likely diagnosis? ★

A Hirschsprung's disease

B Malrotation of the bowel

C Oesophageal atresia

D Pyloric stenosis

E Urinary tract infection

18. A 54-year-old railway worker is hit by a train. He has an open injury to his right thigh, with a fractured femur clearly visible in the wound. There is arterial bleeding from the wound, and his systolic blood pressure is 70 mmHg. Which is the single most appropriate immediate action? ★

A Activate the major haemorrhage protocol

B Apply a tourniquet proximally

C Apply pressure to the wound

D Ask the surgeon to cross-clamp the femoral artery

E Explore the wound to clamp the bleeding vessel

19. A 35-year-old man has acute pain in his upper abdomen, radiating through to his back, and he is vomiting. Which single factor is most likely to support a diagnosis of pancreatitis? ★

A Contact with gastroenteritis

B Excessive alcohol intake

C History of foreign travel

D History of renal colic

E Use of cocaine and amphetamines

20. A 25-year-old woman has vaginal bleeding. Her husband tells you that they have been undergoing fertility treatment, and she is thought to be 2 months pregnant after implantation of fertilized eggs. She has some bleeding from her vagina, with mild left-sided abdominal tenderness. She has a pulse rate of 60 bpm and a systolic blood pressure of 80 mmHg. Which is the single most appropriate action to take in the Emergency Department? ★

A Arrange an urgent ultrasound scan of her pelvis

B Arrange for her to go to theatre

C Give her O-negative blood

D Give her O-positive blood

E Perform a speculum examination

21. A 41-year-old cyclist is brought into the Emergency Department after a collision with a motor vehicle. He appears pale and clammy. His blood pressure is 65/30 mmHg, and his heart rate is 145 bpm. He has a grossly hyper-expanded left hemithorax, with tracheal deviation to the right. The neck veins are visibly distended. Which is the single most appropriate initial management? ★

A 1 L bolus of colloid

B Insert a chest drain

C Perform needle thoracocentesis

D Perform pericardiocentesis

E Transfuse 2 U of O-negative blood

22. A 45-year-old man presents with tachycardia, and the electrocardiogram (ECG) is shown in Figure 9.1 (see Colour Plate section). Which single feature is an adverse sign in patients with this condition? ★★

A Abdominal pain

B Agitation and confusion

C Systolic blood pressure higher than 180 mmHg

D Redness of the extremities

E Basal crepitations and raised jugular venous pressure

23. A 25-year-old woman has taken 40 paracetamol tablets (20 g). She is refusing to accept medical treatment, stating that she wishes to die. Which is the single most appropriate immediate course of action? ★★

A Allow her to go home, as everyone has a right to die

B Assume that she is mentally incompetent and treat her against her wishes

C Contact her general practitioner (GP) for more information about her

D Formally assess her capacity to refuse treatment

E Request psychiatry to section her for medical treatment

24. A 95-year-old woman has a leg ulcer on the medial aspect of her lower leg. It is weeping, with necrotic tissue in the centre of the ulcer. After debridement under local anaesthesia, the wound looks pink and has some minor bleeding areas. Which is the single most appropriate dressing to apply? ★★

A Alginate dressing

B Flamazine cream

C Hydrocolloid dressing

D Iodine-impregnated dressing

E Non-adherent dressing

25. A 43-year-old woman is in a coma. To a painful stimulus, she opens her eyes, groans, and extends her arms. Which is her single Glasgow Coma Scale score? ★★

A 3

B 6

C 9

D 12

E 15

26. A 12-year-old boy presents to the Emergency Department 1 hour after clashing heads while playing football. Which single aspect of his presentation warrants computed tomography (CT) imaging of his head? ★★

A He has vomited twice in the Emergency Department

B He has a Glasgow Coma Scale (GCS) score of 14

C He has had a seizure in the Emergency Department

D He is bleeding profusely from a forehead laceration

E He reports a pain score of 10/10

27. A 22-year-old male student presents to the Emergency Department after a long train journey. He has noticed non-specific chest pain for the last hour and wanted to get it checked out. He is a non-smoker who is normally well and has no previous medical or significant family history. The electrocardiogram (ECG) is normal. Which single blood test would be useful in this situation? ★★

A Coagulation screen

B C-reactive protein

C D-dimer

D Serum amylase

E Troponin T

28. A 68-year-old man is pronounced dead in the Emergency Department after prolonged resuscitation. Which single factor in the history below requires reporting of the death to the coroner/ procurator fiscal? ★★★

A The death is related to a diagnosed terminal illness

B The death is related to travel overseas

C The patient had been in hospital for less than 24 hours

D The patient fell and hit his head earlier in the day.

E The patient is not a UK citizen

29. You are walking home from work as a foundation doctor near the railway line when you hear a massive noise. A mainline train has derailed and is lying on its side. There appear to be multiple casualties. Which is the single most appropriate action? ★★★

A Make your way to the nearest hospital to offer help

B Provide immediate first aid to the nearest casualty

C Telephone 999 and give a formal report

D Telephone the press to give them the news

E Telephone your hospital to let them know

30. An 18-year-old man has been fitting for the last 15 minutes. An oxygen mask is in place and a nasal airway has been inserted by the ambulance crew. One dose of rectal diazepam has been given and a cannula has been inserted. Which is the single most appropriate immediate treatment? ★★★

A Diazepam 10 mg per rectum

B Lorazepam 4 mg intravenously (IV)

C Midazolam 4 mg IV

D Phenytoin 18 mg/kg IV

E Thiopentone 5 mg/kg IV

31. A 75-year-old diabetic woman has a pre-tibial laceration to her right leg that she sustained 45 minutes ago. She has a barely palpable popliteal pulse and no pulses in the foot. Which is the single most appropriate method of closure? ★★★★

A 30 Ethibond (semi-synthetic) sutures

B 40 Vicryl Rapide sutures

C Primary skin grafting

D Steri-strips

E Tissue glue

32. A 72-year-old man is acutely short of breath and unwell; his oxygen saturation on air is 75%, and his blood gases show a mildly raised carbon dioxide level and a low oxygen level with a mild mixed acidosis. Which single factor is a contraindication to the use of non-invasive ventilation (NIV) in this patient? ★★★★

A Epistaxis

B False teeth

C Nausea

D Pneumonia

E Previous respiratory arrest

33. A 75-year-old man has collapsed. He has left-sided facial weakness and a dense left hemiparesis. He is looking towards his right side and appears to have left-sided neglect. There is no obvious visual field deficit. He has severe dysarthria, but no obvious dysphasia. The computed tomography (CT) brain scan performed at 6 hours is suggestive of an ischaemic area in the distribution of the right middle cerebral artery. Which single intervention is most likely to optimize his outcome? ★★★★

A Keep his heart rate between 60 and 100 bpm

B Keep his temperature above 37.5°C

C Keep his systolic blood pressure below 100 mmHg

D Maintain his blood glucose level within the normal range

E Maintain his haemoglobin level above 12 g/dL

34. A 78-year-old man is in shock. After initial resuscitation, the decision is made to insert a central line using the subclavian approach. Which is the single most appropriate landmark to give guidance during the procedure? ★★★★

A Insertion is at the junction of the medial and middle thirds of the clavicle

B The clavicle is superior to the subclavian vein

C The needle should be pointing towards the tip of the contralateral scapula

D The subclavian vein lies medial to the subclavian artery

E The subclavian vein runs under the first rib

35. You are asked to act as team leader during the resuscitation of a 30-year-old man. Which is the single most effective behaviour of a team leader? ★★★★

A Check the identity and skills of all team members when they arrive

B Continually ask team members for their opinion

C Insist on silence during the resuscitation unless questioned directly

D Issue all instructions in a loud voice

E Personally perform all invasive procedures

ANSWERS

1. D ★   OHCS 11th edn → p. 559

In any major trauma, it is important to consider the possibility of a cervical spine injury. Current guidelines recommend full cervical spine immobilization in patients in whom an injury is suspected. Full protection consists of three-point immobilization using a correctly sized semi-rigid cervical collar, blocks to both sides of the head, and tape. Manual in-line immobilization should be used until these are available.

→ http://www.nice.org.uk/guidance/ng41/chapter/Recommendations (National Institute for Health and Care Excellence (2016). *Spinal injury: assessment and early management.* NICE guideline, NG41)

2. A ★

This woman has a markedly raised blood sugar level and is acidotic, which indicates diabetic ketoacidosis. After control of airway and breathing, which should always come first, the next priority is to restore circulating volume with a fluid bolus. Crystalloids are recommended for resuscitation, and sodium chloride 0.9% is the most commonly used. Potassium is only replaced once the patient has an adequate blood pressure and the serum potassium level is less than 5.5 mmol/L. Insulin should be given by a fixed-rate intravenous infusion, started at 0.1 U/kg/hour, once fluid resuscitation has commenced.

→ http://www.diabetes.org.uk/Documents/About%20Us/What%20 we%20say/Management-of-DKA-241013.pdf (Joint British Diabetes Societies Inpatient Care Group guideline (2013). *The management of diabetic ketoacidosis in adults*)

3. C ★   OHCS 11th edn → p. 678

Lidocaine is the anaesthetic of choice, and 1–2 mL of 1% lidocaine is sufficient for the majority of small wounds. Ring blocks essentially use infiltration of a local anaesthetic into the soft tissue around the digital nerve. This results in nerve impulses being blocked before they reach the spinal cord and cerebral cortex, thus achieving anaesthesia. Two injections are required, one on each side of the finger at the base of the finger. The whole skin of the finger will be anaesthetized by such a block, including the nail bed. There is no greater advantage of 2% lidocaine over 1%, and Emergency Departments are recommended to keep only one strength in stock, in order to minimize the risk of confusion when calculating doses. Although prilocaine and bupivacaine could theoretically be used, their much longer onset time makes them impractical for performing wound repairs in the Emergency Department. The use of adrenaline (epinephrine) in any local infiltration around an end artery (in this case, the digital artery) is contraindicated because of the risk of perfusion to the distal finger. Other end arteries include the nasal artery and the artery to the penis. The following website describes how to perform a digital nerve block (it is also an excellent resource for other blocks used in the Emergency Department).

→ https://www.nysora.com/regional-anesthesia-for-specific-surgical-procedures/upper-extremity-regional-anesthesia-for-specific-surgical-procedures/anesthesia-and-analgesia-for-hand-procedures/digital-block/

4. D ★   OHCS 11th edn → p. 394

This patient is most likely to have developed otitis media in association with her viral upper respiratory tract infection, which has led to perforation of her eardrum and discharge of pus. It is unlikely that her symptoms are due to a simple otitis externa, as this rarely gives systemic symptoms such as fever in an adult. Although a foreign body may act as a nidus for infection, it is unlikely that the woman's earpiece would have migrated into her ear without being noticed. Wax should not cause systemic upset. An isolated perforation of the eardrum should not cause continued discharge or temperature.

5. C ★   OHCS 11th edn → p. 532

The objective of immobilization must be considered. This fracture is non-displaced, and as there are no strong forces working across the fracture site to cause displacement, it will heal well in time; therefore, the key aim of immobilization is pain relief. A collar and cuff is the most appropriate form of immobilization. It provides the support needed without being too restrictive and allows early mobilization, which has been suggested to improve long-term function. Some clinicians use a broad arm sling, but this conveys no advantage and is generally more restrictive.

A high arm sling flexes the elbow to over 90° and is therefore uncomfortable in the presence of an elbow effusion. A Futura splint (a removable splint that immobilizes the wrist) is not appropriate for the elbow. Complete immobilization of the elbow is unnecessary, making a back slab unsuitable.

6. D ★

Erythromycin can inhibit the metabolism of warfarin by affecting the cytochrome P450 complex in the liver, and it can therefore enhance its effects. Aspirin and clopidogrel are both antiplatelet agents and could increase the risk of bleeding. However, they would not affect the INR.

7. E ★

This is quite common in the elderly, and consideration should be given to ensuring that it does not keep happening. Occupational therapy services can assess the home environment and daily functioning and can address issues that may predispose to falls.

8. E ★

This patient is having an upper gastrointestinal bleed and is showing clinical evidence of haemorrhagic shock. The clinical priority in the Emergency Department is fluid resuscitation in order to restore the circulating volume. In this case, the most appropriate fluid to use is blood, and this should be given in line with departmental transfusion/major haemorrhage policies. Many Emergency Departments have their own blood fridges. However, if blood is not immediately available, then giving a balanced crystalloid (e.g. Hartmann's solution) would be suitable as a short-term measure. Colloids generally do not convey any benefit over crystalloids in this situation; they are more expensive, and there is some limited evidence that they may be associated with increased morbidity and mortality.

→ http://www.transfusionguidelines.org.uk

→ http://www.nice.org.uk/guidance/CG174/chapter/1-Recommendations (National Institute for Health and Care Excellence (2013). *Intravenous fluid therapy in adults in hospital*. Clinical guideline CG74)

→ http://www.cochrane.org/CD000567/INJ_are-colloids-more-effective-than-crystalloids-in-reducing-death-in-people-who-are-critically-ill-or-injured (Lewis SR, Pritchard MW, Evans DJW, et al. (2018). *Colloids or crystalloids for fluid replacement in critically people*. Cochrane review)

9. A ★

The sudden onset of severe occipital headache suggests a subarachnoid haemorrhage. All of these symptoms may occur in a patient with a subarachnoid haemorrhage, but loss of consciousness suggests rising intracranial pressure and must be treated as an emergency.

10. B ★

This man is significantly shocked and requires fluid resuscitation. A large-bore line is needed in order to provide rapid fluid administration, and a 14G cannula is the most appropriate device to deliver this. Central lines are generally not used for fluid resuscitation, as fluids cannot be given as rapidly down them (due to the length of the line) and they take longer to insert. The use of intraosseous needles in adults is becoming increasingly common, and they are a good alternative if venous access cannot be achieved quickly. However, they should not be the device of choice. Of the options presented, the grey 16G cannula is the most appropriate.

11. B ★

Five people are required to perform a log roll. One person stands at the patient's head and keeps control of the head, neck, and airway and gives commands; one takes the arms and trunk; one takes the upper legs and pelvis; one supports the calves, and the fifth person examines the back and performs a rectal examination. The patient is rolled gently towards

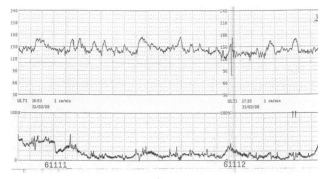

Figure 1.1

Figure 2.1

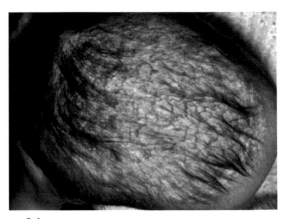

Figure 3.1
Reproduced courtesy of Barts and the London NHS Trust

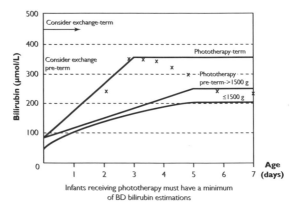

Figure 3.2

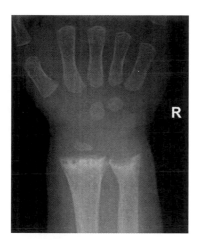

Figure 3.3

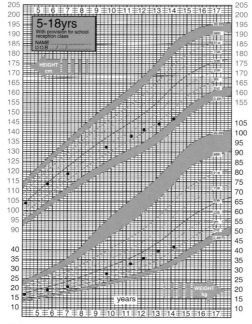

Figure 3.4

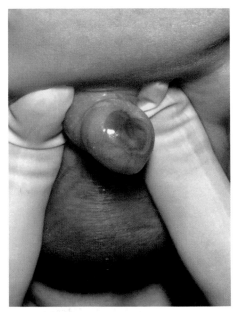

Figure 3.5
Reproduced with permission from Baldwin A. (eds), *Oxford Handbook of Clinical Specialties*, Eleventh edition, figure 5.15, p. 228. Copyright (2020) with permission from Oxford University Press

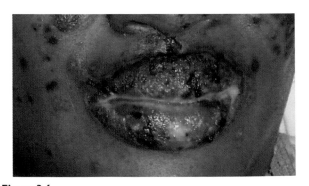

Figure 3.6
Reproduced courtesy of Barts and the London NHS Trust

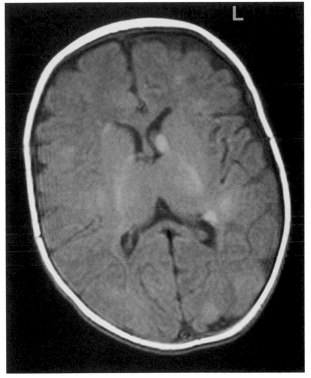

Figure 3.7

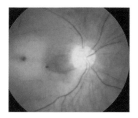

Figure 4.1
Reproduced with permission from Sundaram V, Barsam A, Barker L, Khaw PT, *Training in Ophthalmology*, Second edition, figure 6.31, p. 221. Copyright (2016) with permission from Oxford University Press

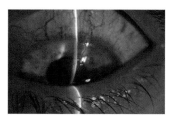

Figure 4.2
Reproduced with permission from Sundaram V, Barsam A, Barker L, Khaw PT, *Training in Ophthalmology*, Second edition, figure 8.26, p. 319. Copyright (2016) with permission from Oxford University Press

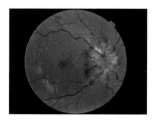

Figure 4.3
Reproduced courtesy of Masoud Teimory

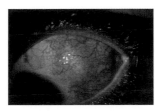

Figure 4.4

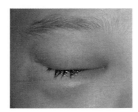

Figure 4.5

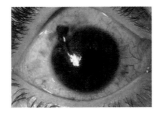

Figure 4.6

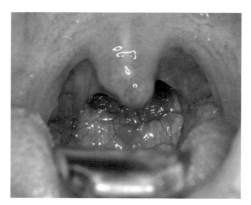

Figure 5.1

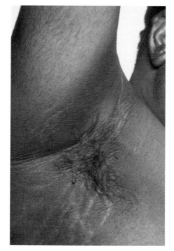

Figure 6.1
Reproduced courtesy of Barts and the London NHS Trust

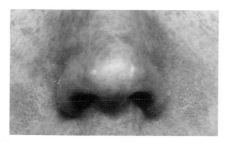

Figure 6.2
Reproduced courtesy of Barts and the London NHS Trust

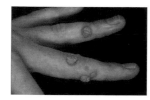

Figure 6.3
Reproduced courtesy of Barts and the London NHS Trust

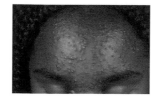

Figure 6.4
Reproduced courtesy of Barts and the London NHS Trust

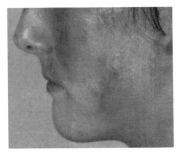

Figure 6.5
Reproduced courtesy of Barts and the London NHS Trust

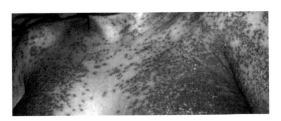

Figure 6.6
Reproduced courtesy of Barts and the London NHS Trust

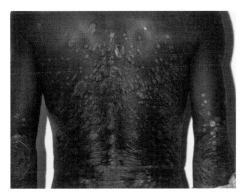

Figure 6.7
Reproduced courtesy of Barts and the London NHS Trust

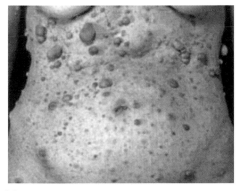

Figure 6.8
Reproduced courtesy of Barts and the London NHS Trust

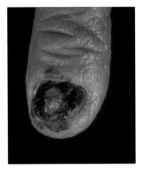

Figure 6.9
Reproduced courtesy of Barts and the London NHS Trust

Figure 6.10
Reproduced courtesy of Barts and the London NHS Trust

Figure 6.11
Reproduced courtesy of Barts and the London NHS Trust

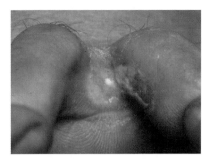

Figure 6.12
Reproduced courtesy of Barts and the London NHS Trust

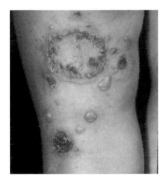

Figure 6.13
Reproduced courtesy of Barts and the London NHS Trust

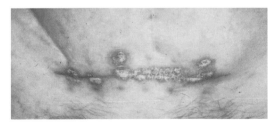

Figure 6.14
Reproduced courtesy of Barts and the London NHS Trust

Figure 6.15
Reproduced courtesy of Barts and the London NHS Trust

Figure 6.16
Reproduced courtesy of Barts and the London NHS Trust

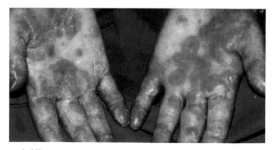

Figure 6.17
Reproduced courtesy of Barts and the London NHS Trust

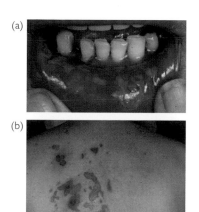

Figure 6.18
Reproduced courtesy of Barts and the London NHS Trust

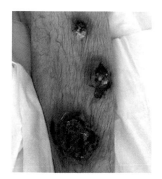

Figure 6.19
Reproduced courtesy of Barts and the London NHS Trust

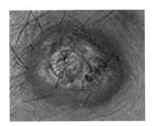

Figure 6.20
Reproduced courtesy of Barts and the London NHS Trust

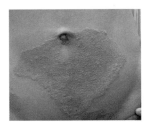

Figure 6.21
Reproduced courtesy of Barts and the London NHS Trust

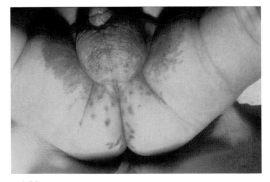

Figure 6.22
Reproduced courtesy of Barts and the London NHS Trust

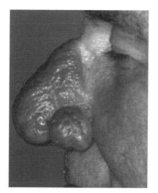

Figure 6.23
Reproduced courtesy of Barts and the London NHS Trust

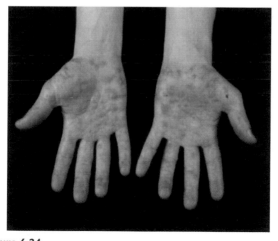

Figure 6.24
Reproduced courtesy of Barts and the London NHS Trust

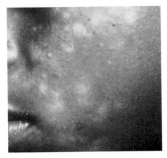

Figure 6.25
Reproduced courtesy of Barts and the London NHS Trust

Figure 6.26
Reproduced courtesy of Barts and the London NHS Trust

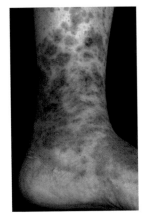

Figure 6.27
Reproduced courtesy of Barts and the London NHS Trust

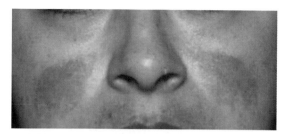

Figure 6.28
Reproduced courtesy of Barts and the London NHS Trust

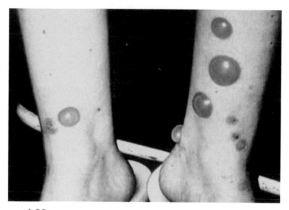

Figure 6.29
Reproduced courtesy of Barts and the London NHS Trust

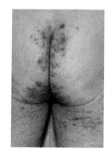

Figure 6.30
Reproduced courtesy of Barts and the London NHS Trust

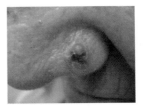

Figure 6.31
Reproduced courtesy of Barts and the London NHS Trust

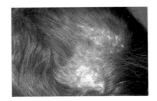

Figure 6.32
Reproduced courtesy of Barts and the London NHS Trust

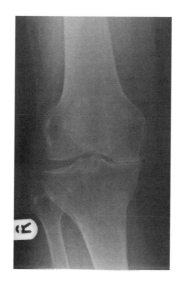

Figure 7.1

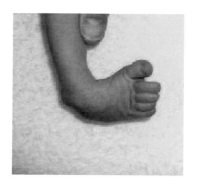

Figure 7.2

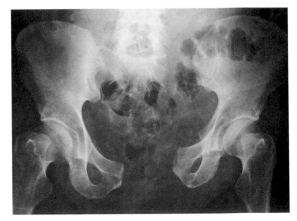

Figure 8.1

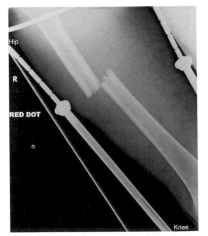

Figure 8.2

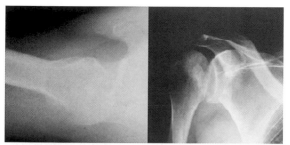

Figure 8.3

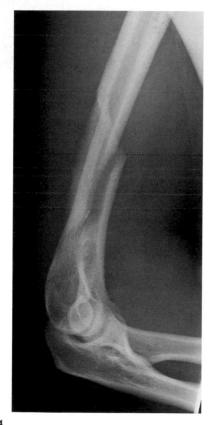

Figure 8.4

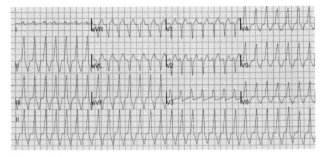

Figure 9.1

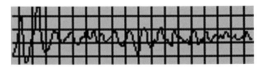

Figure 11.1
Reproduced with permission from Hurley N, Dawson J, Sanders S, and Eccles S, *Oxford Handbook for the Foundation Programme*, 2nd edition, figure 5, p. 187. Copyright (2008) with permission from Oxford University Press

the three supporters of the body and then held in a stable line while the back is examined.

12. A ★   OHCS 11th edn → p. 541

The most important issue in this fracture is to consider what is attached to the fracture site, and therefore what the possible displacement or consequences of not immobilizing might be. The tibial plateau is a weight-bearing surface, so any fracture must be treated as non-weight-bearing at first. In addition, the injury pattern often includes injuries to the menisci or collateral ligaments. If the fracture involves the cruciate ligaments (evidenced by involvement of the tibial spine in the fracture line), minimizing the anteroposterior movement of the tibia on the femur is important. Immobilization techniques must be easy for the patient to manage and maintain their mobility. Therefore, the most appropriate technique for immobilization in the Emergency Department is the above-knee back slab. A below-knee back slab will not restrict the anteroposterior movement of the tibia on the femur. The cast brace is more suitable once the patient has started to mobilize the knee after the initial injury has settled. A cricket bat splint may be useful, as it will allow the patient to wash their leg, but may not be available in the Emergency Department. A wool and crêpe bandage was formerly a useful method but is no longer used because of the extensive resources required and the difficulty for the patient in keeping such a bandage correctly applied.

13. E ★   OHCS 11th edn → p. 196

Accidents are common in toddlers, and it can be difficult to work out which of them are non-accidental. The shins are a very common site for bruising, but the chest, abdomen, and back are not. Small discrete round bruises suggest the use of fingers or an implement. Pulled elbows and greenstick fractures are common in young children, and burns that have splash patterns are more commonly accidental.

→ http://www.nice.org.uk/guidance/cg89 (National Institute for Health and Care Excellence (2009). *Child maltreatment: when to suspect maltreatment in under 18s*. Clinical guideline CG89)

→ https://cks.nice.org.uk/child-maltreatment-recognition-and-management (National Institute for Health and Care Excellence (2019). *Child maltreatment—recognition and management*. Clinical Knowledge Summaries)

14. A ★   OHCS 11th edn → p. 331

This is an ophthalmological emergency, caused by blockage of the flow of the aqueous humour from the anterior chamber, which is exacerbated at night when the pupil dilates. It leads to raised intraocular pressure, which causes severe pain, redness, a fixed pupil, and decreased acuity. Drops are required to cause miosis and open the angle.

15. D ★

OHCS 11th edn → p. 592

Tension pneumothorax is an emergency and should be looked for as part of the primary survey in trauma patients, although spotting it is not always easy. If a patient is in respiratory distress, the most reliable sign that a tension pneumothorax is present is the evidence of haemodynamic compromise due to compression and displacement of the mediastinum, restricting venous return to the heart. Reduced breath sounds could be due to a variety of reasons and do not necessarily indicate a tension pneumothorax. Other signs are tracheal deviation to the opposite side and hyper-resonance to percussion, but these are unreliable signs and can be difficult to elicit. Other causes of circulatory shock in a trauma patient must also be considered.

16. C ★

Patients who are post-ictal may need airway support until they become fully conscious. Guedel (oropharyngeal) airways and suction may trigger a gag reflex. Nasopharyngeal airways are generally well tolerated. Intubation may be necessary if the patient does not regain full consciousness within a reasonable time frame or if there is further airway compromise for any other reason.

17. D ★

OHCS 11th edn → p. 221

This child has a classic presentation of pyloric stenosis. It typically presents at 6–8 weeks with projectile milky vomits during or immediately after feeds. There is constipation and the baby seems to be hungry all the time, as he has had no food. A mass may be felt in the midline during a feed (often described as 'olive'-like) and peristalsis may be seen, but the only reliable way to diagnose pyloric stenosis is with an ultrasound scan.

18. C ★

OHCS 10th edn → pp. 582–3, 587

Haemorrhage control is part of the assessment and initial management of circulation. This should be done by applying direct pressure on bleeding points in the first instance. If this failed to control the bleeding, then applying a tourniquet may be an appropriate measure. Activating the major haemorrhage pathway should be done, along with the above measures, in cases where bleeding is ongoing and the patient is haemodynamically compromised. However, the initial priority should be to control the bleeding.

19. B ★

This is the most likely cause of pancreatitis in a young man. Excess alcohol consumption, both in the form of binge drinking and long-term increased consumption, can cause acute pancreatitis. Some other causes of pancreatitis include gallstones, abdominal trauma, post-endoscopic retrograde cholangiopancreatography (ERCP), steroid use, antibiotics, hyperlipidaemia, and the commonly remembered (but never seen) scorpion venom!

20. E ★   OHCS 11th edn → p. 124

In a miscarriage, products of conception can build up behind the cervical os and cause pressure. The cervix has many stretch receptors, and when it is trying to dilate, it can stimulate the vagus nerve, causing haemodynamic instability. This causes bradycardia because of the vagal stimulation, rather than the tachycardia that is seen in severe blood loss. A speculum examination needs to be performed and these products removed under direct vision with sponge forceps, which may result in an improvement in haemodynamic status. Fluid resuscitation and further surgical treatment may be needed if the blood pressure remains low. An ultrasound scan should be performed to assess the pregnancy, but the haemodynamic instability here (as evidenced by a *relative* bradycardia) makes other options more urgent.

→ https://www.nice.org.uk/guidance/cg154 (National Institute for Health and Care Excellence (2012). *Ectopic pregnancy and miscarriage: diagnosis and initial management.* Clinical guideline CG154)

21. C ★   OHCS 11th edn → p. 592

This is a classic presentation of a tension pneumothorax. This life-threatening condition requires immediate needle thoracocentesis, i.e. insertion of a wide-bore cannula into the pleural cavity, followed by chest drain insertion.

→ https://litfl.com/emergency-thoracocentesis/

22. E ★★

This is a broad-complex tachycardia. If the patient is stable, it can be treated with drugs, most commonly amiodarone. However, in a patient with adverse signs (chest pain, signs of heart failure, or shock), electrical cardioversion should be performed.

→ https://www.resus.org.uk/resuscitation-guidelines/peri-arrest-arrhythmias/#tachy (Advanced Life Support tachycardia algorithm)

23. D ★★   OHCS 11th edn → p. 773

The Mental Capacity Act 2005 (England and Wales) states that everyone should be treated as being able to make their own decisions until it has been shown that they cannot. It also aims to enable people to make their own decisions for as long as they are capable of doing so. In order to have capacity, an individual must be able to understand the information being given to them, to retain and weigh up this information, and to communicate their decision. A lack of capacity could be permanent or temporary, and an individual's capacity to make a decision must be established at the time when a decision needs to be made. A lack of capacity could be due to a severe learning disability, dementia, mental health problems, a brain injury, a stroke, or unconsciousness due to an anaesthetic or a sudden accident. Note that a different Act—the Adults with Incapacity (Scotland) Act 2000—applies in Scotland.

→ http://www.nhs.uk/Conditions/social-care-and-support-guide/Pages/mental-capacity.aspx

→ http://www.scie.org.uk/mca/introduction/mental-capacity-act-2005-at-a-glance

→ http://www.legislation.gov.uk/ukpga/2005/9/contents

24. E ★★

A non-adherent dressing is recommended after debridement. Iodine-impregnated dressings may cause local inflammation and reaction; they are not to be recommended. Alginate dressings have advantages, particularly when the wound has a heavy exudate, but immediately after debridement, these should not be necessary. Hydrocolloid dressings can be used, but they have not been shown to have any benefit over a simple non-adherent dressing.

→ https://cks.nice.org.uk/leg-ulcer-venous#!scenario

25. B ★   OHCS 11th edn → p. 590

The Glasgow Coma Scale score is calculated, as shown in Table 11.2.

26. C ★★   OHCS 11th edn → pp. 590–1

The National Institute for Health and Care Excellence (NICE) guidelines on the management of head injury state that if a post-traumatic seizure occurs, CT imaging of the head is indicated. As this patient is a child, he would need to vomit three times before a scan was indicated, but a single vomit in an adult following a head injury would prompt CT scanning. In a child, a GCS score of 14 on presentation is not an indication for a CT head. However, if the GCS score remains less than 15 after 2 hours, a CT scan would be indicated at this point.

→ https://www.nice.org.uk/guidance/cg176/chapter/1-Recommendations (National Institute for Health and Care Excellence (2014). *Head injury: assessment and early management.* Clinical guideline CG176)

27. C ★★

The D-dimer blood test is only useful if the result is normal, because it can then be used to rule out venous thromboembolism in low-risk patients. D-dimer is a fibrin degradation product which indicates that clotting and subsequent fibrinolysis have been occurring. It is therefore non-specific and will be raised in many situations (e.g. post-operatively). Local protocols may recommend it in a situation where clinical suspicion of pulmonary embolism (based on risk factors and clinical presentation) is low. The D-dimer test can be performed to enable discharge of the patient with more confidence.

Troponin T is only indicated if there is a suspicion that chest pain may have an ischaemic aetiology. There is nothing to suggest this in this case. The other tests have no role in managing this presentation.

28. D ★★★

It is important to know which deaths need to be reported to the coroner/procurator fiscal. Deaths that may be due to an accident should always be reported, even if the cause of death is known. It used to be the case that all deaths occurring within 24 hours of admission had to be reported. However, in 2016, the chief coroner advised that this was no longer necessary, provided a cause of death could be given. The following website provides guidance.

→ https://www.gov.uk/after-a-death/when-a-death-is-reported-to-a-coroner

29. C ★★★   OHCS 11th edn → p. 652

Although it may be tempting to help out at major incidents, these are carefully controlled and managed by trained personnel, and your responsibility, even as a doctor, is to allow these teams to take charge and to act as any other member of the public, unless specifically instructed to do otherwise. Your hospital will have a major incident plan, and they will contact you directly if your help is needed.

30. B ★★★

There are well-established treatment algorithms for the management of status epilepticus. The first-line treatment consists of benzodiazepines. Diazepam is administered per rectum if there is no IV access, but lorazepam is preferred once IV access has been established. Phenytoin and thiopentone may be required, but only if the patient has failed to respond to the use of IV benzodiazepines.

→ https://patient.info/doctor/status-epilepticus-management

→ https://www.nice.org.uk/guidance/cg137/chapter/appendix-f-protocols-for-treating-convulsive-status-epilepticus-in-adults-and-children-adults-published-in-2004-and-children-published-in-2011 (National Institute for Health and Care Excellence (2012). *Epilepsies: diagnosis and management*. Clinical guideline CG137—protocol for treating convulsive status epilepticus in adults and children)

31. D ★★★★   OHCS 11th edn → p. 621

Pre-tibial lacerations are difficult to heal, even when there is no coexisting morbidity. In this patient with both major vessel arterial disease and probable microvascular disease, the blood supply will be severely limited. Any attempt at closure must ensure that the edges are approximated as closely as possible but are not under excessive tension, that there are no foreign bodies in the wound, and that the flap itself is cleaned as thoroughly as possible. Steri-strips under as little tension as possible are the most appropriate method of skin closure in this patient. Some minor 'spot welds' of glue might also help to minimize tension, while still allowing exudate to leave the wound.

Vicryl Rapide is a dissolving suture (after 7–10 days) that is suitable for subcutaneous sutures, but it is not appropriate for this wound as the healing time may be up to 6 weeks. Ethibond can be used to close wounds but would be too heavy and would lead to tissue strangulation between the sutures. Although a proportion of pre-tibial lacerations result in skin grafting, primary grafting is not recommended because of the risk associated with the anaesthetic and the creation of a second wound, particularly in a high-risk patient such as this diabetic woman with arteriopathy.

→ https://cks.nice.org.uk/lacerations

32. A ★★★★

NIV is a method of respiratory support used to reduce the work of breathing and improve ventilation in patients with type 2 respiratory failure. If used in the correct patients, it can prevent the need for invasive ventilation and the complications associated with this. Patients receive positive pressure ventilation via a tight-fitting facial mask or specialist high-flow nasal cannulae. NIV is contraindicated in patients who are unable to wear the mask due to facial trauma or burns, are actively vomiting or have epistaxis, have a reduced conscious level, are unable to protect their airway, or have an untreated pneumothorax. Well-fitting dentures can be left in, as this helps to maintain the facial structure and promotes a good seal with the mask. However, if they are poorly fitting, then they should be removed. A previous respiratory arrest does not prevent the use of NIV. However, it does suggest that it may not be successful and the patient should be monitored closely and the treatment escalated early if appropriate.

→ https://www.brit-thoracic.org.uk/quality-improvement/guidelines/niv/ (British Thoracic Society (2016). *Guidelines for the ventilatory management of acute hypercapnic respiratory failure in adults.*)

→ https://litfl.com/non-invasive-ventilation-niv/

33. D ★★★★

Hyperglycaemia after stroke worsens brain injury. Large randomized controlled trials have shown that keeping blood sugar levels within tight limits leads to better outcomes. Current guidelines advise maintaining a blood sugar level between 4 and 11 mmol/L. Hypotension should be prevented in order to maintain cerebral perfusion and where possible normothermia should be maintained, as pyrexia has been shown to be associated with a worse outcome.

→ Gentile NT, Seftchick MW, Huynh T, Kruus LK, Gaughan J. Decreased mortality by normalising blood glucose after acute ischemic stroke. *Acad Emerg Med.* 2006;**13**:174–80.

★ https://www.nice.org.uk/guidance/cg68 (National Institute for Health and Care Excellence (2008). *Stroke and transient ischaemic attack in over 16s: diagnosis and initial management.* Clinical guideline CG68)

34. B ★★★★

The safest method of obtaining central venous access is to do it under ultrasound guidance, as this improves the chances of successful venous cannulation and reduces complications. However, in some circumstances, this may not be possible, and therefore a landmark technique can be used.

→ https://www.anaesthesiauk.com/SectionContents.aspx?sectionid=128

35. A ★★★★

Being an effective team leader is a skill which requires practice, just like any other. In order to lead a team effectively, it is important to know your team members and their skill set. In medicine, a team can often be working together for the first time, and so checking these things when the team members arrive is essential. The team leader should ideally remain 'hands-off' in order to maintain an overview of the resuscitation. There are numerous publications reviewing the role of the team leader, such as that found at the link below.

→ https://lms.resus.org.uk/modules/m40-v2-decisions/10346/resources/chapter_2.pdf

Pre-hospital emergency medicine

Oliver Harrison

Many doctors are attracted to pre-hospital emergency medicine (PHEM) because of the variety of challenges that it presents. With limited time and resources, the doctor is expected to assess and treat a range of medical and traumatic pathologies in patients of any age, without delaying transport to the most appropriate location for definitive care. This must be done in spite of what is usually a suboptimal environment, e.g. in a ditch at the roadside, on a rainy building site, or in a crowded town centre. Recognizing the limitations of what can be achieved on scene is a key skill that must be balanced against the increasing range of lifesaving interventions at the disposal of pre-hospital teams.

While PHEM has been practised by a variety of doctors for many years, it has only recently gained General Medical Council (GMC) sub-specialty recognition. A formal training programme may now be undertaken by trainees with base specialties of acute medicine, anaesthetics, emergency medicine, and intensive care medicine, leading to a dual certificate of completion of training. The challenging nature of the pre-hospital environment, the high-risk nature of the interventions that can be undertaken, and the lack of availability of immediate assistance on scene mean that PHEM is a service delivered by consultants and senior trainees. Medical students and foundation doctors who may be interested in PHEM training should seek to spend time in the above-mentioned acute specialties, as well as looking for opportunities to observe alongside some of the services that operate nationally.

The following questions represent a small selection of the range of scenarios that may be faced by a PHEM practitioner on a day-to-day basis.

Oliver Harrison, *Pre-hospital emergency medicine* In: *Oxford Assess and Progress: Clinical Specialties*. Edited by: Luci Etheridge and Henry Collier, Oxford University Press. © Oxford University Press 2021. DOI:10.1093/oso/9780198862550.003.0010

QUESTIONS

1. Pre-hospital responders attend a 40-year-old female who is known to have a history of asthma. She is unable to complete full sentences, has a respiratory rate of 30 breaths/minute, a pulse rate of 122 bpm, and an oxygen saturation of 95% on air. Which is the single most appropriate initial management for this patient in the pre-hospital environment? ★

A Administer 5 mg nebulized salbutamol, 500 micrograms nebulized ipratropium bromide, and 10 mg intravenous (IV) hydrocortisone, and transport to the Emergency Department

B Administer 5 mg nebulized salbutamol using an air-driven nebulizer, and transport to the Emergency Department

C Administer salbutamol via a metered-dose inhaler and spacer device, and transport to the Emergency Department

D Administer salbutamol via a metered-dose inhaler and spacer device until symptoms improve, then advise follow-up by the patient's general practitioner (GP)

E Rapid sequence induction of anaesthesia, mechanical ventilation, and transfer to the nearest Intensive Care Unit.

2. A 68-year-old male suffers a cardiac arrest in a public place. Following arrival of the emergency services, the patient is found to be in ventricular fibrillation. The third shock is about to be given. Which is the single most appropriate action after delivery of the third shock? ★★★

A Administer 1 mg adrenaline (epinephrine) and 300 mg amiodarone

B Administer 10 mL 1:10 000 adrenaline (epinephrine)

C Continue cardiopulmonary resuscitation (CPR) for a further 2 minutes before checking for a pulse

D Continue CPR while another responder assesses cardiac activity using subcostal ultrasound

E Pause CPR and check for a pulse

3. A lady who is 36 weeks pregnant delivers her baby unexpectedly at home. On arrival of the emergency services, the baby is found to be floppy, centrally cyanosed, and taking occasional gasps despite being dried and stimulated. Which is the single most appropriate next step in the treatment of the baby? ★ ★ ★

A Commence cardiopulmonary resuscitation (CPR) at a ratio of three compressions to one breath

B Commence CPR at a ratio of 15 compressions to two breaths

C Deliver five inflation breaths using a bag–valve–mask connected to air

D Deliver five inflation breaths using a bag–valve–mask connected to oxygen

E Intubate the baby and ventilate at a rate of 30–40 breaths/minute

4. A male in his 50s is extricated from a house fire. On initial assessment, he displays no signs of airway or breathing compromise, but both his legs appear to have significant burns. Which is the single best initial step in managing this patient? ★ ★ ★

A Apply cling film to all burnt areas, avoiding circumferential wrapping

B Apply water gel dressings to all burnt areas

C Clearly document the extent of full-thickness and partial-thickness burns before applying dressings

D Cool the burns under running water for 20 minutes

E Gain intravenous (IV) access, and administer 0.9% sodium chloride in a volume determined by the Parkland formula

5. A 32-year-old tree surgeon sustains a chainsaw injury to his right anterior thigh. There is significant blood loss from the wound, and the patient is complaining of severe pain. Which is the single most appropriate first step in managing this patient in the pre-hospital environment? ★ ★ ★

A Apply a Combat Application Tourniquet proximal to the area of bleeding, and tighten until haemorrhage stops

B Apply oxygen, and examine the chest before addressing the bleeding

C Gain intravenous (IV) access in order to administer tranexamic acid and analgesia

D Lie the patient supine, apply direct pressure to the wound, and elevate the limb

E Pack the wound with Celox gauze

6. An 11-year-old child who is known to have a peanut allergy develops severe shortness of breath and wheeze while having lunch at school. On arrival of the ambulance crew, the child has oedema of the mouth and appears cyanosed. Which is the single best dose and route of adrenaline (epinephrine) to administer to this child? ★★★

A 300 micrograms intramuscularly

B 500 micrograms intramuscularly

C 300 micrograms intravenously

D 500 micrograms intravenously

E 150 micrograms intravenously

7. A 15-year-old male has sustained a stab injury to the epigastrium with a knife of unknown length. On arrival of the emergency services, he is pale, clammy, and agitated. He has a pulse rate of 128 bpm, a blood pressure of 88/48 mmHg, and a respiratory rate of 34 breaths/minute. Air entry is present and equal bilaterally on auscultation. Which is the single most likely diagnosis? ★★★

A Cardiac tamponade

B Flail chest

C Massive haemothorax

D Simple pneumothorax

E Tension pneumothorax

8. A 65-year-old male patient is extricated from a car by the fire service, following a high-speed road traffic collision. He is suspected of having rib fractures and a humeral fracture and is complaining of tingling in his legs. His Glasgow Coma Scale (GCS) score is 15. To maintain in-line immobilization of the spine, he is transferred onto a long spinal board after removal of the car's roof. Which is the single best way of preparing this patient for onward transport to hospital? ★★★★

A Leave the patient on the long spinal board, and apply a cervical collar, blocks, and tape

B Leave the patient on the long spinal board without further immobilization

C Log roll the patient, and assess for spinal tenderness. If none is present, allow him to get up and lie directly on the ambulance stretcher

D Move the patient to the ambulance stretcher, then log roll to remove the spinal board. Apply a cervical collar, blocks, and tape

E Remove the patient from the spinal board using a scoop stretcher, and transport to hospital on this after applying a cervical collar, blocks, and tape

9. A 25-year-old motorcyclist is attended to by emergency services, having been hit by a car at 30 mph. He is complaining of severe pain to his mid-left thigh, which appears swollen. A closed fracture of the femoral shaft is suspected. Which is the single most appropriate way of managing this injury? ★ ★ ★ ★

A A long box splint to enclose the left lower limb

B Neighbour strapping to the adjacent limb

C No splint required as the fracture appears not to be displaced

D The Kendrick traction device (KTD)

E The SAM pelvic sling

10. Reports are received of an incident developing in a local shopping centre. A number of people have become incapacitated and others are complaining of symptoms, including watery eyes, blurred vision, difficulty breathing, and vomiting. Which is the single most likely chemical agent to have caused these symptoms? ★ ★ ★ ★

A Chlorine

B Cyanide

C Methane

D Phosgene

E Sarin

11. Emergency responders attend a local industrial unit, following reports of a collapsed, unconscious patient. On arrival, the responders notice through a window three patients lying apparently motionless on the floor. Which is the single best course of action for the attending crew? ★ ★ ★ ★

A Cautiously approach the scene, but retreat if any unusual odours are detected or gas clouds seen

B Drag the patients to a central location, so that sequential ABC assessments can be completed and all patients can be monitored

C Remain at a distance from the scene, prevent bystanders from gaining access, and pass a METHANE report to control

D Request backup from the Hazardous Area Response Team (HART)

E Request immediate backup of two further ambulances before proceeding to prioritize patients using the triage sieve system

12. A 32-year-old male weighing approximately 80 kg falls from the roof of his house and lands on the patio. An enhanced care team attends and finds him to have a suspected left-sided femoral fracture, rib fractures, and a boggy swelling to his temporal region. His pulse rate is 115 bpm, blood pressure 90/54 mmHg, and Glasgow Coma Scale (GCS) score E1 V2 M4 (7). The team decides to perform rapid sequence induction of anaesthesia due to his low GCS score. Which is the single best drug and dose to use for induction of anaesthesia in this patient? ★ ★ ★ ★

A Etomidate 25 mg

B Ketamine 80 mg

C Midazolam 16 mg

D Propofol 80 mg

E Thiopentone 400 mg

13. An intercity train derails, causing multiple casualties. Representatives from the three main emergency services gather at a remote location to develop the plans and coordinate the assets required to respond to the major incident. Which is the single most accurate phrase used to describe this group? ★ ★ ★ ★

A Gold coordination group

B Operational coordination group

C Silver coordination group

D Strategic coordination group

E Tactical coordination group

14. A 52-year-old motorcyclist hits the side of a car head on at 40 mph. On arrival of the emergency services, he is complaining of severe lower back pain. His pulse rate is 105 bpm and blood pressure 102/65 mmHg. He is wearing a full set of motorcycle leathers. Which is the single correct way of applying the pelvic binder on this patient? ★ ★ ★ ★

A At the level of the anterior superior iliac spines, following removal of the patient's clothing

B At the level of the greater trochanters, following removal of the patient's clothing

C At the level of the greater trochanters, over the top of the patient's clothing

D Just below the anterior superior iliac spines, following removal of the patient's clothing

E Just below the anterior superior iliac spines, over the top of the patient's clothing

15. An elderly male is found collapsed outside on a winter's night. He is unconscious, hypotensive, and bradycardic. His core temperature is measured as 31°C. A 12-lead electrocardiogram (ECG) is performed which shows an abnormality. Which is the single most likely ECG abnormality to be associated with hypothermia of this degree? ★★★★

A Delta waves

B J-waves

C P pulmonale

D Third-degree heart block

E U-waves

ANSWERS

1. A ★

This patient fulfils the criteria for acute severe asthma. First-line therapy includes β2-agonists, ipratropium, and steroids. Assessment in hospital is needed in case she develops life-threatening or near-fatal asthma.

→ https://www.brit-thoracic.org.uk/quality-improvement/guidelines/asthma/

2. A ★★★

The Advanced Life Support algorithm for shockable rhythms states that 300 mg amiodarone should be given after the third shock, irrespective of whether the shocks have been consecutive or interrupted by CPR. Adrenaline should also be given after the third shock if it has not already been delivered for a non-shockable rhythm, in which case a dose should be given every 3–5 minutes. One milligram adrenaline is the dose contained in 10 mL of 1:10 000.

→ https://www.resus.org.uk/library/2015-resuscitation-guidelines (At the time of publication, the most recent Resuscitation Council UK guidelines were from 2015. They are renewed every 5 years, with the next set of guidelines due for release in late 2020.)

3. C ★★★   OHCS 11th edn → p. 184

If a newborn fails to breathe adequately after birth, the lungs remain filled with fluid and no oxygen is able to reach the heart. The priority is therefore to inflate the lungs—this is achieved by delivering inflation breaths of 2–3 seconds' duration, aiming to generate visible chest movement. In the majority of cases, this should lead to an increase in heart rate and commencement of spontaneous ventilation. If the heart rate fails to improve, CPR should be commenced using a 3:1 ratio.

→ https://www.resus.org.uk/library/2015-resuscitation-guidelines/resuscitation-and-support-transition-babies-birth

4. D ★★★   OHCS 11th edn → pp. 598–9

Cooling burns as soon as possible will stop the burning process, thus limiting the extent of injury. In order to achieve this, any burnt or burning clothes should be removed. Cooling burns will also have a significant analgesic effect. Once cooling has taken place, the burns can be dressed with cling film before transporting the patient to hospital. Accurate calculation of burn extent is difficult in the pre-hospital setting.

→ https://fphc.rcsed.ac.uk/media/1754/burns-patient-management.pdf

5. D ★★★   OHCS 11th edn → p. 587

A wound of this nature is likely to cause severe, if not catastrophic, haemorrhage due to the mechanism and location. Given that the patient is complaining of pain, it can be surmised that the airway is patent. Early control of the haemorrhage is paramount, and this should be carried out in a stepwise approach. This includes: direct pressure, bandaging (e.g. using the Oleas modular bandage), elevation above the level of the heart, packing with haemostatic gauze/granules (e.g. Celox), indirect pressure over a proximal artery, and finally application of a tourniquet if the haemorrhage is occurring from a limb. Blast injuries and traumatic amputations are likely to require immediate application of a tourniquet.

→ https://fphc.rcsed.ac.uk/media/1726/site-of-application-of-tourniquets.pdf

6. A ★★★   OHCS 11th edn → p. 183

The intramuscular route is preferred for administration of adrenaline in anaphylaxis. The use of intravenous adrenaline is only appropriate if the practitioner is experienced in its use and is aware of the appropriate dose to administer. Advanced Life Support guidelines state the dose of intramuscular adrenaline in a child 6–12 years old is 300 micrograms, or 0.3 mL of 1:1000.

→ https://www.resus.org.uk/library/additional-guidance/guidance-anaphylaxis/emergency-treatment

7. A ★★★   OHCS 11th edn → p. 592

Penetrating injuries to the chest and epigastrium can easily result in injuries to the lungs and heart. This patient's rapid deterioration and lack of lateralizing signs suggest that cardiac tamponade is the most likely diagnosis. A massive haemothorax may result in similar haemodynamic changes, but these are unlikely to develop as quickly as when cardiac tamponade is the cause.

→ https://fphc.rcsed.ac.uk/media/1788/management-of-chest-injuries.pdf

8. E ★★★★

The long spinal board is an extrication device only—it should not be used for transport due to the risk of developing pressure sores. The scoop stretcher is recommended for use in transporting patients—it facilitates patient movement without needing repeated log rolls, which are painful and risk disrupting internal clots.

→ https://fphc.rcsed.ac.uk/media/1766/minimal-patient-handling.pdf

9. D ★★★★   OHCS 11th edn → p. 640

The KTD is a portable, easily applied femoral traction splint. A particular advantage is that it can be used in the presence of a suspected or confirmed pelvic fracture. Splinting a suspected femoral fracture will reduce both pain and blood loss, by bringing the open bone ends together.

10. E ★★★★   OHCS 11th edn → pp. 628–9

Sarin is a nerve agent that has previously been used in terrorist attacks. It is an acetylcholinesterase inhibitor that leads to parasympathetic symptoms and motor paralysis, including the respiratory muscles.

11. C ★★★★

The STEP 1-2-3-plus guidance describes the initial operational response to a potential chemical, biological, nuclear, radiological, or explosive incident. The presentation of three or more incapacitated casualties without explanation should prompt suspicion of such an incident and lead to the instigation of appropriate control measures and response escalation as soon as possible. Remaining at a distance from the scene prevents the responders from becoming victims of whatever has caused the casualties to become incapacitated.

→ https://www.ukfrs.com/guidance/search/signs-and-symptoms-exposure

12. B ★★★★

In haemodynamically unstable patients, an induction agent is required that does not cause a further drop in blood pressure. Unlike propofol or thiopentone, ketamine does not cause vasodilatation and also has sympathomimetic effects. Blood pressure is therefore less likely to be adversely affected by its administration. The normal dose is 2 mg/kg, but when patients are severely compromised, a reduced dose of 1 mg/kg should be used.

13. E ★★★★

According to the Joint Emergency Services Interoperability Programme, the three tiers of command are strategic, tactical, and operational. Previously, these tiers were known as gold, silver, and bronze, respectively. The tactical coordination group is concerned with developing the plans required to respond to an incident, while the operational teams on scene execute these plans.

→ http://www.jesip.org.uk/command

14. B ★★★★   OHCS 11th edn → p. 596

This patient has a mechanism and symptoms that would support the diagnosis of a pelvic injury, plus evidence of haemodynamic compromise. A pelvic binder should be placed next to the skin at the level of the greater trochanters. Placing over clothes puts the patient at risk of pressure injury and will necessitate removal of the binder at a later time to remove the clothing, thus potentially exacerbating the pelvic injury.

→ https://fphc.rcsed.ac.uk/media/1765/the-pre-hospital-management-of-pelvic-fractures.pdf

15. B ★★★★   OHCS 11th edn → pp. 588, 600

J-waves, or Osborne waves, are an extra positive deflection on the ECG, occurring just after the normal S-wave, at the J-point. They are commonest in leads II and V3–6. The height of the J-wave is approximately proportional to the degree of hypothermia. Atrial fibrillation is another ECG finding that is commonly seen in hypothermic patients.

→ https://litfl.com/osborn-wave-j-wave-ecg-library/

Anaesthesia and intensive care

Alex Bonner

Anaesthesia is a relatively young specialty by comparison with its counterparts. William Morton administered the first anaesthetic in 1846 in Boston, Massachusetts, and the Royal College of Anaesthetists was cleaved from the Royal College of Surgeons in 1948. Now anaesthetists form the largest group of hospital-based doctors.

Anaesthetists are highly trained physicians whose role is by no means limited to the operating theatre. They oversee the patient journey through the peri-operative period, i.e. preoperative assessment and optimization of the sick surgical patient, ensuring safe intra-operative provision of anaesthesia as well as care of the patient in the early post-operative period. Anaesthetic skills are also requested during management of the critically ill in the Emergency Department, during the care of the parturient mother in providing analgesic, anaesthetic, and intensive care input, and increasingly in the pre-hospital environment. Anaesthetists have an important role in the practice of intensive care where complementary experience in medicine is useful. Other roles of the anaesthetist include provision of acute and chronic pain services, and sub-specialty interests include regional, paediatric, cardiothoracic, and vascular anaesthesia, and neuroanaesthesia.

Anaesthesia is a highly practical specialty, with a strong emphasis on the basic sciences underpinning its practice. Physiology and pharmacology exert their effects with immediacy; therefore, an affinity for these disciplines is desirable. Anaesthetists need to be able to assimilate knowledge of the basic sciences with skills in history and examination, in order to plan for, and respond to, patient needs. In answering these questions, you will be asked to use similar skills.

Alex Bonner, *Anaesthesia and intensive care* In: *Oxford Assess and Progress: Clinical Specialties*. Edited by: Luci Etheridge and Henry Collier, Oxford University Press.
© Oxford University Press 2021. DOI:10.1093/oso/9780198862550.003.0011

QUESTIONS

1. A 70-year-old man has had worsening shortness of breath for 2 days. He has a 50-pack-year history of cigarette smoking but otherwise has no previous medical history. He appears unwell, with a reduced level of consciousness and inadequate respiratory effort. The following arterial blood gas levels are obtained while he is breathing through a face mask with a reservoir bag, with an oxygen flow rate of 15 L/minute:

- pH 7.14
- pO_2 10.1 kPa
- pCO_2 9.8 kPa
- bicarbonate 29.2 mmol/L
- base excess +9.4.

Which is the single best description of the acid–base derangement? ★

A Metabolic acidosis with respiratory compensation

B Metabolic alkalosis with respiratory compensation

C Mixed respiratory and metabolic acidosis

D Respiratory acidosis with evidence of metabolic compensation

E Respiratory acidosis with no evidence of metabolic compensation

2. A 19-year-old man fractured his right lower leg about 30 minutes ago while playing football. He was carried off the pitch on a stretcher. He is in pain and there is some bloodstaining on his sock. His right lower leg is immobilized in a box splint. He has an open fracture of his right distal tibia. There is no distal neurovascular deficit and he is haemodynamically stable; blood loss is estimated to be minimal. He has no other injuries and is fully alert. Which is the single most appropriate initial analgesia to administer? ★

A Intramuscular (IM) diclofenac

B Intravenous (IV) alfentanil

C IV morphine

D IV paracetamol

E Oral codeine phosphate

3. A 19-year-old woman is brought into the Emergency Department by paramedics. She was found unconscious in her bed by her parents who found empty packets of several prescription medications and a bottle of vodka. She does not open her eyes at all but withdraws to pain. She makes no verbal response. Which single number reflects her Glasgow Coma Scale (GCS) score? ★

A 3

B 6

C 9

D 12

E 15

4. A 56-year-old man underwent primary percutaneous coronary intervention (PCI) for an anterior myocardial infarction 6 hours ago. His pain had eased, but he suddenly had severe central crushing chest pain radiating into his left arm. He is now unconscious, with no signs of life. The defibrillator is attached, and the monitor displays the rhythm shown in Figure 11.1 (see Colour Plate section). Cardiopulmonary resuscitation (CPR) with chest compressions and bag–valve–mask ventilation is started. He has intravenous (IV) access. Which is the single next most appropriate management? ★

A Continue CPR for 2 minutes

B Defibrillation

C Endotracheal intubation

D IV atropine

E IV adrenaline (epinephrine)

5. A 24-year-old woman is about to undergo a surgical procedure under a nerve block. Shortly after the anaesthetist finishes the procedure, she feels light-headed and dizzy. She experiences ringing in her ears and tingling around her mouth. Which is the single most likely diagnosis? ★

A Acute labyrinthitis

B Anaphylaxis

C Failure of anaesthetic

D Local anaesthetic toxicity

E Vasovagal attack

6. A 34-year-old woman has been admitted to hospital with cellulitis of her forearm. She has just been given her second dose of intravenous (IV) flucloxacillin. She now has chest tightness and difficulty in breathing, and feels dizzy. She has a diffuse urticarial rash all over her body, and bilateral expiratory and inspiratory wheeze. Her pulse rate is 120 bpm, her blood pressure 80/40 mmHg, and her oxygen saturation 91% on room air. Which is the single most appropriate initial management? ★

A Intramuscular (IM) adrenaline (epinephrine) 0.5 mg

B IV chlorphenamine 10 mg

C IV adrenaline (epinephrine) 1 mg

D IV hydrocortisone 100 mg

E Take blood for serum mast cell tryptase

7. A 76-year-old woman had a left total knee replacement 4 days ago. She is normally fit and healthy. She has had an uncomplicated post-operative recovery, but recent observations give her a Modified Early Warning Score (MEWS) of 6, whereas 1 hour ago, the score was 2. Her pulse rate is 120 bpm, her blood pressure 90/45 mmHg, her oxygen saturation 90% on room air, her respiratory rate 30 breaths/minute, and her temperature 37.5°C. She is alert but has chest pain and shortness of breath. Which is the single most likely cause of her acute deterioration? ★

A Cardiac tamponade

B Myocardial infarction

C Pneumonia

D Pneumothorax

E Pulmonary embolism

8. A 19-year-old man has had a recurrent dislocation of his left shoulder. He has been given 20 mg of intravenous (IV) midazolam and his shoulder is now reduced. He is now unconscious and has stopped breathing. Which is the single most appropriate immediate management? ★

A Connect electrocardiographic (ECG) monitoring

B Give IV flumazenil

C Give IV naloxone

D Intubate the patient

E Open the airway with a jaw thrust

9. A 63-year-old woman had a redo total hip replacement under general anaesthesia 3 days ago. She now has chest pain which developed suddenly and is worse on inspiration. Her pulse rate is 110 bpm, her oxygen saturation 90% on 5 L of oxygen by mask, and her temperature 37.4°C. Which single investigation is likely to confirm the diagnosis? ★

A Chest X-ray

B Computed tomography (CT) pulmonary angiogram

C Electrocardiogram (ECG)

D Echocardiography

E Cardiac enzymes

10. A 64-year-old woman had an inferior myocardial infarction (MI) 12 hours ago and has been successfully revascularized. She suddenly develops a profound narrow complex bradycardia with a rate of 30 bpm. Her blood pressure is 75/39 mmHg, and she feels dizzy and sick. Which is the single most appropriate immediate management? ★

A Intravenous (IV) amiodarone

B IV atropine

C IV isoprenaline

D Transcutaneous (external) cardiac pacing

E Transvenous cardiac pacing

11. A 6-week-old boy, who was born prematurely, has had vomiting and lethargy for 5 days. He has sunken eyes and reduced skin turgor. His capillary refill time is 4 seconds. The following arterial blood gas sample is obtained:

- pH 7.52
- P_aCO_2 5.0 kPa
- P_aO_2 11.0 kPa
- HCO_3 34.2 mmol/L
- base excess +9.1.

Which is the single best description of his metabolic status? ★

A Metabolic acidosis without respiratory compensation

B Metabolic alkalosis with respiratory compensation

C Metabolic alkalosis without respiratory compensation

D Respiratory alkalosis with metabolic compensation

E Respiratory alkalosis without metabolic compensation

12. A 68-year-old man has chronic obstructive pulmonary disease (COPD). He has been involved in a motor vehicle collision and has a fractured femur and signs of a tension pneumothorax. His oxygen saturation is 76% on room air. He is being prepared for a needle thoracocentesis. Which is the single most appropriate means of oxygen delivery to use? ★

A Face mask continuous positive airway pressure (CPAP)

B Immediate intubation and ventilation

C Nasal cannulae

D Non-rebreather mask with reservoir bag

E Venturi mask with 35% oxygen delivery

13. A 55-year-old woman with a history of chronic pain presents to the Emergency Department with morning somnolence, blurred vision, and urinary retention. She states that her general practitioner has recently started a new chronic pain medication, but she cannot remember the name of the drug. Which single drug, used in the treatment of chronic pain, is most likely to cause this group of side-effects? ★ ★

A Amitriptyline

B Carbamazepine

C Gabapentin

D Morphine

E Sodium valproate

14. A 35-year-old man is seen on the day-case unit prior to an arthroscopy for knee pain. He describes himself as 'fit and well' and does not smoke. He takes inhalers for asthma, which is well controlled, and has no other medical problems. Which single American Society of Anesthesiologists (ASA) grade best describes his physical status? ★ ★

A I

B II

C III

D IV

E V

15. A 31-year-old woman is scheduled for an elective laparoscopic cholecystectomy. After intubation, the CO_2 (capnography) trace diminishes; she begins to desaturate, and the anaesthetist is unable to hear air entry when auscultating over the chest despite being able to hand-ventilate her easily. Which is the single most likely cause for this? ★★

A Anaphylaxis

B Cardiac arrest

C Monitoring failure

D Oesophageal intubation

E Bilateral pneumothoraces

16. Urgent help is required in the anaesthetic room. A patient has suddenly become unwell during induction of anaesthesia. He has generalized muscle rigidity and tachycardia, and appears sweaty. His blood pressure is normal. Which is the single most likely diagnosis? ★★

A Acute dystonia

B Anaphylaxis

C Epileptic seizure

D Malignant hyperthermia

E Suxamethonium apnoea

17. A 49-year-old woman has presumed sepsis arising from her biliary tract. She is known to have hypertension and gallstones. The admitting team have obtained intravenous (IV) access and taken blood. The woman has also received a dose of broad-spectrum antibiotics. Her blood pressure is 91/40 mmHg, and her serum lactate level is 3.6 mmol/L. Which is the single most important next management step, according to the Surviving Sepsis Campaign? ★★

A Commence a vasopressor infusion

B Give a minimum 20 mL/kg fluid bolus

C Insert a peripheral arterial line

D Insert a central venous catheter

E Recheck the serum lactate level

18. A new mother on the obstetric ward had a forceps delivery under epidural anaesthesia 2 days ago. She initially made a good recovery and was walking on the ward. However, she now has back pain, leg weakness, and bladder dysfunction. She has lower limb motor and sensory dysfunction on testing. Which is the single most likely diagnosis? ★★

A Bacterial meningitis

B Brown-Séquard syndrome

C Epidural haematoma

D Peroneal nerve palsy

E Prolapsed intervertebral disc

19. A previously fit and well 34-year-old man is undergoing surgery for a fractured right femur. He is under a general anaesthetic and the orthopaedic surgeons have just inserted the femoral nail. Intra-operative blood loss is estimated to be about 2000 mL. He has been given 3000 mL of intravenous (IV) crystalloid fluid throughout the operation. A bedside haemoglobin test reads 6.9 g/dL. His pulse rate is 100 bpm, and his blood pressure is 125/75 mmHg. No further blood loss is anticipated. Which is the single most appropriate next step in management? ★★

A Administration of recombinant activated factor VIIa

B Prescribing post-operative iron tablets

C Transfusion of fully cross-matched blood

D Transfusion of group O rhesus-negative blood

E Transfusion of group-specific blood

20. A 53-year-old woman is transferred to the recovery room after a laparoscopic cholecystectomy. The procedure was technically difficult and lasted longer than anticipated. Her temperature in recovery is 32.9°C. Which single physical process accounts for the greatest heat loss intra-operatively? ★★

A Conduction

B Convection

C Humidification

D Radiation

E Respiration

21. A 31-year-old man has sustained a laceration to his right (dominant) hand while at work. The laceration is on the palm of the hand on the radial aspect. A median nerve block at the wrist is planned to provide sufficient anaesthesia for the wound to be explored and sutured. Which single option most accurately describes where the median nerve lies at the wrist? ★★

A Between the tendons of the palmaris longus and the flexor pollicis longus

B Lateral to the radial artery

C Medial to the ulnar artery

D Medial to the ulnar nerve

E Superficial to the flexor retinaculum

22. A 17-year-old man has HbAS (sickle cell trait). He is undergoing repair of a fractured radius under general anaesthesia. During the procedure, the surgeon uses a tourniquet to create a bloodless field, and K-wires the fracture. The patient receives intravenous (IV) fluid and analgesia, and post-operatively is given oxygen. Which single factor is associated with an increased risk of sickle cell crisis in this case? ★★

A IV fluid therapy

B Opioid analgesia

C Oxygen therapy

D Prophylactic antibiotics

E Tourniquet use

23. An 82-year-old man has had a transurethral resection of the prostate (TURP) procedure under spinal anaesthesia. The procedure was long and the surgeon required large volumes of irrigating fluid. In recovery, the patient becomes increasingly agitated and confused; his Glasgow Coma Scale score falls and he requires intubation. Which is the single most likely metabolic abnormality to account for this? ★★

A Hyperglycaemia

B Hypernatraemia

C Hypoglycaemia

D Hypokalaemia

E Hyponatraemia

24. A 24-year-old woman is 32 weeks pregnant with her first child. She has had pregnancy-induced hypertension. Her booking blood pressure was 125/76 mmHg. She has come to the labour suite with a headache and she has some ankle oedema. Her blood pressure is now 145/92 mmHg, and urinalysis shows 3+ proteinuria. She suddenly loses consciousness and has a tonic–clonic seizure. She is put in the recovery position and given supplementary oxygen. Which is the single most appropriate treatment? ★★★

A Intravenous (IV) lorazepam

B IV magnesium sulfate

C IV phenytoin

D Oral methyldopa

E Sublingual nifedipine

25. A 20-year-old man is undergoing his first ever general anaesthetic for an elective tonsillectomy. Shortly after administration of the induction agents, he becomes unwell. Which is the single most likely first sign indicating that he may be having an anaphylactic reaction? ★★★

A Angio-oedema

B Cough

C Desaturation

D Hypotension

E Rash

26. A 6-year-old child weighing approximately 20 kg is brought into the Emergency Department. She has sustained burns to the torso, covering an estimated 20% of body surface area (BSA). The child is haemodynamically stable. Which is the single correct volume of fluid to administer in the first 8 hours following admission? ★★★

A 250 mL

B 400 mL

C 600 mL

D 800 mL

E 1000 mL

27. A 42-year-old woman had a partial thyroidectomy 24 hours ago. Her preoperative haemoglobin level was 11.4 g/dL. Today's result is 3.8 g/dL. She is pain-free; her pulse rate is 85 bpm, and her blood pressure is 118/76 mmHg. Blood loss was estimated to be about 300 mL, and there is minimal fluid in the surgical drain. Her neck is not distended, and the wound site is clean and dry. Which is the single most likely cause of the anaemia? ★★★

A Bone marrow failure

B Iron deficiency

C Major intra-operative haemorrhage

D Ongoing post-operative haemorrhage

E Spurious result

28. A 29-year-old man has been on the Critical Care Unit for 2 days following a serious motor vehicle collision. He is making no respiratory effort, and tests confirm brainstem death. The medical team is planning to talk to the relatives about the possibility of organ donation. Which single advice is correct in relation to organ donation? ★★★★

A Organs can only be harvested once the donor's heart has stopped beating

B Organ donation can only take place if the donor is on the organ donor register or carried an organ donation card

C Organs of patients who are human immunodeficiency virus (HIV)-positive are usually taken

D Organs will usually be harvested if the donor is on the organ donation register, even if the next of kin do not wish for organs to be donated

E The next of kin can specify if they do not want particular organs to be donated

29. A 35-year-old woman is undergoing a diagnostic laparoscopy for pelvic pain. She is deemed to be at high risk of post-operative nausea and vomiting. Which single class of drugs can be used in the prophylaxis of post-operative nausea and vomiting? ★★★★

A Anticonvulsants

B Benzodiazepines

C Corticosteroids

D Opioids

E Smooth muscle relaxants

30. An 80-year-old woman is undergoing palliative care for inoperable cancer. She has copious secretions in the upper airway that are troublesome, and is requesting something to relieve this symptom. Which single group of drugs is the most appropriate to prescribe? ★★★★

A Acetylcholinesterase inhibitors

B Anticholinergic agents

C Antihistamines

D Dopamine antagonists

E Sympathomimetic agents

ANSWERS

1. D ★

The blood gas shows a marked respiratory acidosis. As is common in patients with smoking-related lung disease, a degree of metabolic compensation for a chronically elevated pCO_2 occurs, shown by the raised bicarbonate level. However, this man is unwell with a grossly elevated pCO_2, which exceeds the buffering capacity of the blood. He has a reduced level of consciousness from carbon dioxide narcosis.

Table 11.1 sets out a step-by-step guide on how to approach blood gases.

Table 11.1 Flow chart

Acidosis: pH 7.35	Alkalosis: pH 7.45
Look at the base excess first. Normal (−3 to +3) = respiratory acidosis, and pCO_2 will be raised (>6 kPa)	Look at the base excess first. Normal (−3 to +3) = respiratory alkalosis, and pCO_2 will be low (<4.5 kPa)
High negative (> −4) = metabolic acidosis. If pCO_2 is normal (4.5–6 kPa), it is just a metabolic acidosis. If pCO_2 is low (<4.5 kPa), there is respiratory compensation. If the pCO_2 is also high, it is a mixed acidosis	High positive (> +4) = metabolic alkalosis. If pCO_2 is normal (4.5–6 kPa), it is just a metabolic alkalosis. If pCO_2 is high (>6 kPa), there is respiratory compensation. If pCO_2 is low, it is a mixed alkalosis
High positive (> +4) = respiratory acidosis with renal compensation. The pCO_2 will be high (>6 kPa)	High negative (> −4) = respiratory alkalosis with renal compensation. The pCO_2 will be low (<4.5 kPa)

2. C ★   OHCS 11th edn → p. 767

Acute severe pain is best managed with strong opioids such as morphine. Common routes of administration include the IV, IM, oral, intranasal, and subcutaneous routes. IV administration will provide the most rapid pain relief and avoids first-pass metabolism by the liver (first-pass metabolism mainly affects orally administered drugs). The strong opioids should be titrated to effect. The IM route is useful in a ward setting, but perfusion to peripheral muscles can be impaired due to the sympathetic activity that follows acute injury. This results in delayed onset of action, with potentially late onset of side-effects once perfusion to muscle is restored, and would be less suitable in this setting. Alfentanil is a very short-acting opioid that is usually only used in the operating theatre or given by infusion for its sedative effect.

The World Health Organization (WHO) analgesic ladder offers a stepwise approach to pain management, although the severity of acute pain needs to be assessed to ensure that treatment begins on the appropriate 'rung' of the ladder.

Treatment of this patient with paracetamol or a weak opioid alone would be insufficient to control his acute pain. Combining a strong opioid with paracetamol and a non-steroidal anti-inflammatory drug (e.g. diclofenac or ibuprofen) will reduce the overall amount of opioid that is needed to control his pain. This is beneficial, as it will minimize the risk of opioid side-effects (sedation, nausea and vomiting, constipation, etc.).

→ https://www.openanesthesia.org/who_analgesic_ladder/

→ https://www.who.int/cancer/palliative/painladder/en/

3. B ★   OHCS 11th edn → pp. 586, 590

The GCS is used to assess and record the level of consciousness of a patient. Although it was developed for use on traumatized patients, the GCS is used to assess virtually all patients who present with a depressed level of consciousness, irrespective of the cause. See Table 11.2.

Table 11.2 Glasgow Coma Scale

Best eye response	Score
No eye opening	1
Eyes open to pain	2
Eyes open to command	3
Eyes open spontaneously	4
Best motor response	
No motor response	1
Extensor posturing to pain	2
Abnormal flexor posturing to pain	3
Withdraws to pain (normal flexion)	4
Localizing response to pain	5
Obeys command	6
Best verbal response	
No sounds	1
Incomprehensible sound	2
Inappropriate speech	3
Confused conversation	4
Normal	5

Reprinted from *The Lancet*, 304, Teasdale G, Jennett B, Assessment of coma and impaired consciousness: A Practical Scale, pp. 81–84, Copyright (1974) with permission from Elsevier.

4. B ★

This man has ventricular fibrillation (VF) and requires immediate electrical defibrillation. The fibrillating heart has electrical activity, but this is uncoordinated and so the heart cannot function as a pump. Passing electricity through the heart (defibrillation) causes transient cessation of all endogenous electrical activity. Once this occurs, the intrinsic pacemakers should take over and result in coordinated contractions of the atria and ventricles being resumed.

Chest compressions alone are very unlikely to cardiovert VF into a perfusing rhythm, and if a defibrillator is immediately available, a defibrillating shock should be given as soon as VF is identified. Once VF has been identified, the initial shock takes precedence over airway, breathing, and the administration of any drugs.

The stepwise management of VF and pulseless ventricular tachycardia (VT) are the same and are outlined in the adult Advanced Life Support algorithm.

→ https://www.resus.org.uk/library/2015-resuscitation-guidelines

5. D ★   OHCS 11th edn → p. 678

Whenever local anaesthetic is used, the possibility of toxicity should be considered. The first symptoms of local anaesthetic toxicity are due to central nervous system (CNS) stimulation (tinnitus, circumoral paraesthesiae, light-headedness, and dizziness), followed by CNS depression and cardiovascular collapse. Injection of local anaesthetic should always follow careful aspiration to ensure that the needle is not in a blood vessel. If a patient complains of symptoms suggestive of toxicity, the operator should immediately stop injecting the anaesthetic. The management of local anaesthetic toxicity can be aided by the administration of Intralipid®.

→ http://www.aagbi.org/sites/default/files/la_toxicity_2010_0.pdf

6. A ★

This patient is having an anaphylactic reaction, probably to the administered antibiotics. The priorities in management should follow the Airway, Breathing, Circulation approach (see the adult Advanced Life Support algorithm).

If anaphylaxis is suspected, the precipitant should be stopped (e.g. stop antibiotic infusion) and the patient given IM adrenaline 0.5 mg (0.5 mL of 1:1000 adrenaline). It is unlikely that IM adrenaline will cause an adverse event if it later transpires that the patient was not having an anaphylactic reaction. If in doubt, IM adrenaline should be given.

Chlorphenamine, hydrocortisone, and taking blood for mast cell tryptase are all indicated in cases of anaphylaxis, but adrenaline takes priority. Common precipitants of anaphylaxis include blood products, colloid fluids, antibiotics, and muscle relaxants.

→ https://www.resus.org.uk/library/additional-guidance/guidance-anaphylaxis

7. E ★

This woman has had lower limb surgery and is likely to have been fairly immobile for the last 4 days. She is at high risk of a deep vein thrombosis and subsequent pulmonary embolism. This is the most likely pathology.

Beck's triad (muffled heart sounds, raised jugular venous pressure, and hypotension) would make cardiac tamponade more likely, but this is not pathognomonic. Equally, there is no history of ischaemic heart disease, and an acute myocardial infarction is unlikely to give rise to desaturation unless there has been gross heart failure. Pneumonia is relatively common in the post-operative population but usually has a more gradual onset of cough, pyrexia, anorexia, and lethargy. Pneumothoraces can be rapid in onset, but again there is no reason (e.g. pre-existing lung disease, positive pressure ventilation, central lines, etc.) to suggest that this patient is at risk from these.

The MEWS is an objective way of highlighting adverse patient physiology, so that appropriate help can be sought (see Table 11.3).

Table 11.3 Modified Early Warning Score (MEWS)

Total score	Action
2	Repeat observations in 30 minutes
3	Inform a junior doctor
>4	Request a junior doctor immediately

Source data from QJM: An International Journal of Medicine, 94, 10, Subbe CP, Kruger M, Validation of a modified Early Warning Score in medical admissions, pp. 521–526, 2001, Oxford University Press.

The MEWS is calculated as shown in Table 11.4.

Table 11.4 MEWS calculation

	3	2	1	0	1	2	3
Respiratory rate (breaths/minute)		<9		9–14	15–20	21–29	≥30
Heart rate (bpm)		<40	41–50	51–100	101–110	111–129	≥130
Systolic blood pressure (mmHg)	<70	71–80	81–100	101–199		≥200	
Temperature (°C)		<35		35–38.4		≥38.5	
AVPU				Alert	Reacts to voice	Reacts to pain	Unresponsive

Reproduced from QJM: An International Journal of Medicine, 94, 10, Subbe CP, Kruger M, Validation of a modified Early Warning Score in medical admissions, pp. 521–526. Copyright © 2001, Oxford University Press.

8. E ★

This patient has respiratory depression secondary to benzodiazepine excess. The immediate approach to any critically ill patient begins with airway assessment and management if indicated. This must take place before moving on to breathing and then to circulation, as outlined in the adult Advanced Life Support (ALS) algorithm. If the patient's airway is not patent or safe after a jaw thrust and use of airway adjuncts (e.g. Guedel airway), they may need intubation. Applying ECG leads is part of the assessment of the circulation.

Naloxone is the reversal agent used in opioid overdose. Flumazenil is the reversal agent used in benzodiazepine overdose, but again airway management takes precedence over flumazenil in this case.

→ https://www.resus.org.uk/library/2015-resuscitation-guidelines/guidelines-adult-advanced-life-support

9. B ★

This history points towards the diagnosis of pulmonary embolism in the post-operative period. Pelvic surgery and orthopaedic surgery are risk factors for pulmonary embolism. Although a chest X-ray and an ECG may point towards pulmonary embolism, in most hospitals, the 'gold standard' investigation for confirming the diagnosis is CT pulmonary angiography.

10. B ★

This patient has a bradycardia, which is probably secondary to her inferior MI and is causing cardiovascular compromise (hypotension). In accordance with the Adult Bradycardia Algorithm, she has adverse signs of her bradycardia, and the first-line treatment should be with IV atropine (an anticholinergic drug). If the bradycardia persists, IV isoprenaline (a β-adrenoceptor agonist) and transcutaneous (external) and transvenous cardiac pacing may all be utilized.

Amiodarone is used to treat tachyarrhythmias and often results in bradycardia.

→ https://www.resus.org.uk/library/2015-resuscitation-guidelines

11. C ★ OHCS 11th edn → p. 221

A child with pyloric stenosis classically presents with a metabolic alkalosis due to loss of acid from the upper gastrointestinal tract. A flow chart giving a step-by-step guide on how to approach blood gases is shown in Answer 1, Table 11.1.

12. D ★

This man's tension pneumothorax is life-threatening. He also needs a high concentration of oxygen to be delivered to his functioning lung, as he is grossly hypoxaemic. Some colleagues may voice concern that a patient with COPD potentially has a 'hypoxic drive' and that giving oxygen will cause the patient to hypoventilate, retain carbon dioxide, and become drowsy. This is not a concern in this life-threatening emergency setting—the patient is likely to die of hypoxaemia or circulatory collapse secondary to the tension pneumothorax first, unless he is treated. The oxygen concentration can be reduced once the patient is more stable.

A face mask with a non-rebreather valve and reservoir bag will deliver about 80% oxygen when the oxygen is turned on to 15 L/minute. Nasal cannulae will deliver about 28%, and the Venturi system will deliver 35%, both of which are insufficient in this setting. Face mask CPAP is likely to expand this pneumothorax further, as would intubation and ventilation. A chest drain must be sited before commencing either of these in this situation.

13. **A** ★★

Amitriptyline is a tricyclic antidepressant, but it is also used in the treatment of neuropathic pain. This class of drugs has an analgesic effect that is independent of any antidepressant effect. The drug blocks many neurotransmitters in the central nervous system, including noradrenaline and serotonin, but it is the anticholinergic actions that would cause the side-effects described here. Drugs that antagonize acetylcholine at cholinergic receptors (e.g. atropine and hyoscine) often cause these effects.

The other drugs are all used in the treatment of chronic pain. All of these agents have significant side-effects. Titrating drugs to achieve the right balance between the desired effect and tolerable side-effects is paramount in this setting. Warning patients about what side-effects to expect and how to manage them is an important aspect of drug prescribing. For example, morning somnolence (tiredness) may be overcome by taking the evening dose 1 or 2 hours earlier.

14. **B** ★★   OHCS 11th edn → p. 659

Class II refers to a patient with a mild systemic disease. The ASA grading of patient status was introduced in the 1960s. Although simple, it has been shown to correlate with the risks associated with anaesthesia and surgery, and therefore forms part of the preoperative assessment of all patients undergoing general anaesthesia. See Table 11.5.

Table 11.5 ASA grading

ASA grade	Description	Mortality rate (%)
I	A normal, healthy patient	0.1
II	A patient with mild systemic disease	0.2
III	A patient with severe systemic disease	1.8
IV	A patient with severe systemic disease that is a constant threat to life	7.8
V	A moribund patient who is not expected to survive without the operation	9.4
VI	A declared brain-dead patient whose organs are being removed for donor purposes	

Adapted from ASA Physical Status Classification System, approved by the ASA House of Delegates on October 15, 2014 © 2017 American Society of Anesthesiologists. All rights reserved. A copy of the full text can be obtained from ASA, 1061 American Lane, Schaumburg, Illinois 60173.

The mortality rates quoted above are an average for both elective and emergency surgery. The suffix E is added to denote an emergency operation.

15. D ★★   OHCS 11th edn → pp. 671–2

Anaphylaxis usually presents with a combination of bronchospasm, rash, tachycardia, and hypotension. As the patient is easy to hand-ventilate, anaphylaxis is unlikely, as bronchospastic lungs require high airway pressures.

Cardiac arrest would cause an absent pulse oximetry trace, and breath sounds would still be audible while the patient was being hand-ventilated.

A failure of monitoring equipment is unlikely to give this picture, as both the capnography and the pulse oximetry modules would have to be faulty at the same time, and the patient might well become cyanotic.

The occurrence of bilateral pneumothoraces would be very unlucky but could give rise to this situation. However, probability dictates that this is very unlikely.

Oesophageal intubation is the most likely cause here and could be confirmed by auscultating over the stomach and hearing air entry when hand-ventilating the patient. Its management involves removal of the misplaced tube, re-oxygenating the patient with mask ventilation, and then intubating the trachea.

16. D ★★   OHCS 11th edn → p. 673

Malignant hyperthermia is an inherited disorder of calcium metabolism that affects skeletal muscle. It is most often triggered by suxamethonium or the volatile anaesthetic agents. Its presentation varies from one individual to another, but it should be considered when there is unexplained tachycardia, especially in the presence of tachypnoea, muscle rigidity, or an increase in end-tidal pCO_2. Malignant hyperthermia can be a life-threatening condition, or it may present more insidiously. Emergency management includes removal of the trigger agent, cooling, and treatment with dantrolene (a drug that interferes with skeletal muscle contraction). Without treatment, the mortality rate is approximately 75%; with treatment, mortality is significantly reduced.

None of the other diagnoses classically present as described here. Acute dystonia is often triggered by neuroleptic agents and typically presents in the first few days of new treatment. It is rarely associated with anaesthesia. Suxamethonium apnoea is an inherited deficiency of plasma cholinesterase, resulting in delayed metabolism of suxamethonium and therefore prolongation of neuromuscular blockade.

→ https://anaesthetists.org/Home/Resources-publications/Guidelines/Malignant-hyperthermia-crisis

17. B ★★

Vasoactive mediators from the infective agent and from damaged endothelium are causing widespread vasodilatation, hypotension, and a resultant tachycardia. The first goal of the management of septic shock is to ensure adequate filling (pre-load), as measured by the central venous pressure (CVP). Once the patient is adequately filled, if hypotension and shock persist, a vasopressor should then be commenced, such as noradrenaline (norepinephrine) which acts predominantly upon α_1-adrenoceptors.

A central line will allow the CVP to be measured, but more important than the specific value recorded is the trend in pressure in response to fluid boluses. If the CVP continues to rise, this usually suggests that more fluid is needed, whereas a plateau in the CVP suggests that adequate filling has been achieved. A central line will also allow some drugs to be administered that would otherwise be irritant to smaller peripheral veins.

An arterial line will be useful in the High-Dependency Unit/Intensive Therapy Unit setting but is not a priority in the first instance. Similarly, rechecking the serum lactate level is unlikely to be of use within the first 6 hours.

18. C ★★

The history points to a rare, but very serious, complication of epidural anaesthesia. A haematoma that is formed following insertion of a catheter into the epidural space can expand and cause neurological compromise. Traumatic insertion or derangements of clotting increase the likelihood of haematoma formation. Despite its rarity, a thorough working knowledge of recognition and management of this condition is essential.

→ https://www.nysora.com/foundations-of-regional-anesthesia/complications/diagnosis-management-spinal-peripheral-nerve-hematoma/

→ https://www.frca.co.uk/article.aspx?articleid=100589

19. C ★★

Loss of more than 20% of the circulating volume is regarded as a significant blood loss, and in most circumstances, this needs to be replaced with a blood transfusion. Circulating volume is approximately 70 mL/kg, so it is around 4900 mL in a 70-kg man. In this case, there is time to obtain fully cross-matched blood, which usually takes up to 45 minutes to become available. This blood will be thoroughly matched for the patient's blood group (A, B, AB, or O), rhesus D status (negative or positive), and the rarer antibodies/antigens. Type-specific blood takes about 20 minutes to become available and is matched for blood group and rhesus D status, but not for the rarer antibodies/antigens. Group O rhesus-negative blood (universal donor blood) should be available immediately in most clinical areas but carries the risk of the patient raising antibodies to the rarer antigens, which can cause problems with future blood transfusions. The decision as to which blood to request will depend upon the level of clinical urgency.

The following link is to the National Blood Service website.

→ https://www.blood.co.uk

20. D ★★

Radiation accounts for approximately 40% of the heat lost from the body. In addition, convection (30%), respiration (including humidification) (20%), and conduction (10%) are all important, and their relative contributions vary, depending on the environment. Space blankets are designed to reduce heat loss from radiation.

21. A ★★   OHCS 11th edn → p. 555

The median nerve lies between the two prominent tendons at the wrist (the palmaris longus and flexor pollicis longus) and is deep to the flexor retinaculum within the carpal tunnel. Swelling within the carpal tunnel gives rise to 'carpal tunnel syndrome', which is caused by compression upon the median nerve.

The ulna bone, ulnar nerve, and ulnar artery are medial to the median nerve, and the radial artery lies lateral to it.

22. E ★★

Use of a tourniquet is associated with precipitation of sickle cell crisis. If a tourniquet must be used, the limb should be thoroughly exsanguinated prior to inflation. All of the other options are associated with minimization of the risk of a crisis and should form part of the peri-operative care where appropriate.

23. E ★★

TURP syndrome is a complication of TURP and is caused by the combination of fluid overload and hyponatraemia, which results from high volumes of hypotonic irrigating fluid being used over the open prostate gland. It can be complicated by hyperglycinaemia (not hyperglycaemia) as a result of the glycine irrigation fluid that is used by the surgeons. Therefore, the mental state of these patients should be regularly assessed peri-operatively, and any sign of confusion should be a cause for concern. Long procedures are a risk factor for TURP syndrome. Management consists of slow correction of the underlying metabolic disturbance. Rapid correction of hyponatraemia can cause permanent neurological disability.

24. B ★★★   OHCS 11th edn → p. 90

This patient initially had pre-eclampsia. This condition is diagnosed after 20 weeks' gestation when there is hypertension (systolic blood pressure greater than 140 mmHg and/or diastolic blood pressure greater than 90 mmHg) or a rise in systolic blood pressure of more than 30 mmHg or a rise in diastolic blood pressure of more than 15 mmHg, compared with the booking blood pressure, and greater than 300 mg/dL per 24 hours of protein in the urine (in practical terms, more than 2+ on urinalysis). Eclampsia is diagnosed when a patient with pre-eclampsia has a seizure. The Magpie Trial demonstrated that patients with pre-eclampsia were less likely to go on to develop eclampsia if they were given IV magnesium. This and other work has also formed the basis of the first-line treatment of eclampsia with IV magnesium.

→ The Magpie Trial Collaborative Group. Do women with preeclampsia, and their babies, benefit from magnesium sulphate? The Magpie Trial: a randomised placebo-controlled trial. *Lancet*. 2002;**360**:1331–2.

→ http://emedicine.medscape.com/article/261435-overview

25. D ★★★   OHCS 11th edn → p. 183

Hypotension is observed more commonly than any other clinical sign in patients who are developing anaphylactic reactions. Any of the other signs mentioned may still occur.

→ https://anaesthetists.org/Home/Resources-publications/Safety-alerts/Anaesthesia-emergencies/Anaphylaxis-and-allergies

26. D ★★★   OHCS 11th edn → p. 598

Approximately 50 000 children present to Emergency Departments with burns every year in the UK. Estimation of the area affected is an important part of the initial assessment and is aided by the use of a Lund–Browder chart. Although fluid resuscitation in burns has been controversial, the Parkland formula is widely used in the management of paediatric burns. The take-home message is that fluid requirements are high because of losses through the damaged skin barrier.

Parkland formula: for the first 24 hours after the burn, give 4 mL/kg per % BSA burn of Hartmann's solution. Give half of this volume in the first 8 hours after the burn, and the other half in the next 16 hours.

27. E ★★★

There is no suggestion that there was significant intra-operative or post-operative bleeding, so major blood loss is unlikely. Iron deficiency anaemia is a chronic pathology and would take longer than 24 hours to develop. Bone marrow failure can result in anaemia but is relatively rare and usually causes a pancytopenia, so it would be important to check the platelet and white cell counts too. Most importantly, this patient has no features of profound anaemia such as circulatory collapse (shock).

The most likely cause is a spurious result due to either an error when taking the blood sample (e.g. taking it from the drip arm and causing dilution) or a laboratory error (this is much less likely). As there are no features of circulatory compromise, a new sample should be taken and analysed. Spurious laboratory results are not uncommon, and if you ever doubt the clinical likelihood of a result, you should consider repeating the investigation.

28. E ★★★★

The majority of organ donations in the UK occur from heart-beating donors. The use of non-heart-beating donors is increasing in the UK but is still relatively uncommon. A patient does not have to be registered on the organ donor register to donate organs, but if they expressed the view that they would not want to donate organs during life, this decision is usually honoured. If a patient expressed the view that they wanted to donate their organs, but their living next of kin were against organ donation, it is unlikely that organs would be taken.

→ http://www.organdonation.nhs.uk

29. C ★★★★

Dexamethasone (a corticosteroid) is commonly used as an anti-emetic. It is usually given intra-operatively, as it is associated with unpleasant side-effects when given to patients who are awake.

→ https://academic.oup.com/bjaed/article/13/1/28/281153

30. B ★★★★

Anticholinergic drugs (e.g. hyoscine) are routinely used for their antisialagogue effect, particularly in the palliative care setting. Acetylcholine is the neurotransmitter at muscarinic receptors of the parasympathetic nervous system, responsible for control of secretions. Therefore, anticholinergic drugs will block this pathway.

Psychiatry

Isabel McMullen

Mental health problems are estimated to affect one in four people each year in the UK, making mental illness one of the commonest presentations to General Practice (GP) surgeries, outpatient clinics, and Emergency Departments. Yet many doctors and medical students feel uncertain about how to approach patients with a psychiatric disorder.

The key to becoming a good psychiatrist lies in the clinical interview. There are few physical signs or investigations that allow doctors to diagnose psychiatric illness, so a detailed history and mental state examination are important. As a psychiatrist, you are in the privileged position of having patients tell you their personal stories, and the skill is in listening attentively and asking relevant questions to help to clarify parts of the story. The best way to practise these techniques is to watch experienced clinicians at work and to interview patients yourself.

Obviously diagnosis is important, so you need to be aware of the types of symptoms that fit with each type of disorder, as well as the medical conditions that may mimic psychiatric illness. Investigations may be necessary to rule out other diseases, and you need to be able to request these appropriately. Psychiatrists have access to a range of treatments—medical (e.g. antidepressants), psychological (e.g. cognitive behavioural therapy), and physical (e.g. electroconvulsive therapy)—and you need to know which ones to recommend. Most of these treatments are delivered in conjunction with the multidisciplinary team, so you should be clear about the roles of each team member.

Finally, there is overlap between psychiatry and the law, which can raise interesting ethical issues. It is sometimes necessary to treat a person against their will, for the safety of that person or others, so you need to know about mental health law. Psychiatrists are also often requested to provide a second opinion in difficult capacity assessments.

Isabel McMullen, *Psychiatry* In: *Oxford Assess and Progress: Clinical Specialties.*
Edited by: Luci Etheridge and Henry Collier, Oxford University Press.
© Oxford University Press 2021. DOI:10.1093/oso/9780198862550.003.0012

QUESTIONS

1. A 53-year-old builder has injured his arm and is admitted to the ward. Late one night, he becomes aggressive, shouting at the nurses and other patients, wanting to leave the ward, and saying that he can see ants running all over the walls. Which is the single most likely cause of these symptoms? ★

A Abnormal reaction to analgesic medication

B Alcohol withdrawal

C Dissocial personality disorder

D Head injury

E Past history of schizophrenia

2. A 20-year-old woman took 40 paracetamol tablets 9 hours ago. Which is the single most appropriate emergency treatment? ★

A Activated charcoal

B Diazepam

C Flumazenil

D N-acetylcysteine

E Naloxone

3. A 34-year-old woman has severe abdominal pain and blood in her stool. Abdominal and pelvic examinations are normal, except for multiple surgical scars over the abdomen, consistent with laparoscopies and an appendicectomy. She provides stool samples obtained at home that contain blood but has not managed to produce one in hospital. Blood and urine investigations are normal, but she insists on further investigation and does not want to leave hospital. Which is the single most likely diagnosis? ★

A Delusional disorder

B Hypochondriacal disorder

C Malingering

D Mild–moderate depressive episode

E Munchausen syndrome

4. A 25-year-old man is disorientated and has slurred speech and respiratory depression. He also has miosis. Which is the single most likely cause? ★

A Alcohol abuse

B Carbon monoxide poisoning

C Opioid abuse

D Paracetamol overdose

E Salicylate overdose

5. A 36-year-old man goes to a plastic surgeon insisting on surgery, stating that his nose is too large and crooked. He says that people stare at him when he goes out, so he prefers not to leave the house. He attributes his recent job loss to his 'deformed nose'. He wears make-up to camouflage it but would like surgery to correct what appears to be a normal nose. Which is the single most likely diagnosis? ★

A Body dysmorphic disorder

B Hypochondriasis

C Mild–moderate depressive episode

D Obsessive–compulsive disorder

E Social phobia

6. A 61-year-old man attends his general practitioner (GP) at the request of his wife who thinks he is drinking too much alcohol. Which single factor is a sign of alcohol dependence? ★

A A wide repertoire of alcoholic drinks

B Decreased alcohol tolerance

C Drinking 28 units of alcohol or more a week

D Drinking despite evidence of its harm to his job and family

E Drinking until late in the evening

7. A 20-year-old man has a first episode of psychosis. Your consultant asks you to prescribe an atypical (or second-generation) antipsychotic. Which single drug should be prescribed? ★

A Chlorpromazine

B Haloperidol

C Lorazepam

D Mirtazapine

E Olanzapine

8. A 64-year-old man is recovering after a myocardial infarction (MI). His recovery is slowed by poor sleep, loss of appetite, lack of motivation, and feelings of hopelessness. Your consultant believes that he is depressed and asks you to commence antidepressant treatment. He has no other medical history. Which would be the single most appropriate class of drug to prescribe? ★

A Benzodiazepine

B Monoamine oxidase inhibitor (MAOI)

C Selective serotonin reuptake inhibitor (SSRI)

D Serotonin and noradrenaline (norepinephrine) reuptake inhibitor

E Tricyclic antidepressant

9. A 52-year-old woman has low mood, tiredness, and weight gain, with decreased appetite. She is tearful and overweight, with dry skin and thin hair. Which is the single most useful test to aid diagnosis? ★

A Chest X-ray

B Electrocardiogram (ECG)

C Full blood count

D Thyroid function tests

E Urea and electrolytes

10. A 35-year-old woman suddenly starts to feel dizzy and short of breath, with chest pains and a tingling sensation in her fingers. These symptoms worsen until she feels as if she is about to die. The episode lasts for about 10 minutes before resolving completely. Which is the single most likely diagnosis? ★

A Acute asthma

B Myocardial infarction

C Panic attack

D Temporal lobe epilepsy

E Transient ischaemic attack

11. A 36-year-old woman is 36 weeks pregnant with twins in England. She has obsessive–compulsive disorder. She is scheduled to have an elective Caesarean section for the delivery of her twins, due to complications in her last delivery and pre-eclampsia in this pregnancy. She has already consented to the operation. She has now become agitated and anxious and is refusing to cooperate, saying that she does not want to have the operation and wants to go home. Which is the single most appropriate course of action? ★

A Arrange emergency detention under the Mental Health Act 2007 (England and Wales), as her health depends on her being treated

B Assess her capacity to consent, and discuss the situation with a senior doctor

C Detain her for treatment, as she has a mental disorder as defined by the Mental Health Act 2007 (England and Wales)

D Prescribe sedative medication, and advise the midwife to call when she is less agitated

E Reassure her and carry on, as she has previously consented to the operation

12. A 44-year-old woman has taken an overdose of 20 paracetamol tablets. Which single factor indicates the highest risk of her going on to complete suicide? ★

A Having a psychotic illness

B Living with a partner

C Taking alcohol with the overdose

D Taking more than 50 tablets as an overdose

E Writing a suicide note before taking the overdose

13. A 58-year-old woman has gastritis. Her general practitioner (GP) is concerned about her possible heavy use of alcohol and arranges some screening questionnaires and blood tests. Which single result would indicate possible problem drinking or hazardous drinking? ★

A A decreased mean corpuscular volume (MCV)

B A low level of gamma-glutamyl transpeptidase (GGT)

C A score of 5 on the Alcohol Use Disorders Identification Test (AUDIT)

D One positive response on the CAGE questionnaire

E Raised urate levels

14. A 34-year-old man is brought to the Emergency Department by the police. He is agitated and elated. His blood pressure is 140/90 mmHg, his pulse rate 120 bpm, and his pupils dilated. Which single substance is he most likely to have been using? ★

A Cocaine

B Heroin

C Organic solvents

D Oxazepam

E Psilocybin

15. A 68-year-old man has a prominent impairment of recent memory with intact immediate recall. He has no evidence of generalized cognitive impairment and no impairment in his level of consciousness. Which is the single most likely diagnosis? ★

A Alzheimer's disease

B Delirium

C Korsakoff's syndrome

D Normal-pressure hydrocephalus

E Post-ictal state

16. A 74-year-old woman has bowel cancer being treated in England. The surgeons say that she requires surgery, which is potentially curative, and that without it she will die. The woman is refusing any surgical intervention. She had postnatal depression 42 years ago but is not currently suffering from any mental illness. Her present Mini-Mental State Examination (MMSE) score is 29/30. She knows about her diagnosis, believes that it applies to her, understands the risks and benefits of the proposed surgery, and is able to retain the information. Which is the single most appropriate course of action? ★

A Detain her under a section of the Mental Health Act 2007 (England and Wales) and perform the operation

B Discharge her from hospital

C Obtain a second opinion, and if that professional considers that the woman has capacity, comply with her wishes

D Restrain her under common law, and perform the operation

E Use the Mental Capacity Act 2005 (England and Wales) to perform the operation

17. A 40-year-old woman is having intrusive and persistent thoughts that she is a 'dirty prostitute'. She recognizes that her thoughts are silly but nevertheless feels ashamed of them. Although these thoughts get her down, she still enjoys life. Which is the single most likely diagnosis? ★

A Depressive disorder

B Generalized anxiety disorder

C Obsessive–compulsive disorder

D Psychotic episode

E Schizophrenia

18. A 28-year-old man is found in an alleyway in a semi-conscious state. He has a respiratory rate of 6 breaths/minute, a pulse rate of 50 bpm, and pinpoint pupils. Which is the single most appropriate drug to give? ★

A Clonidine

B Methadone

C Naloxone

D Naltrexone

E Thiamine

19. An 82-year-old man is forgetful, gets lost when he is out, and has difficulty finding his way home. On occasion, he puts his keys in the microwave, and he does not appear to know how to use it to cook food. His memory problems seemed to get markedly worse around the time when he was admitted to hospital with a stroke 2 years ago, and again earlier this year when he could not speak for several minutes. His speech has since recovered. Which is the single most likely diagnosis? ★

A Alzheimer's disease

B Fronto-temporal dementia

C Lewy body dementia

D Normal ageing

E Vascular dementia

20. A 28-year-old woman has low mood and loss of appetite. She is still coping at work but lacks energy and feels that her concentration is not as good as before. Her sleep is normal, and she enjoys spending time with her friends. She has never had any ideas of self-harm or suicide. Which is the single most appropriate course of action? ★

A Ask her to keep a mood diary and return to see you in 2 weeks' time

B Prescribe citalopram, and see her again in 2 weeks' time

C Prescribe moclobemide, and see her again in 4 weeks' time

D Refer her for cognitive behavioural therapy

E Tell her not to worry and that it is normal to feel like this

21. A 29-year-old woman has recently been diagnosed as having generalized anxiety disorder. Which is the single best initial approach to management? ★

A Advise her to keep a diary of when she feels anxious

B Explain the condition to her, writing down the essential points

C Give her a standard information leaflet

D Provide her with information on the medication that can be used

E Recommend a self-help book

22. A 48-year-old man with alcohol dependence has been found wandering in the street. He has some clouding of consciousness, nystagmus, and ophthalmoplegia. Which is the single most appropriate medication to administer initially? ★

A Acamprosate

B Disulfiram

C Metoclopramide

D Naloxone

E Thiamine

23. A 30-year-old woman with panic disorder has been treated with cognitive behavioural therapy, which has only partially helped her symptoms. She requests further treatment and is prescribed citalopram. Which is the single most likely side-effect profile she should be warned about? ★

A Confusion and memory problems

B Drowsiness, palpitations, and postural hypotension

C Dry mouth, blurred vision, and constipation

D Nausea, gastrointestinal upset, restlessness, and insomnia

E Weight gain

24. A 28-year-old man who has recently been diagnosed with paranoid schizophrenia is started on risperidone. Which single common potential side-effect should he be advised about? ★

A Feeling more alert

B Gynaecomastia

C Hirsutism

D Improved sexual performance

E Weight loss

25. A 79-year-old man has personality change and worsening orientation. He has a tremor, extensor plantar reflexes, and bilateral small pupils that do not constrict in response to light but do constrict on accommodation. Which is the single most useful diagnostic investigation? ★

A Chest X-ray

B Computed tomography (CT) scan of the brain

C Electroencephalogram (EEG)

D Magnetic resonance imaging (MRI) of the brain

E Venereal Disease Research Laboratory (VDRL) test

26. The police bring a 23-year-old man to the Emergency Department who they have detained because he was standing in the middle of the road shouting at the traffic and threatening to stab drivers. The doctor is asked to take a history and examine the patient. Which is the single most appropriate initial action for the doctor to take? ★

A Arrange for the interview to take place in a quiet, private room

B Ask the police to be present during the interview

C Remove from the room any sharp items that could be used as weapons

D Talk to the police about the patient's presentation and behaviour

E Tell another member of staff to note down where the interview will take place

27. A 67-year-old man was diagnosed with dementia a year ago. He has previously been advised, both verbally and in writing, to inform the Driver and Vehicle Licensing Agency (DVLA) of his diagnosis. He says that he has not taken this advice, as he needs his car to get to the shops and to see his friends. The Mini-Mental State Examination (MMSE) reveals that he is not disorientated but does show mild short-term memory loss. Which is the single most appropriate course of action? ★★

A Advise him again verbally that he needs to inform the DVLA

B Advise him verbally of your responsibility to disclose his diagnosis to the DVLA

C Advise him verbally that he should stop driving from now on

D Disclose his diagnosis to the DVLA

E Write to him again, advising that he needs to inform the DVLA

28. A 20-year-old woman has panic attacks when she has to attend formal meetings at work. She also feels anxious when she meets her friends in the pub. Which is the single most likely diagnosis? ★★

A Adjustment disorder

B Generalized anxiety disorder

C Panic disorder

D Post-traumatic stress disorder

E Social phobia

29. A 60-year-old man asks for a repeat prescription for diazepam. He says that his general practitioner (GP) started him on this treatment 3 months ago when he was anxious and depressed after losing his job. Which is the single most appropriate course of action? ★★

A Call his usual GP to arrange an appointment for him in 1 week's time

B Change his prescription to an antidepressant drug, and explain that this would be a more appropriate treatment

C Explain that you cannot re-prescribe diazepam because of the risk of him becoming dependent

D Explain the risk of becoming dependent on diazepam, and then re-prescribe diazepam at half the dose for 4 more weeks

E Explain the risk of becoming dependent on diazepam, and then re-prescribe diazepam in a weekly decreasing dose

30. A 33-year-old woman with bipolar disorder is due to be started on a mood stabilizer. She has some questions about lithium. Which single symptom or sign is a common side-effect of lithium at therapeutic levels? ★ ★

A Coarse tremor

B Dysarthria

C Pigmentation of skin

D Thirst

E Weight loss

31. A 24-year-old man is found acting strangely in the park. He believes that MI5 are behind a plot to harm him and are keeping him under surveillance. He hears himself being commented on by a voice 'reading the news' and thinks that his thoughts are being controlled by devices on buses. Which single symptom is one of Schneider's first-rank symptoms of schizophrenia? ★ ★

A Catatonia

B Ideas of reference

C Persecutory delusions

D Poverty of speech

E Third-person auditory hallucinations

32. A 26-year-old woman has emotional lability and a mildly depressed mood. She feels 'numb' and 'empty', and has recently often acted impulsively (e.g. by shoplifting). She uses recreational drugs regularly. She has no regular partner and is unemployed. She cuts herself in response to distressing feelings but is not suicidal. Which is the single most likely diagnosis? ★ ★

A Antisocial personality disorder

B Avoidant personality disorder

C Emotionally unstable personality disorder

D Histrionic personality disorder

E Mild depressive episode

33. The wife of a patient is in a distressed state. She tells her general practitioner (GP) that her husband is wandering around the house at night and that she is afraid to sleep in case he accidentally harms himself. She says that he has already drawn up a Personal Welfare Lasting Power of Attorney (LPA), which is registered at the Office of the Public Guardian, and that she has appointed her as his 'attorney' to make decisions on his behalf. The GP knows that the patient has a diagnosis of dementia, although it is 6 months since he last saw him. The patient's wife asks the GP to prescribe some sedative medication, adding that her husband is quite happy to take a tablet at night. Which is the single most appropriate response for the GP to make? ★ ★ ★

A Advise the patient's wife that he would need to talk to other members of the family as well before he prescribes any medication

B Explain to the patient's wife that an LPA does not cover decisions about medical treatment

C Explain to the patient's wife that he would need to see her husband to assess whether he lacks the capacity to decide whether or not to take sedative medication

D Explain to the patient's wife that she cannot give consent on behalf of her husband for him to prescribe medication

E Prescribe a small dose of sedative medication for the patient and see him in 1 week

34. A 23-year-old woman has had psychological and somatic symptoms of anxiety for 3 weeks, which mostly occur when she has to drive her car in the city. This is the first time she has suffered from these symptoms. Which is the single most appropriate treatment? ★ ★ ★ ★

A Anxiety management training

B Behavioural therapy

C Brief psychodynamic psychotherapy

D A selective serotonin reuptake inhibitor (SSRI)

E A tricyclic antidepressant

35. A 3-year-old boy has been referred to the paediatrician and child psychiatrist for assessment. He was late in starting to talk and is falling behind his peers at nursery. He is thought to have mild learning disability. His parents have some questions. Which single statement about mild learning disability is appropriate when counselling the parents? ★ ★ ★ ★

A A specific cause cannot be identified in 50% of cases

B Epilepsy occurs in 70% of people with mild learning disability

C Fragile X syndrome is an X-linked recessive condition that can cause mild learning disability

D Only a very small number of people with mild learning disability are capable of working in adulthood

E The expected intelligence quotient (IQ) range is between 20 and 35

36. A 6-year-old boy does not talk and will not play with other children. He is only interested in toy cars and lines them up in a particular order. His teacher says that he cannot read or write like the other children, and that he has temper tantrums for no obvious reason. Which is the single most likely diagnosis? ★ ★ ★ ★

A Asperger's syndrome

B Autistic spectrum disorder

C Normal child

D Obsessive–compulsive disorder

E Rett's syndrome

37. A 30-year-old man with paranoid schizophrenia has not responded to two consecutive 8-week trials of olanzapine and risperidone at therapeutic doses. Which is the single most appropriate course of action? ★ ★ ★ ★

A Combine olanzapine and risperidone

B Commence clozapine

C Commence haloperidol

D Commence risperidone long-acting injection

E Continue olanzapine at a higher dose

38. A 35-year-old man was prescribed an antidepressant 8 months ago for a moderately severe depressive episode. This was his first depressive episode. He now feels that he has almost recovered and wants to know when he can stop taking the antidepressant. Which is the single most appropriate piece of advice? ★★★★

A He must take the tablets for the rest of his life

B He should continue the medication for 1 to 2 months after he has recovered

C He should continue the medication for 4 to 6 months after he has recovered

D He should continue the medication for 1 year after he has recovered

E He should stop the antidepressants immediately if he feels that he is back to normal

39. A 30-year-old man with paranoid schizophrenia on the ward becomes very agitated one night. He is pacing around, talking to himself, and appears to be responding to hallucinations. He is verbally aggressive and hostile to staff and other patients. He has a history of violence when unwell. Simple de-escalation techniques have failed to calm the situation, but he is willing to take medication. Which is the single most appropriate management? ★★★★

A Give clozapine 50 mg orally and review in 1 hour

B Give haloperidol 10 mg intramuscularly (IM) and review in 1 hour

C Give lorazepam 2 mg orally and review in 1 hour

D Give olanzapine 20 mg IM and review in 1 hour

E Request police presence on the ward

40. A 31-year-old single mother discloses that she regularly cuts herself in front of her 6-year-old son and that he often becomes distressed if he thinks he is feeling sad. She is not taking him to school every day. Which is the single most appropriate course of action? ★★★★

A Contact the school to find out whether her son's teacher has any concerns about him

B Find out whether she has any extra support, such as a family member, to help look after her son

C Refer to the police and social services immediately

D Speak to a senior colleague and the designated child protection lead

E Tell her that if she does not stop self-harming, you will have to take action

41. A 22-year-old woman has recurrent depressive episodes. Her main symptoms are low mood, anhedonia, insomnia, and weight loss secondary to poor appetite. She has had adverse reactions to selective serotonin reuptake inhibitors (SSRIs) in the past. Which would be the single most appropriate medication to prescribe? ★ ★ ★ ★

A Citalopram

B Fluoxetine

C Mirtazapine

D Paroxetine

E Sertraline

42. A 47-year-old man with paranoid schizophrenia has been known to his mental health team for 15 years. He has needed eight admissions during that time. He has recently deteriorated due to non-compliance with medication and is threatening his neighbours with violence. He is now in a very similar state to that with which he presented in the past when unwell. He is refusing to agree to admission to hospital for treatment. Which is the single most appropriate section of the Mental Health Act 2007 (England and Wales) to use? ★ ★ ★ ★

A Section 2

B Section 3

C Section 5

D Section 17

E Section 136

43. A 48-year-old woman is admitted to hospital for routine surgery. She takes once-daily lithium for treatment of bipolar disorder. Which is the single correct time to take her blood to check plasma levels of lithium? ★ ★ ★ ★

A Immediately before her dose

B 2 hours after her dose

C 8 hours after her dose

D 12 hours after her dose

E 20 hours after her dose

44. A 35-year-old man who is opiate-dependent is considering tackling his addiction. In discussing treatment options, which is the single most appropriate piece of advice to include? ★★★★

A   Methadone has a shorter half-life than heroin

B   Naltrexone is an opiate agonist and is an alternative to methadone

C   Opiate withdrawal results in death if untreated

D   Opiate withdrawal causes restlessness, abdominal pain, and anxiety

E   The withdrawal syndrome will begin 2 to 3 days after heroin was last taken

45. A previously healthy 78-year-old man has a severe depressive illness. He has not responded to various treatments so far, and his consultant wants to prescribe a tricyclic antidepressant. Which is the single most important investigation before commencing treatment? ★★★★

A   Computed tomography (CT) scan of the brain

B   Electrocardiogram (ECG)

C   Full blood count

D   Urea and electrolytes

E   Urinalysis

ANSWERS

1. B ★ ★   OHCS 11th edn → p. 732

Alcohol withdrawal can cause delirium tremens, which is characterized by florid visual or tactile hallucinations, typically of small creatures. This is relatively common in drinkers who are suddenly admitted to hospital, and a detailed alcohol history should always be taken to try to prevent withdrawal using appropriate medication.

→ http://www.nice.org.uk/guidance/CG115

2. D ★   OHCS 11th edn → p. 278

All patients who have a delayed presentation (more than 8 hours) after paracetamol overdose should have N-acetylcysteine started immediately.

3. E ★

In Munchausen syndrome, or factitious illness, affected individuals fake illness in order to gain medical attention. Often, reasonably serious symptoms, such as blood in the stools or urine, can be falsified. These cannot be reproduced when the person is being directly observed. Malingering is the term used for people who feign illness for another gain (e.g. financial benefit or avoidance of work). Hypochondriasis refers to an excessive worry about illness, and these patients may often have vague medical symptoms such as palpitations or abdominal pain.

4. C ★   OHCS 11th edn → p. 601

These are the classic signs of acute opioid intoxication.

5. A ★

The key here is that the person is excessively concerned with an imagined abnormality in his physical appearance, which is affecting his life. It is not an obsession and is not affecting the mood. The social withdrawal is occurring because of the concern about the feature, rather than because of anxiety. Hypochondriasis is a fear of serious illness, rather than concern about physical features.

6. D ★   OHCS 11th edn → p. 826

It is not the amount drunk, or the quality of what a person drinks, but the effect that it has on their life that characterizes dependence.

→ https://www.drinkaware.co.uk/facts/drinking-habits-and-behaviours/am-i-alcohol-dependent

7. E ★　　　　　OHCS 11th edn → p. 708

Olanzapine is a commonly used atypical antipsychotic drug. These have different side-effects from typical antipsychotic drugs such as haloperidol and chlorpromazine. Lorazepam is a benzodiazepine. Mirtazapine is an antidepressant.

8. C ★　　　　　OHCS 11th edn → p. 714

Depression following an MI is associated with a poor prognosis, although the evidence that treatment of depression improves this is equivocal. Tricyclic antidepressants increase the risk of MI, so they should not be used in patients with ischaemic heart disease. SSRIs may have a protective effect. Benzodiazepines do not treat depression. MAOIs are used only rarely for depression nowadays, due to their potentially lethal interactions.

→ Anon. Depression, antidepressants and heart disease. *Drug Ther Bull.* 2008;**46**:29–32.

9. D ★

Hypothyroidism is a recognized cause of depression, and it also causes physical symptoms, including lethargy, weight gain, constipation, dry skin and hair, and oedema. Recognition of these symptoms should point towards investigation of thyroid function to guide appropriate treatment.

10. C ★　　　　　OHCS 11th edn → p. 718

Although some of these symptoms may occur in any of the options given, the young age, combination of symptoms, and complete resolution within a short time make a panic attack the most likely diagnosis.

11. B ★　　　　　OHCS 11th edn → p. 773

Although this woman has signed a consent form, a patient can withdraw consent at any time. Although she has a history of obsessive–compulsive disorder, which would satisfy the definition of a mental disorder under the Mental Health Act 2007 (England and Wales) or the Mental Health (Care and Treatment) (Scotland) Act 2003, she cannot be detained under the Act to allow medical or surgical treatment to continue. The fact that she has pre-eclampsia does not constitute a danger to herself or others (i.e. her babies) under the Act, as this risk is not arising from her mental disorder.

12. A ★　　　　　OHCS 11th edn → p. 726

→ https://www.hqip.org.uk/resource/national-confidential-inquiry-into-suicide-and-safety-in-mental-health-annual-report-2019/#.XxyO_HuSlPY (key findings (suicide) from the National Confidential Inquiry into Suicide and Safety in Mental Health)

13. C ★   OHCS 11th edn → pp. 826–7

A raised MCV and GGT are indicative of problem drinking. Two or more positive responses are needed on the CAGE questionnaire. Urate levels are raised in about 50% of all people with drinking problems, but they are only useful as screening tests for men, as they are poor discriminators in women. The AUDIT is a simple 10-question test developed by the World Health Organization (WHO) to determine whether a person's alcohol consumption may be harmful. The test was designed to be used internationally and was validated in a study using patients from six countries. Questions 1 to 3 deal with alcohol consumption; Questions 4 to 6 relate to alcohol dependence, and Questions 7 to 10 consider alcohol-related problems.

→ http://apps.who.int/iris/bitstream/10665/67205/1/WHO_MSD_MSB_01.6a.pdf

14. A ★

Cocaine abuse has sympathomimetic effects and causes tachycardia, hypertension, and pupillary dilatation. Heroin has the opposite effect. Solvent abuse causes signs similar to those of alcohol intoxication but may also include hallucinations. Psilocybin, which is found in 'magic mushrooms', also causes hallucinations. Oxazepam is a benzodiazepine.

15. C ★

In delirium and a post-ictal state, there would be alteration in the level of consciousness. In Alzheimer's disease, the person would have generalized cognitive impairment that is progressive. Normal-pressure hydrocephalus usually presents with a triad of ataxia, dementia, and urinary incontinence.

16. C ★   OHCS 11th edn → p. 773

The Mental Capacity Act 2005 (England and Wales) provides a statutory framework to empower and protect vulnerable people who are not able to make their own decisions. It is underpinned by five key principles:

1. Every adult is presumed to have capacity unless it is proven otherwise.
2. Individuals must be supported to make their own decisions.
3. Individuals retain the right to make what might be viewed as unwise or eccentric decisions.
4. Any action taken on behalf of individuals who lack capacity must be done in their best interests.
5. Any action taken on behalf of people who lack capacity must be the least restrictive option.

In this case, the patient has capacity and is not suffering from any mental impairment (e.g. psychotic depression or dementia). Therefore, although it seems an unwise decision, she has the right to refuse surgery. However, in complicated and life-threatening cases such as this, it is always wise to seek a second opinion and, if necessary, to involve your Trust's legal department. Note that Scotland has a separate legal framework—the Adults with Incapacity (Scotland) Act 2000.

→ https://www.gov.uk/government/publications/mental-capacity-act-code-of-practice

17. C ★   OHCS 11th edn → p. 720

An obsession is a stereotyped, purposeless word, idea, or phrase that comes into the mind and that originates from the person, rather than from outside. The patient realizes that it is not true.

18. C ★

Bradypnoea, bradycardia, and pinpoint pupils strongly suggest opioid overdose. The treatment for this is intramuscular and intravenous naloxone.

19. E ★   OHCS 11th edn → p. 734

The history of strokes, together with the progressive dementia, points to vascular dementia caused by multiple infarcts. Alzheimer's disease is a possibility, but the vascular history suggests otherwise. Lewy body dementia is characterized by hallucinations, visuo-perceptual defects, and a fluctuating course. Fronto-temporal dementia, or Pick's disease, is characterized by frontal lobe signs such as disinhibition.

20. A ★   OHCS 11th edn → p. 710

In mild depression, watchful waiting and review is the first-line strategy. Although this woman has low mood and lack of energy, she is functioning at work and socially, and has no physical symptoms and no suicidal ideation.

→ http://www.nice.org.uk/guidance/CG90

21. B ★   OHCS 11th edn → p. 718

All of these approaches could be used, but as anxiety disorders are maintained by fears about the nature and consequences of symptoms, an explanation of the condition is the first step in treatment. Anxious patients do not concentrate well, especially when given new information. Therefore, writing down the key points so that the patient can read them at home is the optimum approach.

22. E ★

Chronic alcohol consumption can result in thiamine deficiency due to inadequate nutritional intake, impaired uptake in the bowel, and impaired metabolism. Thiamine deficiency can lead to alcohol-induced brain damage, so thiamine should be replaced intravenously if patients with alcohol abuse show signs of possible brain damage. The other medications have roles in treating various addictions but are not appropriate in this case.

23. D ★   OHCS 11th edn → pp. 714–5

All of the other side-effect profiles are prominent in patients who are prescribed tricyclic antidepressants. Confusion is more likely to occur in elderly patients who are prescribed tricyclic antidepressants, and this, together with signs such as dry mouth, is due to the anticholinergic effects of these drugs. Their adrenergic antagonism may cause cardiovascular effects. Citalopram is a selective serotonin reuptake inhibitor (SSRI).

24. E ★

Neurosyphilis is an uncommon cause of psychiatric illness but is suggested by the Argyll Robertson pupils, as described in the question. These are a highly specific sign of neurosyphilis.

25. D ★

Careful consideration has to be given to team safety when assessing potentially dangerous patients. The police may know the patient and be able to provide valuable information such as a history of mental health problems or drug use. In addition, the information that the doctor is given by the police may well influence how and where the patient is seen. For example, it may become clear that the doctor needs to be accompanied by another health-care professional. The police may well have to leave, and their information should be sought early. Although a quiet, private room may help to calm the patient, it may put the doctor in a dangerous situation. Any room that is used should have all potentially dangerous objects removed from it, and the doctor should always place him- or herself between the door and the patient. Although having the police present for the interview may seem a sensible option, it will compromise confidentiality, and if the patient has paranoid thoughts or beliefs, a police presence may well exacerbate these. It is better to ask a member of the health-care staff whether there is a need for the doctor to be accompanied.

26. B ★   OHCS 11th edn → p. 709

Risperidone is an atypical antipsychotic and is associated with hyperprolactinaemia. This may result in gynaecomastia and galactorrhoea in men, and disturbance of the menstrual cycle in women. The side-effects of risperidone sometimes include sexual dysfunction and weight gain.

27. E ★★

The General Medical Council (GMC) has clearly stated that, for several conditions (including dementia), doctors not only should advise patients of the possibility of having to stop driving, but should also take steps to ensure that the relevant statutory authorities are informed of breaches of regulation if there is reasonable concern about public safety. Initially this should be done by informing the patient of the need to let the DVLA know about their condition. The fact that this patient is not disorientated, his short-term memory loss is mild, and he was only diagnosed a year ago would suggest that you do not have to make an immediate clinical decision that he is unfit to continue driving until the DVLA has assessed him.

→ http://www.gmc-uk.org/guidance/ethical_guidance/confidentiality.asp

→ http://www.gov.uk/browse/driving/disability-health-condition

28. E ★★   OHCS 11th edn → p. 718

There are many different types of anxiety disorder. The fact that all of the patient's symptoms occur in social situations makes social phobia the most likely diagnosis.

29. E ★★   OHCS 11th edn → p. 724

Long- term use of benzodiazepines runs the risk of creating dependency. However, suddenly stopping them may cause a withdrawal syndrome. If this man has run out of diazepam, there is a risk that he will develop withdrawal syndrome if he has to wait a week to see his usual GP. Antidepressants will not help the withdrawal. A reducing regime can be used to wean him off the diazepam, but this should be supervised.

30. D ★★   OHCS 11th edn → pp. 716–17

Lithium has a narrow therapeutic index, which means that the difference between effective and toxic doses is small. Thirst is a common side-effect. Fine tremor is also common, and weight gain and skin rash can occur. At toxic levels, dysarthria can occur.

31. E ★★   OHCS 11th edn → p. 714

Schneider's first-rank symptoms of schizophrenia are symptoms that, if present, are strongly suggestive of schizophrenia. They include the following:*

• auditory hallucinations: hearing thoughts spoken aloud, hearing voices referring to oneself in the third person, auditory hallucinations in the form of a commentary
• thought withdrawal, insertion, and interruption
• thought broadcasting
• somatic hallucinations
• delusional perception
• feelings or actions experienced as being generated or influenced by external agents.

*Source data from Schneider K, *Clinical Psychopathology*, New York: Grune & Stratton, 1959.

32. C ★★   OHCS 11th edn → pp. 714–15

There are a number of personality disorders, each of which has its own unique features. They all start in childhood or late adolescence and are patterns of inner experience and behaviour that remain stable throughout life and are different from that which would normally be expected in the society in which the person lives. There are two types of emotionally unstable personality disorder: borderline and impulsive. In the borderline type, the person tends to form intense relationships and have rapid fluctuations in mood, with impulsivity, disturbed self-image, recurrent self-harm, and chronic feelings of emptiness.

33. C ★★★   OHCS 11th edn → p. 773

Under the Mental Capacity Act 2005 (England and Wales), a Personal Welfare LPA does not come into effect until the patient has lost capacity to consent, even though it may be registered with the Office of the Public Guardian. As the GP has not seen the patient for 6 months, he does not know whether he has capacity to decide for himself whether to take medication. Although he has a diagnosis of dementia, which may have affected his capacity under the Act, every adult has the right to make their own decisions and must be assumed to have capacity to make them, unless it is proved otherwise. Until the GP has assessed the patient, he cannot assume that he does not have capacity. If the GP has assessed the patient and has judged that he does lack capacity to decide whether to take this medication, and that prescribing such medication is in his best interests, then the Personal Welfare LPA would allow the patient's wife to give or refuse consent to the administration of treatment by a person providing health-care. Note that a separate Act—the Adults with Incapacity (Scotland) Act 2000—is in place in Scotland.

→ https://www.gov.uk/government/publications/mental-capacity-act-code-of-practice

34. A ★★★★   OHCS 11th edn → pp. 718–19

Anxiety management training is a form of cognitive behavioural therapy that has the best record for the treatment of anxiety. Behavioural therapy with graded exposure to anxiety-provoking stimuli may be useful in some specific cases. Paroxetine (an SSRI) can help to treat social anxiety, but non-pharmacological measures should be tried first.

35. A ★★★★   OHCS 11th edn → p. 742

More often than not, a cause cannot be identified, although genetic causes should be considered, as they may have implications for genetic counselling. Fragile X syndrome is not X-linked recessive but is caused by an expansion of triplet repeats on the X chromosome through successive generations. Epilepsy can occur in learning disability, but only in about 30% of individuals. There is a spectrum of learning disability, and many adults will be able to be supported in finding suitable employment. In mild learning disability, the expected IQ is approximately 50–70; in moderate learning disability, it is 35–50, and in severe learning disability, it is 20–35. However, the IQ provides no information about individual strengths and weaknesses, so it is not the best way of classifying learning disability.

36. B ★★★★   OHCS 11th edn → p. 740

These are all features that suggest a diagnosis on the autistic spectrum. Autism is a pervasive developmental disorder with features that include the following:

- impaired communication: in the most severe cases, there is no language at all, no imaginative play, and echolalia (repeating other people's words)
- impaired social interaction (e.g. not responding to other people's emotions)
- restricted, repetitive, and stereotyped patterns of movement, behaviours, and interests (e.g. liking rigid routines and becoming upset when these do not occur, enjoying activities such as lining toys up or spinning wheels repeatedly)
- onset before the age of 3 years.

Asperger's syndrome is classified by some as being at one end of the spectrum. However, language is retained in Asperger's syndrome, although it is qualitatively different. Rett's syndrome occurs in girls.

37. B ★★★★   OHCS 11th edn → p. 708

In England and Wales, there are published guidelines on the use of clozapine in the treatment of resistant schizophrenia.

→ http://www.nice.org.uk/guidance/CG82

38. C ★★★★

If antidepressants are stopped too soon, about 50% of patients will relapse. Antidepressants should be withdrawn over a period of several weeks.

→ http://www.nice.org.uk/guidance/CG90

39. C ★★★★   OHCS 11th edn → p. 731

You should familiarize yourself with your local Trust's rapid tranquilization policy for cases such as this. In general, start with simple de-escalation techniques (talking calmly, using non-hostile body language, etc.) and, if necessary, offer oral medication first, only moving on to IM administration if the patient refuses oral treatment. A benzodiazepine such as lorazepam is a good starting point, and you should review the situation regularly. If this is not effective, an antipsychotic should be prescribed. First-generation antipsychotics, such as haloperidol, are no longer the first-line approach, because of the risk of dystonic side-effects. Olanzapine would be an appropriate choice, but note that it cannot be given within 1 hour of lorazepam.

40. D ★★★★

In the interest of safeguarding children, concerns like this should not be ignored. According to recommendations from *Good Medical Practice*, all doctors have a duty to consider the interests of children who may be in the care of adult patients. There are local systems in place to discuss non-urgent concerns, and all Trusts will have a designated lead for child protection.

→ https://www.gmc-uk.org/ethical-guidance/ethical-guidance-for-doctors/protecting-children-and-young-people

41. C ★★★★   OHCS 11th edn → p. 714

Fluoxetine, paroxetine, sertraline, and citalopram are all SSRIs. For patients who cannot tolerate SSRIs, the next choice would be mirtazapine, which is a reuptake inhibitor and receptor blocker that affects the levels of noradrenaline (norepinephrine) and serotonin in the synapses.

→ http://www.nice.org.uk/guidance/CG90

42. B ★★★★   OHCS 11th edn → p. 770

The Mental Health Act 2007 applies to England and Wales. Scotland has a separate Act—the Mental Health (Care and Treatment) (Scotland) Act 2003.

- Section 2 is a (maximum) 28-day section for assessment of a patient with a mental disorder. It is used if the diagnosis is not clear.
- Section 3 is a (maximum) 6-month section for treatment. It is only used if the patient is well known to the health-care professionals and the symptoms are consistent with the type from which they suffer when unwell.
- Section 5 is an emergency holding power, used by nurses (Section 5(4)) or doctors (Section 5(2)) to detain an informal patient who is already an inpatient.
- Section 17 is the part of the Mental Health Act that allows the Responsible Clinician to grant a detained inpatient leave from the hospital.
- Section 136 is an emergency section used by the police to bring a person in a public place whom they suspect is suffering from a mental disorder to a place of safety in order that they may be assessed.

→ https://www.nhs.uk/using-the-nhs/nhs-services/mental-health-services/mental-health-act/

→ http://www.gov.scot/Publications/2008/09/24090333/1

43. D ★★★★   OHCS 11th edn → p. 716

Drug levels may need to be checked for a number of drugs which have a narrow dose range—a small window in which the drug is effective, but not toxic. To be effective, peak levels should be within the therapeutic range, but not be so high as to cause toxic side-effects, and trough levels should stay within therapeutic range. The metabolism of a drug can be affected by a number of factors, e.g. the person's metabolism, their physical health, other drugs that they take, etc. Trough levels are checked just before a dose. Peak levels are checked at some point soon after a dose. Study of different drugs has determined when levels should be checked for different dosing regimes, and most organizations will have protocols for the testing of common drug levels, guided by the *British National Formulary* (*BNF*). Lithium is a commonly used psychiatric drug that requires monitoring, especially at a time of change in the patient's circumstances.

→ http://www.bnf.org (registration required)

44. D ★★★★   OHCS 11th edn → p. 829

Opiate withdrawal is an unpleasant experience but does not result in death in healthy individuals. Symptoms include restlessness, anxiety, insomnia, abdominal pain, nausea, diarrhoea, yawning, and piloerection. Methadone is a long-acting opiate, with a long half-life, which is taken orally once a day and so reduces the 'rush' that is caused by injecting heroin. Naltrexone is an opiate antagonist that can be used after completing detoxification, to reduce the risk of relapse.

45. B ★★★★

Tricyclic antidepressants can slow cardiac conduction and may cause arrhythmias and heart block. This is particularly dangerous in the elderly, in whom the side-effect of postural hypotension may also be a problem.

General practice

Philippa Edwards

General practitioners (GPs) are the gatekeepers of the National Health Service in the UK, and virtually all referrals to secondary care are made through them. The breadth and depth of the discipline can at times seem overwhelming, although the old adage 'common things occur commonly' still holds. GPs need to be confident in the diagnosis and management of conditions from birth to the grave, and to know their boundaries of competence and when to refer to secondary care. The complexity of the GP consultation includes the following two points:

1. Many conditions present in a relatively undifferentiated form to the GP, whose job it is to try to identify whether the condition is normal or abnormal, and whether it is serious or minor.
2. GPs develop a close professional relationship with many of their patients and may also be the point of contact for other members of the family, neighbours, and friends of the patient. This knowledge is an important aspect of their holistic approach to medicine and is much valued by their patients. As the nineteenth-century physician Sir William Osler (1849–1919) said, '*The good physician treats the disease; the great physician treats the patient who has the disease.*'

The commonest presentations to GPs in the UK are for respiratory problems, chronic disease management, musculoskeletal disorders, and psychological problems. Health promotion, in particular smoking cessation and the management of obesity, is also important in preventing chronic illness. Although many presentations are minor and self-limiting, serious illnesses also occur, and GPs need to be able to recognize them, sometimes in the early stages.

The questions in this chapter will assess your knowledge in the common areas that present, testing diagnostic skills and reasoning. They also test negotiating skills to ensure patient compliance, teamworking within the primary care setting, and risk management.

Philippa Edwards, *General practice* In: *Oxford Assess and Progress: Clinical Specialties*. Edited by: Luci Etheridge and Henry Collier, Oxford University Press. © Oxford University Press 2021. DOI:10.1093/oso/9780198862550.003.0013

QUESTIONS

1. A 26-year-old woman has registered as a new patient, and her New Patient Health Check reveals a body mass index (BMI) of 32 kg/m². Which is the single best explanation to the patient of what the BMI means? ★

A It is a measure of cardiovascular risk

B It is a measure of how much weight a person needs to lose

C It is a representation of weight for height

D It is a way of calculating how fat the body is

E It is the ratio of hip circumference to waist circumference

2. A 44-year-old builder has acute low back pain, following heavy lifting at work the previous day. He is finding it difficult to walk. Which single feature of his presentation would warrant an urgent referral to hospital? ★

A Difficulty in passing urine

B Inability to perform a straight leg raise beyond 20°

C Pain down the back of both legs

D Reduced ankle jerks

E Use of inhaled steroids for his asthma

3. The mother of a 16-year-old girl is worried that her daughter is becoming depressed, and she knows that the girl came to see you last week. The daughter's behaviour at home has been deteriorating, and there have been a lot of arguments. The mother wants to know what the recent consultation was about and to seek your opinion about what to do. Which is the single most appropriate course of action? ★

A Advise her that she can apply to the Clinical Commissioning Group for access to her daughter's medical record

B Do not discuss her concerns about her daughter at all, as the daughter is over 16 years of age

C Listen to her concerns, but do not reveal information about the daughter, as the daughter has not given you consent

D Tell her a little about the recent consultation, and ask her to come back later with her daughter

E Tell her what transpired in the recent consultation, as she has a right to know as a parent

4. A 65-year-old man has had a previous small myocardial infarction. He wants advice on modifying his risk factors to prevent further health problems. Which is the single most important modifiable risk factor for stroke in this patient? ★

A Alcohol intake of 40 units per week

B Atrial fibrillation

C Body mass index of 35 kg/m²

D Previous myocardial infarction

E Raised blood pressure of 165/105 mmHg

5. A 44-year-old businessman has recently been diagnosed with high blood pressure. He does not want to take any medication. Which is the single best approach to take in the consultation to try and come to a resolution? ★

A Allow him to do what he wants to do, but tell him that he will have to see another doctor in the future

B Be friendly towards him, so that he is more likely to come back if he changes his mind

C Identify and consider his viewpoint, bringing this into the decision-making process

D Tell him all about the different medications and their side-effects, so that he has all of the information

E Tell him that he needs to take the medication which has been chosen for him or he may be at risk of harm

6. A 35-year-old woman is unable to sleep, is tired during the day, and is having problems at work as a result. Which single aspect of her history is the most likely to have a significant bearing on her presenting complaint? ★

A She drinks about 20 units of alcohol per week

B She has a 9-year-old daughter

C She has a stressful job as a teacher

D She is tearful and cannot concentrate

E She smokes ten cigarettes a day

7. A 17-year-old girl is going away to college next year. She is seeking information about the human papillomavirus (HPV) vaccine, as she missed the programme at school and is now considering having the vaccination. Which is the single most appropriate piece of information to give her about the vaccine? ★

A If she has already had sexual intercourse, she has probably already been exposed to HPV and it is not worth having the vaccination

B If she has the vaccination, it will protect her against HPV and she will not need cervical smear testing later in life

C If she suffers from eczema or asthma, she will not be able to have the vaccination because of the risk of severe allergic reactions

D The vaccination is only available as part of a primary immunization course for infants, and she is too old to be included in the 'catch-up' cohort

E The vaccination is effective in preventing cervical abnormalities caused by HPV types that can lead to cervical cancer, and she is eligible to have it

8. A 52-year-old woman wants advice about mammography breast screening before her appointment. She has read a newspaper article which suggests that it may not be valuable and could even be potentially harmful. You are not aware of this evidence and have not seen any recent literature on the subject. Which is the single most appropriate response to give in this situation? ★

A Advise her that there is a financial penalty for practices if patients do not attend screening appointments, so she should make every effort to keep her appointment

B Agree with her that there are reasonable concerns about the benefits of mammography, and advise her not to take any further part in the screening programme

C Explain that you are not aware of the evidence that she has raised with you, so you are going to refer her to a specialist breast surgeon for up-to-date advice

D Explain that you are not aware of the evidence that she has raised with you, but that you could help her to interpret it once you have looked at it yourself

E Explain that you are not aware of the evidence that she has raised with you, so it is unlikely to be true and she should attend for screening

9. A 48-year-old woman has recently moved into the practice area. At her induction health check, the practice nurse notes that her weight is 85 kg and her height is 160 cm. Which single health factor would you consider in advising her about her weight? ★

A She is at increased risk of stomach cancer and needs to lose weight to a body mass index (BMI) of 25 kg/m² to bring her risk down to acceptable levels

B She is at increased risk of stomach cancer and needs to lose 20 kg to bring her risk down to acceptable levels

C She is at increased risk of hypertension and should lose 5 kg to bring her risk down to acceptable levels

D She is at increased risk of kidney stones and needs to lose 10 kg to bring her risk down to acceptable levels

E She is at increased risk of type 2 diabetes and should lose 20 kg to bring her risk down to acceptable levels

10. A 22-year-old student has muscle aches, malaise, headache, and anorexia that started 2 days ago. Today he has a temperature of 39.4°C. Which is the single most important direct question to ask him as part of history taking in order to confirm the likely diagnosis? ★

A Has he been bitten by an animal recently?

B Has he had close contact with anyone else with similar symptoms?

C Has he recently eaten any food that he thinks might have 'gone off'?

D Has he travelled overseas recently?

E Is he taking any medication at present?

11. A 55-year-old diabetic man asks for the vaccines he had last year against flu and pneumonia. His records show that he had the influenza and pneumococcal vaccines last year. Which is the single most appropriate piece of advice to give him? ★

A The influenza vaccine that he had last year will protect him against influenza for another 5 years

B He does not need another influenza vaccine this year but should have it next year

C He does not need another pneumococcal vaccine this year but should have it next year

D He is in a high-risk category for influenza and should have this vaccine every year

E He is in a high-risk category for pneumonia and influenza and should have both vaccines every year

12. A 50-year-old man with convictions for violence comes to the surgery reception, smelling of alcohol and demanding dihydrocodeine. Which is the single best way of managing this situation? ★

A Ask him to take a seat in the waiting room to be seen in order with the other patients

B Immediately show him to the next available doctor

C Phone the police and ask them to remove him

D Physically eject him from the premises and lock the surgery door

E Place him in a vacant room and ask a doctor to see him when they are available

13. An 84-year-old woman is in hospital recovering from a total hip replacement, following a fall in her flat. She was previously independent, despite living on the first floor, and drove her own car to the nearby shops. Who is the single best professional to ensure that she is safe to return to her flat? ★

A Age Concern worker

B General practitioner

C Health visitor

D Occupational therapist

E Physiotherapist

14. An 18-year-old man has a sore throat, fever, and malaise. A monospot test is sent and comes back positive. Which is the single most important element to avoid at this stage? ★

A Alcohol

B Contact sports

C Fatty foods

D Kissing

E Paracetamol

15. A 21-year-old student comes for a repeat prescription of her combined oral contraceptive pill (the Pill). She has been having bad one-sided headaches, with flashing lights lasting a few minutes prior to the headache since starting the Pill. She has a past history of migraine when stressed and has some exams coming up. Her blood pressure is 100/70 mmHg, and her clinical examination is normal. Which is the single most appropriate management? ★

A Advise her that the headaches are most probably caused by exam stress

B Advise her to stop taking the Pill if the flashing lights last longer than 60 minutes

C Stop the Pill she is taking, and try a different combined oral contraceptive pill

D Stop the Pill she is taking, and consider a progestogen-only pill instead

E Stop the Pill she is taking, and refer her urgently to a neurologist

16. A 65-year-old woman, who lives alone, has chronic knee pain and is prescribed a course of non-steroidal anti-inflammatory drugs (NSAIDs) for the first time. After she has left the surgery, you notice from her record that she is asthmatic. Which is the single most appropriate way to communicate to the patient not to take the medication? ★

A Ask the receptionist to make her a routine appointment for the next day

B Phone her and give her the appropriate advice

C Phone the local chemist and instruct them not to issue the prescription

D Phone the police and ask them to go to her house

E Write to her, requesting her to make an urgent appointment

17. A 21-year-old single mother has a 2-month-old baby who is not sleeping and seems perpetually hungry. She is still breastfeeding but thinks that she will have to change her baby to bottle-feeding. She wants some advice about this. Who is the single best person from the health-care team to advise her? ★

A District nurse

B General practitioner

C Health visitor

D Midwife

E Social worker

18. A 22-year-old woman has persistent headaches, nausea, and disturbed sleep and feels tired and cold all the time. She appears very thin, and her body mass index (BMI) is 16 kg/m². She tells you that this is the right weight for her. Which single health-care professional would be most appropriate to follow her up? ★

A Dietitian

B Endocrinologist

C General practitioner

D Neurologist

E Psychiatrist

19. A 32-year-old woman is 33 weeks pregnant with her second child. She has come for a routine antenatal appointment. During her first pregnancy, she had pre-eclampsia and required a hospital admission and early delivery. Today she is feeling tired and 'off colour'. Which single combination of clinical features would suggest that she could be suffering from pre-eclampsia requiring immediate hospital referral? ★

A Raised blood pressure alone

B Raised blood pressure and proteinuria

C Raised blood pressure, proteinuria, and headache

D Raised blood pressure, proteinuria, and peripheral oedema

E Raised blood pressure, proteinuria, and seizures

20. A 17-year-old man has had a sore throat, fever, malaise, and headache for 4 days. He has bilaterally enlarged tonsils with exudate, and cervical lymphadenopathy. Which single complication of his illness may be prevented by treatment with oral penicillin? ★

A Drug eruption

B Glomerulonephritis

C Mesenteric adenitis

D Otitis media

E Sinusitis

21. A 65-year-old woman with osteoarthritis affecting both knees is in need of some pain relief. However, she is unwilling to take anti-inflammatory drugs, as she says that they make her feel ill and other painkillers make her constipated. She asks whether there is anything other than standard painkillers that could help her pain. Which is the single most appropriate therapy to recommend? ★★

A Glucosamine and chondroitin

B Homeopathy

C Modern acupuncture using trigger points

D Reflexology

E Transcutaneous electrical nerve stimulation (TENS) machine

22. A man has a chest infection. He is prescribed a course of amoxicillin for 1 week. He also wants a repeat prescription of his blood pressure medication. Under which single circumstance is he eligible to obtain the medications without paying prescription charges for them? ★

A He earns less than £25 000 per annum

B He has a partner and more than three children at home

C He has been unwell for more than 4 weeks

D He has diabetes

E He is aged over 50 years

23. A 35-year-old woman is 12 weeks pregnant. She has significant dysuria, urinary frequency, and offensive-smelling urine. A dipstick test shows 3+ blood, 3+ leucocytes, and 2+ nitrites. Which single treatment regime is most appropriate? ★★

A Amoxicillin for 7 days

B Encourage oral fluids and simple analgesia

C Nalidixic acid for 7 days

D Nitrofurantoin for 7 days

E Trimethoprim for 3 days

24. A 36-year-old woman attends the surgery for her 'pill check'. She has been on the combined hormonal contraceptive (CHC) Microgynon® for 18 years and wants to continue it as she has had no problems with it. She smokes ten cigarettes a day. Her blood pressure is 140/88 mmHg, and her body mass index (BMI) is 30 kg/m². Which is the single most appropriate management? ★★

A Explain that her blood pressure is too high for the CHC and she needs to consider changing to an alternative method of contraception

B Explain that her BMI is too high for the CHC and she needs to consider changing to an alternative method of contraception

C Explain that she has an increased risk of ovarian cancer on the CHC and she needs to consider changing to an alternative method of contraception

D Explain that smoking increases the risks associated with the CHC and she needs to consider changing to an alternative method of contraception

E Give her a further prescription for Microgynon®, and arrange a review in 6 months

25. A 50-year-old man seeks advice about his father, who has mild dementia and is living in a nursing home. The father is becoming increasingly unwell with a chest infection, and the son wants him to be admitted to hospital, but the father wishes to stay where he is. Which is the single best summary of the legal situation? ★★

A As the father has dementia, he is not competent and therefore the son can and should decide on his treatment

B The father is competent and can therefore decide on his own treatment, regardless of the son's opinion

C The father is not competent and therefore decisions about his care must be made by his doctor, based on the patient's best interests

D The father's competence should be assessed and, if he has capacity, he can accept or decline treatment himself, regardless of the consequences

E The father's competence should be assessed, but his doctor may insist on admission, should his condition deteriorate, on the grounds of necessity

26. A 35-year-old woman with persistent irritable bowel syndrome asks to see a complementary therapist to help her with her symptoms. She understands that she may need to pay for this privately and that there may not be good evidence for the effectiveness of some complementary treatments, but she says that she is convinced that this is what she would like to do. Which is the single most appropriate action to take in response to her request? ★★

A Ask her to identify a practitioner whom she would like to see, and then provide a written referral if this is requested

B Decline to refer her on the grounds that this will avoid the need to pay private care fees

C Refer her directly to a colleague who runs a private complementary clinic

D Refer her to a gastroenterologist because she is more likely to achieve better symptom control with the help of a conventional specialist

E Refer her to a therapist selected from the Yellow Pages on the basis of geographical proximity to her home

27. A 65-year-old woman, who regularly attends with symptoms related to chronic depression, has some vague muscle ache and headache. She has been told before that her symptoms may well be related to her depression, but she requests further assessment. Which single aspect of her history is the most likely to point to a significant alternative diagnosis? ★★

A She has been experiencing pain in her hip when walking

B She has been experiencing some stinging pain on passing urine

C She has noticed a deterioration of her vision

D She has noticed some hearing loss in her left ear

E She has recently started taking herbal remedies for her depression

28. The local pharmacist has sent back a prescription written this morning. He says a controlled drug has been prescribed wrongly—a patient with intractable chronic back pain has been given a prescription for morphine modified release (MST Continus®). Which single element must be on a prescription for a controlled drug? ★★

A The date must be written in words and figures

B The diagnosis must be specified

C The full name and address of the patient must be handwritten, not typed

D The prescriber's General Medical Council registration number must be given

E The total quantity to dispense must be expressed in words and figures

29. A medical student is sitting in on a general practitioner (GP) surgery. One of the patients says that he would rather not have a student present. Which is the single most appropriate way of handling this? ★ ★ ★

A Before calling the patient in, ask the student to wait in another room

B Emphasize the importance of student teaching, hoping that the patient will reconsider

C Introduce the student and confirm that the patient would prefer the student to leave

D Rebook the patient for another surgery when you do not have students present

E Reschedule the patient to the end of surgery

30. A 62-year-old woman has had a unilateral painful rash, highly suggestive of shingles, for 36 hours. She asks if she could pass it on to her grandson, who is 7 days old. He lives in the same town and she last saw him yesterday. The baby's mother does not think she has ever had chickenpox. Which is the single most appropriate piece of advice to give to the grandmother? ★ ★ ★

A As the baby has been in contact with her, he should receive zoster immunoglobulin (ZIG) as soon as possible

B It is better to get chickenpox during childhood than later in life, and she need not worry about contact

C It is better to get shingles during childhood than later in life, and she need not worry about contact

D The baby could get chickenpox, and she should avoid seeing him until the blisters have crusted over

E The baby will be protected by maternal antibodies and will not be affected

31. A 50-year-old woman has hypertension and is on ramipril. She has dizziness, imbalance, and nausea. It can occur during the day or night, but she has noticed that it often happens when she looks up and she has had difficulty getting out of bed in the mornings. There are no headaches, visual symptoms, or any problems with her hearing. In surgery, she is not feeling dizzy. Her blood pressure (BP) is 116/70 mmHg, with no postural drop. Cranial nerve examination is normal, with normal speech and gait. There is no tremor, past pointing, or dysdiadochokinesia. Which is the single best course of action for this lady? ★ ★ ★

A Admit her to hospital for a head computed tomography (CT) scan

B Perform the Epley maneuvre

C Prescribe prochlorperazine 5 mg three times daily (TDS)

D Refer for vestibular rehabilitation exercises

E Stop her antihypertensive

32. A 40-year-old woman has heavy periods. Her periods have always been heavy, but now they are getting worse and she wants to discuss possible treatments. She has no inter-menstrual or post-coital bleeding, and she is up-to-date with her cervical smears. She is otherwise well, with no significant past medical history. She has two children and does not want any more. Her husband has had a vasectomy. Which is the single most appropriate management? ★ ★ ★ ★

A Arrange blood tests, including a full blood count, a thyroid and hormone profile, and a pelvic ultrasound scan

B Conduct a pelvic examination and offer insertion of the Mirena® coil

C Conduct a pelvic examination and offer the combined hormone contraceptive pill

D Refer her to gynaecology for consideration of endometrial ablation

E Refer her to gynaecology for consideration of hysterectomy

33. A 68-year-old man was watching television 10 days ago when his wife noticed that the right side of his face was drooping, his speech was slurred, and he could not move his right hand. This only lasted for 10 minutes, so he did not seek any medical help at the time. He has no other medical problems and is not on any medication. His blood pressure is 130/70 mmHg and examination is unremarkable. Which is the single most appropriate management? ★ ★ ★ ★

A Admit him to hospital, as he has had a transient ischaemic attack (TIA) and is at high risk of progression to having a stroke

B Commence 75 mg aspirin and arrange blood tests, including cholesterol and glucose

C Commence 75 mg aspirin and refer him routinely to a medical clinic for further investigations

D Commence 300 mg aspirin and refer him routinely to a medical clinic for further investigations

E Commence 300 mg aspirin and refer him to a TIA clinic to be seen within 1 week

34. A 58-year-old man attends for his annual diabetic review. As well as diabetes, he has a history of a myocardial infarction (MI) 5 years ago, from which he recovered well. He now works as a delivery driver. In clinic, his body mass index (BMI) is 32 kg/m² and blood pressure (BP) 126/70 mmHg, and a urine dipstick shows protein 1+ and blood 2+. His recent blood results show:

- HbA1c 68 mmol/mol
- glomerular filtration rate (GFR) 54 mL/min/1.73 m² (stable)
- liver function tests (LFTs) normal
- full blood count (FBC) normal.

His current medications are ramipril 10 mg once daily (OD), metformin 1 g twice daily (BD), aspirin 75 mg OD, and atorvastatin 80 mg OD. He has been advised on optimizing his lifestyle. Which is the single most appropriate step in improving his diabetic control? ★ ★ ★ ★

A Refer to the local diabetic clinic for consideration of insulin therapy

B Start a dipeptidylpeptidase-4 inhibitor such as sitagliptin

C Start a sodium–glucose co-transporter-2 (SGLT2) inhibitor such as canagliflozin

D Start a sulfonylurea such as gliclazide

E Start a thiazolidinedione such as pioglitazone

ANSWERS

1. C ★

The BMI is calculated as weight in kilograms divided by height in metres squared (kg/m^2). It is a measure of weight for height and does not represent body fat or other ratios.

2. A ★   OHCS 11th edn → p. 487

Retention of urine and faeces should raise suspicions of cauda equina syndrome (compression of the cauda equina in the spinal canal). Pain and inability to perform a straight leg raise can be caused by muscular back injury or sciatica, and ankle jerks are usually brisk in cord compression.

→ http://patient.info/doctor/low-back-pain-and-sciatica

→ https://cks.nice.org.uk/sciatica-lumbar-radiculopathy#!diagnosis Sub:1

3. C ★

All competent patients have a right to confidentiality, and you should not break this unless the patient specifically gives consent for you to share the information. However, if the mother wants to express her concerns about her daughter, it is acceptable to listen to these without revealing any information.

→ http://www.gmc-uk.org/guidance/ethical_guidance/confidentiality. asp

4. E ★

There are several risk factors for stroke, some of which can be modified and some of which cannot. Hypertension is considered to be an important risk factor for stroke, with well-documented relationships between blood pressure and the occurrence of stroke. There is also good evidence that treating hypertension reduces the risk of stroke. Atrial fibrillation is the most important risk factor for stroke, being that atrial fibrillation increases the risk of stroke by 480% (hypertension by 140%). However, there is no mention that this man is in atrial fibrillation.

5. C ★   OHCS 11th edn → p. 786

An approach that is patient-centred and which identifies, acknowledges, and respects the patient's decisions and feelings ensures a better long-term result. It is important to realize that all patients have different life factors that may influence their decision-making. Respecting these is vital for building a lasting relationship.

6. D ★   OHCS 11th edn → p. 710

All of these are possible risk factors for poor sleep, apart from moderate cigarette smoking. However, the suggestion of low mood and possible depression is an important presenting symptom that needs to be followed up.

7. E ★   OHCS 11th edn → p. 166

HPV can cause cervical abnormalities that may progress to become cancer. There are hundreds of HPVs, of which types 16 and 18 cause 70% of HPV-related cervical cancers. HPV types 6 and 11 are associated with genital warts. In the UK, two vaccines are currently used. Cervarix® immunizes against types 16 and 18, and Gardasil® immunizes against types 6, 11, 16, and 18. The current programme schedule involves three doses given at 0, 1–2, and 6 months. The Department of Health recommends that any women under the age of 18 years with unknown or incomplete immunization status should complete the course. Those from overseas who are not protected should be offered protection.

→ https://www.gov.uk/government/publications/human-papillomavirus-hpv-the-green-book-chapter-18a

8. D ★

A common-sense approach to difficult situations such as this that respects the main principles of patient autonomy, beneficence, and non-maleficence is needed here. General practitioners may have to help patients to interpret health information, especially now that they have access to so much more information via the Internet.

9. E ★   OHCS 11th edn → p. 830

Type 2 diabetes is greatly increased in overweight people and is a major cause of morbidity. A healthy BMI is in the range of 20–25 kg/m². If this woman lost 20 kg, her weight would be 65 kg. Her BMI would therefore be $65/1.6^2$, which is 25.4 kg/m². This is a much healthier BMI and an achievable range to aim for.

→ http://www.nice.org.uk/guidance/cg43

10. D ★

A possible diagnosis is malaria, which would be suspected if the patient had travelled to a region where malaria is prevalent.

11. D ★

The influenza vaccine is prepared each year from viruses of the three strains that are thought most likely to cause flu that winter. It is about 70% effective, and protection lasts for 1 year. Pneumococcal vaccine only needs to be given once. Both are recommended for high-risk groups of patients, including individuals with diabetes.

→ https://www.gov.uk/government/publications/influenza-the-green-book-chapter-19

→ https://www.gov.uk/government/publications/pneumococcal-the-green-book-chapter-25

12. E ★

Although all patients are entitled to appropriate treatment, you should not place other patients or practice staff at risk of harm. This patient has the same right to treatment as do others, but you should not disadvantage other patients by seeing him first simply because he is demanding. It may be necessary to call the police, but you may well be able to advise and treat him without difficulty, and you should endeavour to do this before taking more drastic action.

13. D ★

The occupational therapist's role is to assess patients with regard to their activities of daily living and to advise on how to make these activities achievable.

14. B ★

Glandular fever, or infectious mononucleosis, caused by Epstein–Barr virus, can cause splenomegaly. A rare, but serious, complication is splenic rupture, the risk of which is increased by contact sports and trauma to the area. The splenomegaly usually lasts for 6 to 8 weeks.

15. D ★   OHCS 11th edn → p. 153

The Pill can increase the risk of ischaemic stroke. Women who have a history of migraine should stop the Pill immediately if they develop aura and worsening headache, and they should have an ischaemic event excluded if these symptoms persist. The progestogen-only pill is a safe alternative, as it contains no oestrogen, which is the component that leads to the increased risk.

→ http://www.bnf.org/bnf (see Section 7.3.1; requires registration)

→ https://www.fsrh.org/standards-and-guidance/documents/combined-hormonal-contraception/

16. B ★

NSAIDs may cause worsening of asthma, although this is not always the case. However, the patient should be warned about the risk and advised not to take the medication. The most effective way to ensure that this is done is to speak to her yourself. A further appointment can be offered to discuss alternative treatments later.

17. C ★   OHCS 11th edn → p. 784

The health visitor is a qualified nurse with a health visiting qualification (which includes public health nursing and health promotion). She takes over home visiting of new mothers from the midwife when the baby is 10 days old.

18. E ★   OHCS 11th edn → p. 746

There is a high probability that this woman has anorexia nervosa. She has symptoms of underweight and starvation, a persistently low BMI below 17 kg/m², and a belief that this is the right weight despite symptoms. She needs to be assessed and managed by an eating disorders specialist team, led by a psychiatrist, as part of mental health services. You may of course continue to see her as a GP, but she needs specialist help to direct her treatment.

19. C ★   OHCS 11th edn → p. 50

Pre-eclampsia is defined as hypertension plus proteinuria, with or without peripheral oedema. However, the presence of symptoms such as headache makes hospital referral important here. The presence of seizures would make the diagnosis eclampsia, rather than pre-eclampsia.

20. B ★

Although there is no clear evidence to support the use of antibiotics to reduce the incidence of post-streptococcal glomerulonephritis, antibiotics are often given in primary care for this reason.

21. E ★★

Many patients seek complementary therapies and alternative to prescribed medicines, so it is useful to have some idea of these. Initial trials for glucosamine showed some improvement in osteoarthritis; however, these were using different preparations which are not available to the public, and more recent trials have shown no benefits. The National Institute for Health and Care Excellence (NICE) does not recommend glucosamine for osteoarthritis. NICE does state that TENS machines should be offered as an adjunct in the treatment of osteoarthritis.

→ https://pathways.nice.org.uk/pathways/osteoarthritis# path=view%3A/pathways/osteoarthritis/management-of-osteoarthritis. xml&content=view-node%3Anodes-minimally-invasive-and-non-invasive-therapies

22. D ★

This patient would qualify for free prescriptions if he was aged over 60 years and if he had a low income and less than £16 000 in savings or investments, or if he had one of a number of chronic diseases. Help is based on a comparison between an individual's weekly income and assessed requirements at the time when the claim is made (or the date on which the charge was paid if a refund is claimed).

→ http://www.nhsbsa.nhs.uk/healthcosts

23. D ★★

This patient clearly has a significant urinary tract infection and needs anti-biotic treatment. Trimethoprim and nalidixic acid are contraindicated in the first trimester of pregnancy, and amoxicillin, although safe, is likely to be ineffective due to widespread resistance. Nitrofurantoin is safe in early pregnancy but is best avoided near term, because of the possible risk of haemolytic anaemia in newborn babies.

24. D ★★   OHCS 11th edn → p. 152

When re-prescribing 'the Pill', the blood pressure and BMI should be re-corded, as well as the smoking history and whether the patient is having any problems. A smoking history is important because both smoking and the oral CHC can increase the risk of venous thromboembolism. The cut-off age for prescribing the Pill in a smoker is 35 years. There is no evidence that a lower-strength pill decreases this risk. Although this woman's BMI is raised and she is obese, the cut-off BMI for prescribing the Pill is 35 kg/m². CHC use may be associated with a small increase in the risk of cervical cancer, which is related to duration of use, and a small increased risk of breast cancer, which will reduce with time after stop-ping, but a reduced risk of ovarian and endometrial cancer that continues for several decades after stopping. A persistently raised blood pressure over 160/95 mmHg would mean that this patient should stop the Pill and consider an alternative, which could include a progesterone-only pill, depot, or implant, or an intrauterine device (IUD) or intrauterine system (IUS).

→ https://www.fsrh.org/standards-and-guidance/documents/combined-hormonal-contraception/

25. D ★★   OHCS 11th edn → p. 773

The patient may have capacity, but it needs to be assessed. If he is com-petent, he can refuse or accept any treatment that is offered. However, he cannot insist on treatment that is not considered appropriate by his doctor. This legal situation is covered by different Acts in England and Wales, and in Scotland.

26. A ★★

Provided that you are happy that the patient is not at risk of harm, it is appropriate to facilitate a referral to a complementary therapist if they request it. However, because this is a private referral, you need to ensure that it is done professionally, that the patient has as much choice as possible, and that there is no suggestion that you have a personal interest in the referral.

27. C ★★

A wide variety of symptoms can occur in depression. However, it is important always to revisit the diagnosis and to assess every presentation fully. In an elderly woman with headaches and myalgia, loss of vision may occur in giant cell arteritis, and prompt treatment can save sight.

28. E ★★

Prescriptions for controlled drugs must be indelible and include:

- the name and address of the patient
- the form and strength of the preparation
- the total quantity in both words and figures of the preparation, or the number in both words and figures of dosage units, to be supplied
- the dose to be given
- the prescriber's name, signature, and address
- the date of the prescription.

Pharmacists cannot dispense, unless the prescription is filled in correctly.

→ http://www.bnf.org (requires registration)

29. A ★★★

When asking a patient whether they will allow a student to be present, you should have an appropriate mechanism to ensure that this does not pressurize the patient, embarrass either them or the student, or disadvantage the patient in any way.

30. A ★★★   OHCS 11th edn → p. 40

Neonates with significant exposure to chickenpox or shingles should receive ZIG as soon as possible. The fact that the mother has probably never had chickenpox means that she has no varicella antibodies to pass across the placenta, and the baby therefore has no protection.

31. B ★★★   OHCS 11th edn → pp. 404–5

This lady has benign paroxysmal positional vertigo (BPPV). This is the commonest vestibular disorder seen in primary care. It is provoked by certain movements of the head, such as looking up or rolling over and getting out of bed. It can be associated with nausea, but not usually vomiting, and patients are well in between episodes. BPPV can settle without treatment but may last a long time. Repositioning manoeuvres, such as the Epley manoeuvre, are more effective than vestibular suppressant medication, which should not be used long term. If this lady's symptoms persist and are debilitating, it may be appropriate to refer her to a specialist clinic, but trials of simple treatment should be done first.

→ https://cks.nice.org.uk/benign-paroxysmal-positional-vertigo

32. B ★★★★   OHCS 11th edn → p. 117

The National Institute for Health and Care Excellence (NICE) has provided guidelines on the management of heavy periods. These suggest that in simple heavy menstrual bleeding, the only investigation required is a full blood count to rule out anaemia. A pelvic examination is only required if a structural or histological abnormality is suspected or an intrauterine device is being considered. The first-line recommended treatment is a Mirena® coil, with treatments such as non-steroidal anti-inflammatory drugs, tranexamic acid, and combined hormone contraceptives being second-line treatment. Surgical management is considered if pharmaceutical treatments have failed and/or there is a severe impact on the woman's quality of life, after full discussion of the risks.

→ https://pathways.nice.org.uk/pathways/heavy-menstrual-bleeding

33. E ★★★★

A TIA is defined as stroke symptoms and signs that resolve within 24 hours. Patients who present with a TIA need to be assessed to determine whether they are at high or low risk, using the validated $ABCD^2$ (Age, Blood pressure, Clinical features, Duration of symptoms, and Diabetes) tool. A patient with an $ABCD^2$ score higher than 4 is at high risk and should have specialist assessment and investigations, such as cholesterol and carotid Dopplers, within 24 hours. Patients with a score of 3 or less or who present more than 1 week after the event should have specialist assessment and investigation within 1 week. This man has a score of 3 and is therefore at lower risk. All patients should be started on 300 mg aspirin, unless this is contraindicated.

34. B ★★★★

This gentleman is obese, has chronic kidney disease stage 3 (CKD3) and established cardiovascular disease (CVD). His occupation is driving, so he needs to avoid hypoglycaemic attacks. A dipeptidylpeptidase-4 inhibitor, such as sitagliptin, would be the most appropriate option here, as it is weight-neutral and safe to be used in all stages of CKD and with established CVD. It also carries a low risk of hypoglycaemia. SGLT2 inhibitors are not licensed for initiation with a GFR less than 60. Sulfonylureas cause weight gain, carry a risk of hypoglycaemia, and can increase the risk of cardiovascular death. Pioglitazone can also cause significant weight gain and has been associated with bladder cancer, so this man's haematuria would need to be fully investigated before commencing pioglitazone.

→ http://pathways.nice.org.uk/pathways/type-2-diabetes-in-adults

Eponymous syndromes

Luci Etheridge and Alex Bonner

Eponyms are still widely used in medicine. Most commonly, they describe collections of clinical features (i.e. a syndrome) or particular clinical signs but are also used to name procedures, anatomy, and equipment. As our understanding of pathophysiology and genomics has improved, naming of diseases and clinical signs has tended to reflect that. However, many eponyms still persist from an era when naming patterns of disease or illness presentation enabled clinicians to gather data, recognize problems, and decide on treatments before the pathology or treatment was fully understood. In this chapter, you will be asked questions challenging your ability to recognize clinically relevant eponyms that you may well encounter in your practice as a doctor.

Luci Etheridge and Alex Bonner, *Eponymous syndromes* In: *Oxford Assess and Progress: Clinical Specialties*. Edited by: Luci Etheridge and Henry Collier, Oxford University Press.
© Oxford University Press 2021. DOI:10.1093/oso/9780198862550.003.0014

QUESTIONS

1. A 16-year-old girl is referred to the gynaecology clinic as she has never menstruated. She is 140 cm tall. She has small breast bud development and sparse pubic and axillary hair present. Inspection of the external genitalia is normal. A trans-abdominal ultrasound scan shows her ovaries and uterus to be present, but are small and physiologically quiescent. Her initial blood tests are as follows:

• follicle-stimulating hormone (FSH) 60 IU
• luteinizing hormone (LH) 48 IU
• prolactin 410 IU.

What is the single most likely diagnosis? ★

A Congenital paramesonephric duct obstruction

B Hypothalamic hypogonadism

C Mayer–Kuster–Hauser–Rokitansky syndrome

D McCune–Albright syndrome

E Turner's syndrome

2. A 6-hour-old term baby boy weighs 2.54 kg. He has microcephaly, a flat occiput, upward-slanting palpebral fissures, a protruding tongue, a single palmar crease on the right hand but normal palmar creasing on the left, and a wide sandal gap. Which is the single most likely finding on neurological examination? ★ ★

A Absent Moro reflex

B Exaggerated Moro reflex

C Generalized hypertonia

D Generalized hypotonia

E Selective hypertonia of the lower limbs

3. A 68-year-old man with a history of alcohol abuse presents with an acute abdomen. He has a 12-hour history of back pain. On examination, Grey Turner's sign is present. Which is the single most likely pathophysiological process to account for this? ★ ★

A Obstructive jaundice

B Pleural effusion

C Polycythaemia

D Retroperitoneal haemorrhage

E Ureteric colic

4. A previously fit and well 50-year-old man has left-sided facial weakness, which he first noticed that morning. There is no history of any associated pain or rash. On examination, he has a lower motor neurone weakness, power 0/5 on the left side of his face, and he is unable to fully close his left eye. Examination is otherwise normal, and his blood pressure is 132/84 mmHg. Which is the single best next course of action? ★★

A Admit to hospital for an urgent head computed tomography (CT) scan

B Prescribe 20 mg prednisolone for 14 days

C Prescribe 60 mg prednisolone for 5 days

D Prescribe 60 mg prednisolone with 800 mg aciclovir for 5 days

E Refer urgently to ear, nose, and throat (ENT)

5. A 57-year-old man has had worsening pain in his left shoulder blade for 2 weeks which is keeping him awake at night. It is now spreading along the medial side of his left arm, and he has numbness and tingling in the little finger of his left hand. On examination, he has reduced power in the fourth and fifth fingers on the left, drooping of his left eyelid, and constriction of the left pupil. What is the single most important investigation to confirm the likely diagnosis? ★★

A Bone scan

B Chest X-ray

C Computed tomography (CT) scan thorax

D Magnetic resonance imaging (MRI) scan brain and neck

E Nerve conduction studies

6. You are asked to perform an arterial blood gas sample on a 20-year-old man who has been admitted to hospital with pneumonia. In preparation, you perform Allen's test. Which is the single most likely anatomical explanation of a positive test? ★★★

A Impaired digital blood flow

B Incomplete palmar arch

C Raynaud's disease

D Subclavian vein thrombosis

E Thoracic outlet obstruction

7. A 53-year-old man has sudden-onset leg weakness and altered sensation. A magnetic resonance imaging (MRI) spine has revealed a lesion consistent with a partial Brown-Séquard syndrome. Which single answer best describes the signs expected on clinical examination? ★★★

A A spastic paralysis on the contralateral side of the body below the level of the lesion, with contralateral loss of fine touch sensation, vibration touch, and proprioception, and ipsilateral loss of pain and temperature sensation

B A spastic paralysis on the contralateral side of the body below the level of the lesion, with contralateral loss of pain and temperature sensation and ipsilateral loss of fine touch sensation, vibration touch, and proprioception

C A spastic paralysis on the same side of the body below the level of the lesion, with ipsilateral loss of fine touch sensation, vibration, proprioception, pain, and temperature

D A spastic paralysis on the same side of the body below the level of the lesion, with ipsilateral loss of fine touch sensation, vibration, and proprioception, and contralateral loss of pain and temperature sensation

E A spastic paralysis on the same side of the body below the level of the lesion, with ipsilateral loss of pain and temperature sensation, and contralateral loss of fine touch sensation, vibration, and proprioception

8. A patient is admitted to the Medical Admissions Unit with a provisional diagnosis of Ludwig's angina. What is the single most likely anatomical site of the presenting problem? ★★★

A Anterior neck

B Central chest

C Floor of mouth

D Left arm

E Mandible

9. A 10-month-old boy is admitted to hospital with a chest infection. He has always had difficulty feeding, but this seems to have worsened and he coughs and splutters with his feeds and often sounds 'chesty'. He has faltering growth, having dropped from the 75th centile at birth to the 9th centile now. He has developmental delay and is not yet rolling and is unable to sit. On examination, he has lots of upper airway sounds apparent. He has a flat, broad nasal bridge, a prominent forehead, and a prominent tongue. He has contractures of his wrists and elbows, with truncal hypotonia. He has marked hepatosplenomegaly. What single finding would you expect on analysis of his urine? ★ ★ ★ ★

A Altered organic acid pattern

B Excess glycosaminoglycans

C Generalized aminoaciduria

D Microscopic haematuria

E Presence of reducing substances

10. A 10-year-old boy has a small, deformed right-sided chest wall. His right middle and ring finger are fused together. A computed tomography (CT) scan shows absence of his right pectoralis major muscle. What is the single most likely diagnosis? ★ ★ ★ ★

A Down's syndrome

B Muscular dystrophy

C Pectus carinatum

D Pectus excavatum

E Poland syndrome

11. A 75-year-old woman with a history of rheumatic fever presents with worsening breathlessness and features of acute heart failure. On examination, you notice that her head is nodding in synchrony with the heartbeat—De Musset's sign. Which is the single most likely valvular lesion to account for this? ★ ★ ★ ★

A Aortic regurgitation

B Aortic stenosis

C Mitral stenosis

D Mitral regurgitation

E Pulmonary stenosis

12. A 76-year-old man presents to the Emergency Department with a chronically discharging left ear and pain behind his left eye. His temperature is 38.5°C. On examination, he has a sixth cranial nerve palsy on the left side. Which is the single most likely syndrome to explain these findings? ★★★★

A Ganser syndrome

B Gilbert's syndrome

C Goldenhar syndrome

D Gradenigo's syndrome

E Guillain–Barré syndrome

13. A 45-year-old man is involved in a motorcycle accident. He presents to the Emergency Department, complaining of pain in his right forearm. X-rays demonstrate a Galeazzi fracture. Which is the single best description of the abnormalities seen on the X-ray? ★★★★

A A dorsally angulated fracture of the distal radius

B A fracture of both the mid-shaft radius and ulna

C A fracture of the proximal ulna with a dislocation of the radial head

D A fracture of the radius with an associated dislocation of the distal radio-ulnar joint

E An intra-articular fracture of the distal radius

ANSWERS

1. E ★   OHCS 11th edn → pp. 855, 859

Turner's syndrome is a common cause of primary amenorrhoea and should be considered in all girls presenting with this. It is caused by a chromosome abnormality, with a karyotype of 45,XO. Girls are typically short and, if left untreated, will only grow to less than 5 feet on average. They have typical features, which include webbing of the neck, lymphoedema, a low posterior hairline, wide-spaced nipples, and a wide carrying angle. Ovaries do not develop properly, causing post-menopausal levels of gonadotrophin hormones and affecting the development of secondary sexual characteristics. In hypothalamic hypogonadism, the levels of FSH and LH are low. Congenital paramesonephric duct obstruction is an example of a congenital Müllerian duct abnormality, which causes anatomical abnormalities of the uterus and ovaries, as is Mayer–Kuster–Hauser–Rokitansky syndrome. McCune–Albright syndrome affects bones and endocrine tissues and causes precocious puberty, rather than delayed puberty. If left untreated, this can also cause short stature.

2. D ★★   OHCS 11th edn → p. 273

These are the classic phenotypic features of a baby with trisomy 21 (Down's syndrome). The consistent neurological finding in babies with trisomy 21 is generalized hypotonia—they are floppy babies.

3. D ★★★

Grey Turner's sign describes bruising present on the flanks of a patient following retroperitoneal haemorrhage. It is often described in association with acute pancreatitis, but there are other causes of retroperitoneal haemorrhage. Cullen's sign is peri-umbilical discoloration, and Fox's sign describes discoloration of the inguinal crease, both caused by haemorrhage tracking along tissue planes.

4. C ★★   OHCS 11th edn → pp. 424–5

This man has Bell's palsy (Charles Bell). This is treated with a course of high-dose prednisolone; it is not recommended to treat with antiviral treatment. There is no history of a rash that would suggest Ramsay Hunt syndrome, which is treated with aciclovir. Diagnosis is a clinical one, so no investigations are needed. The majority of cases resolve within 9 months. Urgent referral should be done if there is any doubt about the diagnosis, or in recurrent or bilateral Bell's palsy. Routine referral should be considered if there is no improvement clinically within 1 month.

→ https://cks.nice.org.uk/bells-palsy

5. C ★★   OHCS 11th edn → p. 366

The description on examination is of an ulnar nerve palsy—paraesthesiae and weakness in the fourth and fifth fingers—and Horner's syndrome (Johann Friedrich Horner, Swiss ophthalmologist, 1869)—ipsilateral ptosis and miosis. The third part of the triad in Horner's syndrome is anhidrosis, loss of facial sweating, but this is often not reported and harder to find on examination. The story of severe shoulder pain, in combination with the ulnar nerve palsy, would lead you to think about a lesion in the shoulder region affecting the brachial plexus. The combination of Horner's syndrome should raise the suspicion of a lesion interfering with preganglionic sympathetic fibres in the cervical sympathetic chain. If all this is put together, it is highly suspicious of a Pancoast tumour (Professor Henry Pancoast, American physician, 1932), a malignant tumour in the apex of the ipsilateral lung. Horner's syndrome, in the presence of shoulder pain, should always lead you to think of an apical lung cancer. Pancoast tumours are rare—less than 5% of lung cancers—and can be hard to spot as they often do not show up on X-ray. Therefore, a CT scan of the thorax, or sometimes an MRI scan, should be arranged if suspicion is high. Horner's syndrome can occur with dissection of the carotid artery, but in this case pain is usually facial and with an acute onset, so an MRI scan of the neck would be less helpful. Central lesions can also lead to it but are usually longer-standing and not associated with shoulder pain. Given that the bony pain is so localized, a bone scan would not be indicated. Nerve conduction studies may outline an ulnar nerve dysfunction but would not help find a cause.

→ https://www.cancerresearchuk.org/about-cancer/lung-cancer/stages-types-grades/types/pancoast-tumours

6. B ★★★

Allen's test assesses the integrity of the palmar arch and helps to identify patients in whom there would be additional risk of distal ischaemia associated with the insertion of a radial artery cannula, performance of radial arterial blood sampling, or harvest of radial artery for surgical grafting.

→ http://www.euro.who.int/__data/assets/pdf_file/0005/268790/WHO-guidelines-on-drawing-blood-best-practices-in-phlebotomy-Eng.pdf?ua=1

7. D ★★★

Brown-Séquard syndrome describes a rare incomplete spinal cord lesion. It can present both in primary and secondary care as either an acute injury or a consequence of disease such as a tumour or an infection. The clinical presentation is often a cause for difficulty due to hemisection of the cord and, as such, its effect on different tracts of the cord. Two key facts regarding the neurology need to be recalled in order to understand the clinical presentation—firstly, the crossover of the descending corticospinal tract (containing motor signals) and ascending dorsal columns (containing proprioception and fine touch input) which occurs at the level of the medulla; also the ascending spinothalamic tracts (containing pain and temperature input) which cross one to two levels above their dorsal root at the spinal cord itself. An injury causing a hemisection of the cord will lead to loss of motor function, proprioception, and fine touch on the same side as those fibres have already crossed at a higher level. However, the contralateral pain and temperature sensation is affected for areas below the level, as they cross at the spinal cord itself. Any patient presenting with an incomplete spinal cord injury can be called a Brown-Séquard. However, not all patients present in the same way, depending on the exact cause and site of lesion. The syndrome was first described by Charles-Edouard Brown-Séquard who documented injuries in sugar cane farmers in Mauritius in the nineteenth century.

→ http://patient.info/doctor/brown-sequards-syndrome

8. C ★★★★

Ludwig's angina is a rare bacterial infection of the floor of the mouth, often associated with a dental abscess or recent oral trauma. It can progress rapidly and threaten airway patency, so it needs to be assessed and treated promptly.

→ https://medlineplus.gov/ency/article/001047.htm

9. B ★★★★   OHCS 11th edn → pp. 848, 850

This baby has typical features of a mucopolysaccharidosis (MPS) such as Hurler's (Gertrude Hurler, 1919) or Hunter's (Charles Hunter, 1917) syndrome. These cause a build-up of large sugar molecules—mucopolysaccharides, now known as glycosaminoglycans (GAGs)—in tissues in the body due to an enzyme deficiency. MPS 1—Hurler's—is autosomal recessive and MPS 2—Hunter's—is X-linked. Symptoms are progressive and range in severity. Severe forms present in the first year of life with features due to tissue build-up, e.g. organomegaly, skeletal deformity, coarse facial features and macroglossia, hernias, cardiomyopathy. In this child, the chest symptoms and poor feeding are likely due to the large tongue, bulbar dysfunction, and aspiration. Urine testing is a useful part of a metabolic work-up in children when an inborn error of metabolism is suspected. In this case, excess GAGs will leak out in the urine and give a clue to the diagnosis. White cell enzymes can then be tested for the specific enzyme defect. Urine amino acids will be generally elevated in renal disease. Organic acid patterns will be abnormal in organic acidaemias, such as methylmalonic acidaemia, where specific amino acids build up and leak out. Urine-reducing substances are non-glucose sugars that may leak out in the urine in disorders of sugar metabolism such as galactosaemia. Microscopic haematuria is found in a number of conditions, mostly involving the renal tract.

10. D ★★★★

Poland syndrome is a rare congenital defect characterized by underdeveloped or absence of the pectoralis muscles and ipsilateral syndactyly. Pectus excavatum is characterized by a depressed sternum, giving a concave appearance to the chest wall. Pectus carinatum, also known as pigeon chest, is a congenital defect with prominent sternum and ribs. Down's syndrome (trisomy 21) is a genetic disorder which is characterized by numerous physical and intellectual defects, one of which includes syndactyly.

11. A ★★★★

Severe aortic regurgitation causes a number of eponymous signs, rarely seen nowadays but loved by examiners!

→ https://en.wikipedia.org/wiki/Aortic_insufficiency#Signs_and_symptoms

12. D ★★★★

Gradenigo's syndrome describes the extension of a middle ear infection to the petrous apex. When this occurs, the patient is toxic and can develop an abducens nerve palsy from petrous apicitis and also pain behind the eye due to irritation of the ophthalmic branch of the trigeminal nerve. Ganser syndrome occurs when a person deliberately pretends to have a mental illness. Gilbert's syndrome is a genetic disorder with high levels of bilirubin leading to jaundice. Goldenhar syndrome, also known as OAV syndrome (oculo-auriculo-vertebral syndrome), is associated with abnormal facial development. Guillain–Barré syndrome is a progressive, immune-mediated, ascending peripheral neuropathy.

13. D ★★★★   OHCS 11th edn → p. 848

A Galeazzi fracture is a fracture of the distal radius with a dislocation of the distal radio-ulnar joint. Fractures of the ulna with radial head dislocations are described as a Monteggia fracture. A dorsally angulated fracture of the distal radius is commonly described as a Colles' fracture, and intra-articular fractures of the distal radius as a Barton's fracture.

Index